THE BRITISH LABOUR PARTY AND THE GERMAN SOCIAL DEMOCRATS, 1900–1931

STEFAN BERGER

CLARENDON PRESS · OXFORD

Oxford University Press, Great Clarendon Street, Oxford OX2 6DP
Oxford New York
Athens Auckland Bangkok Bogota Buenos Aires Calcutta
Cape Town Chennai Dar es Salaam Delhi Florence Hong Kong Istanbul
Karachi Kuala Lumpur Madrid Melbourne Mexico City Mumbai
Nairobi Paris São Paolo Singapore Taipei Tokyo Toronto Warsaw
and associated companies in
Berlin Ibadan

Published in the United States by
Oxford University Press Inc., New York

First published 1994

British Library Cataloguing in Publication Data
Data available

Library of Congress Cataloging in Publication Data
Berger, Stefan.
The British Labour Party and the German Social Democrats,
1900–1931 / Stefan Berger.
p.   cm.—(Oxford historical monographs)
Includes bibliographical references (p.   ).
1. Great Britain—Politics and government—1901-1936.
2. Political parties—Europe—History—20th century.   3. Germany—
Politics and government—1871-1933   4. Sozialdemokratische Partei
Deutschlands.   5. Labour Party (Great Britain).   6. Comparative
government.   I. Title.   II. Series
DA566.7B46   1994
324.24107'09'041—dc20   94-18793
ISBN 0-19-820500-7

3 5 7 9 10 8 6 4 2

Printed in Great Britain by
Antony Rowe Ltd, Chippenham, Wiltshire

For my parents
Karl and Inge Berger

Acknowledgements

THIS book is the product of my own intellect, and whatever its short-comings, they are entirely my own. It should also be pointed out that the translations from German are my own where I have not given any other source. Whoever thanks others for their help and encouragement is in danger of trying to find accomplices for his own eccentricities. Yet within the six years of thinking and writing about the British Labour Party and the German SPD, I have benefited from contact with several individuals and help from many institutions, and they should not go unmentioned.

Tony Nicholls and Ross McKibbin have been immaculate and patient supervisors. They have given me the freedom to pursue my own course of studies and were always ready to discuss my ideas at length. Tony Nicholls also proved invaluable, as sub-editor for the Oxford Historical Monographs, in preparing the manuscript for publication. For their time in discussing British and German Labour and reading parts of various drafts of this book thanks are also due to Peter Alter from the German Historical Institute, London, Dieter Dowe from the Friedrich Ebert Stiftung, Bonn, Richard Geary from the University of Nottingham, Eberhard Kolb from the University of Cologne, and to Nick Smart from the University of Plymouth. I would like to thank my colleagues in the School of European Studies at the University of Wales, Cardiff, for pro-viding a stimulating intellectual atmosphere for research. Special thanks are due to David Jackson for his unstinting help and encouragement.

The Rhodes Trust supplied the material means for my three-year stay in Oxford and the money to attend conferences and visit archives. Trinity College, Oxford, provided a home and financial help for three years. Financial help for archive visits was also given by the German National Scholarship Foundation and the German Historical Institute, London. All archives listed in the bibliography gave every possible help. I am grate-ful to the many archivists and librarians who had to put up with me.

My greatest indebtedness, however, is to my wife, Jutta Grub, my daughter Kristina—and to my parents, to whom this book is dedicated.

Table of Contents

Abbreviations

ACIQ	Advisory Council for International Questions
ADGB	Allgemeiner Deutscher Gewerkschaftsbund, General German Trades Union Congress
AfS	*Archiv für Sozialgeschichte*
AfSWP	*Archiv für Sozialwissenschaft und Sozialpolitik*
AG	Aktiengesellschaft
AHR	*American Historical Review*
APSR	*American Political Science Review*
ASE	Amalgamated Society of Engineers
ASU	Anti-Socialist Union
BA	Bundesarchiv, Koblenz
BGB	Bürgerliches Gesetzbuch
BSP	British Socialist Party
BWSA	British Workers' Sports Association
BZG	*Beiträge zur Geschichte der Arbeiterbewegung*
CIU	Workingmen's Club and Institute Union
CLC	Central Labour College
CPGB	Communist Party of Great Britain
DA	*Die Arbeit*
DAS	Deutsche Arbeitersänger, Workers' Singing Association
DLP	Divisional Labour Party
DVP	Deutsche Volkspartei, German People's Party
EC	Executive Committee
EHQ	*European History Quarterly*
EHR	*English Historical Review*
FES	Friedrich Ebert Stiftung, Bonn
GG	*Geschichte und Gesellschaft*
GmbH	Gesellschaft mit beschränkter Haftung
GMC	General Management Committee
GWU	*Geschichte in Wissenschaft und Unterricht*
HWJ	*History Workshop Journal*
HZ	*Historische Zeitschrift*
IFTU	International Federation of Trade Unions

IGA/ZPA	Institut für die Geschichte der Arbeiterbewegung/Zentrales Parteiarchiv, Berlin; now the Stiftung Archiv der Parteien und Massenorganisationen der DDR im Bundesarchiv
IISG	Internationales Institut für Sozialgeschichte, Amsterdam
ILP	Independent Labour Party
IRSH	*International Review of Social History*
ISB	International Socialist Bureau
IWK	*Internationale Wissenschaftliche Korrespondenz*
KPD	Kommunistische Partei Deutschlands, Communist Party of Germany
LCC	London County Council
LLP	London Labour Party
LP	Labour Party
LRC	Labour Representation Committee
LSE	London School of Economics, London
LSI	Labour and Socialist International
LVZ	*Leipziger Volkszeitung*
MP	Member of Parliament
MSPD	Mehrheitssozialdemokratische Partei Deutschlands, Majority Social Democratic Party of Germany
NCF	No Conscription Fellowship
NCLC	National Council of Labour Colleges
NEC	National Executive Committee
NL	Nachlaß
NLR	*New Left Review*
NZ	*Die Neue Zeit*
PLP	Parliamentary Labour Party
PP	*Past and Present*
PRO	Public Record Office, London
PV	Parteivorstand, party executive
RM	Reichsmark
SAI	Sozialistische Arbeiterinternationale, Labour and Socialist International
SAJ	Sozialistische Arbeiterjugend, Socialist Labour Youth
SAP	Sozialistische Arbeiterpartei, Socialist Labour Party of Germany
SDAP	Sozialdemokratische Arbeiterpartei, Social Democratic Labour Party
SDF	Social Democratic Federation
SM	*Sozialistische Monatshefte*

SPD	Sozialdemokratische Partei Deutschlands, Social Democratic Party of Germany
SR	*Socialist Review*
SSLH	*Society for the Study of Labour History*
SSS	Socialist Sunday Schools
SWMIU	South Wales Miners' Industrial Union
TGWU	Transport and General Workers' Union
TUC	Trades Union Congress
USPD	Unabhängige Sozialdemokratische Partei Deutschlands, Independent Social Democratic Party of Germany
WEA	Workers' Educational Association
WETUC	Workers' Educational Trade Union Committee
WTA	Workers' Travel Association
ZfG	*Zeitschrift für Geschichtswissenschaft*
ZfP	*Zeitschrift für Politikwissenschaft*
ZStA	Zentrales Staatsarchiv, Potsdam; now the Bundesarchiv, Abteilungen Potsdam
	Zentrales Staatsarchiv, Merseburg; now part of the Geheime Staatsarchiv Stiftung Preußischer Kulturbesitz

'It is a weakness of much comparative history to exaggerate differences and then to spend much time in explaining these.'

(John Breuilly, *Labour and Liberalism in Nineteenth Century Europe: Essays in Comparative History* (Manchester, 1992), 257.)

'Does *the* "modern socialism" in the singular really exist . . .? Or are there only a multitude of mutually incompatible doctrines . . .? Certainly, these issues may be and are indeed primarily considered from the viewpoint of multiplicity. It is of course so much easier to analyze the socialist systems one by one and explain their manifold differences. . . . However, those who have been able to penetrate the essence of modern proletarianism sense that all the different manifestations are based on the same substance. Conceding mutual disagreements, some kind of homogeneous spirit unites the thinking of the working class and its leaders: Bebel and Jaures, MacDonald and Lenin, Bernstein and Rosa Luxemburg, Turati and Labriola, Branting and Vandervelde, both Adlers, father and son, and it is the same spirit which distinguishes them sharply from all other thinkers.'

(Werner Sombart, *Der proletarische Sozialismus*, i (Jena, 1924), 21 f.)

I

The Pitfalls of Comparative Labour History: How Comrades are Compared

COMPARATIVE historical studies of nation-states can still be seen as a theory without much practice. More than twenty-five years ago Asa Briggs urged historians to break with the insularity of national historiography and to develop comparative Labour history.[1] Although this claim has been frequently reiterated,[2] the actual amount of research produced resembles a rivulet more than a river. This book is a study of two of the most successful working-class political parties—the SPD, founded in 1875/1890, and the Labour Party, which emerged from various groups in 1900/1906. The book focuses particularly on the period 1900 to 1931. A comparative study of what seem at first glance to be two very different types of working-class parties raises a number of interesting methodological points, discussion of which will lead us into the core of the subject.[3]

First, the comparative historian has to take into account the relevant social contexts; he or she has to be familiar with more than one national history. This means overcoming language problems as well as problems of the historian's own national 'mentality'. Second, a further danger facing the comparative historian is that of comparing too many nations.

[1] Asa Briggs, 'Trade Union History and Labour History', *Business History*, 8 (1966), 47.
[2] And in certain areas, including Labour history, comparative social history has made some progress in recent years. See the excellent overview by Hartmut Kaelble, 'Vergleichende Sozialgeschichte des 19. und 20. Jahrhunderts: Forschungen europäischer Historiker', *Jahrbuch für Wirtschaftsgeschichte* (1993), 173–200.
[3] For the theory of comparative history, see Jürgen Kocka, 'Probleme einer europäischen Geschichtsschreibung in komparativer Absicht', in id., *Geschichte und Aufklärung* (Göttingen, 1989), 21–8; John Breuilly, 'Introduction: Making Comparisons in History', in id., *Labour and Liberalism in Nineteenth Century Europe: Essays in Comparative History* (Manchester, 1992), 1–25; Raymond Grew, 'The Case for Comparing Histories', *AHR* 85 (1980), 763–78; H. J. Puhle, 'Theorien in der Praxis des vergleichenden Historikers', in Jürgen Kocka and Thomas Nipperdey (eds.), *Theorie und Erzählung in der Geschichte* (Munich, 1979), 119–36; Charles Tilly, *Big Structures, Large Processes, Huge Comparisons* (New York, 1985); Robert T. Holt and John E. Turner (eds.), *The Methodology of Comparative Research* (London, 1970); Theda Skocpol and Margaret Somers, 'The Uses of Comparative History in Macro-Social Inquiry', *Comparative Studies in Society and History*, 22 (1980), 174–97; Adam Przeworski and Henry Teune, *The Logic of Comparative Social Inquiry* (New York, 1970).

Necessarily he or she will have to be well acquainted with the national histories and the languages of the countries involved in the comparison. Few historians have the linguistic and historical knowledge adequately to cope with more than two countries. Also, if too many cases are taken into account it becomes more and more difficult to formulate questions which can usefully be applied to all countries. And if he or she does not focus on specific key questions, the comparative historian is soon swamped by the mass of data on each individual case. By restricting the scope of this study to the British Labour Party and the German SPD, this problem of cross-national comparative history is avoided.

Furthermore, specific questions which will guide any comparative research can have different underlying aims and objectives. Four different levels of comparison have been suggested: an individualizing comparison which treats each case as unique, and emphasizes its uniqueness by comparing it with other cases. Whatever one case has in common with any other case is consequently minimized in its importance. There are also encompassing comparisons, which accommodate and explain differences between cases within an overarching commonality. More generally, universalizing comparisons aim at identifying similarities between different cases. Lastly, variation-finding comparisons try to identify different cases as variations of one particular phenomenon.[4] In so far as this present study seeks to make the point that similarities between the British and the German labour movements have been underestimated—without at the same time disputing important remaining differences—it can be described as a hybrid between a universalizing and a variation-finding comparison.

Among already existing comparative Labour history, this makes the present study a slightly unusual one. Usually comparative history assumes as its starting-point a causal relationship between two phenomena. It then attempts to verify this assumption by means of an individualizing comparison. The latter is devised to test the correctness of any such assumed causal relationship. If the comparison shows that in two countries different factors could lead to the same results, or if similar factors have led to different results, then the case for any necessary causal relationship between factor and result has been substantially weakened. Max Weber, for example, tried to explain the rise of capitalism and he saw a causal relationship between the emergence of capitalism and what he called the 'Protestant ethic'. In comparing the rise of capitalism in different countries, he could group similar cases where the Protestant ethic and the capitalist spirit were strong and contrast them with other cases where

---

[4] For those four categories of comparative research and a discussion of examples for each of the four categories see Tilly, *Big Structures*, 81–143.

both the Protestant ethic and the capitalist spirit was weak.[5] In his comparative sociology, Weber largely practised individualizing comparisons. The uniqueness of one place/phenomenon was explained in contrast to the difference of another place/phenomenon. Marc Bloch, echoing Weber in his advocacy of individualizing comparisons, argued that the prime aim of comparative history was to 'analyze and isolate the "originality" of different societies'.[6]

Most comparative Labour historians writing about the British and the German labour movement have followed such an individualizing strategy. This is not really surprising, as it is usually thought to be one defining characteristic of Clio to be concerned with a unique time and place. History is usually about the particular and the specific, not about the general or the universal. The question hitherto guiding comparative Labour historians can be described as: why was the labour movement in Britain so different from the labour movement in Germany? In trying to find answers to this question, comparative Labour historians have made a number of assumptions which put the British and the German labour movements at opposite ends of the spectrum of European labour movements.[7] The aim of the present study is to throw doubt upon many of the assumptions which have informed the existing typology of labour movements.

Whether an individualizing or a universalizing comparative framework is adopted, cross-national comparisons of complex structures like labour movements are often built upon broad and sweeping generalizations about the historical development in any one given country. Regional particularities are neglected. Indeed, comparisons have an unfortunate tendency to homogenize the heterogeneity and contingency of different experiences of individuals and organizations at different times in different places. For example, neither Britain nor Germany had a single working-class party. The parties developed in significantly different ways in various regions of the two countries. Over the past decade Labour history in both Britain and Germany has paid far greater attention to regional

---

[5] Max Weber, *The Protestant Ethic and the Spirit of Capitalism* (New York, 1958). Those groups of different cases Weber came to define as 'ideal types' which lay between the contingency of historicism and the dogmatism of history understood as a science which discovers natural laws. For Weber's importance for historiography see Jürgen Kocka, 'Max Webers Bedeutung für die Geschichtswissenschaft', in id. (ed.), *Max Weber, der Historiker* (Göttingen, 1986), 13–27.

[6] Marc Bloch, 'Toward a Comparative History of European Societies', in Jelle C. Riemersma and Frederic C. Lane (eds.), *Enterprise and Secular Change: Readings in Economic History* (London, 1953), 507.

[7] See the short review of existing comparisons at the end of Ch. 1.

developments.[8] Some comparative historians have argued that comparisons should best be undertaken on a regional or local level.[9] The recent influence of post-structuralism on historical writing has further sharpened an awareness of multiplicity and decentring. Efforts to achieve comprehensive generalizations have consequently become more and more suspect in recent years.[10] However, national comparisons between working-class parties can be defended on grounds that both parties after all saw themselves emphatically as national parties. Any purely local comparison would do injustice to the national aspirations of working-class parties.

A further methodological difficulty encountered in cross-national comparisons lies in the fact that sometimes pseudo-similarities and/or pseudo-differences are suggested by the lack of correspondence between the meanings of historical terms in different languages. The existence of homonyms only underlines the importance that should be attached to language in comparative research. An example is the word 'agitation'—in German *Agitation*. These two terms clearly do not mean the same thing. Used positively by Social Democrats to describe the party's propaganda efforts, *Agitation* had none of the derogatory sense of the term 'propaganda' which it carries in English. Campaigning is more specific, functionally oriented, concerning membership or elections. Another example is the word 'functionary'—in German *Funktionär*. Again, the term was used largely in a positive sense by the SPD, whereas members of the Labour Party would rarely speak of 'functionary'. Therefore the term 'official' has been substituted for the term 'functionary'.

[8] The case for a regional/local approach to Labour history has been convincingly made by Michael Savage, *The Dynamics of Working-Class Politics: The Labour Movement in Preston 1880–1940* (Cambridge, 1987). See also Duncan Tanner, *Political Change and the Labour Party 1900–1918* (Cambridge, 1990). For regional/local approaches in German Labour historiography see especially Klaus Tenfelde, 'Wege zur Sozialgeschichte der Arbeiterschaft und Arbeiterbewegung: Regional- und lokalgeschichtliche Forschungen (1945–1975) zur deutschen Arbeiterbewegung bis 1914', in H. U. Wehler (ed.), *Die moderne deutsche Geschichte in der internationalen Forschung 1945–1975* (Göttingen, 1978) and Detlev Peukert, 'Zur Regionalgeschichtsschreibung der Arbeiterbewegung', *Das Argument*, 110 (1978), 546–560. Also Heinz-Gerd Hofschen, 'Recent Developments in Local and Labour History Research in West-Germany', *Llafur: Journal of Welsh Labour History*, 5 (1990), 71–8.

[9] Compare, for example, John Breuilly, 'Liberalism in Mid-Nineteenth Century Hamburg and Manchester', in id., *Labour and Liberalism*, 197–227, and Werner Berg, *Wirtschaft und Gesellschaft in Deutschland und Großbritannien im Übergang zum 'Organisierten Kapitalismus': Unternehmer, Angestellte, Arbeiter und Staat im Steinkohlebergbau des Ruhrgebiets und von Süd-Wales, 1850–1914* (Bielefeld, 1980).

[10] Jane Caplan, 'Postmodernism, Poststructuralism, and Deconstruction: Notes for Historians', *Central European History* 22 (1989), 266. Also generally Lynn Hunt (ed.), *The New Cultural History* (Berkeley, Calif., 1989).

The problem is not confined to words which carry different meanings. It is also a wider problem in relation to similar events and/or institutions having different meanings in different societies. Take for example the problem of regional organization within the Labour Party and the SPD. The regional organizations of the SPD developed into powerful arbiters between the locality and the national centre. A radical SPD local organization within a reformist regional organization was in trouble and vice versa. Comparisons with the Labour Party might draw attention to the fact that the Labour Party built up a regional organization after 1918 as well. However, any closer look immediately reveals the essential difference behind the two levels of organization which carry the same name. Regional organizations in the British Labour Party remained weak. By comparison with their German comrades, they lacked the financial support and personnel required to concentrate all decision-making at the regional level. Within the British Labour Party the gulf between local party and national centre could not be bridged by the regional organizations which remained somewhat inadequate watchdogs for the national centre. Comparative historians should therefore be aware of the possibility that one and the same word (in this case 'regional party organizations') can have different meanings in different national contexts and traditions.[11]

Another related difficulty of comparative history lies in finding a common terminology for related phenomena in different countries. In this study the problem of finding a common term for both the Labour Party and the SPD had to be addressed. 'Socialist' parties would hardly have been correct, as the Labour Party was not socialist before 1918, and even afterwards there remains some doubt. Hence the term 'working-class parties' has been chosen. It avoids ideological connotations, and it stresses that the basis of both parties was largely one of class. Workers were the largest group amongst their rank and file, their activists and their voters. Whenever the term working-class parties appears it refers to the Labour Party and SPD; the wider and more imprecise term 'labour movement' refers to the party, the trade unions, the co-operative movement and cultural, educational, and other ancillary organizations. The liberal, Catholic, and non-German (especially Polish) working-class organizations in Germany as well as conservative, liberal, and Irish working-class organizations in Britain are generally excluded from the comparison.

Clearly and sensibly defining the limits of the comparison poses further

---

[11] For extensive comment on the regional organizations of Labour Party and SPD see 3.2.

problems for the comparative historian. The reader will obviously be struck by the fact that the communist parties of Britain and Germany are not discussed—apart from occasional references—in a comparison of the Labour Party and the SPD. As the CPGB and the KPD respectively influenced the policies and sometimes the structures of Labour Party and SPD after 1918, this may be seen as a serious omission. Germany, after all, saw the development of the biggest Communist Party outside the Soviet Union after 1918. This seems to be in clear contrast to the situation in Britain, where the Communist Party remained relatively small and seemingly insignificant. It has been convincingly argued that the lack of a radical socialist culture in Britain before 1914 was responsible for the lack of support for communism after 1918.[12] Where a radical and militant tradition could be found, as in the Scottish Fife district and the South Wales coalfield, the CPGB had more of an impact than it had nationally. However, it should neither be simply assumed that the CPGB was extremely different in character from the KPD nor that communism was an insignificant part of the British labour movement.

Because of its numerical weakness and its inability to muster support at the polls with the exception of a few places like Rhondda East, Motherwell, and North Battersea, the strength of British communism is easily underestimated. Such influence was most notable within some important trade unions in the 1920s, especially mining and engineering unions. In some Trades Councils, e.g. the influential London one, there existed strong CPGB cells. It required a concerted effort of the 'reformist' TUC leadership after 1927 and the CPGB's suicidal policy of attacking moderate trade unionists as 'social fascists' after 1928 to reduce that influence substantially. Also, the CPGB was capable of building up organizations like the National Unemployed Workers' Movement (NUWM) in the 1920s and 1930s, an organization which was able to mobilize tens, if not hundreds of thousands of people.[13] The miners' union had been particularly impressed by CPGB support for the bitter strike of 1921, and A. J.

---

[12] Dick Geary, *European Labour Politics from 1900 to the Depression* (London, 1991), 64. For the impact of the split of the German labour movement see especially Klaus Schönhoven, *Reformismus und Radikalismus: Gespaltene Arbeiterbewegung im Weimarer Sozialstaat* (Munich, 1989).

[13] There is still considerable debate amongst Labour historians as to the membership figures of the NUWM. R. Croucher, *We Refuse to Starve in Silence: A History of the National Unemployed Workers' Movement* (London, 1987), p. 11 claims hundreds of thousands of members for the NUWM in the inter-war years, while Sam Davies, 'The Membership of the National Unemployed Workers' Movement, 1923–1938', *SSLH* 57 (1992), 29–36 has recently argued for a much lower membership of at best 25,000 members.

Cook of the SWMF became one of the most prominent CPGB members in the 1920s. Furthermore, quite apart from the numerical strength of British communism, it has never been properly researched just how different the outlook of the CPGB and the KPD members, their party structures, and their doctrinal struggles were. Is it not reasonable to assume that both parties were subject to Comintern controls on their policies? Was its membership, like that of the KPD in comparison to the SPD, not far younger than that of the Labour Party? Did not especially the unskilled and unemployed feel attracted to communism in both countries? And if so, why did they not join the party in greater numbers in Britain? The 'Little Moscows' of Maerdy and Bedlinog need comparing with the communist-dominated neighbourhoods in Germany like the Berlin district of Neukölln, the Hamburg district of Barmbeck, and cities like Chemnitz and Dinslaken. Only if such organizational and ideological comparisons between the communist parties of Britain and Germany are actually carried out, can any definite statement be made about the role of communism within the British and German societies. To look only at votes and members is not enough. However, there simply is not enough space in one book to cover the CPGB and the KPD as well as the Labour Party and the SPD. The comparison between the communist parties of Britain and Germany still awaits its historian.

If it is necessary to impose limits on the range of the comparison undertaken, it is equally important to define time limits for any comparative study. Historical comparisons are often differentiated from sociological comparisons by their recognition that time matters. Events and developments, structures and organizations are all linked to a specific time in which they come into existence, in which they thrive and in which they wither away. Drawing particular time caesuras substantially influences the way in which particular events or structures are seen.

For example, it has become rather common in both British and German historiography to stop historical investigations in 1914 and start again in 1918. The First World War, as Arthur Marwick and Jürgen Kocka, amongst others, have argued, was an important watershed for both societies.[14] Social, economic, and political organization changed dramatically as a result of the war. In the course of the war, the composition

---

[14] Arthur Marwick, *The Deluge: British Society and the First World War* (London, 1965). Also J. M. Winter, *The Great War and the British People* (London, 1986); Bernard Waites, *A Class Society at War: England 1914–1918* (Leamington Spa, 1987); Jürgen Kocka, *Klassengesellschaft im Krieg: Deutsche Gesellschaftsgeschichte, 1914–1918* (Göttingen, 1983).

of the working class changed significantly in both countries. There was a definite trend towards deskilling even if skill did not altogether lose its importance. In Germany, the end of the war coincided with a democratic revolution which toppled the political regime of Imperial Germany and made the country a full parliamentary democracy for the first time. In Britain, the war helped to destroy the Liberal Party, which before 1914 commanded very substantial working-class support, as a viable political force.

The war was also an important watershed for the working-class parties. Both reacted in a very similar way to the outbreak of the First World War. They abandoned their pre-war internationalism and contributed to the national war effort. In Germany, the harassment of the labour movement by the authorities stopped. Trade union officials were exempted from military service. The state almost forced reluctant employers to accept trade unions as bargaining partners. State employees could openly join and support the SPD for the first time. In the last stages of the war in 1918, the SPD was even asked to participate in a coalition government. The British Labour Party entered a national coalition already in 1915. Its leader, Arthur Henderson, joined the inner war cabinet, which only consisted of five members. The breakup of the Liberal Party in the war contributed to the Labour Party becoming one of two main parties in the British political system in the 1920s. Furthermore, both working-class parties suffered internal division as a result of their abandonment of pre-war internationalism. The SPD was split by the experience of war, and the Labour Party came very close to a split. Discrimination against those socialists who refused to support the national war effort was severe within both parties. In terms of trade union growth, changing popular attitudes to labour movements, and integration of both working-class parties into their respective societies, these wartime events had wide-ranging consequences and should not be underestimated in their importance.

Yet in other respects the war was more of an accelerator of events than an actual end or starting-point. Strong affinities of both substance and style have been observed between the labour movement of the Weimar Republic and the labour movement of Imperial Germany.[15] Equally, the Labour Party in post-war Britain—despite the 1918 constitution and the emergence as the major opposition party—was in some respects not so

[15] Heinrich August Winkler, *Von der Revolution bis zur Stabilisierung: Arbeiter und Arbeiterbewegung in der Weimarer Republik, 1918–1924* (Berlin, 1984), 245.

different from pre-war Britain in its leadership personnel, in its organizational schemes and its ideological set-up.[16] Comparative studies of inter-war working-class parties in Europe have stressed this continuity in party attitudes and organization.[17] Hence both pre- and post-war periods have been included in the comparison in the hope that it is possible to accommodate the diversity and differences of both periods within the scope of one study.

Quite apart from the difficulties involved in bridging pre- and post-First World War societies in Britain and Germany, there is the general problem as to which precise time limits, if any, should be adopted for a comparative study of Labour Party and SPD. The turn of the century has been chosen as a starting-point. 1900 was the year in which the Labour Representation Committee—which in 1906 became the Labour Party—came into existence. The SPD had been founded a quarter of a century earlier, in 1875, when its predecessors, the Allgemeiner Deutscher Arbeiterverein (ADAV) and the Sozialdemokratische Arbeiterpartei, both founded in the 1860s, joined forces in Gotha to form the Sozialistische Arbeiterpartei Deutschlands, which in 1891 was renamed the Sozialdemokratische Partei Deutschlands (SPD). Comparisons with the British labour movement often stress the comparatively early beginnings of independent political working-class organization in Germany. It should be noted, however, that independent political working-class organization did not start with the Labour Party in Britain. Both the SDF and the ILP were socialist parties, founded in 1883 and 1893 respectively. Also it should be taken into account that the SPD did not start fully to develop as a mass political party until after the end of the anti-socialist law in 1890. The real expansion of its organization came at an even later date, after 1905, when efforts of the Prussian authorities to renew the ban on independent working-class organizations became much less of a threat.

---

[16] Ross McKibbin, 'Labour and Politics in the Great War', *SSLH* 34 (1977), 4. It should be noted that Ross McKibbin, *The Ideologies of Class: Social Relations in Britain 1880–1950* (Oxford, 1990), 297 f. concedes that he may have underestimated the importance of the First World War for the emergence of the Labour Party as one of the two major parties in the British political system. This, however, does not effect continuities in the internal organization and the system of beliefs between the pre- and post-war Labour Party.

[17] Dan S. White, 'Reconsidering European Socialism in the 1920s', *Journal of Contemporary History*, 16 (1981), 254 and especially Carl Cavanagh Hodge, 'The Trammels of Tradition: Social Democratic Parties in Britain, France and Germany 1863–1937' (University of London Ph.D. 1987), who sees the continuity of pre-war organizations and attitudes as one of the major reasons for the failure of working-class parties in the inter-war years.

Although the importance of late nineteenth-century developments for the outlook of the British and German labour movements in the early twentieth century will not be disputed, the turn of the century marked an important point of departure for both the Labour Party and the SPD.

If the turn of the century has been chosen as the starting-point for the present study, the end-point lies in the 1930s: 1933 and the advent of the Nazis to power in Germany marked the end of independent German working-class organizations. In the case of the British Labour Party most historians stress the importance of the year 1931. In that year the second Labour government collapsed under the weight of the economic crisis. MacDonald and a handful of close political friends were expelled from the Labour Party after joining the national government. The rest of the 1930s were dominated by the Conservative Party. The Labour Party, however, quickly recovered from the fiasco of 1931 to establish itself as the major opposition party in the 1930s. The old leadership, which had been in charge almost from the inception of the Labour Party, was replaced by younger men: MacDonald, Henderson, and Snowden left the stage whilst Morrison, Dalton, Bevin, and Bevan stepped into the limelight. If the early 1930s consequently mark some new beginning as far as the leadership personnel was concerned, it was business as usual as far as the organizational aspirations of the Labour Party were concerned. After all, many organizational schemes for a stronger local membership and a better local organization, which had been started in the 1920s, only came to fruition in the 1930s. Ultimately the comparative historian can only note the difficulties involved in emphasizing a few decades within a party history which stretches further back in time and continues up to the present day. Consequently, the 1900s and the 1930s will serve as rough markers rather than exact time limits for the comparison of Labour Party and SPD.

There is, however, another important reason why any comparison of the Labour Party and the SPD should not stop in 1914 and why a relatively broad time span should be adopted for this comparison. Comparative history has to avoid falling into chronological traps: it has to recognize that similar phenomena do not necessarily occur simultaneously. As early as 1874 Lujo Brentano drew attention to the importance of possible time lags for comparative studies, and consequently argued for diachronic rather than synchronic comparisons. According to him the German labour movement of the 1870s and 1880s should best be compared with Chartism and the beginning of the working-class movement in Britain in the first decades of the nineteenth century.[18] He saw both movements as reactions against rapid industrialization, which transformed British as well as German society. Yet, according to Brentano, Germany's industrial take-off lagged about fifty years behind, so that a radical labour movement emerged at a later time than in Britain. For the future he was optimistic that the German labour movement would adapt to the social, political, and economic system in the same way that the British labour movement had done.

Following Brentano's mode of analysis, the present study argues that the date at which independent working-class parties emerged in all industrializing countries was when existing parties could no longer accommodate working-class interests. Because of the inadequate organization of Liberal parties in Germany for a dawning age of mass politics and, possibly even more importantly, because of the inability of the German Liberals to cling to a policy of free trade like their British counterparts, German Liberals had already lost working-class support in the 1860s, when independent working-class parties were established. Looked at from the other way round, the ability of British Liberals to remain champions of free trade and the existence of an elaborate Liberal party machine facilitated cross-class collaboration and delayed the emergence of an independent working-class party until the turn of the century. However, once an independent working-class party had come into existence, it developed along very similar lines to the SPD. To compare the Labour Party before 1914 with the SPD before 1914 would be comparing two different stages in the development of both working-class parties. In many respects only a diachronic comparison of the Labour Party organization in the 1920s and 1930s with the SPD organization before 1914 brings out similarities between the two parties which otherwise are easily overlooked.

Comparing complex organizations like working-class parties over more than three decades poses difficulties of another kind. A merely descriptive framework of comparison would leave the historian sinking into the abyss of excess information provided by secondary literature and archive material. A broad theoretical framework is therefore necessary. Before looking at the material, precise questions have to be asked which will then be

---

[18] Lujo Brentano, 'Die englische Chartistenbewegung', *Preußische Jahrbücher*, 33 (1874), 431–47 and 531–50. For Brentano's position see also Christiane Eisenberg, 'The Comparative View in Labour History: Old and New Interpretations of the English and German Labour Movements before 1914', *IRSH* 34 (1989), 411 f.

examined in the light of the material. Those questions can only be formulated against the background of a chosen theory about the development of
working-class parties and their respective societies. Yet the historian has
to be careful not to prejudge the historical development with hindsight
nor to assume definite historical paths. The danger is all too real that facts
are selected so as to fit an inflexible theoretical framework. Consequently
a flexible relationship between description and theory is required.

The theoretical framework of the present study starts from the assumption that the formation of the working class as class can be linked to
the emergence of an independent labour movement. In all industrializing
countries people who increasingly came to perceive themselves as working class formed their own interest organizations. If such a link, however
complex and difficult to explain, is accepted, then the development of
working-class parties is bound up with the history of class formation. Any
investigation of the history of class formation has to start by asking
questions about the development of the economy, society, and the state.[19]
In trying to answer such questions for Britain and Germany, this study
adopts the results of those historians who have maintained that the differences between the development of the British and the German society in
the nineteenth and early twentieth centuries have at times been grossly
exaggerated.[20] Exceptionalist arguments tend to distort historical reality
in that variations and differences in the outlook of working-class organizations in different countries are easily exaggerated. Comparative labour
history has tended to highlight the uniqueness of particular national
labour movements in the past, thereby neglecting basic similarities between those labour movements.[21] The refutation of either German or
British exceptionalism in a European context will be used on the one
hand to explain similarities between the two working-class parties, similarities which have been neglected by their respective historians so far.
On the other hand the present study will contribute further to the anti-
Sonderweg argument by demonstrating that, with respect to working-class

---

[19] Ira Katznelson, 'Working Class Formation: Constructing Cases and Comparisons', in
Ira Katznelson and Aristide R. Zolberg (eds.), *Working Class Formation: Nineteenth-Century
Patterns in Western Europe and the United States* (Princeton, NJ, 1986), 30.

[20] Especially David Blackbourn and Geoff Eley, *The Peculiarities of German History:
Bourgeois Society and Politics in Nineteenth-Century Germany* (Oxford, 1984).

[21] Aristide R. Zolberg, 'How Many Exceptionalisms?', in Katznelson and Zolberg (eds.),
Working Class Formations, 437–55. Also James E. Cronin, 'Neither Exceptional nor Peculiar: Towards the Comparative Study of Labor in Advanced Society', *IRSH*, 38 (1993), 59–
74. For a lacklustre defence of the exceptionalist framework see Jürgen Kocka, 'Comparative
Historical Research: German Examples, *IRSH*, 38 (1993), 364 f.

parties' organization and ideology, much of the existing historiography, reviewed briefly below, has emphasized the exceptionalism of either Labour Party or SPD too much.

There are only a handful of comparative historians who have worked in the field of Labour history, and there are even fewer who have compared the British and German working-class parties in their respective countries. In fact, this is the most detailed comparison of the development, structure, and ideology of the Labour Party and the SPD so far.[22] Those who have drawn comparisons at all—contemporaries as well as historians of all political convictions—have testified to the differences between the two movements. Oswald Spengler, for example, in his notorious *Preußentum und Sozialismus* wrote: 'The whole English labour movement is based on the difference between rich and poor within the work-force. The iron discipline of a party of millions in Prussian style would be unthinkable here.'[23] For Spengler Prussian ideas were opposed to English ideas, in socialism as in everything else. Englishness for him was individualism leading to egotism and sensualism, parliamentary liberalism, freedom leading to anarchy. Those values were opposed to Prussian ones like 'monarchic' socialism, truthfulness, discipline, asceticism, solidarity, and idealism.

An obsession with alleged national character traits can also be traced in the writings of Werner Sombart on comparative labour history. Not dissimilar in tone to Spengler, he argued that socialism developed in various countries according to the national collective mentality. Trying to trace such illusive mentalities, Sombart established three different historical types of labour movements: (*a*) that of Great Britain and the Anglo-Saxon world, (*b*) that of Germany and the Germanic world, (*c*) that of France and the Latin world. The Germanic socialist is seen by Sombart as the archetypal scholar who acts under the influence of theory and philosophy; the Anglo-Saxon socialist is described as the archetypal shopkeeper, whose only orientation in life is empiricism; and, finally, the Latin socialist is seen as the archetypal artist, influenced by great personalities.[24]

Socialists were generally less concerned with 'national character',

---

[22] It should, however, be noted that there is some progress towards a more systematic comparative approach in the writing of labour movement history. The International Institute of Social History, for example, has embarked on an interesting comparative undertaking. See Marcel van der Linden and Jürgen Rojahn (eds.), *The Formation of Labour Movements 1870–1914: An International Perspective*, 2 vols. (Leiden, 1990).

[23] Oswald Spengler, *Preußentum und Sozialismus* (Munich, 1922), 45 f.

[24] Werner Sombart, *Der proletarische Sozialismus* (Jena, 1924), ii. 358 f.

yet they arrived at the same result. Julius Braunthal, German Social Democrat and leading functionary of the Socialist International after 1918, wrote in 1945:

The labour movement on the Continent . . . developed a profusion of Socialist institutions, and the life of their individual members was intensely interwoven with the life of the movement. The British Labour movement appeared to be no part of the life of its average members. To be quite accurate, it might perhaps be questioned whether it is to be termed a movement, in the sense of an organism of which its cells (the individual members) compose a living whole. It is, in the first place a vast trade union organization, and only in the second place a political organization . . .[25]

And even earlier, in 1908, August Bebel—infuriated by the British socialists' insistence on coming to Berlin on a peace mission—wrote to Molkenbuhr about what he saw as essential differences between British and German socialists: 'I do not want to get mixed up with the English any more. Not only do they speak a different language, they also think differently. Insular isolation has made them special human beings.'[26] Subsequently historians have tended to agree with this judgement without ever undertaking a thorough comparative study of the British and German working-class parties.

Hans Mommsen created a typology of labour movements according to which there was a labour movement of central and eastern Europe and Scandinavia dominated by the SPD, a labour movement of the West European continental states in which the strain of syndicalism was much stronger, and the Anglo-Saxon labour movements which were 'a type of working-class interest organization of their own'.[27] Mommsen's argument was based on a specific perception of the two parties' ideologies and organizational structures. Whereas the Labour Party was seen as ideologically heterogeneous, always rejecting Marxist dogmatism, the German party after 1890 was perceived as a more or less homogenously Marxist party. Organizationally the Labour Party is held to have been little more than a trade union interest group in parliament based simply on local

---

[25] Julius Braunthal, *In Search of the Millenium* (London, 1945), 319.

[26] Institut für die Geschichte der Arbeiterbewegung/Zentrales Parteiarchiv, IGA/ZPA (formerly IML), Bebel papers, NL 22/132, 23: letter Bebel to Molkenbuhr, 28 Sept. 1908. For the misunderstanding between the British Labour Party and the German SPD resulting from the Labour Party's 1908 peace mission see 6.2 below.

[27] Hans Mommsen, 'Zum Problem der vergleichenden Behandlung nationaler Arbeiterbewegungen am Beispiel Ost- und Südostmitteleuropas', *IWK* 15 (1979), 31. Also id., 'Arbeiterbewegung', in C. D. Kernig (ed.), *Sowjetsystem und demokratische Gesellschaft: Eine vergleichende Enzyklopädie*, i (Freiburg, 1966), 274–98.

electoral machines, which had been founded with the aim of securing as many votes as possible. For its part, the SPD is held to have been a social movement providing for its members every facility 'from the cradle to the grave'.

Similar arguments about the essential difference between the British and the German labour movement have been repeated by eminent Labour historians like Klaus Tenfelde, Harvey Mitchell, and Walter Kendall.[28] Where Tenfelde and Mitchell argue for a kind of German exceptionalism, Kendall uses the argument about a kind of *Sonderweg* of British society to substantiate his claim: 'Since labour movements arise as a human response to external social and economic conditions the labour movements of Europe in their turn come to assume forms significantly different from those of either Britain or the U.S.'[29] Dick Geary has forcefully argued that it was mainly the different character of class relationships in Britain and Germany and the different reaction of the British and German state to the labour movement which explains the different developments of the two movements:

the British case differed from developments across the channel . . . Where a national bourgeoisie is weak or tied to an existing and authoritarian state . . . as was to some extent the case in Imperial Germany . . . there the prospects of working-class liberalism appear to be weaker, whilst political radicalism on the part of labour becomes more marked.[30]

Its ability to recruit massive electoral support, its programme of revolutionary Marxism, and its range and size of ancillary organizations all set the German working-class party apart from its British counterpart before 1914. The most recent and probably most pronounced emphasis on the

---

[28] Klaus Tenfelde, 'Geschichte der deutschen Arbeiter und Arbeiterbewegung: Ein Sonderweg', in *Der Aquädukt 1763–1988: Ein Almanach aus dem Verlag C. H. Beck im 225. Jahr seines Bestehens* (Munich, 1988), 469–83; Harvey Mitchell and Peter Stearns, *Workers and Protests: The European Labor Movement, the Working Classes and the Origins of Social Democracy 1890–1914* (Ithaca, NY, 1971), 5.

[29] Walter Kendall, *The Labour Movement in Europe* (London, 1975), 3 f. In 1964 and 1965 a series of essays published by Tom Nairn and Perry Anderson in *NLR* put forward the idea of English exceptionalism, as far as the development of its labour movement and its society was concerned. The argument has recently been restated by Perry Anderson, 'The Figures of Descent', *NLR* 161 (1987), 52: 'The British working class down to the First World War thus remained, in a sense, the mirror opposite of the German.' Also putting forward arguments in favour of British peculiarity in a European context are Bernd Weisbrod, 'Der englische "Sonderweg" in der neueren Geschichte', *GG* (1990), 233–52, esp. p. 243 f., and Breuilly, *Labour and Liberalism*, esp. chs. 4, 6, and 7.

[30] Dick Geary, 'Introduction', in id. (ed.), *Labour and Socialist Movements in Europe before 1914* (Oxford, 1989), 3.

difference between the two countries working-class parties comes from Carl Cavanagh Hodge: 'Britain and Germany produced very different social democratic parties, and much of the similarity between the SPD and British Labour is exhausted with a comparison of membership size and electoral strength.'[31] Of late, Christiane Eisenberg has reviewed the notion of German exceptionalism in labour movement history, coming to the conclusion that although a number of *Sonderweg* arguments no longer stand up in the light of more recent research, it is still possible to speak of two different developments of the labour movement in Britain and Germany.[32]

As this short review of the existing literature on the working-class parties in Britain and Germany has shown, historians have reinforced the classical view established by contemporary observers that the British Labour Party was a different animal from the German SPD. Most of that research synchronically compares the British Labour Party and the German SPD before 1914 when—no doubt—differences prevail. However, sometimes, as in the case of Hodge, the picture is also transferred into the inter-war years, when similarities between the two parties become much more pronounced. Also, as I have argued above, synchronic comparisons between the Labour Party and the SPD before 1914 are fundamentally mistaken, as the parties were in different stages of their respective development. The present study will therefore undertake to challenge or at any rate qualify this received orthodoxy. One of the key contentions will be that, notwithstanding real, lasting, and indisputable differences between the two working-class parties, the chasm of difference between them was not so wide as is often stated in the literature. This first, detailed comparison of the British Labour Party and the German SPD tries to correct what it perceives as the mistaken assumption of placing them at opposite ends of a spectrum of working-class parties between the last decade of the nineteenth century and the beginning of the 1930s.

Blackbourn and Eley have come to the conclusion that the attitude towards the labour movement in both countries can be described as a 'process of attempted political containment with varying degrees of recklessness'.[33] Chapter 2 of this study seeks to give further support to their argument that British and German societies were not so different in their response to Labour as *Sonderweg* theories would suggest. In particular this section focuses on: the ambiguity of state reactions to Labour, including

---

[31] Hodge, 'The Trammels of Tradition', 49.
[32] Eisenberg, 'The Comparative View', 403–32.
[33] Blackbourn and Eley, *Peculiarities*, 26.

outright repression as well as efforts at integration; the possibility of parliamentary alliances with bourgeois parties, and the ambiguous attitude of working-class parties towards parliamentary democracy; the employers' response to the labour movement; the attitudes of both working-class parties to the middle classes and to 'bourgeois' culture.

Once it has been established that the social contexts in which both working-class parties operated were not so very different, the issues of organizational structure and ideology will be examined in Chapters 3 to 5. Chapter 3 outlines the national, regional, and local organizational structure of the two working-class parties. It discusses the character of party leadership, the functions of the party conferences, the nature of the party press, and the organization of party finance and will focus on questions of intra-party democracy, the relations between the party and the trade unions, and the bureaucratic, centralistic, hierarchic nature of both party organizations.

Chapter 4 deals with the crucial importance of notions of solidarity in both parties and focuses on the following aspects: the local organizations as well as the local ancillary organizations of both parties, the implications of belonging to the Labour Party or the SPD, the labour movement culture in Britain and Germany, and the degree of participation of British and German workers in party affairs.

Chapter 5 distinguishes between official ideology and ideology from below. The argument about the basic difference in the official ideology—labourism vs. Marxism—is re-evaluated. Additionally, the ideology of the rank and file is examined. It has to be readily conceded here that it is painfully difficult to reconstruct the world of values and beliefs of the two parties' rank and file. Every effort to do so is overburdened with methodological problems. However, by looking at some of the key words and concepts in popular novels and party literature which the rank and file were likely to read, by investigating the symbolism of both parties' 'festival culture', and by taking into account the results of oral history research, it is possible to arrive at tentative conclusions about the 'ideology from below' of both Labour Party and SPD.

Finally the last chapter deals with the relations between the two parties. By evaluating the scope and quality of existing relations, further light will be shed on the question how far apart or how close the two parties were. If, as I argue throughout, both the British Labour Party and the German SPD were party to a very similar form of socialism, then it is about time to reopen the debate on the existing typologies of labour movements.

2

Integration of the British
and the German Labour Movements
into their Respective Societies

WORKING-CLASS parties everywhere came into existence as a result of claims by the working class to participate in the nation-state's affairs. The nation-state's response to that claim was indicative of the degree of integration of the working-class parties. Existing historiography has stressed the difference in this response between Britain and Germany. The repressive nature of the illiberal, undemocratic, omnipresent German state, it is argued, led to an alienation of organized Labour from that state, whereas the liberal, democratic British state was able smoothly to integrate organized Labour into the traditional framework of government.[1] This argument will be questioned in the first two sections by a re-examination of the relationship between organized Labour and nation-state. Then the investigation moves from the nation-state towards the wider society. The relationship between organized Labour and employers in Britain and Germany forms the subject of the third section and the working-class parties' relations with the middle classes will be discussed in the last. Finally, it should be possible to come to a tentative re-evaluation of the degree of integration of both British and German Labour into their respective societies.

2.1. Working-class parties and the nation-state in Britain and Germany

John Schwarzmantel has recently argued that the attitude of the Labour Party towards the form of the British nation-state was positive, whereas the attitude of the SPD towards the form of the nation-state in Imperial

---

[1] Mommsen, 'Arbeiterbewegung', 273–90; Kendall, *The Labour Movement*, 2–10; Geary, *Labour and Socialist Movements*, 2; Eisenberg, 'The Comparative View', 424; Gordon A. Philipps, 'Britische Gewerkschaften und der Staat', in *Konflikt und Kooperation: Strategien europäischer Gewerkschaften im 20. Jahrhundert* (Essen, 1988), 31; Gregory M. Luebbert, *Liberalism, Fascism or Social Democracy: Social Classes and the Political Origins of Regimes in Interwar Europe* (Oxford, 1991), 159.

Germany was negative. According to him, this had to do with the different character of the nation-state in both countries. Whereas an authoritarian, anti-socialist ethnic nationalism, dominant in Germany, ran counter to the SPD's own democratic nationalism, the British Labour Party could participate in a democratic nationalism based on a consensual framework of government.[2] The following argument about the relationship between organized Labour and the nation-state in Britain and Germany is an attempt to put forward an alternative interpretation to the one provided by Schwarzmantel. Like most *Sonderweg* historians, on whom he incidentally relies heavily in his historical analysis,[3] he overemphasizes the degree of alienation felt by Social Democrats in Imperial Germany, whilst, at the same time, he underestimates the serious cracks in the consensual façade of a less than democratic British state.

The working-class parties in Britain and Germany could look back on a long tradition of commitment towards internationalism. British trade unions were dominant in the setting up of the First International and the British Labour Party played a major role in reconstituting the Second International after 1918, while German socialists dominated much of the theory and programme of the Second International up to 1914.[4] Whilst internationalism and nationalism could and did flourish side by side within many working-class organizations before the First World War, internationalist socialist sentiments had their origin in the rejection of nationalism, in the recognition that other factors, notably class, were a more important bond amongst people than nationality. The danger inherent in the potential juxtaposition of internationalism and nationalism was clearly perceived by revisionist Social Democrats like Wolfgang Heine who condemned the internationalism of the SPD as counterproductive to national integration as early as the 1880s.[5]

The nation-state increasingly came to be perceived as the place where

---

[2] John Schwarzmantel, *Socialism and the Idea of the Nation* (London, 1991), 88–136.

[3] Much of Schwarzmantel's historical argument is based on H.-U. Wehler, *Sozialdemokratie und Nationalstaat: Die deutsche Sozialdemokratie und die Nationalitätenfragen in Deutschland von Karl Marx bis zum Ausbruch des ersten Weltkrieges* (Würzburg, 1962). He also recycles ideas put forward by Günther Roth, *The Social Democrats in Imperial Germany: A Study in Working-Class Isolation and National Integration* (Totowa, NJ, 1963) and Dieter Groh, *Negative Integration und revolutionärer Attentismus: Die deutsche Sozialdemokratie am Vorabend des ersten Weltkriegs* (Frankfurt am Main, 1973). These two classic accounts of pre-First World War Social Democracy both stress the negative attitude of the SPD towards the Wilhelmine state, conceding only a 'negative integration' into Imperial Germany through the vast network of ancillary organizations built up by the SPD.

[4] For a wider discussion of the internationalism of both parties see 6.3.

[5] Wolfgang Heine, 'Persönliche, nur für die Familie bestimmte, Erinnerungen, 1861–1927', in BA Koblenz, Kl. Erw., no. 371–15, p. 341.

labour movements had to frame and enact their policies. Thus the various labour movements in Europe all took shape as national movements.[6] Comparing the attitudes of different European working-class parties towards the nation-state, Marcel van der Linden, contrary to received wisdom, found the British and German working-class parties identifying relatively strongly with their nation-state, whereas the Russian socialists suffered the greatest degree of alienation from its nation-state.[7] Such a view is echoed by Lothar Erdmann, the trade union theorist, who argued that the labour movement, in fostering social reform, was one of the major factors in bringing about a positive attitude by the working classes to the nation-state.[8] Hans-Ulrich Wehler has argued that the SPD was not entirely free of nationalist sentiments before 1914.[9] Karl Kautsky's booklet on 'Patriotism and Social Democracy' with its anti-Slav bias only underlines Wehler's point.[10] Also, the official republican sentiments amongst Social Democrats were increasingly shot through with an acceptance of the monarchy of Imperial Germany.[11] This can be seen as further evidence of the SPD's ambiguous position between integration into and alienation from the German nation-state.

Pre-war British socialists were equally ambiguous in their attitude to the nation-state. Republican sentiments could be found side by side with a widespread acceptance of the monarchy inside the British labour movement.[12] Committed internationalists like Keir Hardie, MacDonald, and Fenner Brockway stood next to rabid nationalists like Blatchford,

---

[6] Although for Britain it has to be said that the Labour Party never really penetrated Ireland.

[7] Marcel van der Linden, 'The National Integration of European Working Classes (1871–1914)', *IRSH*, 33 (1988), 286.

[8] Lothar Erdmann, 'Nationale und internationale Aufgaben der Gewerkschaften', in *Vierteljahrhundertfeier der internationalen Gewerkschaftsbewegung*, ed. by the IFTU (Berlin, 1926), 7 f. See also idem, 'Nation, Gewerkschaften und Sozialismus', *DA*, 10, 1933, 129–161.

[9] Wehler, *Sozialdemokratie und Nationalstaat*, 196. For the advance of nationalism in the SPD before 1914 see also Stanley Pierson, *Marxist Intellectuals and the Working-Class Montality in Germany 1887–1912* (Cambridge/Mass., 1993), 205–28. The most authoritative analysis of the SPD's relationship to the nation-state also stresses the increasing identification of the party with a democratic concept of the nation-state. See Dieter Groh and Peter Brandt, *'Vaterlandslose Gesellen': Sozialdemokratie und Nation 1860–1990* (Munich, 1992), 17–210.

[10] Karl Kautsky, *Patriotismus und Sozialdemokratie* (Leipzig, 1907), 12–15.

[11] Ludwig Quessel, 'Sozialdemokratie und Monarchie', *SM* 16/1 (1912), 271–5. Generally on that topic see Werner K. Blessing, 'Der monarchische Kult, politische Loyalität und die Arbeiterbewegung im deutschen Kaiserreich', in G. A. Ritter (ed.), *Arbeiterkultur* (Königstein im Taunus, 1979), 185–208.

[12] J. A. Thompson, 'Labour and the Modern British Monarchy', *South Atlantic Quarterly*, 70 (1971), 341–9. K. O. Morgan, *Keir Hardie* (London, 1975), 73.

Hyndman, and Grayson.[13] Working-class nationalism—to which the latter appealed—was very real in early twentieth-century Britain (and beyond).[14] However, this should not be taken to imply that nationalist sentiments necessarily precluded a distinct sense of alienation from the nation-state. The existence of 'two nations' in Britain during much of the nineteenth and twentieth century was at least equally real. The British labour movement expressly represented only one of these two nations, and its activists often shared a sense of alienation from the 'other' nation. Labour leaders like Keir Hardie, in their appeal to the working class, played on those feelings of alienation. When Hardie addressed the Barrow Labour Party before 1914, a local report recounted his comments on the typical workingmen's clothes he was wearing that evening:

They were told that the ridiculous dress in which he appeared in the House of Commons . . . was the dress he was wearing that night. (Loud cheers) He did not feel that he need be ashamed of it. (Applause) . . . He had worked for it, and the hand of the sweater had never touched it. (Loud cheers) If every MP could give as good an account of his clothing, his conscience would be pretty clear. He refused, and he would refuse, to change his dress or his opinions to please any man or body of men.[15]

It was also not by chance that Keir Hardie was a Scot representing a Welsh constituency (Merthyr Tydfil) in Parliament before 1914. The British labour movement had strong roots in the Celtic fringe of Britain which found (and, one might add, still finds) it difficult to identify with the British nation-state. Unsurprisingly both the Labour Party in Wales before 1914 and the Scottish Labour Party for some time after 1918 were extremely sympathetic to demands for Home Rule for Wales and Scotland respectively.[16]

In the first World War Wilhelm Schröder's 1911 dictum that 'many a man will be stunned . . ., how enthusiastically Social Democrats will defend

---

[13] Henry Pelling, 'British Labour and British Imperialism', in id., *Popular Politics and Society in Late Victorian Britain* (London, 1968), 82–100; Victor Kiernan, 'Working-Class and Nation in Nineteenth Century Britain', in Maurice Cornforth (ed.), *Rebels and their Causes: Essays in Honour of A. L. Morton* (London, 1978), 123–39. For widespread sentiments of colonialism and imperialism in both the Labour Party and the SPD see Frits van Holthoun and Marcel van der Linden (eds.), *Internationalism in the Labour Movement 1830–1940* (Leiden, 1988), 42–86.

[14] John Benson, *The Working Class in Britain 1850–1939* (London, 1989), 161–3.

[15] *Our Struggle for Socialism in Barrow: 50 Years Anniversary of the Labour Party* (Barrow, 1950), 9.

[16] David Howell, *A Lost Left: Three Studies in Socialism and Nationalism* (Manchester, 1986) and K. O. Morgan, *Rebirth of a Nation: Wales 1880–1980* (Oxford, 1981), 254.

the fatherland, when they are finally forced to . . .'[17] became a sad reality in both Britain and Germany. Masses of socialist articles and pamphlets were published which defended the 'national' war effort. Susanne Miller, Gerald Feldman and Detlef Lehnert have all described the manner in which organized Labour in Germany was absorbed into the nation-state in the First World War.[18] Bethmann-Hollweg, chancellor from 1909 until 1917, wrote to the union leader Carl Legien on 28 February 1918:

That you and the trade unions you lead have a heart for the future of our people, I know from your co-operation with me, which I will always remember with special pleasure and for which the country will have to thank you forever. Out of the experience of this co-operation, I trust that your will to hold fast to the policy of 4 August, will not be swayed . . .[19]

It is also revealing that the official social democratic press in the war did everything to please the authorities: self-censorship was extremely wide-spread.[20] Those socialists who refused self-censorship and remained true to the SPD's pre-war internationalism finally seceded from the SPD in 1917 over the question of continued war support.

Internationalists in the British Labour Party who remained true to their pre-war beliefs were equally isolated and persecuted within their own movement.[21] The jingoism of some British trade union leaders is well known. The Seamen's and Firemen's Union under the leadership of Havelock Wilson, for example, would not allow Arthur Henderson and William Gillies to go to the Stockholm socialist peace conference in 1917.[22] If a split was avoided this was not so much due to the absence of conflicts between internationalists and nationalists in the Labour Party. It had more to do with the character of the Labour Party which only knew affiliated membership of organizations at that time. Some affiliated organizations, like the ILP were overwhelmingly anti-war, whilst others, like some of the major trade unions supported the war. Some members of the

[17] Wilhelm Schröder, 'Sozialdemokratie und Vaterland', *SM* 15 (1911), 1590.

[18] Susanne Miller, *Burgfrieden und Klassenkampf* (Düsseldorf, 1974), 68–74; Gerald Feldman, *Army, Industry and Labor in Germany, 1914–1918* (Princeton, NJ, 1966), 520; Detlef Lehnert, *Sozialdemokratie und Novemberrevolution: Die Neuordnungsdebatte 1918/19 in der politischen Publizistik von SPD und USPD* (Frankfurt am Main, 1983).

[19] ZStA Potsdam, Legien papers, 90 Le 6, 134, 5–6: letter from Bethmann to Legien, 28 Feb. 1918.

[20] IGA/ZPA, PV II 145/13: Berichte des Sozialdemokratischen Pressebüros über Pressekonferenzen.

[21] David Marquand, *Ramsay MacDonald* (London, 1977), 164–237.

[22] Hildamarie Meynell, 'The Second International, 1914–23' (University of Oxford B. Litt. 1956), 179.

Labour Party's NEC joined the war cabinet in 1915 and some went to prison. Consequently, whilst the Labour Party was split over the matter, individual organizations and their active membership remained relatively unified in their stance. ILP members might well have deplored the pro-war stance of the majority of those organizations which were affiliated to the Labour Party. However, they did not have to found a new party, as the ILP already existed—affiliated but separate from the Labour Party.

After the First World War Germany experienced a revolution, Britain did not. Does that not point to a different degree of radicalism in the working-class parties in Britain and Germany? First of all, one should stress the obvious impact of military defeat in Germany. The German government simply did not have the adequate means of dealing with the revolutionary unrest in 1918. Its authority was eroded and the suffering of the population due to the Allied blockade was intense. By contrast, the victorious British government, not faced with similar forms of economic hardship, found effective means of dealing with the revolutionary potential which was showing in post-war Britain as well.[23] And secondly, it remained true after the war that the SPD was not, in the words of Kautsky, a revolution-making party. Quite the contrary, the wartime commitment of the SPD to the nation-state continued. If anything, it was substantially strengthened by many of the radicals having left the SPD for the USPD. In the revolutionary turmoil of 1918 and 1919 the SPD put itself at the head of the radicalized masses to defuse the situation and calm troubled waters. At the Weimar party conference in 1919 Eduard Bernstein was heavily criticized for having condemned the nationalism of the party during the war. Scholich denounced Bernstein as 'anti-national Socialist',[24] and Kummer saw Bernstein's fault in his 'mania for truth (*Wahrheitsfimmel*) . . . For this one-sided search for truth (*Wahrheitssucherei*) the German workers will never be able to have any understanding.'[25] At the same conference Otto Wels argued that to be proud of one's nation was 'something great and colossal. We Germans must learn to feel German.'[26] Social Democrats and trade unionists came to identify fully with the German nation as the SPD's position on the treaty of Versailles and on the occupation of the Ruhr were to demonstrate. Hilferding's theory

---

[23] James E. Cronin, 'Coping with Labour, 1918–1926', in James E. Cronin and Jonathan Schneer (eds.), *Social Conflict and the Political Order in Modern Britain* (London, 1982), 113–45.

[24] *Protokoll des SPD Parteitags 1919 in Weimar* (Berlin, 1919), 268.   [25] Ibid. 271.

[26] Ibid. 159. Also on the post-war stand of the SPD towards the nation-state: Winkler, *Von der Revolution*, 206–26.

of organized capitalism, already formulated before the First World War, became the dominant party theory in the Weimar Republic. The consequence of this for the SPD's relations with the state was positive, because the state, according to Hilferding, could be used to achieve economic democracy and finally socialism. It had thus been transformed from a Marxist 'superstructure', which had to be smashed, into a useful means of reform.[27]

Nevertheless the ambiguous tension between isolation and integration continued after 1918. It is mirrored by the historiographical debate: whereas Heinrich August Winkler and Michael Stürmer, for example, have argued that the SPD was not willing to commit itself fully to the parliamentary democracy of the Weimar Republic, Richard Breitmann has emphasized the SPD's readiness to co-operate with other democratic parties and to attract support from non-working-class voters.[28] It can scarcely be denied that many Social Democrats found it difficult to leave behind the memory of persecution under the Anti-Socialist Law and develop a positive attitude towards the nation-state. On the other hand, the law did not only alienate Social Democrats. It created a determination to work within the legal limits defined by the nation-state.[29] However, as H. A. Winkler has argued in a comparison between the policies of the French and the German socialists in the inter-war years, the electoral strength of the KPD in Germany put the SPD under pressure to strengthen its class appeal to the more radical elements of the German working class; thus the SPD's inability to overcome its ambiguous stand somewhere between revolutionary rhetoric and reformist practice.[30]

As the electoral strength of the CPGB remained negligible, one would expect it to be much less difficult for the British Labour Party to develop

---

[27] Hilferding's speech on the 1927 party conference clearly shows the effort to develop a more positive theory of the state. See *Protokoll des SPD Parteitags in Kiel 1927* (Berlin, 1927, repr. Bonn, 1974), 165–89.

[28] Richard Breitmann, *German Socialism and Weimar Democracy* (Chapel Hill, NC, 1981), 8. Heinrich August Winkler, *Der Schein der Normalität: Arbeiter und Arbeiterbewegung in der Weimarer Republik, 1924–1930* (Berlin, 1985), 334 characterized the attitude of the SPD as 'reserved republicanism'; Michael Stürmer, *Koalition und Opposition in der Weimarer Republik, 1924–1928* (Düsseldorf, 1967), 140 talked of 'self-elimination of the SPD' from political power. Susanne Miller, *Die Bürde der Macht: Die deutsche Sozialdemokratie, 1918–1920* (Düsseldorf, 1978), 446 stressed the fact that the Social Democrats did not take full responsibility for the state because they lacked skill and experience to do so due to their widespread exclusion from power in the Kaiserreich.

[29] Willi Guttsman, *The German Social Democratic Party, 1875–1933: From Ghetto to Government* (London, 1981), 57–60.

[30] H. A. Winkler, 'Klassenkampf vs. Koalition: Die französischen Sozialisten und die Politik der deutschen Sozialdemokraten', *GG* 17 (1991), 186.

into a well-integrated people's party after 1918. Indeed, some Labour activists of the inter-war years stressed the positive integration of Labour into British society: 'trade unions have never come into conflict with the State on claims to provide an alternative government to the one in power, but only on claims that in respect of certain questions in dispute their members must obey their unions and not the State.'[31] Yet, after the First World War up to the 1926 General Strike, when industrial unrest and rank-and-file radicalism were riding high, it seemed to many onlookers that a positive integration of the British labour movement was threatened for the first time, that a turn to revolutionary attitudes was conceivable. Reports of local demonstrations in 1920 show that there was strong anti-state sentiment: 'We are out for the overthrow of the capitalist system in this country. We are not going to be dictated to by that fraternity any longer, nor accept their rotten system of piecework . . . Three cheers for the Socialist Revolution.'[32] Although it never had a chance of seriously influencing the Parliamentary Labour Party (PLP), this kind of statement fell within an acceptable range of Labour Party rhetoric after the First World War. The firm commitment to internationalism, as shown in the 'Hands off Russia' campaign,[33] the radical commitment to 'pacificism',[34] the propagation of the League and the rejection of traditional diplomacy after 1918 all indicated a growing anti-nationalist feeling in the Labour Party.

The strong identification of sections of both movements with their nation-state was somewhat surprising given the long tradition of repression of organized Labour in both countries. Comparing levels of repression in various European nation-states in the nineteenth century R. J. Goldstein has come to the conclusion that repression in both Britain and Germany can be described as significant. It was the pervasiveness and frequency of political repression in Germany which set the German case

---

[31] W. Milne-Bailey, *Trade Unions and the State* (London, 1934), 21. For a more recent view of the argument of slow and constant integration of Labour into the state see Hugh Clegg, *A History of British Trade Unionism since 1911*, ii: *1911–1933* (Oxford, 1985), 558 and Ross M. Martin, *TUC: The Growth of a Pressure Group, 1868–1976* (Oxford, 1980), 58.

[32] A speaker from the Operative Builders' Society at a Sept. 1920 demonstration at Hatfield; see Peter Kingsford, *The Labour Movement in Hatfield, 1918–1970* (Hatfield, 1988), 10.

[33] L. J. MacFarlane, 'Hands off Russia: British Labour and the Russo-Polish War, 1920', *PP* 38 (Dec. 1967), 126–52.

[34] Martin Ceadel, *Pacifism in Britain, 1914–1945: The Defining of a Faith* (Oxford, 1980), 3 distinguished pacifism from pacificism. Pacifism is 'the belief that all war is always wrong and should never be resorted to', whereas pacificism is based on 'the assumption that war, though sometimes necessary, is always an irrational and inhumane way to solve disputes'.

apart from the British one.[35] One can find similar juxtapositions of a liberal British state vs. a repressive German state in the work of J. P. Nettl,[36] and more recently in the work of Jürgen Kocka, Mary Nolan, Aristide R. Zolberg, and John Breuilly.[37] These interpretations are in line with a recent trend in British historiography to emphasize the liberal character of the British state, neglecting its more repressive features.[38]

The evidence for the repressive nature of the German state is overwhelming. When the anti-socialist law finally elapsed in 1890, the German labour movement had gone through eleven years of severe state repression, which led to a strong radicalization of the SPD's attitude towards the state.[39] The state bureaucracy, especially the police and the courts, came to be seen as instruments of the ruling class by the SPD.[40] However, the British labour movement had experienced a similar period of severe persecution in the first half of the nineteenth century. The disregard of the customary legal decencies, the widespread use of police spies and *agents provocateurs*, the extensive use of imprisonment and deportations was an indication that the British state, just like its German counterpart, was reacting ruthlessly to any challenge to the existing political and economic system.[41]

The years between 1850 and the 1870s are usually described as the classical years of working-class reformism in Britain.[42] The Tories and the Liberal Party under Gladstone from 1868 to 1874 managed to soothe working-class radicalism by pushing through Parliament important legislation, for instance, the 1867 extension of the franchise to all male householders within the towns and the 1872 recognition of trade unions. From then on organized Labour saw little reason for independent

[35] R. J. Goldstein, *Political Repression in Nineteenth Century Europe* (London, 1983), 333.

[36] J. P. Nettl, 'The State as a Conceptual Variable', *World Politics*, 20 (1968), 560–92.

[37] For Kocka, Nolan, and Zolberg see their respective contributions in Katznelson and Zolberg, *Working-Class Formation*; for Breuilly see his recent *Labour and Liberalism*.

[38] Such tendencies can be found in the work of Alastair Reid, *Social Classes and Social Relations in Britain, 1850–1914* (London, 1992) and E. F. Biagini and Alastair Reid (eds.), *Currents of Radicalism: Popular Radicalism, Organized Labour and Party Politics in Britain 1850–1914* (Cambridge, 1991).

[39] For anti-state propaganda material under the anti-socialist laws, see the collection of pamphlets in IGA/ZPA, Handbill Collection, V DF/3/11.

[40] H.-G. Haupt, 'Staatliche Bürokratie und Arbeiterbewegung: Zum Einfluß der Polizei auf die Konstituierung von Arbeiterbewegung und Arbeiterklasse in Deutschland und Frankreich zwischen 1848 und 1880', in Jürgen Kocka (ed.), *Arbeiter und Bürger im 19. Jahrhundert: Varianten ihres Verhältnisses im europäischen Vergleich* (Munich, 1986), 221–54.

[41] John Saville, *1848: The British State and the Chartist Movement* (Cambridge, 1987).

[42] Neville Kirk, *The Growth of Working Class Reformism in Mid-Victorian England* (London, 1985).

political representation in Parliament, and it increasingly came to rely on the Liberal Party as a mouthpiece for labour's demands. The 1880s saw the beginning of the end of that alignment in Britain with the emergence of the New Unionism and small socialist organizations like the SDF. As soon as working-class radicalism threatened to raise its head again, the British state's repressive potential came to the forefront again. A common interest in the suppression of what was perceived as radical working-class organizations was revealed in the correspondence between the Imperial Ministry of the Interior of the Reich and the British government. In a letter of 12 February 1902, Lord Lansdowne declared his government's willingness to take part in a common international fight against revolutionary organizations. In a further memorandum of 2 June 1902 he assured the Berlin government that the Metropolitan Police Force in London would already closely monitor every step of the capital's revolutionaries.[43] In the light of this one can only endorse David Howell's warning not to underestimate the authoritarianism of the British state.[44]

The yearly reports of the Prussian police to the Minister of the Interior are full of allegations of the revolutionary character of Social Democracy, right through to 1914:

German Social Democracy has refrained from revolutionary deeds within the last few years, so that one might be tempted—at first sight—to believe in a transformation of Social Democracy from a revolutionary into a radical reform party. In reality there can be no doubt that the revolutionary character of the movement has remained unchanged.[45]

Because the German government failed to acknowledge the changing mood within the SPD towards strict legality, a whole series of efforts were made to produce some sort of anti-socialist legislation after 1890. It is significant though that none of these plans succeeded, because the majority of the Reichstag parties were not willing to carry them. Social Democracy was no longer faced with a monolithic anti-socialist bloc in parliament. Nevertheless the hard line taken by the government, the Conservative parties, and the Kaiser created bitter feelings amongst Social Democrats who long remembered 'the constant persecutions, with

---

[43] ZStA Potsdam, 15.01: RMdI, nos. 13688, 28–35, and 88–90. Even if it is clear that Lansdowne did not mean by 'revolutionaries' what his German counterpart meant, the exchange shows that both governments viewed working-class organizations as potentially dangerous to the political stability of their respective governments.

[44] Howell, *A Lost Left*, 285.

[45] ZStA Merseburg, Rep. 77/656 I: Bericht über den Stand der sozialdemokratischen und anarchistischen Bewegung im Allgemeinen, p. 18.

which the government . . . after the fall of the anti-socialist laws opposed the demands of the working class for equality and participation'.[46]

Apart from legislative measures, the freedoms of association and assembly were very much restricted in Germany: many social democratic gatherings could not be held, because the authorities withheld permission.[47] On even more occasions social democratic events had to be cut short, as the obligatory policeman would shut the assembly for minor offences against the state or its institutions. The schools and universities and the army as well as the militaristic organizations of Imperial Germany were exploited for anti-socialist propaganda.[48] If necessary the state authorities were willing to use police and army against organized Labour. In the event of large-scale demonstrations, troops were often under alert, as, for instance, in Berlin in 1908.[49] German Labour activists could not but experience the omnipresent state as a repressive agent for more sinister forces.[50] Unsurprisingly Richard Evans found the pub talk of Hamburg workers full of complaints about police harassment, unfair imprisonment, and dubious legal proceedings.[51]

The 1918 revolution in Germany changed the situation: repression of the SPD, so significant a feature of Imperial Germany, stopped almost completely in the Weimar Republic. However, the post-revolution SPD was not the same as the pre-war SPD. The wartime split of the party was also a split between those socialists for whom integration into any capitalist nation-state seemed impossible and those who had embarked on the difficult path towards such integration. The former smaller part of the pre-war SPD now formed the KPD, and the full force of the democratic German state came down on the KPD in the Weimar Republic. Repression of working-class parties did not disappear, it only concentrated on another party. The KPD and the SPD both suffered terribly under

---

[46] BA Koblenz, Kl. Erw. no. 371-15, Wolfgang Heine, 'Erinnerungen', 372.

[47] ZStA Potsdam, 01.01, nos. 2855-63: suppression of social democratic associations and their assemblies 1872-1928.

[48] G. A. Ritter and Klaus Tenfelde, *Arbeiter im deutschen Kaiserreich 1871-1914* (Bonn, 1992), 680 f., 724 f., and 737 ff. See also Thomas Rohrkrämer, *Der Militarismus der 'kleinen Leute': Die Kriegervereine im deutschen Kaiserreich 1871-1914* (Munich, 1990).

[49] IGA/ZPA, St. 22/68. For police action against the labour movement see Dieter Fricke, *Bismarcks Prätorianer: Die Berliner politische Polizei im Kampf gegen die deutsche Arbeiterbewegung (1871-1898)* (Berlin, 1962).

[50] Dick Geary, 'Identifying Militancy: The Assessment of Working Class Attitudes towards State and Society', in Richard J. Evans (ed.), *The German Working Class 1888-1933: The Politics of Everyday Life* (London, 1982), 220-46.

[51] Richard J. Evans, *Proletarians and Politics: Socialism, Protest and the Working Class in Germany before the First World War* (New York, 1990), 151.

National Socialism. It was, without any doubt, the worst form of persecution the German labour movement had ever experienced. All the SPD
in particular had striven for and had been partially successful in implementing in the Weimar Republic (key elements of a welfare state and a
parliamentary democracy, to name just the two most important) was lost
in the Nazi dictatorship.

There was never a remotely similar effort in Britain completely to
destroy the labour movement and murder its activists. This is not to say,
however, that repression of the labour movement was altogether absent
from the British scene. There are indications that the relations between
the police and British Labour were far from harmonious. The police were
widely perceived as an instrument of class rule: 'Along the dividing line,
there they stand, taking their orders, together with pay and promotion,
from the one class, and executing them for the most part on the other, as
any police court records will show.'[52] The years between 1900 and 1939
saw the development of 'a national police force designed to counter either
a local or a nation-wide threat from labour.'[53] Robert Roberts has dismissed the working men's love of the policemen in Britain as myth,
describing the ruthless action of British police against striking trade unionists.[54] In Pontypridd, for example, after the General Strike had collapsed
in 1926, the police raided the home of the Secretary of the General Strike
Committee to seek out seditious literature.[55] In Leeds, at the end of the
nineteenth century, strikers were repeatedly prevented from holding
meetings by co-ordinated attempts of the chief constable, the town clerk,
the mayor, and a watch committee.[56] Equally the police and the army were
introduced in strikes.[57] Victimization against teachers who were active on
behalf of the labour movement was not unknown in Britain.[58] Dan Griffiths

---

[52] Stephen Reynolds, Bob and Tom Woolley, *Seems So! A Working-Class View of Politics* (London, 1913), 85.

[53] Jane Morgan, *Conflict and Order: The Police and Labour Disputes in England and Wales, 1900–1939* (Oxford, 1987), 276.

[54] Robert Roberts, *The Classic Slum: Salford Life in the First Quarter of the Century* (Manchester, 1971), 71.

[55] Brynmor John, 'Introduction to the Archive of the Pontypridd Labour Party', in *Origins and Developments of the Labour Party* ed. by D. G. Clark (EP Microfilm, Wakefield, 1980), 8.

[56] E. P. Thompson, 'Homage to Tom Maguire', in Asa Briggs and John Saville (eds.), *Essays in Labour History* (London, 1960), 307.

[57] John Saville, 'Trade Unions and Free Labour: The Background to the Taff Vale Decision', in Briggs and Saville, *Essays*, 326 f.

[58] *The Burston School Strike*, ed. by the ILP (London, 1915). Also: *Labour Leader* (26 Feb. 1909), 130, 'Socialist Teacher Dismissed'; and ibid. (12 Mar. 1909), 164, 'Political Persecution at Burnley: Socialist Woman Teacher Dismissed'.

has claimed that schools were as instrumental to the British as to the German ruling class: 'The enemies of the workers in Germany . . . made a cult of inculcating subservience and "patriotism" in their schools. . . . The same thing is being done . . . in this country. The celebration of Empire Day, for example, is a part of this process.'[59]

Not only at the state level, but also at the municipal level, state authorities discriminated against the labour movements in both countries wherever possible.[60] Boards of Guardians in Britain, for instance, would sometimes change their time of meeting from evening to morning so as to make it impossible for working men to attend,[61] and municipal councils in Germany would make sure that Social Democrats were not elected to important committees.[62] Yet, before 1914, there remained a decisive difference in that the Labour Party was involved in municipal government in at least some localities, whereas the SPD was widely excluded from power in the localities. After the First World War—with changes in the franchise system in both countries and an altogether different political situation—both parties became heavily involved in the running of local government. The German Social Democrats consciously adopted British ideas of 'municipal socialism' and sought to adapt them to the German framework of municipal politics.[63] Socialist controlled municipalities in the 1920s like Berlin and Sheffield implemented similar programmes aimed at providing services ranging from the municipal provision of gas, electricity, and water to cheap public transport facilities to better and cheaper housing to the provision of educational facilities to the supply of milk, and so on.[64]

So far the reaction of both the British and the German state towards their respective labour movements has been described as one of

---

[59] Dan Griffiths, *The Real Enemy and Other Socialist Essays* (London, 1923), 65.

[60] For Britain see *Labour Organizer* (Dec. 1929), 244 f.; for Germany see generally Robert Michels, 'Die deutsche Sozialdemokratie: Parteimitgliedschaft und soziale Zusammensetzung', *AfSWP* 23, NS 5 (1906), 485. A local example is given by Bernd Rabe, *Der sozialdemokratische Charakter: Drei Generationen aktiver Parteimitglieder in einem Arbeiterviertel* (Frankfurt am Main, 1978), 32 f.

[61] *Report and Balance Sheet of Barrow-in-Furness LRC, 1905–06* (Barrow-in-Furness, 1906), 5.

[62] Erhard Lucas, *Zwei Formen von Radikalismus in der deutschen Arbeiterbewegung* (Frankfurt am Main, 1976), 131.

[63] Edmund Fischer, 'Der Gemeindesozialismus', *SM* 14 (1910), 181–6 and Max Fechner, 'Municipal Socialism in Germany Since the War', *Labour Magazine*, 8 (1929–30), 364–7.

[64] For Sheffield see E. G. Rowlinson, 'Triumph of Municipal Enterprise: Why Sheffield is a Labour Stronghold', *Labour Magazine*, 6 (1927–8), 353–5. For Berlin, Frankfurt, Hamburg, and other SPD strongholds of municipal socialism in the 1920s see the reports in the SPD's monthly municipal periodical *Die Gemeinde*.

repression. However, both states followed a double strategy which can best be described as a 'carrot and stick' policy. Persecution, especially in the law courts, was mixed with efforts to integrate the working classes into the framework of the nation-state by means of social policy measures, aimed at undermining the position of the labour movement in the working class. This argument should, however, not be taken to imply that a strictly instrumentalist interpretation is adopted by the present study. It shall be readily conceded that the development of both the nation-state's legal system and its social policy had a number of reasons. Their function as instruments in the hands of a ruling élite to minimize the importance of independent working-class organizations was just one amongst other functions. What is really at issue here, then, is the potential of both countries' social policy and law enforcement procedures to demote the working-class parties in Britain and Germany respectively.

Both countries were pioneers of the modern welfare state.[65] In the second half of the nineteenth century questions of social reform surfaced in both societies and quickly were to take the centre stage in public discussion, partly because an impoverished underclass was more and more perceived as a revolutionary threat.[66] The aim of creating a kind of state control over the whole spectrum of working-class life was propagated as a remedy.[67] In Britain discussions about the necessity of social reform were additionally promoted by the 'national-efficiency' debate after the Boer War. Welfare was meant to reduce social tensions, to maintain and develop the work ethic, and to bring a solution to the social problems of the time without challenging the political, social, and economic system.[68]

It is interesting to note that the labour movements in Britain and Germany were both rather reluctant to accept welfare legislation at first. In Germany this was primarily due to the anti-Labour bias of Bismarck's legislation but it was also important that the social welfare legislation still

---

[65] Wolfgang J. Mommsen and Wolfgang Mock (eds.), *The Emergence of the Welfare State in Britain and Germany, 1850–1950* (London, 1981); G. A. Ritter, *Der Sozialstaat im internationalen Vergleich* (2nd edn., Munich, 1991).

[66] For Germany see James J. Sheehan, *The Career of Lujo Brentano: A Study of Liberalism and Social Reform in Imperial Germany* (Chicago, 1966), 46–94. For Britain see Pat Thane, *The Foundations of the Welfare State* (London, 1982), 38, 61, 107–11, 217.

[67] Jürgen Reulecke, 'Formen bürgerlich-sozialen Engagements in Deutschland und England im 19. Jahrhundert', in Kocka, *Arbeiter und Bürger*, 284 has argued that ideas of social control cannot be found in Britain. That this is not necessarily so has been shown by John Brown, 'Social Control and the Modernisation of Social Policy 1890–1929', in Pat Thane (ed.), *The Origins of British Social Policy* (London, 1978), 126–46.

[68] G. V. Rimlinger, *Welfare Policy and Industrialization in Europe, America and Russia* (New York, 1971), 9 f.

only benefited a minority of workers. In Britain trade union leaders before 1914 were reluctant to see the state taking over the functions the unions had so far provided for their members, such as unemployment benefits or pensions.[69] Yet, especially within the Fabian Society, the Labour Party, and increasingly within the big industrial trade unions, a form of collectivist state socialism, in which the provision of social welfare played a central part, came to be the accepted doctrine, even before 1914.[70]

Despite and because of Bismarck, the SPD and the socialist trade unions looked to the state for support in their demands for social welfare. In the Reichstag before 1914 it was in the area of social policy that the Social Democrats were most active. Already before the war, as the issue of the *Arbeitsnachweise*[71] shows, the unions had come to see the state as an ally against the all-too-powerful German employers' associations.[72] The labour movement also co-operated with 'bourgeois' social reformers when they tried to devise social policies.[73] In the war it was the government at all levels which supported the movement's commitment to an industrial truce, whereas most employers remained hesitant to accept trade unions as bargaining partners.[74] After the war, the trade unions tried more and more to use the state for the adoption of its social and economic policies.[75]

If social policy was the carrot, then the law, it is usually argued, was the stick. It is portrayed as one of the most potent weapons of the German ruling élites in their endeavour to keep the Social Democrats at

---

[69] Henry Pelling, 'The British Working-Classes' Attitude to the Extension of State Powers, 1885–1914', *SSLH*, 13 (Autumn 1966), 17 f.

[70] Arthur Marwick, 'The Labour Party and the Welfare State in Britain, 1900–1948', *AHR* 73 (1967), 380–403. Barry Jones and Michael Keating, *Labour and the British State* (Oxford, 1985) have pointed out that demands for state provision of social welfare became an almost unchallenged orthodoxy in the Labour Party of the 1930s.

[71] *Arbeitsnachweise* were employment agencies, set up by employers to control their workforce; those workers known to be social democrats or trade unionists would be blacklisted by the employment agency. Therefore trade unions, with little success, set up their own employment agencies. Only in the Weimar Republic did the employment agencies become state-run institutions.

[72] Anselm Faust, 'State and Unemployment in Germany, 1890–1918 (Labour Exchanges, Job Creation and Unemployment Insurance)', in Mommsen and Mock, *The Emergence*, 154–6.

[73] ZStA Merseburg, Rep. 77, no. 106, I, 126: article about the international congress for health and safety at work in Zürich, 1897.

[74] Jürgen Reulecke, 'Der erste Weltkrieg und die Arbeiterbewegung im rheinisch-westfälischen Industriegebiet', in id. (ed.), *Arbeiterbewegung an Rhein und Ruhr* (Wuppertal, 1974), 215–20.

[75] Ursula Hüllbüsch, 'Gewerkschaften und Staat: Ein Beitrag zur Geschichte der Gewerkschaften zu Anfang und zu Ende der Weimarer Republik' (University of Bonn Ph.D. 1958), 240.

arm's length from power.[76] The judiciary is usually described as tightly controlled and rigidly loyal to the political system. It is seen as a wilful object in the state's efforts to suppress the German labour movement. From September 1897 to August 1898, for example, German Social Democrats were sentenced to nearly 55 years' imprisonment and nearly 20,000 marks in fines.[77] Wolfgang Heine, who was busy defending Social Democrats in the courts,[78] stated in his memoirs: 'The judiciary . . . said "yes and amen" to all forms of harassment [by the authorities], and their growing subtlety in interpreting the law encouraged the authorities to even more harassment.'[79] This negative view of the judiciary can be seen in numerous pamphlets and booklets, of which Karl Liebknecht's *Rechtsstaat und Klassenjustiz* is one of the most comprehensive examples.[80]

Nevertheless one should be careful before endorsing a view of the British judiciary as an independent arbiter of social conflict and contrasting it with a view of the German judiciary as the repressive instrument of social élites.[81] It is indicative of the more complex situation that antisocialist organizations in Germany were frequently furious about what they perceived as laxness towards socialists on the part of the German judiciary: 'it is well known that the public prosecutors in Germany, with very few exceptions, refuse to prosecute cases of libel by the social democratic press on the ground that this would not be in the public interest . . .'.[82] Judges, particularly in southern and western Germany, were not blindly loyal to the Imperial authorities, but retained a remarkable

---

[76] H.-U. Wehler, *Das deutsche Kaiserreich 1871–1918* (Göttingen, 1973), 131–3.

[77] ZStA Merseburg, Rep. 77, no. 656, I. The average yearly income of a worker in the printing industry was 1,317 marks whilst a worker in the textile industry earned 594 marks a year. See Ritter and Tenfelde, *Arbeiter*, 476. In 1900 20,000 marks would have been the equivalent of £965.25, which in 1991 would have been worth about £50,801. For the mark–£ exchange rates see London and Cambridge Economic Service, *The British Economy: Key Statistics 1900–1970* (London, 1971), table L. For the purchasing power of the £ sterling in the 20th century see: *Lloyds Bank Economic Profile of Great Britain 1992* (London, 1992). I am grateful to Trevor Boyns for providing me with this information. Henceforth, whenever I give rough equivalents of the current values of marks and £ sterling, it will be based on these sources.

[78] FES, papers of Heine, nos. 133–76 reports about innumerable cases against Social Democrats.

[79] Wolfgang Heine, 'Erinnnerungen', in BA Koblenz, Kl. Erw., no. 371–16, p. 480.

[80] Karl Liebknecht, *Rechtsstaat und Klassenjustiz: Vortrag, gehalten zu Stuttgart am 23. August 1907* (Stuttgart, 1907). Also Ernst Fraenkel, *Zur Soziologie der Klassenjustiz* (Berlin, 1927).

[81] Michael John, 'The Peculiarities of the German State: Bourgeois Law and Society in the Imperial Era', *PP* 119 (1988), 105–31 stresses the independence of the legal profession in Germany from political pressure of social élites.

[82] ZStA Merseburg, Rep. 77, no. 819, I, 117: newsletter of the Reichsverband, 15 Sept. 1906. Similar charges can be found in: ZStA Potsdam, 07.01, no. 1395/4, 70/71.

degree of independence in their judgements.[83] It is also significant that
the SPD, despite denouncing the Civil Code (BGB) as class based, worked
hard to insert their own ideas into it. The social democratic press high-
lighted the debates of 1896 in the Reichstag, and in 1899 *Vorwärts*
declared: 'Any chaotic, colourful state of the law leads to an imprecision
of the law (*Rechtsunsicherheit*)... The one who suffers most from this
state of affairs is the worker... The unity of law is therefore an undeniable
political progress...'.[84] G. A. Ritter has underlined the fact that repression
of Social Democracy in the Kaiserreich had its limits in the rule of law.[85]

Not only was the German judiciary not as wilful an instrument of state
repression as has often been believed, but the British judicial system was
itself extraordinarily biased against Labour and the working class as such.[86]
Julius Motteler, who lived in London from April 1888 to the early 1900s,
wrote in 1900: 'The police and the whole judiciary here [in Britain] is
according to my opinion much more infamous than in Germany.
Liebknecht in his time here... probably saw and experienced very little
of English conditions, otherwise he would not constantly stress their
virtues...'.[87] Motteler had witnessed the massive attack on socialism that
was taking place in Britain in the 1890s and early 1900s. Besides anti-
socialist campaigns in the press and by employers' federations, a series of
court rulings, leading to the Taff Vale decision of 1901[88] and further to
the Osborne judgement in 1909,[89] demonstrated a firm belief amongst the
British judiciary that the law should be used to enforce repressive controls upon trade unions.[90] Despite the fact that the nineteenth century

---

[83] Martin Martiny, *Integration oder Konfrontation? Studien zur Geschichte der sozialdemokratischen Rechts- und Verfassungspolitik* (Bonn, 1976), 197.

[84] *Vorwärts*, 230 (1 Oct. 1899). For the SPD's attitude to the BGB see Michael John,
Politics and the Law in Late 19th Century Germany: The Origins of the Civil Code (Oxford,
1989), 231–8.

[85] G. A. Ritter, 'Die Sozialdemokratie im deutschen Kaiserreich in sozialgeschichtlicher
Perspektive', *HZ* 249 (1989), 300.

[86] Henry Pelling, 'Trade Unions, Workers and the Law', in: id., *Popular Politics*, 62–81.

[87] FES, papers of Julius Motteler, no. 1836/3, letter from Motteler to [unknown], 15
July 1900. At that time Motteler feared that British judges would agree to shut down the
Communistischer Arbeiterbildungsverein in London.

[88] For Taff Vale see Frank Bealey and Henry Pelling, *Labour and Politics, 1900–1906: A
History of the LRC* (London, 1958), 55–97.

[89] Michael J. Klarman, 'The Osborne Judgement: A Legal/Historical Analysis' (University of Oxford D.Phil. 1987) stresses the point that the judges—heavily hostile to the labour
movement—largely implemented their own views of what they perceived as sound labour
law. The implications of Taff Vale for the German trade union law are discussed in
Wilhelm Rütten, 'Der Taff Vale Case und das deutsche Gewerkschaftsrecht', *AfS* 31
(1991), 103–21. Rütten also remarks on the overall similarity of British and German trade
union law at the time.

[90] J. A. G. Griffith, *The Politics of the Judiciary* (Manchester, 1977), 200.

statute law saw a gradual expansion of trade union rights in Britain,[91] the judiciary was under the spell of class prejudices concerning organized Labour. Their whole world-view and self-understanding seemed threatened by the emergence of a political force which went against most of the values in which the judiciary as a relatively coherent social group believed. After 1890 elements of 'public opinion' in Britain turned against trade unionism. As the courts generally followed closely the changes in public opinion towards the trade unions, the law 'by judge-made decisions, was being turned against them'.[92] These decisions by individual judges were often dependent on whether the particular judge was sympathetic or inimical to trade unionism as such. It was exactly that insecurity of the law (*Rechtsunsicherheit*) which had been overcome in Germany with the adoption of the BGB in 1900.

As has been argued in this chapter, the ambiguous attitude of the British and the German labour movement towards their respective nation-state was not overcome in the period under discussion here. Both movements were caught between a desire to end their isolation in the nation-state and the aim of transforming what they saw as the 'capitalist' nation-state. The 'carrot and stick' approach of the state only furthered such ambiguity, as the Labour Party and the SPD found themselves confronted with repression as well as efforts by their respective states to solve the social question. To view the relationship Labour–state in Britain and Germany as one of positive vs. negative integration simplifies the matter too much. Certainly the state was less present in the everyday existence of the British labour movement, yet the British state was by no means absent from British Labour's reality and its attitude towards Labour was often hostile in a way which does not foster any straightforward assumption that British Labour was 'positively integrated' into the nation-state. Conversely, there were numerous signs even in Imperial Germany that the SPD made serious efforts to redefine its relationship to the existing nation-state in a more positive way.

2.2. The working-class parties in Britain and Germany, the parliamentary system, and relations with other parties

The previous section dealt with the integration of British and German Labour into their respective nation-states. The present one deals with

---

[91] Keith D. Ewing, *Trade Unions, the Labour Party and the Law: A Study of the Trade Union Act 1913* (Edinburgh, 1982), 7–68.

[92] John Saville, 'Trade Unions and Free Labour', in Briggs and Saville, *Essays*, 341–4.

the narrower issue of their integration into their political systems. The exceptionalist viewpoint is that the SPD was completely excluded from participation in the half-democratic political system of Imperial Germany and that it was not fully committed to the democratic system of the Weimar Republic. By contrast, the British Labour Party is held to have been well integrated into a stable and successful democracy, developing a strong belief in the virtues of parliamentary government.[93] It is this view which shall be re-evaluated in the present section by examining the attitude of Labour Party and SPD towards parliamentary forms of government, towards other political parties, and towards taking over government responsibility.

The argument about Britain being a fully democratic political system before 1918 overlooks the existence of extensive franchise restrictions based on property up to 1918 and on gender up to 1928 (when all women aged 21 to 30 got the vote for the first time). Additionally there was plural voting. It has been estimated that about 40 per cent of adult men and all adult women remained disfranchised before 1914. A geographical analysis of levels of enfranchisement shows that working-class areas had the lowest levels of enfranchisement in the country. The pre-war British franchise not only discriminated by gender but also by class.[94] Despite Duncan Tanner's recent argument that age, marital status, and residential mobility were all more important in disfranchising a substantial part of the British population than class, there can be no doubt whatsoever that a number of working-class constituencies had extremely low levels of enfranchisement.[95] At an LRC conference in London on 14 and 15 April 1904 the undemocratic franchise was discussed with a view to thorough reform according to 'the principle of one man one vote'. Widespread corruption and the improper system of registration were heavily criticized. Keir Hardie drew attention to this state of affairs again in his 1910 Labour Party Conference presidential address: 'The election has again forced upon our attention the need for a great scheme of electoral reform whereby the nation, and not merely a fraction of it, would be able to

---

[93] Ira Katznelson, 'Working Class Formation', in Zolberg and Katznelson, *Working Class Formation*, 29; Hodge, 'The Trammels of Tradition', 124–58, 191–226, 274–309, and 310–51; Luebbert, *Liberalism*, ch. 5.

[94] H. C. G. Matthew, Ross I. McKibbin, and J. A. Kay, 'The Franchise Factor in the Rise of the Labour Party', *EHR* 91 (1976), 724 and 726. The authors have estimated that half the industrial working class remained disfranchised before 1918.

[95] Tanner, *Political Change and the Labour Party 1900–1918*, 99–128. For a criticism of Tanner see Stefan Berger, 'The Decline of Liberalism and the Rise of Labour: The Regional Approach', *Parliamentary History*, 12 (1993), 84–92.

express its opinions at the ballot box'.[96] On the municipal level in Britain disenfranchisement was also widespread. In many places like Wolverhampton only about 1 per cent of the town's inhabitants were eligible to vote in 1900, in 1903 18 per cent, in 1912 19 per cent, and even in 1921 only 38 per cent were eligible to vote.[97] On the whole Rowett has argued that throughout the inter-war years the local government franchise was not decisively transformed from a right dependent on the ownership of property to a citizen's right.[98]

In Germany the participation of the working class in national elections was much broader. The franchise for national elections was extended to all males over the age of 25 years on the basis of the direct, universal, and equal franchise of 1867/71. The distribution of constituencies which ensured equal representation for rural and urban areas (despite of the fact that only one-third of the population lived in rural areas) certainly discriminated against the SPD, but the distribution of constituencies also disadvantaged the Labour Party. However, the German franchise in the different states (*Länder*) had a definite anti-working-class bias. For example, there was the *Dreiklassenwahlrecht* in Prussia or the equally unjust case of Saxony, where manhood suffrage was actually abolished by Conservatives and National Liberals afraid of a social democratic majority in the state parliament (Landtag).[99] On a municipal level numerous franchise systems existed which were almost all based on property regulations, thereby excluding the majority of working men.[100] While Germany remained undoubtedly far from implementing a democratic franchise on all levels of political decision-making, such a franchise was equally absent in Britain. Consequently both the SPD and the Labour Party suffered from undemocratic franchises before the war.

Somewhat surprisingly perhaps this did not lead to a rejection of

[96] *Report of the Annual Conference of the Labour Party 1910* (London, 1910), 55. For the LRC conference in 1904 see Labour Party Archive, Labour Party Pamphlets and Leaflets 1894–1912, no. 18, p. 3.

[97] G. W. Jones, *Borough Politics: A Study of the Wolverhampton Town Council* (London, 1969), 30. For similarly low levels of enfranchisement in inter-war Oxford see R. C. Whiting, *The View From Cowley: The Impact of Industrialization on Oxford 1913–1939* (Oxford, 1983), 22.

[98] J. S. Rowett, 'The Labour Party and Local Government: Theory and Practice in the Inter-War Years' (University of Oxford D.Phil. 1979), 5–9.

[99] On the different franchise systems in different German *Länder* and their effects on the SPD see Gerhard A. Ritter (ed.), *Der Aufstieg der deutschen Arbeiterbewegung: Sozialdemokratie und freie Gewerkschaften im Parteiensystem und Sozialmilieu des Kaiserreichs* (Munich, 1990).

[100] Dieter Fricke, *Handbuch zur Geschichte der deutschen Arbeiterbewegung, 1869–1917* (Berlin, 1987), ii. 761–80.

parliamentary government as such by either party. On the contrary, parliamentary government was more and more endorsed by the working-class parties, although there were strong anti-parliamentary minorities. In Germany this minority was more influential before 1918, mainly because of the different nature of British and German parliamentary systems. In Germany parliament had only limited powers before the complete transformation of the political system before 1918. Therefore it was difficult to view it as an effective instrument of social reform. As Ramsay MacDonald argued: 'The German *Reichstag* is not a parliament . . . [It] is . . . little more than a debating society . . . Whilst the eyes of the parties in an irresponsible legislature like the *Reichstag* are fixed upon the horizon, those of the parties in a responsible legislature like our own House of Commons are fixed at their feet.'[101]

Despite the comparative weakness of the German parliament, MacDonald underestimated the pragmatism of many Social Democratic politicians. Their eyes were not necessarily fixed upon the horizon of revolution but upon the not unreasonable hope of a slow process of parliamentarization of the political system in Imperial Germany which would make Germany more like Britain. Manfred Rauh has argued that the Reichstag became stronger in relation to government before 1914. He has spoken of 'a process of silent parliamentarization' after Bismarck's resignation.[102] The two columns, on which Bismarck's constitution had rested, the monarchic principle (*monarchische Prinzip*) and Prussian hegemony, were undermined step by step. Parliament was able slowly to extend its powers, while the upper house, the Bundesrat, where the various states sent non-elected representatives, gradually became less powerful in the time of the 'personal rule' of Wilhelm II. Between 1900 and 1906 the Imperial government came to co-ordinate its policies with supporting parliamentary parties. A process of 'slow parliamentarization' helped the pro-parliamentary wing of the SPD to overcome anti-parliamentary sentiments within its own party. Richard Evans has found a growing belief amongst the Hamburg working class that some form of parliamentarization was taking place in Imperial Germany.[103] Almost certainly a substantial part of the party supported the parliamentarization of the

---

[101] Ramsay MacDonald, *The Socialist Movement* (London, 1911), 108 f.

[102] Manfred Rauh, *Föderalismus und Parlamentarismus im Wilhelminischen Reich* (Düsseldorf, 1973), 7. Also Manfred Rauh, *Die Parlamentarisierung des Deutschen Reiches* (Düsseldorf, 1977). A similar argument can be found in Thomas Nipperdey, 'War die Wilhelminische Gesellschaft eine Untertanen-Gesellschaft?', in id., *Nachdenken über deutsche Geschichte* (Munich, 1986). Also Groh and Brandt, *Vaterlandlose Gesellen*, 158.

[103] Evans, *Proletarians*, 162 f.

political system in Imperial Germany, thereby hoping for an evolutionary development in which the SPD could finally play its part.[104]

Noticing that the party succumbed more and more to parliamentarism, Kautsky wrote to Bernstein in 1895: 'I believe no social-democratic party suffers more from parliamentary cretinism than German Social Democracy. This is understandable, as it is only in Parliament that the party achieves great things.'[105] A few years later Bernstein was pointing to the parliamentary orientation of the British Labour Party as a model for the SPD to follow.[106] From 1 June 1894 onwards, when the German Social Democrats in the Bavarian parliament for the first time agreed to the state budget, many small steps paved the way of the SPD into the parliamentary system: 'Step after step the majority of the party came over to the pragmatic-reformist view. After the successful elections of 1890 positive co-operation was made the final basis of social-democratic work in parliament.'[107] The heavy involvement of the SPD in local politics before 1914 further demonstrated the willingness of the party to participate constructively in the framework of politics in the Second Reich. 13,000 local and municipal councillors and an estimated 100,000 Social Democrats sitting on administrative and representative bodies such as industrial and commercial courts, industrial insurance, and certificate of employment agencies show a considerable degree of integration of the SPD into the political system of the Wilhelmine state. Where Social Democrats found a more liberal political climate, especially in the states of southern Germany, they were willing to co-operate with the authorities in the state diets (Landtage). They did so in Hesse and Baden from 1891 and in Bavaria from 1894 onwards.[108] It was also in Southern Germany that co-operation between the state's factory inspectorate and the trade union officials was generally good.[109] In Baden, the SPD's MPs even declared their overall

---

[104] Elfi Pracht, *Parlamentarismus und deutsche Sozialdemokratie 1867–1914* (Pfaffenweiler, 1990). Vernon Lidthe, *The Outlawed Party* (Princeton, 1966), 153 f. speaks of 'ambivalent parliamentarianism' of the early SPD.

[105] IGA/ZPA, papers of Eduard Bernstein, 23/8, 171: letter from Kautsky to Bernstein, 18 Oct. 1895.

[106] Eduard Bernstein, *Parlamentarismus und Sozialdemokratie* (Berlin, 1906), 54–60.

[107] Hermann Teistler, *Der Parlamentarismus und die Arbeiterklasse* (Berlin, 1892), 3. Teistler does not speak for a clear majority within the party in 1892, yet the mere fact that such a view could be printed as official party propaganda shows the existence of pro-parliamentary sentiments in the SPD.

[108] Heinrich Potthoff, 'Social Democracy from its Beginnings until 1945', in Susanne Miller and Heinrich Potthoff, *A History of German Social Democracy: From 1848 to the Present* (Leamington Spa, 1986), 48.

[109] Ritter and Tenfelde, *Arbeiter im Deutschen Kaiserreich*, 387.

satisfaction with the state of policing.[110] Clearly, similar things cannot be said about Prussia.

Ambiguity between acceptance and rejection of parliamentary democracy was also at the basis of the Erfurt programme of the SPD of 1891. The first part of that programme, written by Kautsky, was essentially arguing for the transformation of the present political, economic, and social system, whereas the second part, written by Bernstein, was parliamentary oriented and introducing specific reform proposals. Indeed, from 1877 onwards the party fought in the Reichstag for the establishment of an extensive factory inspection system and broad-ranging housing and health regulations. Furthermore there were legislative proposals by the social democrats in the Reichstag to broaden the parliamentary immunity of Reichstag members, to extend the legal reforms, to establish the traditional liberal freedoms, to eliminate indirect taxation, to limit the work day, to prohibit child and female labour in certain industries, to protect workers against unhealthy and unsafe working conditions, and to establish an imperial labour office.[111]

Another example of that ambiguity was the attitude of the party towards the regular and formal cheering of the Imperial head of state within the Reichstag ('Hoch der Kaiser'). There was increasing opposition from within the parliamentary party against non-participation in what came to be seen as a formality.[112] The degree of integration of the SPD can be seen in the 1912 debate about whether or not Philipp Scheidemann should take his place as vice-president of the Reichstagspräsidium to which he had been elected with the votes of the liberals. It had been the Social Democrats who approached the liberals for their support, and it was August Bebel who was most worried that Scheidemann should be properly dressed when he attended court ceremonies (as would have been his duty as member of the Reichstagspräsidium).[113] If, in the end, Scheidemann did not take his place in the Präsidium this was more due to the intransigent position of the Centre Party than to the position of Social Democracy.[114]

---

[110] Peter Brandt and Reinhard Rürup, *Volksbewegung und demokratische Neuordnung in Baden 1918/19: Zur Vorgeschichte und Geschichte der Revolution* (Sigmaringen, 1991), 41.

[111] For the activity of the party in the Reichstag before 1914 see Gary P. Steenson, *'Not One Man—Not One Penny': German Social Democracy, 1863–1914* (Pittsburgh, 1981), 54–65.

[112] Wolfgang Heine, 'Präsidentenwahl, Hofgang, Kaiserhoch', *SM* 16/1 (1912), 335–40.

[113] Brigitte Seebacher-Brandt, *Bebel: Künder und Kärrner im Kaiserreich* (Berlin, 1988), 364.

[114] Beverly Heckart, *From Bassermann to Bebel: The Grand Bloc's Quest for Reform in the Kaiserreich, 1900–1914* (New Haven, Conn., 1974), 198–206.

A general orientation towards participation in the political system was also mirrored by the development of the party organization of the SPD—as later that of the Labour Party—according to electoral boundaries rather than on industrial or socio-economic units.[115] Additionally the press of the labour movement in both countries was anxious to give as much coverage as possible to parliament and elections. As the SPD had not developed any constitutional theory of its own[116] it slowly adopted key elements of a liberal constitutional theory.[117] This only served to strengthen the commitment of the party towards parliamentary democracy. In the First World War the paper of the reformist wing of the party, the *Sozialistische Monatshefte*, ran a campaign to increase the dedication of the SPD to the parliamentary system.[118] As the great majority of the anti-parliamentary forces within the SPD joined the KPD after 1918, the overwhelming majority within the SPD emphatically endorsed the new parliamentary system of government in the Weimar Republic. At the time of the presidential cabinets at the end of the Weimar Republic it was the SPD that most energetically defended the democratic constitution and the parliamentary system.[119] However, at the same time the party was not entirely successful in overcoming all internal opposition towards parliamentary democracy in the Weimar Republic.[120]

If Britain had an undemocratic franchise, it nevertheless did have an extremely stable form of parliamentary government. The British Labour Party did not have to help bring it about nor did it ever have to fear for its existence. These were very different preconditions from the ones which confronted the SPD. Partly as a result of the stability of parliamentary government in Britain, there was a very strong belief in

---

[115] Bernd Faulenbach and Günther Högl (eds.), *Eine Partei in ihrer Region: Zur Geschichte der SPD im westlichen Westfalen* (Essen, 1988), 73.

[116] Dieter Grosser, *Vom monarchischen Konstitutionalismus zur parlamentarischen Demokratie* (The Hague, 1970), 33–60.

[117] Peter Steinbach, *Sozialdemokratie und Verfassungsverständnis: Zur Ausbildung einer liberal-demokratischen Verfassungskonzeption in der Sozialdemokratie seit der Mitte des 19. Jahrhunderts* (Opladen, 1983), esp. pp. 19 and 39.

[118] See for example articles like Hermann Kranold, 'Die Pflicht zum Parlamentarismus', *SM* 23/2 (1917), 1215–20 or Wilhelm Kolb, 'Was nun?', *SM* 22/3 (1916), 1025–8. Already before the war: Edmund Fischer, 'Sozialdemokratie und Regierungsgewalt', *SM* 16/1 (1912), 278.

[119] Hans Mommsen, 'Die Sozialdemokratie in der Defensive: Der Immobilismus der SPD und der Aufstieg des Nationalsozialismus', in id. (ed.), *Sozialdemokratie zwischen Klassenbewegung und Volkspartei* (Frankfurt am Main, 1974), 106–33.

[120] Peter Lösche and Franz Walter, 'Auf dem Weg zur Volkspartei? Die Weimarer Sozialdemokratie', *AfS* 29 (1989), 75–136. Also Peter Lösche and Franz Walter, *Die SPD: Klassenpartei—Volkspartei—Quotenpartei* (Darmstadt, 1992), 1–76.

parliamentarism within the British Labour Party—especially within the PLP.[121] The Fabian theory of the state, which came to be widely accepted amongst the PLP, the ILP, and local Labour Party activists, saw the state as a politically indifferent body which could be used either for or against the working class. The task of the Labour Party was described as instituting social and economic changes by parliamentary means. MacDonald argued:

The Master of Parliament is the nation, and if Parliament does not do its work, it is no use smashing it . . . Parliament is an expression of public opinion . . . and the duty of a Socialist Party inside is to see that it does not lag behind public opinion; whilst the duty of the party outside is to see that public opinion is properly educated.[122]

The other major leader of the Labour Party, Arthur Henderson, can also be described as a staunch believer in parliamentary democracy.[123]

The Labour Party's endorsement of parliamentary government has been either applauded or lamented by historians according to the latter's own political convictions. It is, however, rarely questioned. And yet, even within the British labour movement there was the same split between those socialists accepting the parliamentary system and those rejecting it well into the twentieth century. The anti-parliamentary section of British socialists was especially strong within the early labour movement.[124] Clarionettes, syndicalists, guild socialists, and SDF members were in the forefront amongst those who demanded delegate democracy, direct legislation, and a general change in the structure of society.[125] The view of Keir Hardie that parliament in the late nineteenth century was becoming an annex of the Stock Exchange is well known, and it has been pointed out that this was not only his personal view.[126] The four members of the

[121] Ralph Miliband, *Parliamentary Socialism* (London, 1961); Stanley Pierson, *British Socialists: The Journey from Fantasy to Politics* (Cambridge, Mass., 1979), 149–53; John Shepherd, 'Labour and Parliament: The Lib-Labs as the First Working-Class MPs, 1885–1906', in Biagini and Reid, *Currents of Radicalism*, 187–213.

[122] Ramsay MacDonald, *Socialism Today: The Chairman's Address Delivered at the Synod Hall, Edinburgh 1909* (Edinburgh, 1909), 7.

[123] Ross McKibbin, 'Arthur Henderson as a Labour Leader', *IRSH* 23/1 (1978), 92.

[124] Nigel Young, 'Prometheans or Troglodytes? The English Working Class and the Dialectics of Incorporation', *Berkeley Journal of Sociology*, 12 (1967), 8.

[125] Judith A. Fincher, 'The Clarion Movement: A Study of a Socialist Attempt to Implement the Co-operative Commonwealth' (University of Manchester MA 1971), 241 f. Also Ian Bullock, 'Socialists and Democratic Form in Britain, 1880–1914' (University of Sussex Ph.D. 1981), 187 and 230–51.

[126] Frank Bealey, 'Keir Hardie and the Labour Groups I', *Parliamentary Affairs*, 10 (1956–7), 83. For the strength of anti-parliamentary feeling in the Labour Party before 1914 see also J. H. Steward Reid, *The Origins of the British Labour Party* (Minneapolis, 1955), chs. 12 and 13.

ILP National Council who in 1910 condemned the revisionist policies of the PLP and called the parliamentary road to socialism a cul-de-sac or memories of ILP left-wingers like those of David Kirkwood and John Paton testify to the existence of a section within the Labour Party who mistrusted the party's parliamentary orientation.[127] More mainstream figures like G. D. H. Cole, R. H. Tawney, and H. Laski, not to mention Stafford Cripps, all at some time had reservations about the parliamentary way to socialism.[128]

The British parliament, it is often said, was very much run like a gentlemen's club, which helped Labour MPs become 'absorbed into that close and closed community' of parliament.[129] However, this view is questioned by David Clark, himself a Labour MP:

In spite of the commonly-held myth, there is little cross-party friendship; voluntary segregation is evident in the tea and dining-rooms for even today the class-divide throws up parties composed of MPs drawn largely from different classes and with little in common socially. Thus friendships are invariably within party ranks.[130]

Similarly contrasting statements can be found in the SPD. Whereas Bebel was reported to be shocked when Bethmann in 1911 addressed him in the corridors of the Reichstag: 'I have belonged to this house from its very beginning since 1868. This was the first time that a member of the government had addressed me outside the assembly hall.'[131] Philipp Scheidemann reported about a rather relaxed club-like atmosphere in the Reichstag before 1918: 'It should be expressly stated that the personal relations of *Reichstag* members were quite friendly . . . There existed a feeling of mutual esteem in spite of political differences . . . There was frequently quite a pleasant atmosphere of sociability . . . at the reserved tables . . .'.[132] It therefore needs to be stressed that the full development of democratic parliamentary systems in both countries after 1918 helped the working-class parties to overcome resistance against representative

---

[127] *Let Us Reform the Labour Party* (London, 1910); David Kirkwood, *My Life of Revolt* (London, 1935), John Paton, *Left Turn* (London, 1936).

[128] J. M. Winter, *Socialism and the Challenge of War: Ideas and Politics in Britain, 1912–1918* (London, 1974). Also A. H. Hanson, 'The Labour Party and the House of Commons Reform', *Parliamentary Affairs*, 10 (1956/7), 463 f.; Harold Laski, *The Crisis and the Constitution: 1931 and after* (London, 1932); Stafford Cripps, *Can Socialism Come by Constitutional Methods* (London, 1932).

[129] James MacGregor Burns, 'The PLP in Great Britain', *APSR* 44 (1950), 862.

[130] David Clark, *Labour's Lost Leader: Victor Grayson* (London, 1985), 50.

[131] Quoted from Gustav Mayer, *Erinnerungen: Vom Journalisten zum Historiker der deutschen Arbeiterbewegung* (Munich, 1949), 179.

[132] Philipp Scheidemann, *Memoirs of a Social Democrat*, (London, 1929), i. 92.

government, even if full integration into their respective parliamentary systems could not be achieved: uneasiness towards the parliamentary system remained within both parties.

A second test for the degree of integration of the Labour Party and the SPD into their respective political systems can be seen in the ease or difficulty with which alliances and electoral agreements with other parties were forged. The conservative parties were generally hostile, but on the whole German conservatives were more so than their British counterpart. German conservatives increasingly before 1914 turned to popular politics to ensure the party's survivals at the polls.[133] 'Tory democracy', a phrase coined by Randolph Churchill in his effort to mobilize popular support from all classes, consisted of a well-organized and successful form of demagogic populism.[134] The Conservative Party relied on a superb electoral machine which paid special attention to the mobilization of the working-class vote by presenting itself as 'above party' and 'against state interference in workers' lives'. Furthermore it was quick to taint the Labour Party with labels such as 'bolshevist' and 'unconstitutional' to whip up fear amongst the electorate.[135] However, the populism of British and German Conservatives aimed at different social groups. Whereas the German Conservatives tried successfully to rally the rural labourers and small farmers behind their cause, the British Conservatives could not follow a similar strategy, for the agricultural sector was so insignificant as to be almost meaningless. Instead British Conservatives successfully appealed to the industrial working class, especially in northern textile districts like Lancashire.[136] The enmity of conservative parties in both Britain and Germany towards independent working-class parties is not difficult to trace. In Germany before 1914 the Conservatives were the party arguing the case for a renewal of the anti-socialist law throughout the 1890s. After 1918 the Conservatives, now under another name, remained adamant not to join any coalition with 'the Reds'. In Britain, the Conservatives put through parliament blatant anti-Labour legislation

---

[133] The fact that the political right turned towards aggressive populism before 1914 has been stressed by Geoff Eley, *Reshaping the German Right; Radical Nationalism and Political Change after Bismarck* (New Haven, Conn., 1980).

[134] On the modernity of the Tories see especially Martin Pugh, *The Tories and the People, 1880–1935* (Oxford, 1985), 160–2.

[135] Maurice Cowling, *The Impact of Labour, 1920–1924: The Beginnings of Modern British Politics* (Cambridge, 1971), 416.

[136] Savage, *The Dynamics of Working Class Politics*, and Jon Lawrence, 'Popular Politics and the Limitations of Party: Wolverhampton 1867–1900', in Biagini and Reid, *Currents of Radicalism*, 65–85.

as late as 1927 when the Trades Disputes Act aimed at crippling the trade union link with the Labour Party.[137]

The relation of the working-class parties to the Liberal parties in both countries was not such a clear-cut case of enmity.[138] After all, programmatically and personally the SPD and the Labour Party were standing in a liberal political tradition. Many of their beliefs and their leaders had a Liberal background.[139] Independent working-class parties had only come into being when Liberalism was deserting its former ideals, and when class was becoming more and more an issue in the political allegiance to one or another party. In Germany the Liberals increasingly abandoned key liberal values in their alliance with the conservatives.[140] Most importantly, they renounced demands for free trade and for a more democratic political system. Social Democrats frequently reminded the Liberals of this treachery: 'If the National Liberals really wanted to pursue an honest liberal policy, we certainly would be their best friends, because at all times we were willing to support real liberal demands, it was only the gentlemen of the Liberal Party who were not.'[141] It has been pointed out that there was a lack of Lib-Lab or progressive alliances in Imperial Germany, because a number of factors were standing in the way of such a pact. First and foremost, there was the limited importance of popular politics in Imperial Germany.[142] Important as this undoubtedly was, there remains the point that there was some significant co-operation between

[137] For the pre-history of the Act see Patrick Renshaw, 'Anti-Labour Politics in Britain, 1918–1927', *Journal of Contemporary History*, 12 (1977), 698. The effect of this act as a symbol of Labour's ostracism was high, as has been pointed out by Melvin C. Shefftz, 'The Trade Disputes and Trade Unions Act of 1927: The Aftermath of the General Strike', *Review of Politics*, 29 (1967), 387–406. The Act was only repealed by the post-1945 Labour government.

[138] I do not discuss the relations of the SPD to the Centre Party, mainly because the Centre Party has no real English counterpart. It should be noted, however, that relations between the SPD and the Centre were not necessarily inimical, as the case of Bavaria shows. See Heinrich Hirschfelder, *Die bayerische Sozialdemokratie, 1864–1914* (Erlangen, 1979), ii.472–9.

[139] For Germany see Shlomo Na'aman, *Die Konstituierung der deutschen Arbeiterbewegung, 1862–1863: Darstellung und Dokumentation* (Assen, 1975) and Arthur Rosenberg, *Democracy and Socialism: A Contribution to the Political History of the Past 150 Years* (London, 1939), esp. pp. 161 and 328. For Britain see K. D. Brown, 'The Edwardian Labour Party', in id., (ed.), *The First Labour Party* (London, 1985), 8–11; Michael Freeden, *Liberalism Divided: A Study in British Political Thought 1914–1939* (Oxford, 1986), 294.

[140] John Breuilly, 'Liberalism or Social Democracy: A Comparison of British and German Labour Politics, c. 1850–1875', *EHQ* 15 (1985), 3–42.

[141] *Der nationalliberale Parteitag und die Sozialdemokratie: Rede des Reichstagsabgeordneten August Bebel in der Volksversammlung vom 16. Oktober 1907 in 'Kellers Festsälen' in Berlin* (Berlin, 1907), 12. For similar sentiments see Franz Mehring, 'Ein Spinnwebfaden', *NZ* (1904–5), 258.

[142] Breuilly, *Labour and Liberalism*, 141.

Liberals and Social Democrats in the south-western states in Germany. In the Weimar Republic the Weimar coalition of SPD, the Liberal DDP and Centre Party was probably the nearest equivalent to the progressive alliances in many British municipalities before 1914.

In Britain the Liberal Party slowly abandoned its Gladstonian past before the First World War. Gladstone had remained a hero figure with much of the British working class, as he was seen as upholding non-conformist moral principles, a fighter for free trade, for the political rights of the working people and for the ideal of a meritocracy. Yet the post-Gladstonian party became split between those who supported imperialism and those who supported social reform as remedies against working-class poverty. Where the latter attitude, which soon came to be known as 'New Liberalism', prevailed, Labour found it difficult to break the Liberal hegemony over politics.[143] Whatever position one takes in the wider argument on the decline of Liberalism, the end of 'Gladstonianism' and the unwillingness of 'Old Liberalism' to accommodate the working-class interest contributed to the rise of independent Labour politics in Britain after the turn of the century.[144] The secession of independent working-class parties from the Liberal Parties happened at different times in both countries. In Britain such a secession was delayed by the fact that the Liberals were able to remain the champions of free trade for much longer than their German counterparts. Consequently the British Liberal Party could present itself as a truly cross-class alliance for much longer than the German Liberals. Besides, it was not until the beginning of the twentieth century that at least some British trade unions began to support the issue of social reform. Therefore the Liberal Party was able to keep itself open to the left as well as to the right to a degree which was simply impossible to the German liberals.[145]

The second reason for the foundation of independent working-class parties in Britain and Germany can be found in the emergence of class as a decisive factor in determining party allegiance. Christiane Eisenberg has pointed to the emerging class consciousness of the British and German working-class in the mid-nineteenth century. Increasingly the working class resented liberal middle-class patronage and set up their own

---

[143] The best summary on the debate about the decline of the Liberal Party and the rise of Labour is now given by Tanner, *Political Change*.

[144] Henry Pelling, *The Origins of the Labour Party, 1880–1900* (London, 1954), 222. Alun Howkins, 'Edwardian Liberalism and Industrial Unrest: A Class View of the Decline of Liberalism', *HWJ* 4 (1977), 143–61.

[145] Gustav Schmidt, 'Politischer Liberalismus, "Landed Interests" und organisierte Arbeiterschaft, 1850–1880. Ein deutsch-englischer Vergleich', in Hans-Ulrich Wehler (ed.), *Moderne deutsche Sozialgeschichte* (Berlin, 1966), 266–88.

organizations.[146] The growing class consciousness of the working class can be perceived especially on the local level of politics. Here, in the localities, electoral alliances between the Labour Party and the Liberal Party rarely functioned properly. Rather, there was increased hostility between Liberals and independent working-class parties, although the relationship could vary substantially from locality to locality.[147] The SPD in Leipzig, for example, had to face a closed phalanx of liberal and conservative parties hostile to the SPD.[148] Despite recent efforts to de-emphasize the importance of class for pre-war British politics and to stress the strength of working-class Liberalism,[149] there is still overwhelming evidence that the relationship between Liberal and Labour Parties in the constituencies in Britain was deteriorating fast in the years before the war. MacDonald found it increasingly difficult to keep the rank and file at bay and prevent wildcat candidatures in those constituencies where the antagonism between Liberalism and independent Labour organizations was strong. The local Liberal Party was all too often regarded as the party of the local employers, and the continued reference to the Gladstonian aim of keeping class out of politics was to become more and more a façade barely hiding class conflicts towards the turn of the century.[150] Liberal intransigence to co-operate with the forces who demanded independent Labour representation also contributed to the rise of independent Labour organizations before 1914. As Ellen Wilkinson wrote in her General Strike novel of 1929, 'Was there another country in the world where the class barriers were so high as in England, and where it was so loudly proclaimed that none existed at all?'[151]

Despite such hostility at the local level—essential in setting up

---

[146] Christiane Eisenberg, 'Arbeiter, Bürger und der "bürgerliche Verein", 1820–1870. Deutschland und England im Vergleich', in Jürgen Kocka (ed.), *Bürgertum im 19. Jahrhundert: Deutschland im europäischen Vergleich* (Munich, 1986), ii. 187–219.

[147] George L. Bernstein, 'Liberalism and the Progressive Alliance, in the Constituencies, 1900–1914: Three Case Studies', *Historical Journal*, 26 (1983), 617–40; Pat Thane, 'Labour and Local Politics: Radicalism, Democracy and Social Reform 1880–1914', in Biagini and Reid, *Currents of Radicalism*, 244–70, Tanner, *Political Change*.

[148] Richard Lipinski, *Bericht des Bezirksvorstandes der sozialdemokratischen Partei Leipzigs im Jahr 1913/14* (Leipzig, 1914), 133.

[149] Biagini and Reid, *Currents of Radicalism*, 3 f.

[150] Evidence for the issue of class gaining more and more importance before 1914 can be found in: Ross McKibbin, *The Evolution of the Labour Party, 1910–1924* (Oxford, 1974), 71; Bill Lancaster, *Radicalism, Co-operation and Socialism: Leicester Working-Class Politics, 1860–1906* (Leicester, 1987); K. Laybourn and J. Reynolds, *Liberalism and the Rise of Labour* (London, 1984); Cyril Parry, *The Radical Tradition in Welsh Politics: A Study of Liberal and Labour Politics in Gwynedd, 1900–1920* (Hull, 1970); Howkins, 'Edwardian Liberalism and Industrial Unrest'.

[151] Ellen Wilkinson, *Clash* (London, 1929, repr. 1989), 303.

independent working-class parties in the first place—both SPD and Labour Party found it necessary to come to some sort of alliance with the Liberal Parties in national and local politics. Beverly Heckart has shown how close the non-conservative parties in the German Reichstag came before the war in forming an alliance against the conservatives and against the semi-democratic state.[152] Individual Social Democrats enjoyed good relations with individual Liberals. Wolfgang Heine, for example, organized a private circle of left liberals and Social Democrats at his home before the war. He and Albert Südekum were good friends with Theodor Barth, Eugen Diederichs, and other leading left liberals.[153] Bebel and Bernstein were corresponding with Barth and Naumann,[154] and the influential Lujo Brentano—in contact with Social Democrats like Bebel, Bernstein, Eisner, and Ebert before 1914—was active amongst Liberals to bring about an alliance with Social Democracy.[155] There can be little doubt that in the south of Germany such an alliance was already functioning before the First World War.[156]

In the war the 'bourgeois'–socialist coalition was finally forged in the Reichstag. In becoming part of the Interfraktioneller Ausschuß in 1917, the SPD was part of a party coalition which would have formed the government in a responsible parliamentary system.[157] That the war was seen as a turning-point in the relationship between Social Democrats and Liberals becomes very clear in the correspondence between Wolfgang Heine and Theodor Barth/Eugen Diederichs.[158] The improved relationship can also be seen from the publication of a book in which leading Liberals and Social Democrats commented on their vision of a post-war Germany.[159] After the war the maintenance of this consensus between

---

[152] Heckart, *From Bassermann to Bebel.* For Friedrich Naumann's conception of an alliance between bourgeois parties and SPD, its possibilities and limits, see also Peter Theiner, *Sozialer Imperialismus und deutsche Weltpolitik* (Baden-Baden, 1983), esp. 129–217. Also important: U. Ratz, *Sozialreform und Arbeiterschaft: Die 'Gesellschaft für soziale Reform' und die sozialdemokratische Arbeiterbewegung 1900–1914.* (Berlin, 1980).

[153] BA Koblenz, papers of Albert Südekum 190, 91/31; ZStA Potsdam, papers of Wolfgang Heine, 90 He 1, nos. 6, 15, and 37;

[154] ZStA Potsdam, papers of Barth, 90 Ba 4, nos. 27 and 7–8; IGA/ZPA, papers of August Bebel, 22/132, 59.

[155] James J. Sheehan, *The Career of Lujo Brentano: A Study of Liberalism and Social Reform in Imperial Germany* (Chicago, 1966), 138 f.

[156] Ludwig Quessel, 'Der Block der Linken und unsere Agitation', *NZ* 28 (1909–10), 827–30.

[157] Miller, *Burgfrieden und Klassenkampf*, 299–308.

[158] ZStA Potsdam, papers of Wolfgang Heine, 90 He 1, no. 6.

[159] Friedrich Thimme and Carl Legien (eds.), *Die Arbeiterschaft im neuen Deutschland* (Leipzig, 1915), especially pp. iii–iv.

bourgeois parties and Social Democrats seemed possible for a short time, but soon it became clear that the old antagonisms between the right wing of the National Liberals, who were now organized in the DVP, and the Social Democrats were not overcome by war and revolution. In many ways the gulf between the SPD and the other parties had widened again.[160] In Britain the position was in many ways reversed. It was not so much a problem of bringing about an alliance between Liberals and Labour, but of Labour seeking to steer clear of the Liberals' deadly embrace. The Labour Party under the leadership of Arthur Henderson and Ramsay MacDonald decided on a two-edged strategy: they would fight the Liberals tooth and nail in the trade unions, in order to win the trade unions for the cause of independent Labour representation, but they would agree to co-operate with the Liberal Party in elections, in order not to split the progressive vote. As in Germany the Labour Party pursued common political aims in parliament and formed electoral alliances with the Liberal Party. The Gladstone–MacDonald *entente* of 1903 led to a number of progressive parliamentary tickets, where Labour and Liberal candidates would run side by side in the elections.[161] Yet it is indicative of the anti-Liberal mood within the Labour Party that MacDonald found himself permanently under pressure to justify this increasingly unpopular *entente* inside his own party. In 1913 he even referred to the German Social Democrats and their *Stichwahlbündnisse* (electoral agreements) to demonstrate that it was not against socialist principles to form such agreements with other parties.[162] After 1918 the resistance within the Labour Party against any compromise with the Liberals was even stronger and now it also comprised the leadership.[163]

It has been argued that in relation to parliamentary government and alliance strategy the SPD and the Labour Party followed similar trajectories. The same ambiguities over constructive participation on the one hand and outright rejection on the other were characteristic of both up to 1933. The ultimate test for the degree of integration of independent working-class parties into their respective political systems is their willingness to take over government responsibility. In doing so, they publicly

[160] Breitman, *German Socialism*, 192. For the ambiguous relationship of the SPD with the DVP see: Winkler, *Von der Revolution*, 458 and id., *Der Schein der Normalität*, 305. For the strong differences between Stampfer and Crispien over the question of co-operation with bourgeois parties, see id., *Von der Revolution*, 587.

[161] Bealey and Pelling, *Labour and Politics*, 125–59.

[162] Ross McKibbin, 'James Ramsay MacDonald and the Problem of the Independence of the Labour Party, 1910–1914', *Journal of Modern History*, 42 (1970), 231.

[163] Sidney Webb, 'The Party Today', *Labour Magazine*, 1 (1922–3), 150 f.

declare their acceptance of any constraints of the framework of government they are acting under. Without wanting to go too much into detail,
here, as in the other two areas of investigation, one is struck by the
ambiguity of Labour Party and SPD towards the issue of participating in
a government. After both parties had made essentially unfavourable experiences with coalition and minority governments in the early 1920s, there
were similar debates in both parties, as to whether it was worthwhile to
take responsibility in a society which was still based on the capitalist
production process. A kind of attentiveness continued to run through
both parties in the 1920s. A belief that nothing could be done before the
economic and social system had not been significantly changed mixed
with a conviction that working-class parties should act as principled
opposition parties to make at least some sections within the SPD and
Labour Party hesitant to form alliances and take government responsibility in the 1920s.[164] The established parties in Britain and their political
élites might have been trying harder than their German counterparts to
accommodate the working-class interest,[165] but in the light of the above
evidence, one must conclude that neither the Labour Party nor the SPD
achieved full integration into their parliamentary systems.

2.3. The labour movement in Britain and Germany vs. employers and anti-Labour organizations

Integration of the labour movement into society did not only depend on
the reaction of the nation-state to the emergence of independent working-
class organizations. The reaction of employers was also important. Recognition and non-recognition of trade unions by employers could decisively
foster or hinder the integration process. The exceptionalist view on the
matter has been one of tolerant British employers who came to accept
trade unions as bargaining partners in the second half of the nineteenth
century and who stood in marked contrast to authoritarian German employers who tried everything to keep trade unionism out of the workshops and factories well into the twentieth century.[166] By comparing the

---

[164] For Germany this is a major topic in Winkler, *Von der Revolution*; id., *Der Schein der
Normalität*; id., *Der Weg in die Katastrophe*. For Britain see Robert Skidelsky, *Politicians and
the Slump* (London, 1967) and also H. M. Drucker, *Doctrine and Ethos in the Labour Party*
(London, 1979), 37.

[165] Breuilly, *Labour and Liberalism*, 151.

[166] Geary, *European Labour Politics*, 18 f. A slight modification of his views can be found
in Dick Geary, 'Arbeiter und Unternehmer im deutschen Kaiserreich', in *Konflikt und
Kooperation*, 177 f., where he concedes that 'master in one's own house' attitudes could be
found in Britain as well.

reaction of employers to trade unionism in both countries it should be possible to re-evaluate the correctness of such a view.

The different features of German industry, with its higher levels of concentration and cartelization, vertical and horizontal integration, and the interpenetration of financial and industrial capital were important in shaping different industrial relations from those of Britain. Political pressure groups of industry could be much more centralized in the framework of the German economy than in the British one. The Centralverband deutscher Industrieller (1876–1919) (Central Organization of German Industrialists), where heavy industry was dominant, and the more liberal Bund der Industriellen (1895–1912), where small export-oriented industries were prevalent, had no real parallel on the British side before 1914, where a whole array of employers' organizations of the various British industries could be found. British employers were more vulnerable to trade union pressure, not the least because bargaining remained highly decentralized. The localized nature of much industrial bargaining did not change significantly with the emergence of national employers' organizations in 1916 (Federation of British Industries, FBI) and 1919 (National Confederation of Employers' Organizations, NCEO). Other factors which strengthened the hand of German employers against the trade unions were protection after 1879 and the technological orientation of much of German industry with its low dependence on highly vulnerable unskilled workers. Big industrialists in Britain found it more difficult and costly to keep trade unions out of the workshops.[167] Yet Britain's small industry often put up a fight against trade unionism: '. . . also in England there exist quite a few mini-Stumms, who refuse any bargaining with their workers.'[168] Even if levels of trade unionization in Britain were higher than in any other European country, absolute figures remained low. Around the turn of the century, nearly 80 per cent of the male work-force remained non-unionized.[169] On the eve of the First World War levels of unionization in the manufacturing industry in Britain and Germany were not so different, with 30–40 per cent of the work-force being unionized in Britain and 25–30 per cent unionized in Germany. These levels compared favourably with both the USA (20 per cent) and France (15 per cent).[170]

---

[167] For a convincing argument to this effect see Dick Geary, 'Socialism and the German Labour Movement Before 1914', in id., *Labour Movements*, 122–4.

[168] Eduard Bernstein in *Vorwärts*, 110 (12 May 1901). See generally A. E. Musson, *The Growth of British Industry* (London, 1978), 255.

[169] Benson, *The Working Class*, 190–3.

[170] A. R. Zolberg, 'How Many Exceptionalisms?', in Katznelson and Zolberg, *Working Class Formation*, 398.

Regional and local differences within both countries were just as important as the size of the industry in determining the character of industrial relations. In Germany the Ruhr and Saar employers were especially hostile to independent working-class organizations,[171] whereas trade unions were widely accepted in other areas.[172] The Krupps and Stumms of Germany stood side by side with the Abbés and Boschs.[173] Trade unions in Germany were far from powerless in Imperial Germany. Werner Abelshauser has argued that the rise in real wages after the 1880s was not the least due to trade union pressure.[174] Well before 1914, two out of three industrial conflicts ended in compromise, another indication of a growing readiness of employers to accept trade unions as representative organizations of the working class.[175] In Wales the intransigence of the coal owners led to a complete defeat of the miners' union in the 1898 strike, and the Penrhyn lockout from 1900 to 1903 was to become a symbol of employers' reluctance to deal with trade unions. After the 1926 defeat of the miners a yellow union, the South Wales Miners Industrial Union (SWMIU) was founded and immediately recognized by the mine management.[176] The non-acceptance of unions by almost all railway companies at the beginning of the century finally triggered off the Taff Vale dispute which showed Ammon Beasley holding opinions similar to the famous German *Herr-im-Haus* viewpoint of the Ruhr industrialists.[177]

If regional autocrats could be found amongst British and German industrialists, the more widespread recognition of collective bargaining procedures in the British industry cannot be denied. Sir Alfred Mond,

---

[171] See David F. Crew, *Town in the Ruhr: A Social History of Bochum, 1860–1914* (New York, 1979), 146. For the Saar see Ulrich Borsdorf, *Hans Böckler: Arbeit und Leben eines Gewerkschaftlers von 1875–1945* (Cologne, 1982), 79 ff.

[172] The notion that unions were widely accepted by employers was for example expressed in Georg Schmidt, 'Die Anerkennung der Gewerkschaften einst und jetzt', *SM* 14 (1910), 814–17.

[173] Ritter and Tenfelde, *Arbeiter*, 417–24.

[174] Werner Abelshauser, 'Lebensstandard im Industrialisierungsprozeß: Britische Debatte und deutsche Verhältnisse', *Scripta Mercaturae*, 16 (1982), 87.

[175] Hartmut Kaelble, *Nachbarn am Rhein: Entfremdung und Annäherung der französischen und deutschen Gesellschaft seit 1880* (Munich, 1991), 92.

[176] For the development of the South Wales coalfield and the intransigence of employers towards trade unions see Hywel Francis and David Smith, *The Fed: A History of the South Wales Miners in the Twentieth Century* (London, 1980).

[177] Bealey and Pelling, *Labour and Politics*, 55 and 71. For the widespread use of the 'services' of the Free Labour movement see W. Collison, *The Apostle of Free Labour* (London, 1913), 139–157, esp. 145. For the attitudes of the Ruhr captains see Bernd Weisbrod, *Schwerindustrie in der Weimarer Republik: Interessenpolitik zwischen Stabilisierung und Krise* (Wuppertal, 1978).

the very model of a liberal entrepreneur, voiced the opinion of at least some of his fellow industrialists when writing to Lujo Brentano in December 1912: 'I assure you . . . that in England nobody thinks of abolishing trade unions, on the contrary employers have become used to co-operating with working–class organizations. Many of the big industries . . . have their conciliation boards, federations, or unions, and work under collective wage agreements . . .'.[178] His statement preceded his 1927 initiative to base the trade union–employer relationship on a footing of mutual understanding and co-operation, the so-called Mond–Turner talks.[179] However, it would be a grave mistake to see Mond as representative of British employers at large. The Mond–Turner talks were not supported by the major employers' federations in Britain, and, if anything, the talks only served to demonstrate the profound differences in opinion between employers and organized Labour about how the economy should be run.[180]

Nevertheless it can be argued that British employers found that they were obliged to tolerate strong unions as long as they posed no threat to the existing economic order, whilst German employers on the contrary used their substantial power to keep unionism out of the workshop.[181] As a consequence trade unions in Great Britain were more apprehensive of state intervention in industrial relations than their German counterparts. It was the basic weakness of the German trade unions which made them look to the state even before 1914, and favour strong state intervention in the sphere of industrial relations after 1918.[182] Domestication of industrial conflict was, however, the ultimate rationale of employer strategies in both countries.

Although these explanations go some way in accounting for differences

---

[178] BA Koblenz, papers of Lujo Brentano, map 73, 221–3: letter from Sir Alfred Mond to Lujo Brentano, 2 Dec. 1912, p. 1.

[179] Hugh A. Clegg, *A History*, ii. 464–71.

[180] John Turner, 'The Politics of Business', 8 and Michael Dintenfas, 'The Politics of Producers' Co-operation: the FBI–TUC–NCEO Talks 1929–33', 91, both articles in John ' Turner (ed.), *Businessmen and Politics: Studies of Business Activity in British Politics 1900–1945* (London, 1984).

[181] M. C. Rowlinson, 'Cadbury's New Factory System, 1879–1919' (University of Aston Ph.D. 1987), 15 and 62 f. has argued convincingly that British employers were able to channel much rank and file unrest into peaceful negotiations by recognizing trade unions.

[182] For the basic difference of trade union attitudes towards state intervention in the sphere of industrial relations see: Jutta Rabenschlag-Kräußlich, *Parität statt Klassenkampf? Zur Organisation des Arbeitsmarktes und Domestizierung des Arbeitskampfes in Deutschland und England, 1900–1918* (Frankfurt am Main, 1983), 293–314; Bernd-Jürgen Wendt, 'Industrial Democracy: Zur Struktur der englischen Sozialbeziehungen', *aus politik und zeitgeschichte*, 46 (1975), 3–47, esp. his comparative remarks, pp. 5–13.

between employer–trade union relationships in both countries, basic similarities should not be overlooked. The reactions of employers to the emergence of trade unions varied widely in Britain and Germany, and British as well as German industrialists developed similar systems of rigid economic and social control. In Germany they tried to control their workforce by so-called employers' employment agencies which operated on the basis of blacklisting any known trade unionist.[183] Employers tried to set up their own trade unions, so-called yellow trade unions, which would work closely with the management.[184] They tried to put pressure on publicans not to give rooms to trade unions or socialists, and if they knew of workers who held assemblies privately in flats or elsewhere, they were immediately sacked.[185] On 1 May the employers would answer industrial action by unions with large-scale lockouts or dismissals, and even in the Weimar Republic employers did not drop their enmity towards Labour Day.[186] Quite the contrary, many employers were not willing to accept the enlarged role of organized Labour in the Republic and bitterly fought against the welfare state, 'factory councils', and state arbitration.[187] Social patriarchy also revealed itself in the foundation of factory sports clubs[188] and, indeed, the provision of every social and other facility the worker could think of.[189]

In Britain, certainly victimization and blacklisting was a popular method amongst employers to keep a check on trade unions.[190] In Barnsley, it was

---

[183] For Bavaria see Robert Kandler, 'The Effects of Economic and Social Conditions on the Development of the Free Trade Unions in Upper Franconia, 1890–1914' (University of Oxford D.Phil. 1986), 241.

[184] K. Mattheier, *Die Gelben: Nationale Arbeiter zwischen Wirtschaftsfrieden und Streik* (Düsseldorf, 1973).

[185] Lucas, *Zwei Formen*, 128.

[186] For harassment of workers by employers celebrating 1 May see Dieter Fricke, *Kleine Geschichte des 1. Mai: Die Maifaier in der deutschen und in der internationalen Arbeiterbewegung* (Frankfurt am Main, 1980), 113–15, 130–33, and 181 f. and also Udo Achten, *Illustrierte Geschichte des 1. Mai* (Oberhausen, 1979), 206 f., 246 f. and 256 f. See also IGA/ZPA, St. 22/75.

[187] Dick Geary, 'Employers, Workers and the Collapse of the Weimar Republic', in Ian Kershaw (ed.), *Weimar: Why did German Democracy Fail?* (London, 1990), 100 f.

[188] Rainer Stübling, *Kultur und Massen: Das Kulturkartell der modernen Arbeiterbewegung in Frankfurt am Main, 1925–1933* (Offenbach, 1983), 70.

[189] 'Die "Polypenarme" betrieblicher "Wohlfahrtseinrichtungen": Beobachtungen eines Gewerkschaftsredakteurs in der chemischen Industrie (1911)', in Klaus Saul, Jens Flemming, Dirk Stegmann, Peter-Christian Witt (eds.), *Arbeiterfamilien im Kaiserreich: Materialien zur Sozialgeschichte in Deutschland, 1871–1914* (Königstein im Taunus, 1982), 113–15. See also the oral history evidence in Lothar Steinbach, *Mannheim: Erinnerungen aus einem halben Jahrhundert: Sozialgeschichte einer Stadt in Lebensbildern* (Stuttgart, 1984), 49, 63 f., 78, 147.

[190] J. D. Young, *Socialism and the English Working Class: A History of English Labour, 1883–1939* (Hemel Hempstead, 1989), 110–22.

claimed that 'ordinary people . . . were virtually controlled by their employers'.[191] Socialists generally met secretly, 'fearful of being victimized and rough handled'.[192] After Victor Grayson's 1907 election victory in the Colne Valley 'a number of his ardent supporters were discharged from the mills. In addition, tradesmen who had identified themselves with the party were boycotted and suffered commercially'.[193] George Hodgkinson, for instance, remembered distinctly that trade unions before 1914 were not at all recognized in Coventry workshops: 'They [the workers] might have been undercover members, but if they were, they kept it very secret, since trade unions were frowned upon by the employers.' And coming down from Ruskin College in 1919 he found: 'I could not immediately find work. The bar was down and I was on the black list of the employers . . .'.[194] Social patriarchy among employers was far from absent in Britain. Provision of social and recreational facilities, housing, or work trips were means of keeping relations between the work-force and the employer stable. Welfare schemes in the 1890s were often linked to anti-union, no strike clauses.[195] The dependence of workers on their employers was often so strong 'that resistance to political domination was precluded'.[196] Ultimately, British and German employers found it extremely difficult to come to terms with trade unionism. They finally did so only where it was either profitable or unavoidable.

It is therefore not surprising that many employers in both countries

---

[191] Judith Watts and Donald Nannestad, *The First 50 Years: Half a Century of Labour Rule in Barnsley* (n.p., n.d.), n. pp.

[192] *Socialism in West Sussex: A History of the Chichester Constitutional Labour Party* (Chichester, 1983), 2.

[193] *History of the Colne Valley Labour Party, 1891–1941: Jubilee Souvenir* (Colne Valley, 1941), 25.

[194] George Hodgkinson, *Sent to Coventry* (London, 1970), 23 and 60.

[195] A. Jowitt, 'Late Victorian and Edwardian Bradford', in R. K. S. Taylor and J. A. Jowitt (eds.), *Bradford, 1890–1914: The Cradle of the ILP* (Bradford, 1980), 7 f.; Patrick Joyce, *Work, Society and Politics: The Culture of the Factory in Later Victorian England* (London, 1980), 219, Bob Morris and Jim Smyth, *Paternalism as an Employer Strategy 1800–1960* (Edinburgh, 1989); Thane, *The Foundations*, 12 f.; W. R. Garside and H. F. Gospel, 'Employers and Managers: Their Organizational Structure and Changing Industrial Strategies', in C. Wrigley (ed.), *A History of British Industrial Relations* (Brighton, 1982), 106–8; S. G. Jones, 'The Survival of Industrial Paternalism in the Cotton Districts: A View from the 1920s', *Journal of Regional and Local Studies*, 7 (1987), 1–13. Robert J. Waller, *The Dukeries Transformed: The Social and Political Development of a Twentieth-Century Coalfield* (Oxford, 1983), chs. 4–9.

[196] Alan Warde, 'Conditions of Dependence: Working-Class Quiescence in Lancaster in the 20th Century', *IRSH* 35 (1990), 71–105. For the intransigence of Scottish employers to organized Labour see R. Duncan and A. McIvor (eds.), *Militant Workers: Labour and Class Conflict on the Clyde, 1900–1950* (Edinburgh, 1992).

supported organizations which were directly anti-Labour. The most obvious ones were the Reichsverband zur Bekämpfung der Sozialdemokratie (Imperial League against Social Democracy), founded in 1904 and the Anti-Socialist Union (ASU), founded in 1907. Both organizations came into being after the working-class parties had proved themselves powerful forces in the national elections of 1902 in Germany and 1906 in Britain respectively. Other organizations in Germany which were opposed to social-democratic leadership of the working class included the Bund vaterländischer Arbeitervereine, founded in May 1907 as a rival organization to the socialist trade unions, and the Alldeutsche Verband (Pan-German League).[197] Besides there were smaller groups, mainly concerned with publishing anti-socialist literature. They carried illustrious names such as Vaterlandsverein (Fatherland Club), Wirtschaftlicher Schutzverband (Economic Defence League), or Arbeitsgemeinschaft für praktische Aufklärung und Volksgesundung (Association for Practical Instruction and Healthy Public Attitudes).[198]

In Britain the Liberty and Property Defence League had been set up in July 1882.[199] In 1893 William Collison founded the Free Labour Protection Association which during the following years organized an effective anti-trade union campaign in Britain with the full support of a number of British employers.[200] In 1906 the Middle Class Defence League was founded with the prime aim of combating those forces advocating state intervention and higher taxation. Additionally many ratepayers' associations throughout the country also had a decidedly anti-socialist tinge.[201] After the First World War Middle Class Unions were set up in many British towns. As in the case of Bedford they were mainly concerned 'with combating the growth of socialism and communism, and with the organization of the maintenance of essential supplies in case of an emergency, such as a general strike or worse'.[202] Other organizations which worked more or less closely with the Anti-Socialist

---

[197] For the Alldeutsche Verband see Roger Chickering, *We Men, Who Feel Most German: A Cultural Study of the Pan-German League, 1886–1914* (Boston, 1984). On other nationalistic pressure groups see Jürgen Kuczynski, *Studien zur Geschichte des deutschen Imperialismus*, ii: *Propagandaorganisationen des Monopolkapitals* (Berlin, 1950), esp. 7–160.

[198] Some of their publications are contained in BA Koblenz, ZSg. 2/13–14.

[199] N. Soldon, 'Laissez-Faire as Dogma: The Liberty and Property Defence League', in K. D. Brown (ed.), *Essays in Anti-Labour History* (London, 1974), 208–33.

[200] Collison, *The Apostle* 92–103 and 139–57.

[201] Kenneth D. Brown, 'The Anti-Socialist Union, 1908–1949', in Brown (ed.), *Essays*, 242.

[202] *Bedford Politics 1900–1924*, pub. by Bedfordshire Record Office (Bedford 1986), 15.

Union were the Primrose League, the British Constitution Association, the Imperial Sunday Alliance, and the Nonconformist Anti-Socialist Union.[203]

For reasons of space we will compare only the two major anti-socialist organizations, namely the Anti-Socialist Union and the Reichsverband. How were they structured, what were their activities and aims? The Reichsverband tried hard to copy the elaborate organization of the SPD. It was planned as a mass organization based on local groups which were united in district organizations. In 1906 it had already 120,000 individual members[204] and in 1914 they were organized in 800 local groups with special regional strength in Prussia.[205] The ASU also tried hard to become a viable force in the country. It set up numerous local branches which were organized in county divisions.[206] It employed sixty well-paid full-time provincial agents in 1911.[207] They usually organized anti-socialist activities within their particular areas. The Union also set up an Intelligence and Statistical Department in 1909 in order to collect data on the socialist movement in the country.[208] A women's branch was inaugurated in 1910.[209] It soon was building up settlements in working-class areas. An education branch was set up in 1911, including in its membership 'about nine hundred prominent educationalists . . .'.[210] In 1911, the 'Liberty Wheelers', a cycling club formed by the Liverpool members of the ASU, was reported to be 'in full swing',[211] indicating that the Union was also socially active.

On the whole the activities of both organizations looked remarkably similar. Both published innumerable booklets and pamphlets amounting to a rather similar ideological campaign against the working-class parties

---

[203] For these organizations see *Anti-Socialist*, 2 (Mar. 1909), 28; 3 (Apr. 1909), 30; and 8 (Sept. 1909), 90; Pugh, *The Tories*; for the strength of anti-socialism in Britain see J. N. Peters, 'Anti-Socialism in British Politics, c.1900–1923: The Emergence of a Counter-Ideology' (Oxford University D.Phil., 1992).

[204] ZStA Potsdam, 07.01, no. 1395/4, 42, letter Reichsverband to von Loebell, 14 Sept. 1906.

[205] *10 Jahre Reichsverband: Festgabe der Hauptstelle des Reichsverbandes gegen die Sozialdemokratie in Berlin zum 9. Mai 1914* (Berlin, 1914), 58. The Reichsverband was virtually non-existent in the southern states Baden, Württemberg, and Bavaria, where its raging anti-socialism found fewer supporters.

[206] *Liberty*, 5 (Aug. 1910), 39.

[207] Brown, 'The Anti-Socialist Union', in id., *Essays*, 242.

[208] *Anti-Socialist*, 8 (Sept. 1909), 93.   [209] *Liberty*, 4 (July 1910), 43.

[210] *Liberty*, 1 (Jan. 1911), 18. For the spreading of settlements see ibid., no. 34 (8 Nov. 1911).

[211] *Liberty*, 14 (21 June 1911), 177.

of both countries.[212] The ASU published a newspaper, the *Anti-Socialist* from 1909 to 1910. This paper was continued as *Liberty* from 1910 onwards. The Reichsverband published a press service, the *Anti-Sozialdemokratische Korrespondenz* from 1 August 1904 onwards. At the end of 1906 1,225 papers and journals subscribed to it.[213] Additionally the Reichsverband financially supported the paper *Deutsches Volksblatt*.[214] Apart from written propaganda both organizations concentrated on the spoken word. They saw their prime task in the education of the masses against socialism and therefore wished to provide speakers to bring the message to the people. So they founded speakers' classes, at first in the capitals, Berlin and London, and later in other towns. Speakers were especially useful at election times, when they were dispatched to the constituencies in order to help the 'anti-Labour' candidate win support. The Anti-Socialist Union also had special campaigns between elections to bring the anti-socialist message to the country.[215]

Although both organizations claimed to be above party politics in the sense that they would support anybody who was not socialist, they both failed to bring about such a broad anti-socialist coalition. This becomes clear when both organizations were forced to abandon their party neutrality in attacking non-socialists who looked favourably towards co-operation with working-class parties, like Lloyd George or Cadbury in Britain and Sombart in Germany, and accused them of fostering the socialist cause. In Germany only the right wing of the National Liberals and the Conservative Party and in Britain only the Liberal Unionists and the Conservative Party worked closely with the respective anti-socialist organizations. Both groups were largely financed by a few notables from industry and right-wing political parties.[216] In addition, the Reichsverband got a considerable amount of money from membership fees, whereas the Union started public appeals for money, like the Million

---

[212] ZStA Potsdam, papers of Wolfgang Heine, 90 He 1, no. 28: for some of the Reichsverband publications, for example *Handbuch für nichtsozialdemokratische Wähler* (1st edn. Berlin 1906, 2nd edn. 1909, 3rd edn. 1911). For similar material of the ASU see *The Failures of Socialism* (London, 1909) and *Socialism Exposed* (London, 1914).

[213] Klaus Saul, *Staat, Industrie und Arbeiterbewegung im Kaiserreich: Zur Innen- und Sozialpolitik des Wilhelminischen Deutschland, 1903–1914* (Düsseldorf, 1974), 129.

[214] ZStA Potsdam, 07.01, no. 1395/1, 153.

[215] See for example the report about a summer campaign at the seaside in *Liberty* (3 June 1910), 27 or about a special campaign in Yorkshire and Lancashire in *Liberty* (1 Apr. 1910), 3.

[216] Dieter Fricke, 'Der Reichsverband gegen die Sozialdemokratie von seiner Gründung bis zu den Reichstagswahlen von 1907', *ZfG* 7 (1959), 244 and 250; Brown, 'The Anti-Socialist Union', in id., *Essays*, 248 f.; both stress the fact that business interests were heavily represented on the organizations' councils.

Shillings Fund which was supported by many respectable papers, like *The Times*, throughout the country.[217]

Both organizations had informal contacts with the government. The contact of the Reichsverband in the Reichskanzlei (chancellor's office) was secretary von Loebell, himself a founding member of the Reichs-verband.[218] Max Lorenz, the editor of the *Anti-Sozialdemokratische Korrespondenz*, visited von Loebell frequently, and von Loebell seems to have helped the Reichsverband, whenever state authorities proved uncooperative. Yet, there are also indications that the government was not too keen on close contact with the Reichsverband. The Reichsverband frequently complained to von Loebell that authorities were openly hostile to their efforts. Bethmann's letter to von Loebell of 27 October 1905, thanking him for asking the Reichsverband to be more cautious in its relations with public authorities, can be seen as another indication of the government's hesitation in co-operating openly with the Reichsverband.[219] The ASU was not only generously supported by the Conservative Party and the Liberal Unionists, but it is also likely that it influenced the government's decisions when the Tories were in power. During the 1926 General Strike, for example, several members of the Conservative government were active ASU supporters and members, and the Prime Minister himself had taken a keen interest in the work of the ASU.[220] What is more, not only could the business interest make itself felt indirectly through organizations like the ASU, there was a distinct group of industrialists in parliament who combined on issues like anti-trade union legislation.[221] Consequently it can hardly be surprising if government 'increasingly appeared to be on the side of the employers'.[222]

In ideological terms differences can be perceived between the anti-socialist organizations in Britain and Germany. The Reichsverband was explicitly against social reform:

German social reform has done nothing for the maintenance of social peace, on the contrary, it has been damaging for social peace. . . . It wanted to create satisfaction, but it raised covetousness . . . the social reform had a deeply demoralizing

---

[217] *Anti-Socialist*, 10 (Nov. 1909), 118–20.
[218] Fricke, 'Der Reichsverband', 254. For the co-operation of government and Reichsverband in the notorious 1907 election see Kuczynski, *Propagandaorganisationen*, 177.
[219] ZStA Potsdam, 07.01, 1395/2, 76.
[220] Brown, 'The Anti-Socialist Union', in id., *Essays*, 259.
[221] John Turner, 'The Politics of Business', in id., *Businessmen*, 15 f. has calculated that between 1924 and 1939 35 per cent of the parliamentary Conservative Party were businessmen.
[222] Chris Wrigley, *David Lloyd George and the British Labour Movement: Peace and War* (New York, 1976), 234, who has drawn attention to anti-Labour sentiments within the Liberal Party.

effect on the masses. The sense of duty, the energy of will to care for oneself, have seriously deteriorated in the people . . .[223]

The ASU (in contrast to other anti-socialist organizations in Britain like the British Constitution Association or the Liberty and Property Defence League, which campaigned against social reform) was in favour of social reform: 'Today in the UK the crying need—a need recognised by all parties—is Social Reform.'[224] The Union was championing schemes for co-partnership and profit-sharing in industry and it endorsed the Whitley councils after the First World War. If the social background of anti-socialist leadership figures like Collison or von Liebert is compared, another interesting difference emerges. Whereas Collison was actually representative of a highly individualistic British working man, von Liebert was part and parcel of the reactionary Prussian officer-caste. As representative of the working class, Collison was much more willing to accept the necessity for an improvement in his class's standard of living than Liebert. Yet these ideological differences should not be overemphasized. The Union looked full of admiration to Germany. Here they saw the model of a strong anti-socialist government.[225] The major function of the two movements was to strengthen the politically right-wing parties against a perceived tide of socialism. Their programme and organization indicate the degree of antipathy with which the labour movement was received not only by employers and their interest groups but also by the middle classes in Britain and Germany who formed the core of support for anti-socialist organizations in both countries. It is to the relationship between the middle classes and the labour movement in Britain and Germany that attention is turned in the next section.

2.4. Labour and the middle classes

Both the Labour Party and the SPD had been founded as class parties: they appealed to a particular social class whose interests they claimed to represent. However, once working-class parties decided to participate in elections to representative bodies, they appealed also to non-working class groups for electoral support. In the light of this, *Sonderweg* historians have argued that the British Labour Party was successfully appealing to

[223] *Das Schuldkonto der deutschen Sozialreform*, Pamphlet no. 1 of the Reichsverband, pub. 5 Jan. 1906.
[224] *Exposure of the Socialist Conspiracy: The Socialist Secret Plan of Campaign*, ed. by the Anti-Socialist Union (London, 1911), 16.
[225] See caricature in *Liberty* (4 Oct. 1911), or the passionate call for a Bismarckian statesman in Britain in *Liberty* (29 Nov. 1911).

parts of a non-working-class vote, whereas the SPD was either not willing to do the same or was prevented from doing so by the existence of a more rigid class structure in Germany. Whereas all classes in British society were heavily divided internally, German classes were comparatively homogeneous in their political behaviour. Such differences in the class structure were consequently reflected in a very different relationship between middle and working classes. According to Ernst Dückershoff, a German miner employed in Britain before the turn of the century, relations were friendly in Britain, whereas the German worker, due to state repression, 'trusts no one who is not a workman'.[226] Arguments like this have been taken up by historians like G. A. Ritter, Klaus Tenfelde, and Dick Geary, who all stress that sharper social differences between blue- and white-collar workers (*Kragenlinie*) marked unbridgeable political differences in Germany. The clearer class divide in Germany led to a middle class neurosis about the 'red peril' which was exploited to the full by extreme reactionary political forces.[227]

The SPD is sometimes portrayed as having played into the hands of the reactionaries, because of its insistence to remain the very model of a class party rejecting non-working class people in its organizations and frightening them off with its Marxist ideology as late as the 1920s.[228] Other historians have not blamed the SPD for frightening off the middle classes, but rather the middle classes for their slavish orientation towards their social superiors. The problem with the latter view is that it relies heavily on impressionistic evidence such as Heinrich Mann's novel *Der Untertan*.[229] Less literary-oriented interpretations have either stressed the similarity of the entrepreneurial ethos in Britain and Germany and argued against any serious feudalization of the entrepreneurial middle classes,[230] or they have maintained that the industrial middle classes became feudalized almost everywhere in Europe, including Britain and

---

[226] Ernst Dückershoff, *How the English Workman Lives* (London, 1899), 76 and 81.

[227] Geary, *European Labour Politics*, 19; Dick Geary, 'Sectionalism in Britain and Germany before the First World War', unpublished paper presented to the 1988 Lancaster conference on working-class culture in Britain and Germany; Ritter and Tenfelde, *Arbeiter*, 145–7; Heinz-Gerhard Haupt, 'Zur gesellschaftlichen Bedeutung des Kleinbürgertums in westeuropäischen Gesellschaften des 19. Jahrhunderts', *GG*, 16 (1990), 304.

[228] Theodor Geiger, 'Die Mittelschichten und die Sozialdemokratie', *DA* 13 (1931), 619–35. See also Michael Prinz, 'Wandel durch Beharrung: Sozialdemokratie und "neue Mittelschichten" in historischer Perspektive', *AfS* 29 (1989), 38 f.

[229] Wehler, *Das deutsche Kaiserreich*, 93; R. Alter, 'Heinrich Manns "Untertan": Prüfstein für die "Kaiserreich-Debatte"?', *GG* 17 (1991), 370–89.

[230] Hartmut Kaelble, 'Wie feudal waren die deutschen Unternehmer im Kaiserreich? Ein Zwischenbericht', in Richard H. Tilly (ed.), *Beiträge zur quantitativen vergleichenden Unternehmensgeschichte* (Stuttgart, 1985), 148–74.

Germany.[231] In either case Britain and Germany would belong to a European 'norm' rather than an exception. What is really at issue in the present section is the exceptionalist argument that antagonistic relationships between German Labour and the middle classes are to be contrasted with the more harmonious relationships between British Labour and the middle classes.

SPD leaders from Wilhelm Liebknecht to Wolfgang Heine frequently warned against an influx of middle-class individuals, especially academics and intellectuals. In 1899 Liebknecht wrote: 'if bourgeois elements get so numerous and important in the party that there is a real danger of the proletarian elements getting pushed to the side . . . the danger of bourgeoisification becomes real . . . But all that is bourgeois is diametrically opposed to all that is socialist.'[232] In 1928 Heine wrote to Julie Braun: 'I, myself, judge the activities of certain middle-class academics in the party as not at all positive . . . The danger which is imminent with academics, lies in the doctrinal fervour of people who know no other work than political journalism and agitation.'[233] August Bebel's injunction to the 1903 party conference to look thoroughly at every new party member, but to look twice or even thrice as thoroughly at every middle-class academic, is probably the most famous indication of SPD reservations against middle-class intellectuals. Bebel's view seems representative of more widespread dislike within the SPD of members of the educated middle classes, whereas the members of the petty bourgeoisie were more readily accepted.[234] At the same time, however, Bebel stressed frequently that the party needed brain workers as well as manual workers, and privately conceded: 'The only disappointment that I have experienced since the fall of the anti-socialist law, is the fact that far fewer useful and competent members of the intelligentsia have joined the party than I expected.'[235] However, men with a middle-class background were by no means absent from the SPD leadership and they could even be amongst the most popular leaders, as demonstrated by Paul Singer before the First World War.

The SPD's belief in historical determinism[236] did not help the party to

---

[231] A. J. Mayer, *The Persistence of the Old Regime: Europe to the Great War* (London, 1981).

[232] Wilhelm Liebknecht, *Kein Kompromiß, kein Wahlbündnis* (Berlin, 1899), 7.

[233] ZStA Potsdam, papers of Wolfgang Heine, 90 He 1, no. 229, 79–84: letter Heine to Julie Braun, 16 July 1928.

[234] Evans, *Proletarians*, 139, 149–151; Pierson, *Marxist Intellectuals*, chs. 4 and 7.

[235] IGA/ZPA, papers of August Bebel, 23/137, 149: letter from Bebel to unknown, 16 Jan. 1893.

[236] See 5.2.

win over substantial parts of the middle classes: 'We do not care much where most of the educated persons stand. . . . surely, they will finally come to the proletariat, when it is proven that the consequences of our sciences, the forces which drive forward our culture cannot be enforced differently.'[237] Additionally it proved to be difficult to reach the middle classes via working-class *Agitatoren*. As the social milieu was so different, this only led to 'unfruitful discussions'.[238] If the willingness of the SPD to integrate the middle classes was hesitant, although by no means absent, before 1914, this seems to have changed slightly in the Weimar Republic. Efforts were now made to include elements of the *Mittelstand* and small farmers into the party,[239] yet the SPD proved still to be unable to leave the skilled working-class ghetto, as they found it difficult to get accepted by other strata of society.[240]

The British Labour Party is held to have profited from an influx of mostly non-working class Liberal politicians in and after the First World War. These prominent Liberals, having often fought side by side against the war with anti-war Labour Party members, had been received with much goodwill.[241] Indeed, there were several efforts in the 1920s, including a *Daily Herald* campaign, to win over the middle classes to Labour:

The labour movement has not devoted sufficient attention to the trials, troubles and grievances of that section of the community usually known as 'the middle classes'; they are no less workers because they work with their heads rather than their hands. Politically and industrially it is of the greatest importance that the middle classes shall be won for Labour.[242]

---

[237] Max Maurenbrecher, *Die Gebildeten und die Sozialdemokratie* (Leipzig, 1904), 7.

[238] Heinrich Knauf, 'Aus der Praxis der Agitation', *NZ* 30 (1911–12), 674.

[239] William Harvey Maehl, *The German Socialist Party: Champion of the First Republic, 1918–1933* (Philadelphia, 1986), 208 f. It is significant that the SPD's perception of the Liberal influx into the Labour Party after 1918 was positive. See for example *Freie Presse*, Elberfeld-Barmen, 8 Jan. 1925. For the increasing number of white-collar employees and civil servants in the ranks of the SPD in the Weimar Republic see Lösche and Walter, 'Auf dem Weg zur Volkspartei', 86–90. For the town of Harburg, where the SPD could mobilize substantial lower middle-class support already before 1914 see Peter Christian Witt, 'Die Entstehung einer sozialdemokratischen Stadt: Harburg zwischen preußischer Annektion 1866/67 und Erstem Weltkrieg', in Ritter, *Der Aufstieg*, 259–316. Also more generally R. Blank, 'Die soziale Zusammensetzung der sozialdemokratischen Wählerschaft Deutschlands', *AfSWP* 20 (1905), 513–24.

[240] Guttsman, *The German Social Democratic Party 1875–1933*, 122–7.

[241] Ramsay MacDonald, 'Outlook', *SR* 15 (1918), 10 f. W. J. Brown, 'Labour and the Middle Classes', *Labour Magazine*, 1 (1918), 330 f., Catherine Ann Cline, *Recruits to Labour: The British Labour Party, 1914–1931* (Syracuse, NY, 1963), 130, Tanner, *Political Change*, 403.

[242] *London News* (May 1925), 3: 'Hearty Welcome to the Daily Herald Campaign'.

Yet, it remains doubtful, if, apart from a number of Liberals in the top echelons of the party, many middle-class Liberals were actually recruited to the Labour Party on a ward level. The gulf which existed also in Britain between the lower middle classes of white-collar workers and the skilled or unskilled workers made any such efforts almost futile.[243]

Within British clerks, snobbishness about their own social standing was such as to preclude any identification with blue-collar workers. Anti-proletarian and anti-Labour sentiments were extremely widespread amongst British clerks.[244] When the early 1980s saw the emergence of a Social Democratic alternative to the Labour Party, Gareth Stedman Jones advised the Labour Party to seek to become an interclass alliance. Maintaining that such an alliance had been working before the First World War, he had to admit that the British Labour Party failed to revive such an interclass alliance in the inter-war years.[245] Consequently it can hardly be surprising if local studies have pointed out that membership in local Labour Parties remained largely working class in the 1920s and 1930s.[246] Apart from the membership, it has been shown that the Labour Party, throughout its history and with the exception of the 1945 elections has had to rely on working-class votes which usually contributed at least around two-thirds of its overall vote.[247] The main reasons for the party's attachment to a social milieu, which so resembled the SPD's situation, were to be found in the combined employers'/state counter-attack against independent Labour in the 1890s and the 1920s, two crucial times for the Labour Party's existence. Furthermore the defection of non-working class Labour leaders to other parties, like Mosley's and Strachey's in 1931, strengthened an inverted snobbery of the working-class members of the

[243] For the substantial difference between the lower middle classes and even the labour aristocracy in Britain see Eric Hobsbawm, *Worlds of Labour* (London, 1984), 242.

[244] Peter Behringer, *Soziologie und Sozialgeschichte der Privatangestellten in Großbritannien* (Frankfurt am Main, 1985), 155, 234, 236 f.

[245] Gareth Stedman Jones, 'Why is the Labour Party in a Mess', in *Languages of Class* (Cambridge, 1983), 244.

[246] Michael Savage, 'The Social Bases of Working-Class Politics: The Labour Movement in Preston, 1890–1948' (University of Lancaster Ph.D. 1984) 187; John Boughton, 'Working-Class Politics in Birmingham and Sheffield, 1918–1931' (University of Warwick' Ph.D. 1985), 253. German local studies point into the same direction of a working-class based party. See for example Adelheid von Saldern, *Auf dem Wege zum Arbeiter-Reformismus: Parteialltag in sozialdemokratischer Provinz, Göttingen 1870–1920* (Frankfurt am Main, 1984), 141 f., Michels, 'Die deutsche Sozialdemokratie I', 518, and H. Müller, *Geschichte der Arbeiterbewegung in Sachsen-Altenburg* (Jena, 1923), 60.

[247] Willi L. Guttsman, *The British Political Elite* (London, 1963), 242; W. L. Miller, *Electoral Dynamics in Britain since 1918* (London, 1977), 22 f., 225; John Bonham, *The Middle Class Vote* (London, 1954), 162–76.

party, stressing their workplace experience rather than any form of further education. This is evident in statements like the one by James Sexton of the Dock Labourer's Union on the 1918 Labour Party conference: 'It was reported that Lord Haldane was now a member of the Labour Party, and they had Outhwaites, Ponsonbys and Morels to whom he decidedly objected. It had been their experience that these men would not subscribe to the Labour Party and carry out its mandates.' Equally, Bruce Glasier's less than charming characterization of Lady Warwick, the flamboyant aristocratic convert to socialism, can serve as another example of the mistrust with which members of other social classes were greeted in the British labour movement: 'we have had "Comrade Warwick" with us for three days . . . I was introduced to her—. . . but I made it a point to leave her soon. . . . She is very handsome but mostly made up— false . . . hair, and much powder and henna die.' George Bernard Shaw's disappointment with the discrimination against middle-class socialists in the Labour Party, and the preference for trade union candidates,[248] is but one example of the somewhat difficult relationship between middle-class intellectuals and the labour movement in Britain.

Both parties tried to broaden their appeal to recruit middle-class supporters. Yet the evidence presented here would support Przeworski's argument that, however much working-class parties try to appeal to the entire electorate, their success is limited, because it is impossible for any party to appeal to conflicting interests and values of different sections of society at the same time.[249] Certainly, for much of the time under discussion here, the time for a genuine people's party which was to replace a class party had not yet come in either Britain or Germany.

The ambiguous attitude of both labour movements towards the middle classes can also be seen in the historiography on both labour movement cultures and their attitudes towards 'bourgeois' culture. A fervent debate centred around the question whether labour movement culture was deferential to the dominant modes of bourgeois culture or not. A majority of historians argued for a widespread *embourgeoisement* of the labour movement, whilst some maintained the importance of an original

---

[248] Pierson, *British Socialists*, 323. Neil Blewett, *The Peers, the Parties and the People: The General Elections of 1910* (London, 1972), 230 has found that 84 per cent of all Labour candidates in 1910 belonged to the manual working classes. For Sexton's remark see *Report of the Annual Conference of the Labour Party, 1918* (London, 1918), 28. For Glasier's remarks on Lady Warwick see Liverpool University Library, Glasier Papers, 1904/15 and 1904/25, letters Glasier to his wife from 16 Aug. 1904 and to his sister Lizzie from 17 Aug. 1904.

[249] Adam Przeworski, *Capitalism and Social Democracy* (Cambridge, 1985), 129.

proletarian culture.[250] In any case, little distinction can be made between the SPD and the Labour Party in this respect. Guttsman has come to the conclusion that the German labour movement culture was not a crystallization of anti-capitalist sentiment, and that no real efforts had been made to create a new culture on an ideological basis, despite sections of the movement propagating a new lifestyle.[251] Roth sees the subculture of the SPD enmeshed in a bourgeois world of ideas and sentiments.[252] Robert Michels argued: 'a cards' club remains a cards' club, even if it is called cards' club "freedom".'[253] For the area of *Arbeiterdichtung* (workers' poetry) after 1918 Christoph Rülcker has demonstrated that bourgeois values came to dominate this poetry, whose main readers were social democratic officials.[254] Ritter and Tenfelde for Imperial Germany and Winkler for the Weimar Republic have found the social democratic official to be a man of the bourgeois world order,[255] and Peter Stearns has argued that with rising living standards, German artisans developed a bourgeois consumption pattern.[256] These are only a few examples of historians who have argued that the SPD had failed to produce a culture of their own which stood in marked contrast to the 'bourgeois' culture.

The British labour movement emerges in much of the literature just as deferential to the culture of the middle classes as its German counterpart. Raphael Samuel and Ralph Miliband, amongst others, have tried to track down non-working-class modes of behaviour and value systems in Labour Party activities.[257] It has been argued that the Labour Party took over bourgeois values of 'high' art.[258] In its most vigorous form the argument goes that it was precisely the labour movement (not the early one, but its

---

[250] The whole area of labour movement culture in Britain and Germany is discussed with more reference to the actual organizations in 4.2.

[251] Guttsman, *The German Social Democratic Party*, 207–15 and 331, W. L. Guttsman, *Workers' Culture in Weimar Germany* (Oxford, 1990), 287–313.

[252] Roth, *The Social Democrats in Imperial Germany*.

[253] Robert Michels, *Zur Soziologie des Parteiwesens in der modernen Demokratie: Untersuchungen über die oligarchischen Tendenzen des Gruppenlebens* (first pub. 1911, repr. of the 2nd edn., Stuttgart 1957), 278.

[254] Christoph Rülcker, *Ideologie der Arbeiterdichtung, 1914–1933* (Stuttgart, 1970), esp. 11 and 39–42.

[255] Ritter and Tenfelde, *Arbeiter*, 542, 667; Winkler, *Der Schein der Normalität*, 648.

[256] Peter N. Stearns, 'Adaptation to Industrialization: German Workers as a Test Case', *Central European History*, 3 (1970), 322.

[257] Raphael Samuel, 'The Middle Class Between the Wars', *New Socialist*, (Mar./Apr. 1983), 28–32; Miliband, *Parliamentary Socialism*, 95 f.

[258] Boughton, 'Working-Class Politics in Birmingham and Sheffield', 298; see also: Ian Britain, *Fabianism and Culture: A Study in British Socialism and the Arts, c.1884–1918* (Cambridge, 1982).

post-1900 successor), which killed a sense of separate identity within the British working class by developing into an electoral machine on constitutional lines.[259] The key word for the labour movement's alleged domination by bourgeois value systems is 'respectability'.[260] The sharp dividing line that both working-class parties usually drew in relation to the *Lumpenproletariat* and their orientation towards the petty bourgeoisie in life-style and habits is usually cited as evidence for the force of this concept. The foreign correspondent of the *Sozialistische Monatshefte* in 1931 noticed the following scene which he found archetypal for the orientation of the Labour Party towards 'respectability':

Birmingham celebrates May Day. The Labour Club organizes a festive evening. Lady Cynthia . . . comes in full red dress, the colour of socialism. And with a certain disappointment she recognizes nowhere a red badge: people have come in their usual Sunday dress, sit together and drink their pint of beer, as usual.[261]

The smaller group of historians who claim that the labour movements of both countries were able to create a certain frame of an independent culture have collected much valuable information. In following up the activities of the numerous cultural organizations of the SPD, Horst Groschopp has maintained that the German labour movement made a conscious effort to develop a genuine proletarian culture which stood in marked contrast to bourgeois concepts of culture.[262] Vernon Lidtke stressed the fact that the labour movement culture in Germany differed from bourgeois forms of culture in its determination to symbolize the SPD's ideology.[263] And for the time of the Weimar Republic Burns and van der Will have closely examined the *Sprechchor* (speaking choir) as an original socialist contribution to culture. Both have further maintained that all other cultural activities of the Social Democrats, much as they may have resembled bourgeois cultural forms, were in fact different, because

[259] Nigel Young, 'Prometheans or Troglodytes? The English Working Class and the Dialectics of Incorporation', *Berkeley Journal of Sociology*, 12 (1967), 2, 8, and 24 f.

[260] Robert Michels has commented on the similarity of the 'persönliche Ehrenhaftigkeit' of the German socialist with the 'respectability' of his British counterpart, see Michels, 'Die deutsche Sozialdemokratie I' 512. For the importance of notions of respectability in the British Labour Party see B. Harrison, *Peaceable Kingdom* (Oxford, 1982), 200–7.

[261] 'Rundschau', *SM* 37 (1931), 284. He went on to note that he had experienced similar scenes in Germany, commenting on the similarity of notions of respectability in the British Labour Party and the German SPD.

[262] Horst Groschopp, *Zwischen Bierabend und Bildungsverein: Zur Kulturarbeit in der deutschen Arbeiterbewegung vor 1914* (2nd edn., Berlin, 1987), 23.

[263] Vernon L. Lidtke, *The Alternative Culture: Socialist Labor in Imperial Germany* (New York, 1985), 24.

they were inspired by 'a historical hope for freedom from repressive rule'.[264]

For the British labour movement Eileen and Steven Yeo have frequently argued the case for a strong tradition of labour movement and working-class resistance to the dominant modes of bourgeois culture and society. Both have presented evidence for the diverse forms of a genuine labour movement culture which working people created within the framework of mostly local activities.[265] The rich arsenal of the British labour movement's symbols, metaphors, badges, flags, and banners all point in that direction.[266] In 1924 the editor of the *Daily Herald*, Hamilton Fyfe, warned Labour Party Members of Parliament against the danger of getting tamed by existing social values. Court dress, the modes of behaviour within the House of Parliament, social invitations to society parties, if accepted, would in the long run corrupt the transformatory aims of the Labour Party.[267] The same ambiguity between integration and isolation, that we have already seen in other areas of society, can be observed here as well. The labour movement in both countries was taking over bourgeois norms and values, but it was also actively engaged in finding outlets and expressions for an original proletarian self-consciousness.

2.5. Conclusion

The *Sonderweg* notion that the Labour Party was well integrated into British society, whereas the SPD was not well integrated into German society, does not stand up to critical examination. The borders of both labour movements with the rest of their respective societies were blurred and fluctuating, and their attitude towards 'society' remained ambiguous. On the one hand, there was much positive identification with the nation-state and its institutions, like parliament, and there were serious efforts to work within these institutions for the emancipation of the working class. Alliances with other parties were sought and forged in order to achieve this aim, and there were efforts to attract members of the middle classes, although members of the middle classes often remained rather hostile.

---

[264] Rob Burns and Wilfried van der Will, *Arbeiterkulturbewegung in der Weimarer Republik* (Frankfurt am Main, 1982), 167–232 and 248.

[265] Eileen Yeo, 'Culture and Constraint in Working-Class Movements, 1830–1855', in Eileen and Stephen Yeo (eds.), *Popular Culture and Class Conflict, 1590–1914* (Brighton, 1981), 155.

[266] Hobsbawm, *Worlds of Labour*, esp. 68–79 about Labour rituals.

[267] Hamilton Fyfe, 'The House of Rimmon', *SR* 24 (1924), 109–116.

Finally, the emerging labour movement culture was partly geared to and dependent upon bourgeois models of culture.

On the other hand, both labour movements were committed to internationalism and deeply suspicious about the state and its instruments. Anti-parliamentary sentiments emerged in both movements, discriminatory franchise practices, the activities of anti-socialist organizations, the anti-Labour attitude of a section of the judiciary and employers, as well as government repression, alienated both labour movements from the nation-state and created a self-assertive labour movement culture in both societies, which remained deeply suspicious of the middle class and its value system.

3
Party Organization

Sonderweg arguments often include references to the very different organization of Labour Party and SPD. The Labour Party was founded as a trade union pressure group in parliament. As such it did not emphasize the systematic buildup of a strong party organization. Instead it relied on trade union money and the enthusiasm of local activists to win elections. Conversely, the SPD developed an 'organizational patriotism' which led to the formation of an extensive party machine which has been described as a way of life as much as a vehicle for electoral victory. The highly bureaucratized and centralized SPD is held to have been in stark contrast to the haphazard and amateurish party organization of the Labour Party.[1] It is this exceptionalist view which shall be tested in the present chapter. At first the national, regional, and local organization of the Labour Party and the SPD will be compared before more specific organizational topics, such as the finance of the two parties, their press, their concept of leadership and intra-party democracy, and their relationship with the trade unions are discussed.

Before plunging into a comparative analysis it will be helpful to look at a simplified schematic overview of the Labour Party and SPD organization from 1890 to 1933:[2]

SPD organization according to its 1890 statute:	Labour Party organization before 1918:
party conference	party conference
↓	↓
party executive (Parteivorstand and Kontrollkommission)	party executive (NEC)
↓	↓
system of local men of confidence (in 1890s more and more replaced by local party committees)	constituency organization (consisting of affiliated organizations only)
↓	
party members (in constituency organizations and ancillary clubs)	

---

[1] Tenfelde, 'Sonderweg', 476–480; Mommsen, 'Arbeiterbewegung', 279; Luebbert, *Liberalism*, 159.

[2] Compare the more detailed schematic overview of the SPD after 1918 in Guttsman, *The German Social Democratic Party*, 151.

SPD organization according to its 1905
statute:
   party conference
          ↓

   party executive (Parteivorstand and
   Kontrollkommission, separate bodies from
   1900 onwards, Parteiausschuß after 1912)
          ↓

   state and area party (process of setting
   them up began in 1890s)
          ↓

   district party (from 1893 onwards built up
   by uniting several constituency
   organizations)
          ↓

   constituency organization (397)
          ↓

   local/ward parties
          ↓

   party members

SPD organization according to its 1919 and 1924 statutes:	Labour Party after 1918:
party conference	party conference
↓	↓
party executive (Parteivorstand, Kontrollkommission, and Parteiausschuß)	party executive (NEC)
↓	↓
area party organization (no state parties)	nine regions
↓	↓
constituency organization (35)	constituency organization
↓	
sub-constituency organization	
↓	↓
local/ward parties	local/ward parties
↓	↓
party members	party members

3.1. Party organization on a national level

The national centres of decision-making within the Labour Party and the SPD were the National Executive Committee (NEC) and the Parteivorstand (PV). Both institutions were characterized by a slow but continuous expansion and an extraordinary stability as far as their personnel was concerned. There were twelve members on the NEC in 1900, the number increasing to twenty-three in 1918 and twenty-five in 1929. Important political figures of the party served nearly continually on the NEC. J. R. Clynes, Arthur Henderson, J. R. MacDonald, Hugh Dalton, and Herbert Morrison all served twenty-five years or more on the most important party institution. The NEC elected the party secretary, who was responsible to the NEC for all matters regarding party organization. From 1900 to 1912 Ramsay MacDonald held this important post, for the most part concentrating on winning over the unions to the Labour Party. After the party had succeeded in doing so, Arthur Henderson presided over the organizational buildup of the party as secretary from 1912 to 1934.

Similar to the NEC of the Labour Party, the PV of the SPD grew over the years. It originally consisted of five members: two chairmen, two secretaries, and a treasurer. In 1900 a second executive organ, the control commission (Kontrollkommission), was set up as a separate body.[3] It had seven members whose task it was to control the executive and to function as an institution that would deal with complaints about party decisions. Furthermore it discussed all important matters with the PV.[4] After 1905 the number of paid secretaries to be elected onto the executive in any given year was left open, so that new secretaries could be appointed according to administrative needs. Friedrich Ebert was elected secretary in 1906 and in 1911 two more secretaries were elected to the executive. After 1918 the PV increased its numbers from twelve members in 1919 to twenty members in 1933.[5]

Contemporary SPD observers like Alexander Schifrin already saw that the SPD had an even more remarkable record of continuity of its leadership personnel than the Labour Party. To prove his point he referred to the fact that of twenty-three members of the Labour Party's NEC in 1924 only ten retained their seats in 1928.[6] In the entire period of the Weimar Republic only thirty-one persons served on the twenty man strong (in 1933) executive of the SPD. Eleven persons left the executive during that time; eight died in office, two resigned in order to take up ministerial posts, and just one was defeated in an election. Executive members of the SPD nearly always had lifetime tenure. The PV in Imperial Germany elected two chairmen rather than one. This was a control mechanism

---

[3] After 1890 control commission and executive were nominally one body, because of the restrictive German laws of association, but they already performed their different functions.

[4] Thomas Nipperdey, *Die Organisation der deutschen Parteien vor 1918* (Düsseldorf, 1961), 368.

[5] Richard N. Hunt, *German Social Democracy, 1919–1933* (New Haven, Conn., 1964), 76.

[6] Alexander Schifrin, 'Parteiapparat und Parteidemokratie', *Die Gesellschaft*, 7 (1930), 526.

designed to prevent any misuse of power by any one individual. However, their position was similar to that of secretary of the Labour Party. Before the First World War Paul Singer and August Bebel and, after their death, Hugo Haase and Fritz Ebert were the chairmen of the party. Their authority in the Vorstand rested on their personality and their record as Labour leaders. In the Weimar Republic *three* chairmen of the party divided the main organizational tasks between them: Otto Wels was responsible for the inner organization of the party, Hermann Müller was responsible for propaganda and at the same time he was the leader of the parliamentary party, and Arthur Crispien was responsible for the SPD's contacts with the International.[7] No chairman of the SPD was ever again to reach the authority of August Bebel who, not unlike Henderson, ruled supreme over party affairs.

The NEC developed a sub-organizational structure to deal with the day-to-day work, the so-called head office. In 1910 the Labour Party's head office was located in two rooms in Victoria Street and it employed seven persons. Most of the daily routine work was done by the Assistant Secretary, James Middleton. On the eve of the First World War the staff at Labour Party head office consisted of eleven persons, in 1930 there were thirty employees at head office and another seventeen working throughout the country. By then also a fairly elaborate departmental organization had been set up: head office was subdivided into the Secretary's office, the Assistant Secretary's office, the National Agent's department (the National Agent had been appointed for the first time in 1908), the Chief Woman Officer's department, a Press and Publicity department, an Information Bureau and an Enquiry Office.[8] The reorganization of the party in 1918 set up four standing subcommittees at head office for (*a*) organization and elections, (*b*) policy and programme, (*c*) literature, research, and publicity and (*d*) finance and general purposes. Much of the routine administrative work was done by the head office, which was steadfastly loyal to the party secretary.

Despite such efforts it has been pointed out that the organization of the Labour Party head office still left much to be desired. As John Silkin, former chief whip of the Labour Party, has argued:

the staffing structure of the Labour Party headquarters has never been thought through. There is little effort to direct resources intelligently. Failing any clear

---

[7] Winkler, *Der Schein der Normalität*, 647.
[8] R. T. McKenzie, *British Political Parties: The Distribution of Power within the Conservative and the Labour Party* (2nd edn., London, 1963), 563.

direction from the Executive, staff often wander off in what ever direction suits them, developing some aspects of policy at the expense of others . . . The staffing structure has just grown over the years in response to various pressures. Departmental heads fight tooth and nail to maintain their empires . . .[9]

Another difficulty of the Labour Party head office before 1914 resulted from the fact that it had to operate through existing groups, mainly trade unions and socialist societies which affiliated to the Labour Party. Consequently it found it impossible to enforce its authority upon the affiliated organizations and centralize all decision-making effectively in the party leadership. In fact, the party leadership itself, the NEC, consisted of representatives elected by the constituent bodies of the Labour alliance. Only independent local groups could have been a power base of a Labour Party leadership which was not responsible to sectional interests of affiliated organizations. In asking the conference in 1912 to allow individual membership of the Labour Party MacDonald and Henderson made an effort to set up such a power base, yet the trade union and socialist vote on the conference defeated the proposal.[10] Head office was only able to encourage the growth of individual membership organizations in the country with a view to building a more homogeneous movement and freeing the party from sectional interests after the 1918 constitutional change.[11]

If the Labour Party found it difficult to set up an efficient administrative apparatus at the national level of organization, the SPD's central party organization never looked too impressive either. Even in the mid-1920s, its staff numbered only sixty-four, a number of which were responsible for the party's ancillary organizations.[12] Before the First World War, the PV of the SPD had two sessions weekly, in which it mainly dealt with correspondence from local parties. It had no clerical staff of its own (apart from a typist after 1905), most clerical work had to be done by the members of the PV themselves. This was only possible because the vast SPD organization was subdivided into regions, and the major work of organizing and supervising the party at local level was done by the regional headquarters of the SPD. We will have to return to this feature of the SPD organization in the next section.

PV and NEC had the task of supervising and co-ordinating the work of the party outside parliament. Both institutions had to expand their

[9] John Silkin, *Changing Battlefields: The Challenge to the Labour Party, 1923–1987* (London, 1987), 18.

[10] McKibbin, *Evolution*, 95.

[11] *Labour Organizer* (Oct. 1923), 15.

[12] Guttsman, *The German Social Democratic Party*, 246.

personnel and refine their organizational structure in order to meet the needs of a growing party. The national bureaucracies of Labour Party and SPD undertook various efforts not only to keep in constant touch with the local bureaucracies, but also to direct and enhance the growth and development of local parties. Both parties edited several organizational handbooks as well as special journals for local officials,[13] giving advice to party workers on such subjects as how to administer local organization, to organize *Agitation,* and to fight elections. Labour Party as well as SPD publications emphasized the importance of a well-organized bureaucracy. The SPD handbook stressed: 'The party administration is head and soul of the organization. . . . Where there is no order in the party organization, there is no fighting strength . . .'.[14] And the Labour Party's trust in organization is reflected in many such statements as: 'there is no constituency in the country but where with sufficient propaganda and tactful organization one may not be able to establish a powerful party'.[15]

If necessary, the PV reminded MPs that they not only had parliamentary duties, but that they also had duties in their constituencies, especially at election times, when local organizations were keen to secure well-known MPs as speakers.[16] Naturally, the different electoral systems of Britain and Germany after 1918 had an impact on the relationship between MP and local party. Whereas proportional representation in Germany tended to weaken the contact between elected representative and local party, the single constituency system in Britain ensured that it remained strong.[17] Despite those institutional differences it is fair to say that both Labour Party and SPD MPs were keen to develop good relations with their own constituencies and reserved a substantial amount of their time for party work. Peter Grassmann, for instance, although he was deputy chairman of the ADGB, found much time not only for an extensive

---

[13] Arthur Henderson and Ramsay MacDonald, *Notes on Organization and the Law of Registration and Elections* (London, n.d.); *Handbuch für die Ortsvereine: Eine Anweisung für die Erledigung der Aufgaben der Ortsvereine* (Berlin, 1930). The Labour Party published *Labour Organizer: The Official Journal of the National Association of Labour Registration and Election Agents,* ed. Herbert Drinkwater from 1920 onwards. The SPD published *SPD Nachrichten für die Funktionäre* in 1921–2 and the *Mitteilungsblatt der VSPD* from 1924 to 1928.

[14] *Handbuch für die Ortsvereine,* 61 and 75.

[15] *Labour Organizer* (June 1922), 12.

[16] Historische Kommission, NB 471, no. 172: letter from Vorstand to SPD Reichstagsfraktion, 13 Apr. 1931. Also IGA/ZPA, papers of Paul Löbe, 110/97, no. 4: letter from Wels to all national and state MPs, 8 June 1921.

[17] Maurice Duverger, *Political Parties: Their Organization and Activity in the Modern State* (2nd edn., London, 1959), 193, Winkler, *Von der Revolution,* 245 f.

correspondence with his Hamburg constituency, but also for frequent travels to Hamburg. When, in 1925, he could not come personally to give a talk in Hamburg, he wrote a three-page letter to explain why he could not come, adding: 'This is the first time that I have to ask you to release me from giving a talk.'[18] Friedrich Ebert was another case of an important party official who nevertheless found time for a 'close and responsible relationship to the constituency'.[19] Not only was he often personally present in Elberfeld-Barmen, but he also gave a yearly report to his constituency about his parliamentary work, in which he tried to foster specific interests of his constituency.

One of the tasks of the Society of Labour Candidates in Britain was to discuss ways of maintaining good relations with the constituencies. In a meeting on 10 June 1929, for example, it was agreed that 'an endeavour should be made during the summer months to provide propaganda assistance to Divisional Labour Parties. . . . candidates or MPs should spend their holidays or week-ends in places where they were needed . . .'.[20] Philipp Noel-Baker, for example, was a Labour MP who spent much time in his Coventry constituency. He engaged himself in municipal elections, corresponded regularly with George Hodgkinson, the local party agent, kept a cuttings file concerned with information on Coventry and came frequently to Coventry to give speeches there on disarmament, education, and unemployment.[21] The National Labour Club in London, a club set up for the benefit of Labour MPs, organized a series of receptions at the club premises for representatives of London Borough and Divisional Labour Parties with the aim of improving contact between the top and the bottom of the organization.[22]

The good relations between local parties and MPs gave little opportunity to the national executives of either the Labour Party or the SPD to gain a significant influence on parliamentary candidate selection. The influence of the NEC of the Labour Party on candidate selection was potentially high. Its statutory powers included the rejection of any

---

[18] Historische Kommission, NB 466, no. 51: letter Grassmann to Hamburger SPD, 15 Aug. 1925.

[19] D. K. Buse (ed.), *Parteiagitation und Wahlkreisvertretung: Eine Dokumentation über Friedrich Ebert und seinen Reichstagswahlkreis Elberfeld/Barmen, 1910–1918* (Bonn, 1975), p. xiii.

[20] Churchill College, Noel-Baker collection, NBKR 2/2: Minutes of the Committee Meeting of the Society of Labour Candidates, 10 June 1929.

[21] Churchill College, Noel-Baker collection, NBKR 2/13.

[22] Beatrice Webb, 'The Parliamentary Labour Club: Its Origins and Use', *Labour Magazine*, 3 (1924–5), 12–14.

candidate proposed from a constituency. Yet, the difficulty the national leadership had in stopping constituency parties from contesting parliamentary seats under the Gladstone–MacDonald agreement before 1914 indicated the degree of autonomy that local parties were willing and keen to exercise. Because of the fact that a candidature was largely financed locally by socialist societies and trade unions, head office in London had very limited powers of preventing such independent action. Direct interventions of head office in the affairs of local parties were therefore limited to resolving 'difficulties' over candidatures, particularly when communists were nominated by local parties.[23] Within the SPD the selection of a Reichstag election candidate was expressly a task of the constituency organization before 1914. In the Weimar Republic candidates were proposed by a conference of subdistricts and formally selected by the area party conference.[24] The PV seldom interfered, although from 1905 the PV had the last say in the nomination of parliamentary candidates in cases where the local and district parties could not agree on a candidate.[25]

If we now turn our attention from the top party institutions to the parliamentary parties, the PLP of the Labour Party and the Fraktion of the SPD, certain organizational similarities can be observed. Both parliamentary parties decided to set up a kind of parliamentary executive. From the time of the anti-socialist law the Fraktionsvorstand gave political leadership and direction to the Fraktion. The official titles of its members were more or less unimportant formalities, as the chairman of the Fraktion (*Fraktionsvorsitzender*) only had real power according to his authority in the party.[26] For the ever-rising administrative work a paid clerk (*Fraktionssekretär*) was appointed in 1904. No other administrative machinery of its own was built up by the Fraktion. From 1899 onwards *ad hoc* commissions were set up within the Fraktion to do some of the more specialized parliamentary work. Permanent commissions followed in 1907, yet the only functioning one before 1914 was the one concerned with social policy.[27]

---

[23] On candidate selection within the Labour Party see especially McKibbin, *Evolution*, 134 and J. S. Rowett, 'Labour Party and Local Government', 52 f.

[24] Guttsman, *The Social Democratic Party*, 228.

[25] Nipperdey, *Die Organisation*, 373 f.

[26] Molkenbuhr in 1906 complained to his diary that the title of *Fraktionsvorsitzender* was of little use, as he 'had no legal rights to treat his colleagues as subordinates'; see FES, Molkenbuhr papers, Tagebuchkladde 1, 5 Sept. 1913.

[27] Erich Mathias and Eberhardt Pikart, *Die Reichstagsfraktion der deutschen Sozialdemokratie, 1898 bis 1918* (Düsseldorf, 1966), pp. cxi–cxxiv.

In the case of the PLP, political leadership was provided by the parliamentary committee. Its task was to direct the work of the PLP as a whole, and it met daily except on Fridays to discuss business coming before the House, and to settle Party policy, subject to the decisions of the weekly party meetings.[28] It consisted of the chairman of the PLP, the deputy chairman, the chief Whip, the chairman of the Labour Group in the House of Lords, the Chief Whip of the Labour Peers (since 1925), who were all ex officio members, and of twelve elected representatives of the Labour MPs and one (since 1925 two) Labour Peers.[29] The parliamentary committee of the Labour Party was a more important body than the Fraktionsvorstand of the SPD. It formed a close body and it was difficult for MPs outside this select circle to have much of a say in deciding policy. The SPD members of the Fraktion were more directly involved in the policy-making process. Within the Fraktion of the SPD all parliamentary business was discussed and decided in weekly meetings of the whole Fraktion (often the Fraktion had to meet on several consecutive days). Both parties did not trust individuals to lead the party, but rather gave a collegiate body the power to determine policies. *De facto*, personal dominance over the collegiate body by Bebel in Germany and MacDonald in Britain could at times minimize the control function of that body. As the SPD set up commissions to keep up with the routine of parliamentary work, so did the Labour Party after 1918.[30]

In both parliamentary parties labour movement officials were well represented. In the German case, party officials came to dominate the Fraktion. At the end of the Weimar Republic it could be said: 'The Fraktion of the SPD is a pronounced Fraktion of officials . . . 66 per cent are either officials or editors who are directly employed by the party or by the trade unions.'[31] Within the Labour Party more than 50 per cent of all MPs were union officials in the first half of the 1920s with relatively few MPs on the payroll of the party.[32] Most of its organizing staff had either no parliamentary ambitions or were not given a chance.

Both parliamentary parties managed to centralize much of the political decision-making process in their hands. In the SPD its powers were greatest during Bismarck's anti-socialist law, when the Fraktion was

[28] *Report of the Annual Conference of the LP in 1925* (London, 1925), 90.

[29] McKenzie, *British Political Parties*, 413.

[30] McKibbin, *Evolution*, 216 f.

[31] Viktor Engelhardt, 'Die Zusammensetzung des Reichstages nach Alter, Beruf und Religionsbekenntnis', *DA* 8 (1931), 35.

[32] McKibbin, *Evolution*, 136, Clegg, *A History of British Trade Unions*, ii. 354 f., 364, 379, 478.

the only functioning party institution and in that capacity practically led the party. In future all important party leaders were to sit in the Fraktion as well as having important party functions. The Fraktion was the only party institution without any statutory definitions. Its relationship to other party institutions was to remain a matter of tradition which served to strengthen the hand of the Fraktion.

The PLP was also relatively independent from the decisions of the party in its policies. The Labour Party constitution of 1918 suggested in Clause 4c some sort of responsibility of the PLP to the party conference: 'It shall be the duty of every Parliamentary representative of the party to be guided by the decision of the meetings of such parliamentary representatives, with a view to giving effect to the decisions of the party conference as to the general programme of the party.'[33] Already in the very first years of the LRC, a conflict between party and PLP arose over the reluctance of many former Lib-Lab MPs to give up their Liberal links. Therefore the 1903 Newcastle conference of the Labour Party passed a resolution calling for more discipline amongst the members of the PLP. The setting up of the Parliamentary Fund at the same conference was also undertaken with an eye to centralizing loyalty within the party.[34] However, once the PLP had developed a kind of internal homogeneity, the party increasingly lost a firm grip on it. MacDonald stressed early on the importance of leaving as much freedom as possible to the individual MP,[35] and indeed, as Kenneth Morgan has argued, the PLP could never be effectively bound to adhere to party decisions.[36]

The relationship between the parliamentary parties and the party executives was very strong in both parties. There was a substantial overlap between the leadership of the NEC/PV and the leadership of the PLP/Fraktion. Hardie, Snowden, Henderson, MacDonald, Bebel, Ebert, Scheidemann, Auer, Singer, Molkenbuhr, Müller, and Wels were all leading members of both institutions. Between 1900 and 1912 eight out of fourteen Fraktion members were at the same time members of the sixteen-strong PV.[37] From 1929 to 1931 when sixteen out of twenty-four NEC members were MPs, the NEC acted as a watchdog for the Labour government. Consequently, conflicts between PV and Fraktion were rare

---

[33] *The Labour Party Constitution* (London, 1918), 5.
[34] Frank Bealey, 'Keir Hardie and the Labour Groups', *Parliamentary Affairs*, 10 (1956–7), 92.
[35] Ramsay MacDonald, *Socialism and Government* (London, 1909), i. 83 and 93 f.
[36] Morgan, *Keir Hardie*, 169.
[37] See Mathias and Pikart, *Die Reichstagsfraktion*, pp. cvi f., cxi ff. and cxxvii.

occasions. In the Labour Party one such occasion was the time following the breakdown of the second Labour government in 1931. Between 1931 and 1935, only three MPs sat on the NEC, and the party was trying to reassert its dominance over its parliamentary representatives. Within the SPD, fear of making the party too dependent on its parliamentary representatives and their leaders led to the adoption of a resolution at the 1920 party conference according to which SPD ministers had to give up their PV seats.[38] Ultimately, of course, such measures could not prevent the Fraktion from becoming more and more independent of party controls.[39]

Another indication of the balance of power between party and parliamentary leadership was the inefficiency of conference as a rank-and-file institution controlling the leaders in both parties. First of all, the rank and file were not adequately represented at the party conferences of either party. In the case of the Labour Party, many local parties found it difficult to send delegates to the annual conferences, because they could not find means to raise the money for their delegates. The idea of pooling expenses was severely hampered by the fact that one delegate could only have one vote for his organization, even if other organizations contributed to his costs.[40] The conference of the Labour Party up to 1918 consisted only of delegates from the affiliated organizations. Even thereafter the bulk of the delegates were not rank-and-file activists from the constituencies, but trade union representatives, as over 90 per cent of the Labour Party members were affiliated through trade unions. In addition there were the members of the NEC, the PLP, and the parliamentary candidates, who were all ex officio members of the conference.

In the case of the SPD the bigger constituencies like Berlin and Hamburg found themselves increasingly marginalized at the annual conferences before 1914 by a delegation system which gave clear advantage to the smaller constituencies. The regional organizations, with their power over allocating money, made sure that every constituency, however small, could send its delegate to the annual conference. Rank-and-file representation at SPD conferences was diluted by the fact that members of the Reichstagsfraktion as well as the PV were ex officio also represented at the conference and even had voting rights. Furthermore delegates did not

---

[38] *Protokoll des SPD Parteitags 1920*, 258.

[39] Hunt, *German Social Democracy*, 84.

[40] Organizational Points from the London Labour Party, no. 22, 7 Apr. 1922, contained in: Labour Party Archive, Local Labour Party Files. For the fact that many local parties failed to send delegates see *Labour Organizer* (Oct./Nov. 1925), 8: of 550 affiliated DLPs 357 failed to send a delegate!

come from the constituencies themselves, but well-known leaders, like Eduard Bernstein or Rosa Luxemburg, were nominated by constituencies which they hardly knew at all.

Formally, the party conference was the supreme institution in both the Labour Party and the SPD. Its function in the SPD was regulated by the statute adopted at the Halle conference in 1890. No later changes had any major significance. In the case of the Labour Party not much was said about the functions of the conference until 1918, when the supremacy of the conference over all party institutions was laid down in the constitution. Both statutes set out the right of the party conferences to elect annually the national executive which was itself accountable to the conference. The tasks of the Labour Party and the SPD conferences were broadly similar. They could administer justice, promulgate prohibitions, threaten expulsion in the case of violation, pass resolutions about party tactics as well as political principle and ask or instruct the parliamentary party and the national executive to work for the implementation of specific policies. The conferences fulfilled their functions by considering the various resolutions that were brought before them, either by the national executive or by the delegates to the conference. Until 1912 at the SPD conferences individual members could bring in resolutions. Afterwards only local parties and conference delegates had the right to bring in resolutions. The Labour Party never knew an element of direct democracy like that. It had always been the affiliated organizations, or the delegates representing those organizations, which brought in any resolution. Increasingly, in both parties, it was the NEC/PV which brought in resolutions. Even if conference decisions had not been dominated by party leaders this would not necessarily have made conference decisions more binding on the leadership. As Philip Snowden remarked in his autobiography: 'My experience of conferences has taught me to attach very little importance to their resolutions. Of the hundreds of resolutions I have seen passed by Labour Conferences outlining a drastic programme of reform, I can hardly call to mind one which has had any practical result. Conferences will talk; let them talk.'[41] The leading SPD revisionist Albert Südekum expressed similar sentiments after the 1903 party conference had vigorously denounced revisionism. Ironically he wrote: 'Now that the party has definitely been saved, all continues business as usual . . .'[42]

---

[41] Philip Snowden, *An Autobiography*, i (London, 1934), 87.
[42] Quoted from Nipperdey, *Die Organisation*, 367.

From the first decade of the twentieth century onwards Snowden's and Südekum's disregard for conference decisions was unnecessary: discussions at Labour Party as well as SPD conferences became less and less lively. They were increasingly transformed from a democratic caucus, where different opinions were presented and a consensus was worked out, to dull and predetermined organs of acclamation of the national executive. In the case of the SPD more and more resolutions were brought in by the executive, more and more speakers were nominated by the executive, and speakers opposing resolutions were not allowed the same time as those speaking for them. The pre-war tradition of having two spokesmen for controversial issues was abandoned in the Weimar Republic.[43] The power of the executive over the SPD conference rested on three grounds. First of all, the PV created *faits accomplis* in between conference sessions; secondly, it controlled conference procedures; and, thirdly, it could designate a *rapporteur* for all debates who had the privilege of a *Schlußwort* (a closing speech).[44] Slowly, but surely, party conferences became ritual celebration of party unity rather than lively discussion forums.[45]

In the British case, MacDonald in 1909 stressed the necessity of democratic conference procedures within any political party,[46] and indeed, it has been argued that up to 1922 the political significance of the conference not only as a forum for discussion, but also as an institution for the rank and file, critically scrutinizing the activities of the PLP and the NEC, was impressive.[47] In 1913, after having been heavily criticized at the 1911 and 1912 conferences, the PLP was forced to submit a formal report on its activities for question and debate at future conferences. After 1922, however, the conference procedure underwent a series of changes which rendered it more and more powerless. A substantial increase in its size (there were usually over a thousand delegates in the 1920s conferences) meant that it was losing authority. Its ability to formulate party policy was further reduced by the uncritical support for the leadership by many unions. The procedures of the conference were now pre-arranged by the NEC through a so-called Conference Arrangements Committee. The NEC furthermore had the right to nominate speakers

---

[43] Hunt, *German Social Democracy*, 76–8.

[44] Carl E. Schorske, *German Social Democracy, 1905–1917: The Development of the Great Schism* (Cambridge, Mass., 1955), 136.

[45] Peter Nettl, 'The German Social Democratic Party 1890–1914 as a Political Model', *PP* 30 (1965), 80.

[46] MacDonald, *Socialism and Government*, 24–7.

[47] Lewis Minkin, *The Labour Party Conference: A Study in the Politics of Intra-Party Democracy* (London, 1978), 7.

who were restricted by no time limit, whereas all other speakers were restricted to five minutes. Given the careful tutelage of the NEC, it is hardly surprising that in the 1920s the conference seldom rejected the advice of the leaders of the party.[48] Conferences became more stage-managed and the parliamentary and party leadership became more influential, as the rank and file found it more difficult to control it.

3.2. The missing regional link

The existence of broad similarities between the national organizations of the Labour Party and the SPD having been established, this section compares the regional organizations of both parties. Regional party organizations of the SPD (*Landes-* or *Bezirksorganisation*) had already developed in the 1890s, but it was only in the 1905 statutes of the SPD that these organizational forms were formally recognized.[49] They were to become an additional organizational layer between the electoral district party and the national party, closely reflecting the strong federal structures and traditions of Germany. The federalization of the party structure meant in fact the recognition of the impossibility of centralizing the party at the national level. The regions were better suited to reflect the different legal and political position of the party in the various German *Länder*. Consequently, the most effective centralization of power took place at the regional level. There were not one but several centres of power in the SPD.[50] The rapporteur on the new statutes at the 1924 SPD conference underlined the federal attitude of the party: 'The constitution [of the Weimar Republic] did not create a unitary nation; the states have retained some sovereignty. The same must be granted to the organizations in the states; they must have the possibility of fully using their sovereignty. The centralization of the party does not mean uniformity.'[51] That all elections were fought on decentralized campaigns from 1893 onwards surely is another sign of the importance of regional parties in the SPD. The growing importance of regional parties is also mirrored by the replacement of the control commission by a new party council (*Parteiausschuß*) in 1912 which was made up of representatives of the regional parties.

Consequently the most effective forms of bureaucratization and centralization were found in the regions. The region consisted of either one

---

[48] McKenzie, *British Political Parties*, 515.
[49] Fricke, *Handbuch*, i. 274–83.
[50] Nipperdey, *Die Organisation*, 390.
[51] *Protokoll des SPD Parteitags 1924*, 142.

(Baden, Hesse) or several (Bavaria, Saxony, Prussia) district parties (*Agitationsbezirke*). The number of fully-paid party secretaries increased from sixteen to fifty-one in the regional organizations of the SPD between 1905/6 and 1913/14.[52] The tasks of the regional bureaucracies of the party were manifold and important: they influenced and controlled the *Agitation* and organization of the electoral districts, organized rural *Agitation*, influenced the nominations of delegates to the national party conference and usually ensured that weaker local organizations would be well represented at the conference. They had a say in the nomination of parliamentary candidates and were partly responsible for the campaigns in constituencies where there was to be a second ballot. Last, but not least, they controlled the press through a press commission which controlled the employment of journalists on the district party newspaper.[53] If a local SPD organization wanted to set up any enterprise of its own (a newspaper, printing press, hall, etc.), it had to have the approval of the regional or national executive to do so.[54] Founded as transmission organs which would make it easier for the national party leadership to stay in contact with the local parties in the country, the regional parties emancipated themselves from this purely functional task and had an increasingly important influence on the national party. The regional bureaucracies closely resembled the respective national institutions. There was a state/district Vorstand and an Ausschuß, which was to control the Vorstand. Both were elected by regular state/district conferences.

The Labour Party had been at pains to suppress efforts at regional organization right from the start. When a Scottish Workers' Parliamentary Elections Committee was set up seven weeks prior to the LRC in 1900, MacDonald in the following years spent much energy on its dissolution and the centralization of its activities in the hands of the LRC. He finally succeeded in 1909, when the Committee voted itself out of existence. Yet at the end of 1912 head office had to accept Scottish peculiarities and set up the Scottish Advisory Council.[55] The party gave only nominal autonomy to Scotland in 1919 and no autonomy was granted to Wales or the London party. Between 1917 and 1920 Morrison and Henderson clashed frequently over the degree of autonomy that the

[52] Fricke, *Handbuch*, i. 284.
[53] Nipperdey, *Die Organisation*, 351.
[54] Schorske, *German Social Democracy*, 253–6.
[55] W. H. Fraser, 'The Labour Party in Scotland', in Brown, *The First Labour Party*, 38–63.

executive would grant to the London party.[56] As the German party mirrored the federal German Reich, the Labour Party in its organization mirrored the centralized London-based system of government in Britain.

However, already before the First World War, the secretary and the National Agent of the Labour Party found it an increasing strain to act as channels of communication between the local Labour Parties and the National Party.[57] From 1911 onwards Henderson spent a good deal of his time touring the country teaching organizational techniques and encouraging local efforts to build up Labour Parties.[58] His aim was to make the local parties more uniform, as they had developed without much guidance from above and were rather varied in outlook and structure. The streamlining of the party by the 1918 constitution was already on Henderson's agenda before the First World War. Yet the task of keeping up constant lines of communication with hundreds of local organizations became too much for a few travelling organizers before 1914 and head office was only an inadequate substitute after 1918.

So it is hardly surprising that Henderson's 'General Scheme of Organization', adopted in 1920, mirrored the realization of the plain fact that a mass party could not be run without any institutional channels of communication between the organization in the country and head office. From now on the country was divided into nine party districts. Yet there were no major organizational changes connected with that manœuvre. No regional head offices and no permanent regional organizations (permanent regional executives or annual regional conferences) were set up.[59] The newly appointed regional organizers (and the regional propagandists in 1922) would work from their homes in the districts reporting back regularly to head office.[60] Their prime task was to help local parties in their organizational efforts, such as the planning of election campaigns, the nomination of party agents or the very foundation of a local party. Indeed, a more rapid and efficient organization of the constituencies has been attributed to the appointment of regional organizers. Between 1918 and 1922 regional conferences had been organized as supplements of

---

[56] On the problems of centralization connected with the three regions Scotland, Wales, and London, see McKibbin, *Evolution*, 163–74.

[57] G. R. Shepherd, 'The National Agent on Present Problems', *Labour Organizer* (Oct. 1929), 188 f.

[58] McKibbin, *Evolution*, 22.

[59] It was only in 1938 that permanent regional organizations were set up, and even then their powers remained distinctly limited. See McKenzie, *British Political Parties*, 532–9.

[60] Only the organizers for London and Southern Counties had their offices at head office in London.

annual national gatherings. By 1922 regular delegate conferences were
held in each of the regions, providing for an intermediate layer between
constituency and party headquarters in London. The links between the
constituencies and head office were certainly strengthened, but in essence
Henderson's 1920 organization scheme was fiercely opposed to any plans
that smacked of seriously federalizing the party. The Labour Party leaders remained committed to the idea of centralizing as much decision-
making as possible at the national party institutions.[61]

Tentative efforts to set up a more elaborate organization in the 1920s
were consequently bound to fail. Yet, the very effort shows that an improved regional organization was perceived at least by some as a remedy
to the problems of the Labour Party at the time. In 1925, for example, a
Derbyshire Federation of Labour Parties was set up 'with the object of
promoting unity and harmonious action throughout the area'. The federation's tasks included regular visits to the localities by a regional organizer, the arrangement of regional conferences, the encouragement to adopt
a parliamentary candidate for every division and advice for local agents.[62]

Because the regional organizations of the Labour Party were far less
developed than their SPD counterparts, that middle class of party officials, *Bezirkssekretäre* above all, but also the officials of the *Land*, district,
constituency (and later) sub-constituency level, which were so characteristic of the SPD, did not exist in the Labour Party. The efforts after
1918 to streamline the party were seriously hampered by its insistence on
streamlining towards London rather than towards the regions. The more
elaborate structure of the SPD allowed more control of *and* help to local
parties. Whereas London was often distant, the SPD regional organization was close. Consequently local Labour parties found it easier to evade
control and directives from the top, while they could not rely on help
from the top at the same time. In the next chapter it is precisely to the
question of the local organization of the Labour Party and the SPD that
attention is turned.

3.3. Local organization

To create an efficient organization at local level came to be the rallying
cry of the Labour Party and the SPD. Such organization was perceived,
rightly or wrongly, as the ultimate precondition for success. In this section

---

[61] McKibbin, *Evolution*, 176–8, 241.
[62] *Labour Organizer*, 6 (1926), 148 f.

these attempts to find recipes for a steady and continuous growth of local parties and its limits will be discussed.

Before 1899 the conspiratorial system of 'men of confidence' (*Vertrauensmänner*) had been the main channel of communication between the SPD organization in the country and the national party. Although they were elected annually, they acted independently from the local party and were responsible for *Agitation*, the calling of meetings etc.[63] In December 1899 the ban on the combination of political societies was lifted and the SPD was allowed to form legal local party organizations. In many places the local *Vertrauensmann* often continued to hold office as elected chairman/secretary of the local party. If the *Vertrauensmann* had been the only, often voluntary, party official, new offices were now created. Normally there was a secretary, a treasurer, and an executive in every local branch of the SPD. It was mostly in the big cities that these positions were paid ones. Depending on the size of the executive, a smaller executive was appointed which was the leading institution of the local party. Local SPD organization after 1899 became extremely varied and it was not until after 1905 that some sort of streamlining process regarding the structure of local parties started. In the decade before the outbreak of the First World War local parties flourished everywhere. In Chemnitz, for example, the membership was twelve times as high in 1912 as in 1900 and the income was six times as high.[64] Localities were systematically organized. From 2,704 local organizations in 1907 their number nearly doubled to 5,122 in 1914. In 1907 constituency organizations had been set up in only 284 out of 397 constituencies. Five years later not a single constituency remained unorganized.

The local party sometimes was further divided into districts and subdistricts which paralleled the city quarters. The districts and subdistricts had their own executives, which together formed the general executive of the local party. In bigger SPD cities which were SPD strongholds subdistricts were even further divided into streets or blocks for which a representative of the SPD (named differently in different regions: e.g. *Bezirksführer, Reviermann, Blockführer*) was responsible.[65] These representatives were appointed by the general assembly (*Hauptversammlung*)

---

[63] Guttsman, *The German Social Democratic Party*, 149.

[64] Ernst Heilmann, *Geschichte der Arbeiterbewegung in Chemnitz und dem Erzgebirge* (Chemnitz, 1912), 278–80.

[65] For the thriving sub-organizations based on street captains and pay-evenings in local pubs, see for instance the local study on Düsseldorf by Mary Nolan, *Social Democracy and Society: Working Class Radicalism in Düsseldorf, 1890–1920* (Cambridge, 1981), 128 f.

of the local party. They would regularly discuss their problems and experiences with the responsible official on the next level. Those city ward officials were extremely important for the collection of party fees as well as for the solidarity and cohesion of party members. Furthermore they were vital as channels of communication between the local party leaders and the rank and file, ensuring that there remained significant channels for the expression of rank-and-file sentiment. In many places, the SPD managed to install itself within working-class communities as a creditable alternative to other political parties. It did so by developing into a neighbourhood-based party which became meaningful to the everyday lives and struggles of the workers in a particular locality. Party members were given a strong sense of cohesion and belonging by simple organizational innovations such as the introduction of uniform membership booklets after 1907 or the weekly (sometimes monthly) payment of their membership fees.[66]

Because of the remarkable growth of local SPD parties before 1914, its success in mobilizing whole working-class communities can easily be overemphasized. In fact, local parties came to be increasingly dominated by their active officials.[67] The SPD leaders in Hamburg were predominantly recruited from the bureaucracy of trade unions, party, co-operatives, and other labour organizations (64 per cent).[68] Figures describing the number of party officials in the SPD differ widely. At the end of the Weimar Republic Carlo Mierendorff reckoned with only 10,000 officeholders, whereas Alexander Schifrin gave the number of 70,000 to 80,000.[69] John Breuilly has convincingly argued that these figures can easily be inflated by counting, for example, the vast army of printers employed by the party press as officials which, of course, would hardly reflect their position within the party adequately.[70] Indeed, Klaus Tenfelde has found only 157 fully-paid party secretaries of the SPD in the districts by 1914.[71]

---

[66] For cultural and ideological factors contributing to the making of that sense of belonging see Chs. 4 and 5 below.

[67] See for example James Wickham, 'The Working-Class Movement in Frankfurt am Main During the Weimar Republic' (University of Sussex Ph.D. 1979), 27 f.

[68] R. Comfort, *Revolutionary Hamburg: Labor Politics in the Early Weimar Republic* (Stanford, Calif., 1966), 135.

[69] The numbers mentioned in the secondary literature also vary widely. Where Hunt, *German Social Democracy*, 56 f. follows Schifrin, W. H. Maehl, 'The Triumph of Nationalism in the German Socialist Party on the Eve of the First World War', *Journal of Modern History*, 24 (1952), 25 seems to take his numbers from Mierendorff.

[70] Breuilly, *Labour and Liberalism*, 61.

[71] Klaus Tenfelde, 'Germany', in van der Linden and Rojahn, *The Formation of Labour Movements*, 263.

And for 1925 Willy Guttsman counted only 417 full-time employees of the SPD including area secretaries and the staff of the central party organization.[72] Nevertheless the number of officials in the SPD was growing throughout the period under discussion here and the cost of upholding its bureaucratic apparatus was substantial. In 1929 3.2 million marks were spent on the party bureaucracy, more money than was spent in the electoral campaign of 1928.[73]

The rank and file of the party were called to membership assemblies (*Hauptversammlung*) roughly once a month, although there were no clear rules, except that it had to be summoned by the executive whenever important matters had to be discussed concerning the local party as a whole. Small town local SPD parties, like Biberach, only organized regular monthly members' meetings after 1918.[74] Even if regular monthly assemblies took place, reports about lack of interest among members and bad attendance were frequent.[75] Paetau, for example, comes to the conclusion that only 5–10 per cent of all members took part in general assemblies in Kiel.[76] Membership apathy at a local level played an important role for the necessity of appointing paid officials to run local party organizations.[77] Wertheimer's guess of a high participation of SPD members on a local level (according to him 75 per cent of party members were active)[78] thus seems rather unlikely.

Rank-and-file apathy was also visible in the shortage of individuals who were willing and able to fill the relevant positions. Lipinski complained

---

[72] Guttsman, *The Social Democratic Party*, 246.

[73] For the figures see Hunt, *German Social Democracy*, 56 f. In 1929 3.2 million marks would have been the equivalent of £156,870; in 1991 this would have been worth £4.77 million.

[74] Hartwig Abraham (ed.), *Geschichte der Biberacher Arbeiterbewegung und Sozialdemokratie* (Biberach, 1983), 80.

[75] Adelheid von Saldern, *Vom Einwohner zum Bürger* (Berlin, 1973), 126, Alfred Zeitz, *Zur Geschichte der Arbeiterbewegung der Stadt Brandenburg vor dem 1. Weltkrieg* (Potsdam, 1965), 15; Andreas Müller, 'Die groß-hannoversche Sozialdemokratie bis 1. Weltkrieges bis zur Novemberrevolution', *Hannoversche Geschichtsblätter*, NS 33 (1979), 155 f. Also: ZStA Merseburg, Rep. 77, no. 656 l, police report about the social democratic movement from 1897, p. 3 about decreasing numbers in social democratic ward meetings. Complaints about membership apathy can also be found in *Jahresbericht des Sozialdemokratischen Vereins Bremen* (1908–9), 7 and in IML, Polizeipräsidium Berlin, St. 22/12, police reports about membership assemblies of the fourth social democratic constituency, 11 Apr. to 12 Dec. 1906.

[76] R. Paetau, *Konfrontation oder Kooperation: Arbeiterbewegung und bürgerliche Gesellschaft im ländlichen Schleswig-Holstein und in der Industriestadt Kiel, 1900–1925* (Berlin, 1985), 67.

[77] Dieter Fricke, *Die deutsche Arbeiterbewegung, 1869–1914: Ein Handbuch über ihre Organisation und Tätigkeit im Klassenkampf* (Berlin, 1976), 234 f.

[78] Egon Wertheimer, *Portrait of the Labour Party* (2nd edn., London, 1930), 230 ff.

at the 1924 conference: 'Unfortunately some places have so few enthusiastic workers in their organizations that the work falls on very few persons. Through educational work we have to find more workers to prevent the others from being overworked.'[79] Furthermore Lipinski called for more personnel to fill the local, state, and national parliaments. If possible, parliamentary and party double mandates were avoided. Yet Philipp Scheidemann recalled his position in a Hessian town in 1895: 'I was editor, distributor, press and party secretary, advertisement "tout" and treasurer.' Furthermore he did all the electioneering and propaganda work, held hundreds of public meetings and stood as candidate for town council, Hessian diet, and Reichstag.[80] Paid officials often held the highest positions in both local party and municipal parliament and they also tended to dominate the local assemblies.[81] Due to the new electoral law and the greater opportunities for the SPD to influence municipal politics after 1918, the SPD even enlarged and consolidated its local party bureaucracy in the Weimar Republic, and double mandates became even more the rule.[82]

Similar patterns of overlapping membership between local party leaders and municipal party representatives can be found in many local Labour Parties. There was a similar shortage of personnel, so that the warnings of head office to avoid double mandates were often fruitless.[83] In 1924 the *Labour Organizer* wrote: 'What was an excellent policy in the early stages of development [when there were few Labour councillors] now threatens to become an evil and in some places the elected persons do actually possess an improper preponderance on the Executive.'[84] George Lansbury recalled that in 1911, when he agreed to participate in the foundation of the *Daily Herald*, he was not only editor of a newspaper, but also MP, a Poor Law Guardian, Borough Councillor, and a member of the LCC.[85]

[79] *Protokoll des SPD Parteitags 1924*, 143.

[80] Scheidemann, *Memoirs of a Social Democrat*, i. 48 f.

[81] R. G. Huber, *Sozialer Wandel und politische Konflikte in einer südhessischen Industriestadt: Kommunalpolitik der SPD in Offenbach, 1898–1914* (Darmstadt, 1985), 244 f. For the widespread accumulation of offices by SPD officials see also D. Bronder, 'Organisation und Führung der sozialdemokratischen Arbeiterbewegung im Deutschen Reich, 1890–1914' (University of Göttingen Ph.D. 1952), 209.

[82] G. A. Ritter, 'Kontinuität und Umformung des deutschen Parteiensystems', in G. A. Ritter, *Arbeiterbewegung, Parteien und Parlamentarismus: Aufsätze zur deutschen Sozial- und Verfassungsgeschichte des 19. und 20. Jahrhunderts* (Göttingen, 1976), 139–41.

[83] *Labour Organizer* (June 1922), 18.

[84] *Labour Organizer* (Mar. 1924), 5.

[85] George Lansbury, *Miracle of Fleet Street* (London, 1925), 8.

Before 1918 local parties tended to take over the structure of the national party. Only a few parties, Woolwich, Barnard Castle, and Clitheroe, admitted individual members. Most were content with the affiliation of local trade unions and socialist societies, although in some localities this alliance did not work as well as it did at the central level of organization.[86] Local organization got an additional boost when, after the 1910 elections, MacDonald and Henderson pressed ahead schemes for the appointment of full-time agents which were to be dependent upon head office approval.[87] Henderson in 1903 pointed out that bureau-cratization of the local party machine, namely the appointment of paid secretaries, would be necessary to enhance the prospect of a nation-wide network of local Labour Parties.[88] Additionally, selective grants were given to constituencies according to election successes (grants-in-aid schemes from May 1912).[89] Such schemes were particularly necessary in places like Leicester, where the local working-class party had always suffered from not having the means and professional knowledge to de-velop an efficient organization.[90]

In the war, and increasingly from 1918 onwards, an even wider expan-sion of full-time agents took place.[91] Local party activists still did much of the exceptional work voluntarily,[92] yet permanent paid agents were appointed wherever it was financially possible. It was the declared aim of the party after 1918 to create 'a skeleton party in every constituency [and to weld] these parties into intelligent units.'[93] The importance of this change was stressed by Arthur Henderson: 'One important feature of the constitution is that it makes the local groups the units of organization rather than the national societies and thus establishes a more direct relationship with the individual electors in every constituency.'[94] The stronger stress on local parties after 1918 made itself felt. As the national agent stated in May 1922 with some satisfaction: 'Its [the Labour Party's] network of local organization has spread with terrific rapidity from one end of the country to the other since the launching of the new constitution

---

[86] Blewett, *The Peers*, 285.
[87] McKibbin, 'James Ramsay MacDonald', 225 f.
[88] Bealey and Pelling, *Labour and Politics*, 238.
[89] McKibbin, *Evolution*, 31–3.
[90] Lancaster, *Radicalism*, 155.
[91] Silkin, *Changing Battlefields*, 6. Silkin stresses that the full-time agent was the 'key to party organization' (p. 5).
[92] Herbert Drinkwater, 'The Principles of Party Organization', *Labour Organizer* (Dec. 1921), 10.
[93] *Labour Organizer* (June 1930), 97.
[94] Arthur Henderson, 'Labour Looks Ahead', *Daily Herald* (12 Jan. 1918), 5.

in 1918. No longer does the Party fight in its few strongholds, but the battle-line is country-wide . . .'.[95] By 1924 only three constituencies had no sort of local Labour Party and G. D. H. Cole counted the amazing number of 3,000 local parties.[96] Yet, many of those still largely depended on affiliated trade unions or socialist groups and had little individual membership except in some cases a strong women's section.[97] Often also the leaders of pre-war local Labour Parties were rather reluctant to change the structure of the party by introducing paid officials and individual membership. Herbert Drinkwater, the editor of the *Labour Organizer*, blamed the old guard of the party and their conservatism in handling party affairs for much of the apathy that existed in local Labour Parties.[98]

Individual members could affiliate to the local Labour Parties by joining the ward organization. The lack of information about ward organizations mirror the fact that many local parties were slow to set them up.[99] Indeed, one local study about Liverpool stresses the fact that before 1939 in a couple of wards there was a ward secretary, but not necessarily a ward party, mostly due to the lack of activists.[100] Minutes of local parties in the early 1920s often included secretary's reports 'in which he dwelt upon the great need of more active supporters'.[101] Many card-carrying Labour Party members did not bother to turn up at ward meetings or, indeed, to participate in any form of party activity. Even EC or GMC meetings were often attended by few delegates.[102] So, is one to agree with the view that the Labour Party did not have an efficient constituency organization?[103]

This is hardly the whole picture. Already before 1914 well-organized local Labour Parties with paid officials and ward organizations were a

---

[95] Egerton Wake, 'The Principles of Party Organization', *Labour Organizer* (May 1922), 5.

[96] G. D. H. Cole, *A History of the Labour Party from 1914* (London, 1948), 140.

[97] *Labour Organizer* (Dec. 1927), 1.

[98] *Labour Organizer* (Mar. 1928), 52. Drinkwater called the old guards' attitude a 'hanging-on and dog in the manger attitude'.

[99] *Labour Organizer* (Apr./May 1923), 5.

[100] Robert Baxter, 'The Liverpool Labour Party, 1918–1963' (University of Oxford D.Phil. 1969), 223.

[101] Labour Party Archive, Local Labour Party Files: Minutes of Annual Meeting of North-East Kent Divisional Labour Parties, 9 Apr. 1921.

[102] Keith Teanby, ' "Not Equal to the Demand": Major Concerns of the Doncaster Divisional Labour Party, 1918–1939' (University of Sheffield M.Phil. 1983), 24–34. For low turnout at EC and GMC meetings see collection of local Labour Party annual reports in: Labour Party Archive, Local Labour Party Files, and the indictment by *Labour Organizer* (Oct. 1930), 178.

[103] This view was put forward in an influential article by Christopher Howard, 'Expectations Born to Death: Local Labour Party Expansion in the 1920s', in J. Winter (ed.), *The Working Class in Modern British History* (Cambridge, 1983), 65–81.

strong challenge to traditional conservative and liberal organizations. After 1918 the number of those well-organized local Labour Parties increased, especially in the second half of the 1920s.[104] It is noticeable that, where local parties bothered to build up ward organizations, the appointment of ward captains and the holding of cottage and back-door meetings would follow.[105] The holding of annual meetings of all local Labour Parties in any one county in the 1920s is a further sign that efforts to boost local organization were well under way.[106] Rowett has shown for Sheffield how successful a Labour organization could be despite an active anti-socialist propaganda carried out by the local press.[107] Woolwich and Bermondsey were examples of whole geographical areas within a city being more or less identified with the working-class party, just as, for example, the Hammerbrook in Hamburg became identified with the SPD.[108] Certainly not all, but a number of local Labour Parties in the second half of the 1920s managed to do what some (not all!) local SPD parties had already achieved pre-1914, namely to build an organization which could link the party with the everyday experience of workers in a particular locality.[109]

As in the SPD, 'machine-building' in the Labour Party went hand in hand with a growing bureaucratic apparatus and outlook. The exact number of full-time party officials within the Labour Party is unknown. There are no statistics giving a precise count, but the number of full-time agents in the constituencies,[110] of paid head office staff and journalists of the Labour press did probably not amount to more than a few hundred

---

[104] Lists of well-organized local Labour Parties were regularly published in the *Labour Organizer*.

[105] *Labour Organizer* (Jan. 1923), 8 f. For the existence of effective ward steward systems, for example in Westminster Labour Party, see *Annual Report Presented by the GMC to the Individual Members of the Westminster Labour Party 1925* (Westminster, 1925). For the importance attributed to effective ward organizations in the Glasgow ILP before the First World War see Joan Smith, 'Labour Tradition in Glasgow and Liverpool', *HWJ* 17 (1984), 35 f.

[106] *Labour Organizer*, Feb. 1924, p. 18.

[107] John S. Rowett, 'Sheffield under Labour Control', *SSLH* 39 (1979), 12.

[108] For the Hammerbrook see Johannes Schult, *Geschichte der Hamburger Arbeiter, 1890–1918* (Hamburg, 1967), 23–35. For Bermondsey see Fenner Brockway, *Bermondsey Story* (London, 1949), 36. For Woolwich see Paul Thompson, 'London Working-Class Politics and the Formation of the London Labour Party, 1885–1914' (University of Oxford D.Phil. 1963), 437–58.

[109] Savage, *The Dynamics*; G. C. Rose, 'Locality, Politics and Culture: Poplar in the 1920s' (University of London Ph.D. 1989), esp. ch. 4; J. A. Gillespie, 'Economic and Political Change in the East End of London during the 1920s' (University of Cambridge Ph.D. 1984).

[110] According to McKibbin, *Evolution*, 113 the number of full-time agents in the years 1920–4 varied from 111 in 1923 to 133 in 1922.

office-holders. The executive committee of the local party normally consisted of the (unpaid) officers of the party: the president (or chairman), two vice-presidents, treasurer, financial secretary, and secretary. It usually met once a month and set up a number of subcommittees concerned with the social life of the party and the usual range of political activity. The ward secretary was of paramount importance in organizing propaganda meetings of the rank and file, social functions, fund raising, public demonstrations, and electioneering.[111]

The (paid) local agent was even more important in giving guidance and direction to the efforts of voluntary party workers and in guaranteeing some sort of organizational continuity in the locality.[112] The *Labour Organizer* published a series of agents' profiles in the 1920s which gave a picture of what was perceived as an ideal: the local agent had to be a man, 'having a system', he was efficient in creating a 'party machine' and had a clean and well-organized office. He sold a lot of party literature and kept the party successfully out of debt. If he was really good, he would even make a financial profit for the party. Yet, even strongholds of organization, like London, found it difficult substantially to expand the number of full-time agents in the 1920s. From the seventy-seven London Labour Parties at best twenty-seven parties had full-time agents, despite frequent calls on the local parties that 'the maintenance of a constituency party organization at a high state of efficiency requires the full-time services of at least one competent organizer.'[113]

The path followed in active constituencies may have looked similar to the one the Darlington Labour Party took. Its EC wanted to carry out a membership canvass and monthly public propaganda meetings. Furthermore it wanted to buy more suitable premises for the party and the formation of a Labour League of Youth was frequently discussed without coming to any definite decision.[114] Only in 1928, after the appointment of a paid local organizer, a scheme of organization was drawn up:

Central Office as pivot of co-ordinator, ward secretaries with defined duties to regulate the duties of three following district secretaries for each ward . . . These to be in touch with street captains, who in turn would be in weekly contact with individual members. The object of the organization was to obtain a street captain

---

[111] *Labour Organizer* (Dec. 1929), 240 f. Also ibid. (Mar. 1921), 7 f.
[112] McKenzie, *British Political Parties*, 542. See also the extremely lively story of A. C. Powell, 'The Life of a Labour Agent', *Labour Organizer* (June 1930), 110 f.
[113] *Annual Report of the EC of the LLP* (1930–1), 5.
[114] Darlington Labour Party Minutes, 13 Dec. 1926 and 10 Nov. 1926, in Labour Party Archive.

for each street, carrying on collecting, reporting registration changes . . . , removals and new voters, distributing notices and election canvassing . . .'[115]

In a meeting of individual members of the Darlington LP on 3 February 1928 'several members promised to organize streets',[116] demonstrating that the ambitious scheme of the organizer did not just meet with rank-and-file apathy. The newly appointed agent also stepped up the public and party meetings. On 10 December 1928 he reported to the Darlington EC that four Sunday Evening Meetings were to be held at the Theatre Royal before the middle of April; additionally he had arranged regular Sunday evening meetings in the Hall, when there was no speaker at the theatre, and joint meetings with the 'No More War Movement' as well as with the ILP.

John Holford has demonstrated for Edinburgh that 'machine-building' became a big item for local Labour Parties and Trades Councils after the war.[117] For Preston, Michael Savage found in the 1920s, 'the character of Labour politics at the local level changed considerably . . . it changed from a party based on certain trade unions to one based on neighbourhood organizations'.[118] For Bristol it can certainly be said that 'a constituency Labour Party . . . was more than an election machine. Research into the records of the Bristol East Labour Party for the 1930s reveals an astonishing variety of activities in which its members were engaged . . .'.[119] Generally, the Labour Parties in the North-East seemed to have been in 'feverish growth' after 1919.[120] What was increasingly attacked was ineffective election-time-only activity.[121] A good local organization with street captains and regular cottage and back-door meetings, so it was argued, would also be of use at election times.[122] The catastrophic defeat in the 1931 general election stressed the commitment to extending local party organization even more.[123]

---

[115] Darlington LP minutes, 30 Mar. 1928.

[116] Ibid.

[117] John Holford, *Reshaping Labour: Organization, Work and Politics—Edinburgh in the Great War and After* (London, 1988), 179.

[118] Savage, *The Dynamics*, 194.

[119] *A Brief History of Bristol South East Constituency Labour Party* (Bristol, 1979), 7.

[120] Margaret H. Gibb and Maureen Callcott, 'The Labour Party in the North East Between the Wars', *North East Group for the Study of Labour History*, bulletin 8 (Oct. 1974), 13.

[121] *Twenty-Five Years History of the Woolwich Labour Party 1903-1928* (Woolwich, 1928), 10.

[122] *Labour Organizer* (Jan. 1923), 8 f.

[123] *Labour Organizer* (Dec. 1931), 231. See also Emanuel Shinwell, 'Ain't It Grand to be Temporarily Dead?', *Labour Magazine*, 11 (1932–3), 172 f.

Consequently the party undertook throughout the 1920s individual membership campaigns. 'Labour Weeks' were held in many DLP's, in which the party organized 'simultaneous meetings in all parts of the division, some of which would be visited by central speakers, the remainder to be addressed by local speakers and by exchanges from speakers from other localities.'[124] In 1925 Morrison introduced membership canvassing in London: 'to issue to local Labour Parties certificates of merit for each 25 new members secured; and to present a perpetual trophy to the party showing the best results each year in increasing membership'.[125] As in the SPD, regular membership cards were introduced, and the ward secretary would call on the member at least once a month to collect his or her membership fee. It served the same function as the membership collections in the SPD, namely to keep the members in touch with the party's activities.[126] On a national level the NEC's Organizational Subcommittee decided in 1932 to embark on a 'Campaign for the Million Members' with the active help of the local women's sections.[127] By that time the local Labour Parties had already become the most important basis for the party's electoral work.[128] If the Labour Party in 1952, with just over a million individual members was the most powerful working-class party in Western Europe, the groundwork for that success had been laid by the activities in the inter-war years.

One of the prime examples of a Labour Party organization in Britain is Herbert Morrison's London Labour Party in the 1920s and 1930s. Paul Thompson has described the difficulties of the Labour Party in London before 1914 even to get founded.[129] Yet it was precisely on models of organization like the Woolwich Labour Party that the LLP came to rely and which it in turn tried to propagate after 1918. On 18 January 1918 Morrison wrote to the secretaries of all affiliated societies of the LLP that pressing ahead with the scheme for local party organization was the most important present task.[130] Morrison constantly travelled around the local

---

[124] *Labour Organizer* (Sept. 1923), 2.
[125] *Annual Report of the EC of the LLP* (1930–1), 15. See also Herbert Morrison, 'London's Big Push', *London News* (June 1925), 1. For a similar campaign in Coventry in 1924 see Hodgkinson, *Sent to Coventry*, 83.
[126] Drucker, *Doctrine and Ethos*, 16.
[127] Labour Party Archive, Organization Subcommittee Minutes, 27 Jan. 1932.
[128] Stuart Macintyre, 'Socialism, the Unions and the Labour Party after 1918', *SSLH* 31 (Autumn 1975), 111.
[129] Paul Thompson, *Socialists, Liberals and Labour: The Struggle for London, 1885–1914* (London, 1967).
[130] Labour Party Archive, Local Labour Party Files: files on LLP, leaflet, 18 Jan. 1918, signed by Herbert Morrison.

Labour Parties in London so as to improve their organization. Once a week a communication was sent out to all local parties, advising them as to organization and municipal policies. Quarterly meetings of delegates from local parties were held to discuss the same topics.[131] LLP circulars stressed the fact that lack of co-ordination and decentralization meant diffusion of effort and finance.[132] It also encouraged local agents to meet regularly, as did other county divisions, in order to study organizational problems together.[133] Morrison's success was outstanding. In 1914 there had been twenty local Labour Parties in London, in 1924 there were seventy-three. There had been no women's sections in London in 1914, in 1924 there were forty-eight. London sent two Labour MPs to the House of Commons in 1914, in 1924 it elected twenty-two Labour MPs.[134] At the end of the 1920s Herbert Morrison revealed where he took his model of an organizational machine from:

I have never forgotten what Stephen Sanders, MP, told us before the war with regard to Berlin: 'That the Social Democratic Party Executive could sit on the top floor of the *Vorwärts* building, pass a manifesto paragraph by paragraph, have it put into type and circulated to every tenement in the city of Berlin by the next morning.' We cannot quite do this yet in London, but we ought to be able to do it. And some day we will do it.[135]

Not surprisingly, a few years earlier he headed a municipal delegation of the LLP on a visit to the German SPD in the Rhineland.[136]

As has been argued above, local party organizations in both countries were geared towards a similar organizational build up. Whereas the SPD achieved such a buildup already before 1914, the Labour Party did so only in the second half of the 1920s. Both parties were geared towards machine-building at local level, and where the activities of local SPD organizations, especially the involvement of the rank and file, should not be overemphasized, the activities of local Labour Parties were certainly impressive, given the lack of encouragement from regional and national levels. If it appeared to be the case that the SPD was more successful than the Labour Party in building up a cohesive structure, this had little to do with English mistrust of organization but was largely due to the existence

---

[131] B. Donoughue and G. W. Jones, *Herbert Morrison* (London, 1973), 75 f.
[132] Labour Party Archive, Local Labour Party Files, Circular of the LLP, May 1933.
[133] For London, Cheshire, and the West Midlands see *Labour Organizer* (Mar. 1921), 17 f. For Lancashire see *Labour Organizer* (Jan. 1921), 8.
[134] *Labour Organizer* (June 1924), 1.
[135] Herbert Morrison, 'London's Labour Majority', *Labour Magazine*, 8 (1929–30), 68.
[136] *Annual Report of the EC of the LLP* (1926–7), 24.

of a framework for the strengthening of weaker parties. By centralizing much of the finance as well as the decision-making at the regional party level, the SPD managed to balance out some of the unequal political strengths of the local branches. The strong regional organization was a precondition for producing a significant national political force. Territories and parts of the working class could be reached, where 'local conditions' otherwise would have made it difficult for the SPD to penetrate established political patterns. Stronger party bureaucracies were used to organize weak areas and the efficient centralization of decision-making gave the SPD a homogeneous, uniform outlook. It was not as if Labour Party leaders would not have liked to be as centralized, bureaucratized, efficient, and machine-like as the SPD. It was rather that the different set-up of its organization, and especially its neglect for the regions prevented such a set-up. Due to limited financial resources, requests by the local parties to head office for more central co-ordination had to be turned down. Co-ordination remained one of the prime tasks of the regional organizer, who often gave a low priority to this important feature of his job.[137] So the local parties did not receive the support they would have needed in the 1920s and the bureaucratic apparatus to administer a huge local organization was not developed. It proved equally decisive for its organizational deficiencies that the Labour Party never managed to centralize its finances at any level of the Party, i.e. they always remained dependent on the contributions of trade unions at every level of its organization. In the Labour Party the differences between rich and poor constituencies remained decisive for success. It was left to well-organized local Labour Parties to draw up schemes for badly organized ones. The Bermondsey Labour Party, for example, 'adopted' a poor local Labour Party in 1929 and tried to help build up an effective organization there.[138] It is to this question of finance that the next section now turns.

3.4. Party finance

It took the SPD three decades after the merger of 1875 to overcome financial instability.[139] In the 1890s and 1900s the financial success of the party rested largely on profits from party-owned businesses, which were

---

[137] Rowett, 'The Labour Party and Local Government', 38 f.

[138] Brockway, *Bermondsey Story*, 139. See also Egerton Wake's 'appeal to come forward and "adopt" ' the poorer Labour Party constituencies in rural areas, delivered at the 1924 Labour Party Conference, in: *Report of the Annual Conference of the Labour Party 1924* (London, 1924), 181 f.

[139] Roth, *The Social Democrats*, 266.

mostly controlled by the national or regional Vorstände, and on interest rates on capital invested in foreign countries.[140] Party businesses were still bringing substantial profits during the Weimar Republic. In 1928, for example, they brought a net profit of 1.8 million RM (worth £88,265 which would have been approximately £2.6 million in 1991).[141] Individual membership fees were only formally introduced in 1900 (because of the laws of association in Imperial Germany which did not allow centralized and regular party membership fees). Yet it had been a long-standing tradition within most local party organizations to collect 'voluntary' membership contributions. When individual membership fees were finally fixed in 1909 at a minimum monthly rate of 30 pf. for male and 15 pf. for female members (approximately worth £7 and £3.50 in 1991), it was a substantial contribution to party finance,[142] especially as membership rose from 384,000 members in 1906 to 530,000 in 1907, and more than a million members on the eve of the First World War.

With membership figures in the Weimar Republic never dropping below three-quarters of a million and contributions of roughly 38 RM yearly plus 1.85 RM for the International (for 1926; in 1991 this would have been the equivalent of approximately £60), membership fees remained an important means of income for the SPD throughout the period under discussion here. Membership contributions were collected locally and then the money was handed over to the regional organizations. In 1927 the regional organizations' income was 7.4 million RM (£263,000; in 1991 approximately £7.7 million) of which 4.7 million came from ordinary membership dues.[143] After 1912 20 per cent of all locally paid fees had to go to the national party executive (Vorstand).[144] Branches had to produce annual reports covering campaigning activities, membership, and finance. In the 1919 statute of the SPD the income of the Vorstand was raised from 20 to 25 per cent of all membership dues, but as membership numbers in the Weimar Republic fell after initial growth to 806,268 in 1925 and never reached substantially over one million thereafter, this did not amount to much of an increase. During the inflation the

[140] ZStA Merseburg, Rep. 77, no. 656, I: police report about the social democratic movement to the Prussian Minister of the Interior, 15 Jan. 1898, p. 10.

[141] Hunt, *German Social Democracy*, 52.

[142] For the willingness of social democrats to sacrifice a substantial amount of money for the organization see IGA/ZPA, St. 22/38: police report about the agitation district Niederrhein 1911–1913. Also ZStA Merseburg, Rep. 77, CBS no. 35, vol. ii: finances of Social Democracy.

[143] Winkler, *Der Schein der Normalität*, 350.

[144] Nipperdey, *Die Organisation*, 369 f.

executive had to be given emergency powers to raise the dues it received, because of currency fluctuations. In the 1924 statute this emergency power became a permanent one. From then on the executive, together with the control commission, determined its income itself. Despite this increase in power of the PV, the most effective control of finance was still at the regional level. The regional party had the means of boosting the organization of weak local parties by redirecting money from rich and well-organized parties to those which needed financial help. Also, individual party activists who had been persecuted because of their party work could be effectively supported by the regional party.[145]

The Labour Party was financially not as autonomous as the SPD. The trade unions, through a political levy, contributed the lion's share of the Labour Party's finances, nationally as well as locally. In the elections the unions financed their own candidates. A serious consequence of union sponsorship of MPs was that they were more likely to support one of their own men than a non-union candidate, even if the latter was better qualified.[146] As the Manchester and Salford LRC put it in 1920: 'So long as constituency organizations are abjectly dependent on wealthy trade unions to finance their national and local candidates, the party will never command the best brains of the movement to represent them.'[147] The inability of head office to support candidatures in financially weak constituencies had another damaging effect on Labour's organization in the country. Strong personalities, who could have helped to win difficult seats in weaker constituencies, were not willing to stand there, because of obvious financial liabilities. Rather, they chose safe seats, where either trade unions or socialist societies would pay the bill. So for example, MacDonald in 1928 was anxious to leave Aberavon for a better endowed constituency and was only too happy to accept Seaham Harbour.[148] The electoral expenses of the SPD, however, were met out of its central fund and, although the unions additionally contributed to the SPD election fund, they did not have the power to finance their own candidates. The SPD achieved, largely because of its mass membership, its higher membership fees, and also its profitable publishing undertakings (see next section), what the Labour Party struggled in vain to achieve: autonomy in their political expenditure.

---

[145] ZStA Merseburg, Rep. 77, no. 508.

[146] David Howell, 'Introduction to the Stockport Labour Party Archive', in *Origins*, ed. Clark, p. 21.

[147] Manchester and Salford LRC, *Annual Report and Balance Sheet for 1920*, in Labour Party Archive, Local Labour Party Files.

[148] PRO, MacDonald Papers, 30/69, 1710–1713.

In the 1920s Labour's head office came to adopt and actively propagate the idea of individual membership as a means of sound finance which would decrease the party's dependence on trade union money: 'Individual membership should be a real source of income to local parties, and should produce for the party nationally, at least enough to pay for the outside organizational staff.'[149] It was especially after the 1927 Trade Union Act had crippled the trade union link with the Labour Party that efforts to increase individual membership were stepped up. Paid membership canvassers were thought necessary, as voluntary work seemed less and less satisfactory.[150] Collectors were appointed who would often be paid a certain percentage of the collected fees, so as to raise their interest in a proper collection of party fees.[151] Southampton Labour Party even decided to start a five-year plan with the aim of 'thirty per cent organization as a minimum for all wards'.[152] Individual membership of the party in fact rose from nil in 1918 to 447,000 in 1937.[153] Whether the Labour Party was copying a specifically German model of party organization seems difficult to establish, although the adopted schemes, like the quota system, uniform membership cards, systems of collecting membership fees, and the regular local membership campaigns (in Germany they were dubbed 'red weeks') were suspiciously similar to the SPD organization.[154] The major difference up to 1945 was that the Labour Party set a trifling membership fee of 1s. per annum for male members and 6d. for female members (in 1991 approximately £3.50 and £1.75 respectively). Even the *Labour Organizer* agreed that local parties should make an effort to collect more than that minimum fee.[155] The willingness of many party members to contribute a more substantial amount than

---

[149] *Labour Organizer* (Mar. 1921), 14.

[150] *Labour Organizer* (Jan. 1921), 2.

[151] For example Minutes of Special EC meeting of the Stockport Labour Party, 4 Aug. 1927, in *Origins*, ed. Clark. Also Sheerness Labour Party, Balance Sheet 1932, in Labour Party Archive, Local Labour Party Files. The interest attached by the Labour Party leadership to the question of how efficiently to collect individual members' contributions can be seen very clearly from a paper by Honley Atkinson, 'The Collection of Individual Members' Contributions', in Labour Party Archives, NEC Minutes, 26 Oct. 1932, in which he argued against paid collections, but agreed that the 'factor of organization' is most important in all questions to do with membership.

[152] *Report on Membership Organization*, ed. by the Southampton Labour Party (Southampton, 1936), 1.

[153] Henry Pelling, *A Short History of the Labour Party* (8th edn., London, 1986), 194. The argument that membership numbers are not very reliable can be used for Labour Party and SPD. See David G. Green, *Power and Party in an English City* (London, 1981), 19 and Michels, 'Die deutsche Sozialdemokratie I', 477–9.

[154] Wilhelm Pieck, 'Die Erhebung der Parteibeiträge', *NZ* 30 (1911–12), 778–81.

[155] H. Eastwood, 'Towards that 100 per cent', *Labour Organizer* (Feb. 1925), 10.

that seems evident from the responses to a party call to set up a £100,000 Fighting Fund in 1927.[156]

However, the Labour Party did not fully exploit the financial potential inherent in a larger individual membership. Local Labour Party finance throughout the 1920s remained heavily dependent on contributions by local trade unions. The Stockport Labour Party, for example, had to be largely financed by the Amalgamated Society of Railway Servants, the National Union of Railwaymen, and the Railway Clerks' Association due to the lack of a reliable base amongst the town's working class.[157] And those local parties who had sound financial trade union support could count themselves lucky, as the consequences of limited financial resources were severe in the 1920s. Speakers could not be invited, delegates could not be sent to annual or special conferences, May Day demonstrations could not be held, full-time agents could not be appointed, and decent headquarters could neither be purchased nor rented. The London Labour Party reported in 1927: 'Inevitably things we would like to have done have been left undone owing to the limitation of our financial resources.'[158] Efforts to spread the money flow from the trade unions more equally throughout the country[159] came to nothing.

All efforts of the Labour Party in the inter-war years to put their precarious finance on a sounder footing came to little in comparison with the effective centralization of finances at the regional level within the SPD. The Labour Party's failure to become financially independent of the trade unions had important consequences for the party's inability to direct and control the growth of local parties. Despite the organizational buildup envisaged by many of its national and local leaders, financial constraints all too often put limits on the realization of these plans. For example, despite the Labour Party Organizational Subcommittee's recommendation 'that no reduction in the numbers of the Organizing Staff . . . should be made',[160] the party in 1931 had to consider staff reductions at head office. The comparatively good financial situation of the SPD in turn fostered processes of machine-building.

---

[156] Arthur Henderson, 'Labour's £100,000 Fighting Fund. Why it is Wanted and How it is Being Raised', *Labour Magazine*, 7 (1928–9), 5–8.

[157] David Howell, 'Introduction to the files of the Stockport Labour Party', in *Origins*, ed. Clark, 4.

[158] *Annual Report of the EC of the LLP* (1927–8), 24.

[159] Such moves were discussed in the Labour Party Organization Subcommittee. See Labour Party Archive: Organization Subcommittee Minutes, 17 Feb. 1932, p. 7.

[160] Labour Party Archive: Organization Subcommittee Minutes, 23 Mar. 1932, p. 2.

3.5. The party press

The Labour Party and the SPD both saw the development of their own newspapers as a vital step towards 'making socialists'. In this section the various efforts made and difficulties encountered by both parties in the process of setting up their own newspapers shall be considered. The SPD's party press had difficulties in establishing itself in the second half of the nineteenth century,[161] but especially after 1900 it constantly expanded and became a useful tool for the party's campaigns as well as financially one of the prime assets of the movement.[162] The income from advertisements and from sales increased steadily, so that by 1900 the police reports to the Prussian Ministry of the Interior no longer mentioned any party subsidies to the press.[163] Even before the war most of the SPD's newspapers were printed by its own presses. In 1904 it possessed forty-seven presses and their number steadily increased—by 1927 the party owned 179 printing works. The SPD printed papers for every section of the movement, from intellectual journals to family journals, from papers for women and youth to papers for the blind, from satirical journals to a vast number of regional or local dailies and weeklies. Further contributing to the Labour press in Germany were the separate press empires of the trade unions and the labour movement's cultural, educational, and leisure-oriented ancillary organizations. In 1924 there were 169 SPD papers with a circulation of 1.09 million copies. In 1919 the circulation had rocketed to 1.7 million subscribers, but the momentum was not maintained. In fact, many SPD papers experienced serious crisis in the Weimar Republic.[164] None of the SPD papers could be called a truly national paper. Even the party's official newspaper, *Vorwärts*, always remained very much the local paper of the Berlin party. This is reflected in its circulation: the overwhelming number of *Vorwärts* papers were sold in and around Berlin. The SPD's provincial press was of a very different strength in different regions in Germany. Its strongholds were generally also its electoral strongholds, especially Saxony, Bavaria, and

[161] Jochen Loreck, *Wie man früher Sozialdemokrat wurde: Das Kommunikationsverhalten und die Konzeption der sozialistischen Parteipublizistik durch August Bebel* (Bonn, 1977), 13–15. Also Werner Saerbeck, *Die Presse der deutschen Sozialdemokratie unter dem Sozialistengesetz* (Pfaffenweiler, 1985).

[162] Fricke, *Handbuch*, i. 495–646; see generally Kurt Koszyk, *Die Presse der deutschen Sozialdemokratie: Eine Bibliographie* (Hanover, 1966).

[163] ZStA Merseburg, Rep. 77, no. 656, I, 41.

[164] Guttsman, *Workers' Culture*, 275 f.

Thuringia. On the whole, the numbers of readers of social democratic papers were minimal in comparison to social democratic voters. In 1912 only 2.2 per cent of all German newspapers were social democratic, whereas the SPD received 34.8 per cent of the votes in general elections the same year.[165] The SPD press preached to the converted, because it was bought and read largely by party members.

One of the most striking characteristics of the SPD daily papers was their uniformity. On the one hand the setting up of news agencies which distributed important party and general news to them played an important part in that development. From 1906 to 1922 and from 1929 to 1933 the *Sozialdemokratische Parteikorrespondenz* was published by the executive. In 1921 a social democratic parliamentary press service (*Sozialdemokratischer Parlamentsdienst*) was set up. Some of the news services were run by individual members of the SPD: one of the most influential news services was run by Friedrich Stampfer. To Paul Löbe, who had criticized the deadeningly uniform effect of such news services on the SPD press, Stampfer blamed the local papers for printing every single line of the service rather than just selecting some of its news.[166] Indeed, some responsibility has to be put on the editors of local papers who were often 'chosen not from the point of view of quality, but according to "who could use the salary most".'[167]

Another reason for the uniformity of the SPD's papers lay in their effective streamlining to the dominant party opinion. Dissent was rarely allowed. Before 1918 such streamlining was directed by the district and area organizations who controlled all newspapers in their district/area. In the Weimar Republic the press was controlled jointly by the constituency and local parties. In 1929 there was an important shift of power to the national centre, when the PV decided to establish a national propaganda department which had the following tasks: it should edit the party news service (*Parteikorrespondenz*), and it should collect newspaper articles concerning all important questions of public life.[168] Its main task was the homogenization and streamlining of the party press. Already in the mid-1920s all press undertakings were subsumed under one financial organization, the Konzentrations AG. Such a centralization of funds was

---

[165] For regional and structural problems of the SPD's press see Ludwig Radlof, 'Die Agitation für die Parteipresse', *NZ* 23/2 (1904–5), 295 f.

[166] IGA/ZPA, papers of Paul Löbe, NL 110/93, nos. 1–2: letter from Stampfer to Löbe, 24 Mar. 1908.

[167] Schorske, *German Social Democracy*, 271.

[168] *Jahrbuch der SPD, 1929*, 233.

accompanied by the setting up of the Inseraten-Union GmbH, which had the task of collecting orders for advertisements and arranging for their simultaneous publication in various social democratic papers. Some of these centralizing measures were introduced for purely organizational reasons: to support weaker papers through the surpluses created by those papers which sold well. On the other hand the motive of controlling the provincial party press was of some importance in implementing centralizing measures.

Bebel, for one, was convinced that the party press had to represent party principle rather than serve as a forum for discussion.[169] Kautsky equally stressed the desirability of a unified opinion within the party press. According to him, fractions could not be allowed within Social Democracy:[170] journalists who deviated from the sanctioned party line had to be removed.[171] Social democratic papers, when appointing journalists, were careful to make sure that the applicant had the right ideological views. In 1914, for example, Otto Antrick asked Konrad Haenisch for suggestions, adding: 'I am looking for a left-wing comrade . . . We do not need a revisionist or worse, a politically wavering comrade.'[172] Another example of the intolerant attitude of the SPD leadership to the freedom of opinion of social democratic journalists is the explicit ban on SPD journalists from publishing in non-party journals and newspapers.[173] In the case of the SPD the left's inability to express its views in a party press, controlled by the apparatus, fostered its wartime split,[174] as well as the split of the early 1930s, when the Rosenfeld–Seydewitz group formed the SAP.[175]

Whenever the question of a Labour newspaper came up at conferences or elsewhere in the British labour movement, inevitably the example of the SPD would be mentioned. At the 1922 TUC conference Ben Tillett

[169] Loreck, *Wie man früher Sozialdemokrat wurde*, 66–73.

[170] Karl Kautsky, 'Der Journalismus in der Sozialdemokratie', *NZ* (1905–6), 218.

[171] Karl Kautsky, 'Die Freiheit der Meinungsäußerung', *NZ* (1905–6), 154.

[172] ZStA Potsdam, papers of Konrad Haenisch, 90 Ha 4, no. 5: letter from Otto Antrick to Konrad Haenisch, 6 Nov. 1914, p. 2.

[173] See the complaints about the ban by Friedrich Stampfer, 'Gewissensfragen', *NZ* 21 (1902–3), 825–7 and by Konrad Haenisch, ZStA Potsdam, papers of Haenisch, 90 Ha 4, no. 412: exchange of letters with Otto Wels about articles that Haenisch had written for a *bürgerlich* paper in Berlin.

[174] For the wartime conflict about the *Schwäbische Tagwacht* in Stuttgart and for the events surrounding the *Vorwärts* see Miller, *Burgfrieden und Klassenkampf*, 82–7 and 143–7.

[175] H. U. Ludewig, 'Die "Sozialistische Politik und Wirtschaft": Ein Beitrag zur Linksopposition in der SPD, 1923–1928', *IWK* 17 (1981), 14–41.

expressed his admiration for the German newspaper network: 'The German movement runs something like 75 if not something like 78 daily newspapers, and they are run exactly on the lines now proposed by the council. There is only this difference, that they are paying more in a week than we are asking you to pay in six.'[176] In 1925, responding to a questionnaire from the Socialist International concerning the organization of the Labour press in all member countries, Hamilton Fyfe, the editor of the *Herald*, wrote: 'We should particularly like to have in writing information from our German colleagues regarding the co-ordinated efforts of the Social Democratic Party . . .'.[177]

Throughout this period the Labour Party struggled to support one national Labour daily. Until 1915 the undercapitalized *Daily Citizen* served the purpose, but it made heavy losses before the war and was forced to cease publication in 1915.[178] After the war the hopelessly undercapitalized *Daily Herald*, an independent Labour daily from 1912 to 1919, founded and run by George Lansbury, ran into financial trouble, and Lansbury tried to save it by inducing the labour movement to take over responsibility for it.[179] It finally did so in 1922, when the paper became the joint property of the General Council of the TUC, the Executive of the Labour Party, and shareholders (mainly trade unions).

Yet, throughout the following years it continued to produce heavy losses and the labour movement became more and more reluctant to finance what seemed a bottomless pit. In 1928/9 the Labour Party's shares were transferred to the TUC and in 1930 the TUC decided to hand over the financial responsibility for the *Herald* to a private firm, Odhams, retaining the political control over the paper, including the appointment of the editor. Finally the newspaper began to make profits. As the Labour Party actively campaigned for new subscriptions, the circulation rose to 1,500,000 and a separate northern edition came out in Manchester.[180] If the Labour Party faced difficulties in setting up a national daily, it should be remembered that the SPD never had a national

---

[176] *Report of the Annual Conference of the TUC in 1922*, 95.

[177] IISG, Amsterdam, SAI files 950/1, p. 5.

[178] For the failure of the *Daily Citizen*, rooted in limited financial resources, lack of commitment, and the impact of the First World War see Tomoko Ichikawa, 'The Daily Citizen, 1912–1915: A Study of the First Labour Daily Newspaper in Britain' (University of Wales MA 1985).

[179] For the post-war development of the *Herald* up to 1924 see generally McKibbin, *Evolution*, 221–34. For a thoughtful comparison of the *Herald* and the *Citizen* see Deian Hopkin, 'The Socialist Press', *SSLH* 44 (1982), 8 f.

[180] For details of the campaign see *Labour Organizer* (Jan. 1930), 2–8.

daily of its own. In fact, all the dailies of the SPD taken together had roughly similar circulation figures as the *Herald* in the 1930s. Furthermore, other papers, more loosely connected with the labour movement fared better. There was the ILP's *Labour Leader* which became the *New Leader* in 1925. In that year George Lansbury founded a new left-wing journal, *Lansbury's Labour Weekly* which merged with the *New Leader* two years later. The *Clarion*, founded in 1891, was the paper of the Clarion movement which, in its heyday, had a circulation of 70,000 a week. *Reynolds' Newspaper*, founded by the chartist G. W. M. Reynolds in 1850 and often connected in its later stages with the co-operative movement, could claim a mass circulation of over 300,000 already in the 1860s. The left-wing intellectual papers, like the *New Statesman*, founded by the Fabians in 1913, and *Tribune*, founded in 1937, quickly gained recognition also outside the narrow boundaries of the movement. The ILP even owned four very profitable printing presses.[181]

Besides these national papers, there was a remarkable number of provincial journals.[182] Most of them existed only for a limited amount of time, but the local parties relentlessly tried to provide their faithful with their own paper. As early as the 1870s a network of local Labour papers was successfully established.[183] In 1900 forty periodicals supported the LRC, and by 1915 a further 113 periodicals had been started. In the 1920s head office regarded the provincial Labour press as a more useful propaganda vehicle than the *Herald*. It assisted local party efforts by publishing a memorandum which gave advice and hints as to the costs and the organization of a local paper.[184] Will Henderson, the press secretary of the party, declared in 1922: 'The local weekly papers wield a far greater political influence than the dailies, especially in rural areas . . . '.[185]

One of the best examples of a thriving local Labour press before 1914 was Woolwich.[186] In 1899 the *Woolwich Labour Notes* were published and in 1901 the monthly *Woolwich Labour Journal* came out. In 1904 the latter was transformed into the weekly *Woolwich Pioneer* which ceased publication in 1922. The *Pioneer* was printed on the local party's own printing

---

[181] Pat Francis, 'The Labour Publishing Company, 1920–1929', *HWJ* 18 (1984), 120.

[182] For lists of local papers in the 1920s see the *Labour Organizer*.

[183] For these early efforts see Aled Jones, 'Local Labour Newspapers', *SSLH* 44 (1982), 7 f.

[184] *Labour Organizer* (Mar. 1924), 11.

[185] W. W. Henderson, 'The Press and Labour', *Labour Organizer* (Apr. 1922), 7.

[186] See for the Woolwich Labour press before 1914 Thompson, 'London Working-Class Politics', 441 f. and 456 f.

press, which was also at the disposal of other local Labour Parties who wanted to use its service. The example of the Woolwich press makes the difficulties of the Labour press in Britain clear: reluctance of local trades- men to advertise and shifting party sympathies in the constituency. There was no national advertisement bureau like the Inseraten Union GmbH which would supply the papers with advertisements, and party members did not have to subscribe to the local newspaper as most of their German comrades were expected to do. Without that, even in a model constitu- ency like Woolwich, the paper was only kept alive by subsidies from rich sympathizers such as Joseph Fels.

With a view towards overcoming such financial difficulties through closer co-operation between papers, Will Henderson advertised plans to hold local Labour newspaper conferences. The setting up of regional centres from which a number of journals could be run would ease the financial burdens of a Labour paper.[187] Furthermore, the *Labour News* service was established at head office in 1920. Its task was analogous to the *Sozialdemokratischer Pressedienst*. It was primarily to inform the local papers about the activities of the national movement and about national politics, but by 1924 only thirteen local parties were using the *Labour News*. In 1926 the news service was abandoned. There were other attempts in the 1920s to bring about some sort of centralization of the provincial press: Will Chamberlain, editor of the Birmingham *Town Crier*, for example argued: 'With up-to-date Labour printing establishments in Lon- don, Manchester, the Midlands and South Wales, the possibilities of the extension of the Midland scheme over the whole of the country are enormous.'[188] These promising paths were not further explored and most of the experiments broke down already in the 1920s. The inward-looking approach of many local Labour Parties was not, as in the case of the SPD, broken by a powerful regional party which could have organized co- ordinating measures, such as newspaper editorial conferences and staff conferences. Certainly the local Labour Press, unlike the *Herald*, could at no time mobilize a mass readership.[189] Some local parties were even obliged to advertise their programmes and meetings in the local capitalist press.[190]

[187] *Labour Organizer* (Jan. 1921), 1 and 6; *Labour Organizer* (June 1921), 17 f.

[188] W. J. Chamberlain, 'The Provincial Labour Press Problem: How it May Be Solved', *Labour Organizer* (June 1921), 24.

[189] Deian Hopkin, 'The Labour Party Press', in Brown, *The First Labour Party*, 106 and 124.

[190] *Labour Organizer* (Mar. 1921), 2.

The unsuccessful efforts to establish an effective news service for the local party press, and the overall failure to centralize the local press effectively, also meant that the Labour press in Britain remained much more diversified and at the same time localized than its German counterpart. The more centralized and homogeneous the party press was, the greater was the danger that the press was to become a means by which party leaders could rule autocratically.[191] Some of the bigger national papers, like the *Citizen*, showed a striking similarity to the German socialist papers. Lack of discussion was one of their most distinctive features. The *Labour Leader*, for example, after it ceased to be the personal property of Keir Hardie, became the mouthpiece of the National Administrative Council of the ILP in the first decade of the twentieth century and by and large reflected the leadership's views on politics.[192] Yet the local Labour Party press remained largely free from national interventions. Here grassroots feelings could not be bullied and streamlined, as they could by regional press commissions in the case of the SPD.

As well as a press both parties tried to set up publishing houses. The Dietz publishing house in Berlin published the party's books, pamphlets, and leaflets. More than 60 million pieces of literature were distributed in 1929 alone.[193] Nothing as huge as the Dietzverlag existed in Britain. One of the most remarkable efforts of the Labour Party to create something similar led to the foundation of the Labour Publishing Company which lasted from 1920 to 1929, when financial and distributional problems put an end to it.[194] It was only in the 1930s that another effort was made to set up some sort of publishing house for Labour. This time it did not come from the labour movement itself, but from an individual publisher with socialist convictions, Victor Gollancz, who established the Left Book Club in 1932. Once again, it proved to be a financial failure (if certainly a great success in other ways), and was just kept alive by the financial genius of Gollancz, who made his money with other books.[195]

Both the British and the German working-class parties wanted a strong

[191] For the SPD this aspect of a centralized press has been stressed by Michels, *Zur Soziologie*, 125–31; Nipperdey, *Die Organisation*, 321 f. Kurt Laumann, 'Organisation und Apparat' in Franz Bieligk (ed.), *Die Organisation im Klassenkampf* (Frankfurt am Main, 1967, 1st edn. Berlin, 1931), 147 f., Maehl, *The German Socialist Party*, 222 and Schorske, *German Social Democracy*, 201.

[192] T. G. Ashplant, 'The Working Men's Club and Institute Union and the ILP', (University of Sussex Ph.D. 1983), 186.

[193] Hunt, *German Social Democracy*, 51.

[194] Francis, 'The Labour Publishing Company', 115–23.

[195] Sheila Hodges, *Gollancz: The Story of a Publishing House, 1928–1978* (London, 1978), 117–143.

and lively press in order to influence their membership and have a public voice with which to speak to the electorate. However, despite considerable efforts, both parties' successes remained limited. The SPD papers never even reached the majority of SPD voters, whilst the Labour Party struggled nationally and locally to uphold its papers. It is sometimes assumed that the Labour Party's press empire remained comparatively weaker than that of the SPD, because sport and entertainment was not so important to the German worker, or, conversely, because the German worker was much more politicized than his British counterpart. Ross McKibbin, for example, has argued that 'the Labour leaders . . . seriously overestimated the part that politics normally played in the lives of the British working classes. Britain was not Germany: the British working class was enmeshed in its national culture in a way the German working class was not.'[196] Yet working-class culture and labour movement culture should not be mixed up. The people involved in the labour movement of Britain and German were probably equally politicized, and the working class of Britain and Germany was probably equally uninterested in politics and 'enmeshed in its national culture'. There is little evidence that either the British or the German working class at large read the socialist papers.

The Labour press in Britain certainly suffered more from lacking centralization and finance. Most papers were issued before problems of production, costs, and distribution had been properly thought out. Amateurism prevailed in the running of Labour newspapers and the conditions under which, nationally and locally, Labour newspapers were produced, were astonishingly bad.[197] Additionally the politically fragmented character of the movement has to be taken into account. A unified Labour Party did not exist. There were several socialist societies and many trade unions which were loath to loose control over their own independent press.[198] Hamilton Fyfe, in 1923/4 criticized, above all, the lack of centralization within the Labour press in Britain.[199] However, the most important reason for the difficulties of the Labour Party's press was the degree of concentration that mass publishing had achieved in Britain. The localized character of the German press was important for

[196] Ross McKibbin, 'Why was there no Marxism in Britain?', *EHR* 99 (1984), 234.

[197] W. J. Chamberlain, 'The Provincial Press Problem', *Labour Organizer* (June 1921), 21–4 and (July 1921), 12–14. H. M. Richardson, 'The Press Problem: How Labour Should Tackle it', *Labour Magazine*, 1 (1922–3), 102 f.

[198] Deian Hopkin, 'The Labour Party Press', Brown, *The First Labour Party*, 105.

[199] Hamilton Fyfe, 'Our Most Urgent Task Today', *Labour Magazine*, 2 (1923–4), 493.

the stability of the SPD's newspapers. There were no national papers in Germany like the *Daily Mail* or *The Times* (many Germans read local papers which also carried the major national and international news).[200] The development of a national 'yellow' press in Britain from the middle of the nineteenth century onwards successfully targeted the working-class market for newspapers. The sales figures of the popular press exploded in Britain between 1850 and 1880: a 33 per cent increase between 1816 and 1838, a 70 per cent increase between 1836 and 1856, and a 600 per cent increase between 1856 and 1882 meant that at the end of the nineteenth century there was simply no market into which non-mass-circulation Labour newspapers could have expanded with relatively little capital investment.[201] Labour newspapers could therefore only be successful either if they adhered to certain key features of the new popular press,[202] or if they decided to be designed for a very particular audience in the manner of a weekly like the *New Statesman*. Yet even in the latter case, the paper could only survive its first years through the generosity of some of its financiers.[203] Despite these 'peculiar' difficulties of the British Labour press, it has been shown that it reached an impressive scope and variety. It was smaller in scope, but more diverse in character than the regimented SPD press, which had its own difficulties (most notably of enlarging its circulation) despite being regarded as a model by many Labour Party leaders.

3.6. The relationship between the leaders and the rank and file of the working-class parties of Britain and Germany

So far in this chapter processes of organization-building within the Labour Party and the SPD have been compared. These processes were combined with a certain degree of centralization and bureaucratization

[200] Modris Eksteins, 'The German Democratic Press and the Collapse of Weimar Democracy' (University of Oxford D.Phil. 1970), 26–42. For Britain see Lucy Brown, 'The Growth of a National Press', in Laurel Brake, Aled Jones, and Lionel Madden (eds.), *Investigating Victorian Journalism* (London, 1990), 133: 'There can be no doubt, on any definition, that by the 1890s the British press operated on a national scale.'

[201] Hugh Cunningham, *Leisure in the Industrial Revolution, c.1780–1880* (London, 1980), 176.

[202] Deian Hopkin, 'The Left-Wing Press and the New Journalism', in Joel H. Wiener (ed.), *Papers for the Millions: The New Journalism in Britain, 1850s to 1914* (New York, 1988), 225–42.

[203] Edward Hyams, *The New Statesman: The History of the First 50 Years, 1913–1963* (London, 1963), 75 f.

in both parties. From this observation, many past observers, the most famous of whom were Lenin and Michels, have concluded that such developments opened up a gulf between the leadership of the party and its rank and file. The party leaders became a kind of political labour aristocracy who—in their everyday reality—showed themselves more and more removed from the social experiences of workers who formed the majority of the party's ordinary members. It is to this immensely influential hypothesis that attention is turned in the present section.

Party leaders on a local, regional, or national level seem to have had a very similar social background to the party's rank and file in the Labour Party and the SPD. For the SPD Susanne Miller has published statistical material about the social background of MPs in the Reichstag and the Bavarian, Prussian, and Saxon Landtage at the beginning of the Weimar Republic. Most of the MPs were trained as skilled workers. Metal workers, wood workers, and building workers were especially prominent. Few academics and white-collar workers could be found among them. As the SPD was largely a party of skilled workers, there was a relative social homogeneity between leaders and rank and file.[204] Her findings are confirmed by Eberhard Kolb's study of the SPD members in the central council in 1918/19. According to him they can be taken—with some caution—as representative for the middle ranks of social democratic leaders. They were nearly all (84 per cent) from the working classes, mainly skilled workers with very little school education.[205] In the case of the Labour Party, its leaders were—with few exceptions (mostly Liberal converts)—equally working class (notably MacDonald, Henderson, Glasier, Hardie) or lower middle class (Alfred Salter, Herbert Morrison) in origin.[206] It has even been argued that it was because of their working-class origins that they were so unwilling to accept middle-class tutelage in any form and rejected Marxism largely out of distrust for socialist middle-class theoreticians.[207] Autobiographies of party activists almost always contain proud references to their working-class roots. So George

---

[204] Miller, *Die Bürde der Macht*, 459–66 refutes the claims of Bronder that the leadership of the SPD was of 'predominantly middle-class character'. See Bronder, 'Organisation', 5. Bronder's statistical material is not very well chosen, so that it is very likely to carry many misinterpretations about the social democratic leadership.

[205] Eberhard Kolb, 'Zur Sozialbiographie einer Führungsgruppe der SPD am Anfang der Weimarer Republik: Die Mitglieder des Zentralrats 1918/1919', in *Herkunft und Mandat: Beiträge zur Führungsproblematik in der Arbeiterbewegung* (Frankfurt am Main, 1976), 102.

[206] Hobsbawm, *Worlds of Labour*, 69 f. Stephen Yeo, 'A New Life: The Religion of Socialism in Britain, 1883–1896', *HWJ* 4 (1977), 26. Pierson, *British Socialists*, 20 f.

[207] McKibbin, 'Why was there no Marxism', 324–6.

Hodgkinson starts his memoirs: 'My family and social roots are in the working class, with no other desire or ambition than to rise with it.'[208]

However, even if leaders and led had similar social backgrounds, this does not necessarily mean that they continued to have similar social experiences and life-styles. Ellen Wilkinson in her novel *Clash* saw the consequences of bureaucratization as a process of class alienation: 'if [a working class leader] is too rebellious to be collared as a foreman by the boss, the men make him an official and he steps right out of their class.'[209] Processes of bureaucratization and centralization progressively diminished the contact between leaders and rank and file. Less direct contact did not necessarily mean, however, that the rank and file did not have the same interests as the leadership. The old Leninist idea of a political labour aristocracy tends to exaggerate the distance between the party official and the rank and file.[210] Many studies of the German SPD conclude that there is little evidence for severe conflicts between leaders and led.[211] Alan Bullock, writing about Ernest Bevin, could have written for the larger part of working class leaders: 'From beginning to the end of his career he saw himself as the representative of the class from which he sprang . . . ordinary working men and women . . . were "my people" and he understood and felt their problems as his own.'[212]

The distrust of paid officialism which prevailed in both parties demonstrated time and again how far Labour leaders were from perceiving themselves as 'labour aristocrats'. Ramsay MacDonald, for example, agreed to take up the position of secretary of the LRC in 1900, although this post was not connected with a salary of any kind until 1902. And Bruce Glasier, in a heated debate about his abilities as editor of the *Labour Leader* on the 1909 ILP conference, stated: 'He did not want anyone to suggest that the paper was not well edited because the editor was not well paid. . . . He was not in the movement to earn money—(applause) . . .'[213] Herbert Morrison was at great pains to stress similar sentiments in his autobiography when recalling his early work for the party: '. . . I enjoyed

---

[208] Hodgkinson, *Sent to Coventry*, 1.

[209] Wilkinson, *Clash*, 272.

[210] John Breuilly, 'The Labour Aristocracy in Britain and Germany: A Comparison', *SSLH* 48 (1984), 58–71, esp. 67. See also the extended version of the article in id., *Labour and Liberalism*, 26–75, esp. 58–62.

[211] Breitmann, *German Socialism*, 7; Roth, *The Social Democrats*, 261.

[212] Alan Bullock, *The Life and Times of Ernest Bevin*, i: *Trade Union Leader, 1881–1940* (London, 1960), 367.

[213] *Report of the Annual Conference of the ILP in 1909*, 58.

working for nothing, and I would have done the whole job without payment, if I could have afforded it. After all, the Movement depended on the coppers of ordinary people.'[214] Feelings of resentment against any kind of paid officialism ran high in the Labour Party. George Lansbury, for one, recalled that the independence from party officials was one of the most important motives for setting up the *Daily Herald* before the First World War: 'We believed, and I still believe, that all such movements as ours need the stimulus which independent thought and expression alone can give. Officialism always dries up initiative and expression.'[215] Although organizational handbooks of the SPD stressed that payment of officials might be necessary in order to guarantee some sort of continuity in office-holding and work for the party it is indicative that Bebel in 1911 vetoed Otto Braun's becoming chairman of the executive, as Braun would have to be paid.[216] The stress on voluntary work and personal sacrifice in the service of 'the great movement' was similarly upheld in both Labour Party and SPD.

If the relations between leaders and rank and file in the Labour Party and the SPD cannot be defined in terms of the evolution of a 'labour aristocracy', two trends can be detected. The rank and file expressed at times distrust, but were overwhelmingly loyal to their leaders. The leaders themselves had a more profound distrust of the rank and file and often tended to monopolize all activities in their own hands. In Germany and Britain it was especially the party left—frustrated for being unable to achieve dominance within the party—who wished to make distrust of leadership essential. For the German party left Fritz Bieligk in an influential article on the shortcomings of the SPD's organization wrote: 'The basis of any democratic organization has to be not confidence, but distrust.'[217] And in Britain James Maxton spoke against 'great men' theories declaring that 'our movement knows and needs no giants'.[218] Distrust in any form of leadership can also be found in Robert Blatchford, who unsuccessfully sought to eliminate permanent executive officers in the ILP and who spoke up for stronger rank and file participation in the

[214] Herbert Morrison, *An Autobiography* (London, 1960), 73.

[215] Lansbury, *Miracle of Fleet Street*, 1. For further evidence of the critical attitude of many British socialists towards a paid party bureaucracy see Duncan Tanner, 'Ideological Debate in Edwardian Labour Politics: Radicalism, Revisionism and Socialism', in Biagini and Reid, *Currents of Radicalism*, 283 f.

[216] Georg Kotowski, *Friedrich Ebert: Eine politische Biographie* (Wiesbaden, 1963), 171.

[217] Bieligk, 'Die Entwicklung der sozialdemokratischen Organisation', in id., *Die Organisation*, 78.

[218] Quoted from Fenner Brockway, *Inside the Left* (London, 1942), 186 f.

branches.[219] Similar notions of more 'direct' democracy were at the heart of what Stephen Yeo has called 'primitive democracy' at the grass roots of British Labour.[220]

The leaders of the Labour Party and the SPD in turn frequently voiced their opinion that the rank and file should behave loyally to its elected leaders. At the 1924 conference of the SPD, a resolution which planned to give paid party officials no voting rights, so as to increase the rank and file influence on conferences, was rejected after the *rapporteur* of the executive, Lipinski, had vigorously protested against such signs of distrust: 'The resolutions regarding the change of the revised statutes contained a notion of mistrust which is reminiscent of the slogan policy [*Parolenpolitik*] of the communists, aiming at the destruction of confidence in the leaders.'[221] Lipinski was probably underestimating the degree of loyalty that most rank and file felt towards their leaders. As the report of the 1925 district conference in Berlin-Lichterfelde read: 'The whole executive was re-elected by acclamation. This is a happy sign for the good co-operation between executive and officials and for the confidence that the executive enjoys.'[222] It has been shown for Dortmund and Remscheid how after 1905 decision-making shifted more and more from the active rank and file to the local party officials. It became increasingly difficult to control the local leadership's action effectively while at the same time the leadership developed a strong mistrust in all rank-and-file activity.[223]

Despite such leadership attitudes to the rank and file, expulsions from the SPD remained rare cases.[224] The leadership of the Labour Party seemed to have been less tolerant: it set up black lists of organizations which it was not willing to consider for affiliation.[225] After 1918 the right to exclude individual Labour Party members as well as the power of disaffiliation rested with the National Executive, which readily took action whenever it seemed necessary.[226] The party conference had to confirm the decision of the NEC, yet there never was a case in which it did not approve of an expulsion.[227] In the summer of 1925 twenty-three local parties were

---

[219] Fincher, 'The Clarion Movement', 198.

[220] Yeo, 'A New Life', 36.

[221] *Protokoll des SPD Parteitags 1924*, 142.

[222] 'Report about the district conference in Lichterfelde', *Vorwärts*, 10 July 1925.

[223] Ralf Lützenkirchen, *Der sozialdemokratische Verein für den Reichstagswahlkreis Dortmund-Hörde* (Dortmund, 1970), 148, Lucas, *Zwei Formen*, 230.

[224] Fricke, *Handbuch*, i. 292.

[225] Cole, *A History*, 214.

[226] McKenzie, *British Political Parties*, 521.

[227] Miliband, *Parliamentary Socialism*, 59 ff.

disaffiliated, mostly on reasons of Communist infiltration.[228] The LLP from 1925 onwards disaffiliated several organizations, mostly local parties in accordance with instructions received from the NEC of the party.[229]

In both parties, rank-and-file feelings of loyalty far outweighed feelings of distrust. Thousands would come to SPD public meetings with one of the national leaders as visiting speaker.[230] Despite an undeniable readiness of the SPD's rank and file to criticize their leaders in private, they attached the greatest importance to the public unity of the party. Their most scathing criticism was reserved for those party leaders, like Bernstein before 1914, who publicly threatened this party unity.[231] For Baden, it has been shown that the rank and file in local assemblies generally tended to support the regional party leadership.[232] Michels has argued that the strong confidence of the SPD rank and file in the leaders has to do with the extreme loyalty of the SPD leaders to the party. There were virtually no examples of leaders leaving the party to start a better career in a different one.[233] Feelings of loyalty to the leaders in both parties resulted furthermore partly from a feeling of affection and confidence in one's superiors, partly from a deeply rooted sense of solidarity within the movement, and partly from the character of individual leaders who established themselves in positions of authority. As Otto Buchwitz wrote in his memoirs: 'The masses of workers felt traditionally bound to the SPD or they were personally bound to local or district leaders, of whose personal integrity they were convinced.'[234] August Bebel and Keir Hardie were seen by many of their parties' followers as saviours who would free them from their present misery. The Labour Party's rank-and-file loyalty to the leaders was evident in the attitude of the constituencies to official candidates once they were properly selected and endorsed. No ordinary member would think of withdrawing support from such a candidate.[235] Their strong attachment to the party's leaders can also be seen from the fact that no demand seems to have ever been made that the leader should be elected by the mass party outside parliament rather than by the select circle of MPs.[236]

---

[228] Pelling, *A Short History*, 54.
[229] *Annual Report of the EC of the LLP* (1925 ff.).
[230] Guttsman, *The German Social Democratic Party*, 170.
[231] Evans, *Proletarians*, 136, 138, 140, 149.
[232] Brandt and Rürup, *Volksbewegung*, 55.
[233] Michels, *Zur Soziologie*, 101–25.
[234] Otto Buchwitz, *50 Jahre Funktionär der deutschen Arbeiterbewegung* (Düsseldorf, 1949), 107.
[235] Boughton, 'Working-Class Politics in Birmingham and Sheffield', 275.
[236] McKenzie, *British Political Parties*, 355.

The leaders of the Labour Party and the SPD to whom such loyalty was directed were often rather authoritarian personalities. David Clark has argued that strong leadership personalities like Chuter Ede in South Shields had a 'relationship with the local party [that] was almost akin to that of a paternalistic master to trusty retainers'.[237] Indeed, MacDonald, despite his rhetoric about the necessity of a democratic caucus 'saw the Labour leader as a pacemaker and a disciplinarian at the same time . . .'[238] Henderson has been portrayed as 'Labour's Bismarck',[239] and Hardie 'believed, with Carlyle, that history is made by great men, who can provide leadership for others'.[240] Victor Grayson, finally, has been described as 'the spark which set the fire alight. He inspired and infected the local supporters . . . Even now, after all those years, he is still a legend in the Colne Valley.'[241]

For the SPD Otto Wels was 'a perfect stereotype of a party boss',[242] whose pushy leadership style became influential also for the younger generation of party officials.[243] Philipp Scheidemann wrote about Friedrich Ebert: 'He was an autocrat . . . What he wanted done, he got done almost always, though not without a considerable rolling of his eyes.'[244] In Prussia Ernst Heilmann led the party in the 1920s in a style which can only be described as authoritarian.[245] There was a thread of continuity which runs from 'Emperor Bebel' through 'King Ebert' to the 'Red Czar of Prussia', Otto Braun.

The emphasis on strong leadership in both parties also meant that discipline came to be regarded as a high virtue. Party conferences organized by a party minority against policies represented by the party majority came to be seen as heresy in the SPD.[246] Friedrich Stampfer argued that there was no room for different factions within the SPD: 'There can only

---

[237] David Clark, 'South Shields Labour Party', in M. Callcott and R. Challinor (eds.), *Working-Class Politics in North-East England* (Newcastle upon Tyne, 1983), 101.

[238] Guttsman, *The British Political Elite*, 254. According to Guttsman, the history of the Labour Party saw the crystallization of a clearly defined party leadership and the development of traditional leader–follower relationships in the first decades of the 20th century.

[239] Kenneth O. Morgan, *Labour People. Leaders and Lieutenants: Hardie to Kinnock* (Oxford, 1987), 82.

[240] Pelling, *The Origins*, 220.

[241] David Clark, *Colne Valley: Radicalism to Socialism, 1890–1910* (London, 1981), 162.

[242] Hunt, *German Social Democracy*, 72 f.

[243] Brigitte Seebacher-Brandt, *Erich Ollenhauer: Biedermann und Patriot* (Berlin, 1984), 52 f.

[244] Scheidemann, *Memoirs*, i. 82.

[245] Peter Lösche, *Ernst Heilmann: Ein Widerstandskämpfer aus Charlottenburg* (Berlin, 1981).

[246] H. Ströbel, 'Sonderkonferenzen', *NZ* 30 (1911–12), 925–8.

be one single community amongst Social Democrats.'[247] For Karl Kautsky party discipline was the recipe for victory: 'In politics of today only the tactics of the 17th and 18th centuries' wars count, only the closed phalanx will win, which acts according to plan and is unified.'[248] Characteristically, almost all decisions of SPD institutions at all levels were unitary ones before 1914.[249] In the First World War the position of the local minority, left or right, was usually condemned for the breach of discipline involved. As the officials of a Berlin constituency argued in a 1916 resolution: 'any activity based on solidarity . . . is impossible, if every member or official of the party was allowed to act according to his own will against the resolutions and decisions of the majority.'[250] Social democratic conferences and meetings had long been characterized as lacking lively discussion. Adolf Braun wrote: 'The assembly without any discussion, that is the ideal for many chairmen.'[251]

Bernstein can serve as an example of what happened to individuals in the SPD who dared to go against party discipline. He became the target for vicious personal attacks from former party friends. Bebel wrote to Plekhanow in 1898: 'Kautsky and myself have made it very clear . . . that we do not regard him [Bernstein] as a party comrade any more . . . .'[252] Bernstein himself realized how important this intolerance was for the slow progress of his revisionist ideas within the party: 'what I personally find most sad is the fact that many brave, otherwise courageous comrades crack, as soon as it concerns party affairs. . . . the lies of the opponents throw everyone into the dirt who dares to talk against the authority of the party leaders.'[253] Klenke has shown for the SPD how little democratic theory the party had absorbed and how high its autocratic potential was.

---

[247] Friedrich Stampfer, 'Richtung und Partei', *NZ* (1905–6), 294.

[248] Karl Kautsky, 'Wahlkreis und Partei', *NZ* 22 (1903–4), 46.

[249] Dieter K. Buse, 'Party Leadership and the Mechanisms of Unity: The Crisis of German Social Democracy Reconsidered, 1910–1914', *Journal of Modern History*, 62 (1990), 485 ff.

[250] IGA/ZPA, SPD, PV, II, 145/6: protocol of the officials' conference of the constituency Teltow-Beeskow-Charlottenburg, 30 Jan. 1916, no. 50.

[251] Adolf Braun, *Gewerkschaftliche Betrachtungen und Überlegungen während des Weltkrieges* (Leipzig, 1915), 132 f. For the general tendency to discourage discussions after lectures and speeches 'as being just a nuisance' see Roth, *The Social Democrats*, 271. Yet Paul Göhre in his reports about the SPD organization stressed the fact that it was expected from workers attending assemblies to take a view and defend it. See Paul Göhre, *Drei Monate Fabrikarbeiter und Handwerksbursche* (Leipzig, 1891), 89–92.

[252] IGA/ZPA, papers of August Bebel, 22/132, nos. 95–6: letter from Bebel to Plekhanow, 30 Oct. 1898.

[253] IGA/ZPA, St. 22/28, no. 4: police report about a confidential interview of Berlin party officials with Eduard Bernstein in Berlin-Charlottenburg in 1909.

Anti-pluralistic tendencies could be found in the determination of the SPD to avoid intra-party conflicts, in its assumption of an essential identity of interest between leadership and rank and file and in its endless efforts to homogenize various interests within the party.[254]

The adherence to rigorous forms of party discipline can also be observed within the SPD Fraktion. Speeches and votes against a majority decision of the Fraktion were not allowed, and in fact did not occur before the First World War, when the movement split over the question of war credits. Of course, there was substantial dissent in the Fraktion, especially over questions of agricultural and foreign policy, but when it came to voting in parliament, such dissent never manifested itself in a split vote. There was no tradition in the SPD to see the individual MP as responsible only to his conscience. Quite on the contrary, the SPD MP was encouraged to see himself as part and parcel of a highly disciplined body carrying out the programme of the party as laid down by the party conference. In regard to the latter point, of course, there always remained considerable room for interpreting or even disregarding conference decisions.[255]

In contrast it has been observed: 'As a group, the PLP lacked discipline . . .'[256] The Labour Party's standing orders in fact included a so-called conscience clause which allowed MPs to express their disagreement with the majority of the PLP, or so dissenters would claim.[257] Already in 1907 the party conference dropped its demand that the MP should pledge himself to resign when he found himself in opposition to the majority of the PLP.[258] However, at the same time, a widespread belief could be found within the party that the party conference was a means of controlling the party leaders and ensuring that they would bow to conference decisions. The tension between the freedom of MPs from party interference and the demands of party discipline and the statutory right of party conference to impose binding manifestos on the party's leaders in Parliament remained unresolved long beyond the period under discussion here.

The Labour Party as a coalition between various socialist groups and trade unions badly needed tolerance, as there was a distinct lack of

---

[254] Dietmar Klenke, *Die SPD-Linke in der Weimarer Republik: Eine Untersuchung zu den regionalen organisatorischen Grundlagen und zur politischen Praxis und Theoriebildung des linken Flügels der SPD in den Jahren 1922–1932*, 2 vols. (Münster, 1983), 510–88.

[255] Hunt, *German Social Democracy*, 85.

[256] Guttsman, *The British Political Elite*, 229.

[257] Pelling, *A Short History*, 21.

[258] McKenzie, *British Political Parties*, 392 f.

ideological unity. Therefore party discipline was less rigorous than it was in the SPD. MacDonald found: 'the ordinary friction between a left and a right wing [was] a healthy and progressive malady which . . . was no sign of weakness but of growth'.[259] Such a statement contrasted sharply with those of Stampfer or Kautsky. Indeed, not only MacDonald stressed the virtues of pluralism within the party. Calls upon the local parties to avoid autocratic practices and keep intra-party discussion and democracy alive can be found in the pages of *Labour Organizer*[260] as well as in the writings of party theorists, like G. D. H. Cole and Harold Laski.[261] However, despite a greater willingness to tolerate dissent, the reality of local Labour Party life often did not stand up to such aspirations. Party discipline was regarded as essential: 'It was always a guiding principle that the Party is bigger than any individual in it, and loyalties held firm. . . . To go "agin the Group" is one of the deadly sins . . . a voluntary discipline [is established] the absence of which can endanger the very existence of the [council] group and the party.'[262] Leaders like George Lansbury certainly regarded the movement as their essential guiding light. Lansbury 'believed that the identity of the socialist candidate was secondary, that whoever was selected to stand was merely a representative of a movement which was greater than any individual.'[263] Others thought that discipline had not to be paid to the movement but to their own personalities. Bevin was regarded by many as a person who 'could not face opposition without losing his temper. . . . a dictator who shouted down his opponents'.[264] MacDonald and Cole themselves were known to be ill-tempered, to say the least, if they found themselves heavily criticized.[265] Beatrice Webb noted about Cole:

he has an absurd habit of ruling out everybody and everything that he does not happen to like or find convenient . . . Cole indulges in a long list of personal hatreds. The weak point of his outlook is that there is no one that he does not like except as a temporary tool; he resents anyone who is not a follower and has a contempt for all leaders other than himself . . .[266]

[259] Ramsay MacDonald, 'The ILP and the Labour Party', *SR* 15 (1918), 185 f.
[260] See for example *Labour Organizer* (Sept. 1927), 99.
[261] Adolf M. Birke, *Pluralismus und Gewerkschaftsautonomie in England: Entstehungsgeschichte einer politischen Theorie* (Stuttgart, 1978), 191–215.
[262] Hodgkinson, *Sent to Coventry*, 104 and 127. Also G. W. Jones, *Borough Politics: A Study of the Wolverhampton Town Council, 1888–1964* (London, 1969), 163–70.
[263] Jonathan Schneer, *George Lansbury* (Manchester, 1990), 37.
[264] Alan Bullock, *Ernest Bevin*, i. 364.
[265] For MacDonald see Hamilton Fyfe, *Sixty Years of Fleet Street* (London, 1949), 195, for Cole see A. J. P. Taylor, 'Bolshevik Soul in a Fabian Muzzle', in id., *Politicians, Socialism and Historians* (New York, 1982), 170.
[266] *The Diaries of Beatrice Webb*, ed. by Norman and Jeanne MacKenzie (London, 1984), iii. 222 f.

It has been argued that both the attitudes of leadership to the rank and file as well as the attitudes of rank and file towards the leadership were remarkably similar in Labour Party and SPD. There was no big social gap between leaders and rank and file in either party. On the one hand there was a development in both parties towards a situation where the leaders demanded loyalty and discipline (and largely got it). On the other hand the leadership remained distrustful of the rank and file, thus reflecting the high authoritarian potential in both parties.

3.7. Party and trade unions in Britain and Germany

A comparison between the organization of the Labour Party and the SPD would hardly be complete without considering the role of the trade unions in the life of the parties. Trade unions were closely allied with the working-class parties in Britain and Germany. Whereas the foundation of trade unions preceded the existence of any working-class political party in Britain, the development of trade unions and working-class party in Germany was a parallel process. Since the SDAP in Germany helped to set up trade unions in the 1860s, party activists often saw trade unions as prep schools for socialism. In 1898 Kautsky maintained that the SPD had the leading role in the class war and the trade unions were just supplementary organizations, while Eduard Bernstein in 1901 called the SPD the highest institution in the labour movement.[267] However, since the 1890s the socialist trade unions under Carl Legien successfully steered a more independent course. The trade unions became equal partners by the Mannheim agreement of 1906 and in the debates about the mass strike and May Day activity they managed to hold their own against the party.[268]

At the beginning of the First World War the free trade unions set the pace for the labour movement's reaction to the war in calling for an industrial truce, before the party had even made up its mind on how to react. As Susanne Miller argued, the party objectively could not do much

---

[267] Rolf Thieringer, 'Das Verhältnis der Gewerkschaften zu Staat und Parteien in der Weimarer Republik: Die ideologischen Verschiedenheiten und taktischen Gemeinsamkeiten der Richtungsgewerkschaften. Der Weg zur Einheitsgewerkschaft' (University of Tübingen Ph.D. 1954), 30. It should be noted here that U. Engelhardt, *'Nur vereinigt sind wir stark': Die Anfänge der deutschen Gewerkschaftsbewegung 1862/63–1869/70* (Stuttgart, 1977) has stressed against older views that German trade unionism developed out of local initiatives quite independently from political groups. He has been criticized for going too far in discounting the influence of political groups on the creation of trade unions by Christiane Eisenberg, *Deutsche und englische Gewerkschaften: Entstehung und Entwicklung bis 1878 im Vergleich* (Göttingen, 1986), 138–91.

[268] See for example the programmatic and symptomatic defiance of party superiority by Ludwig Rexhäuser, *Gewerkschaftliche Neutralität* (Leipzig, 1908).

else but share in the trade union policy of *Burgfrieden*.[269] In the war the outlook and policy decisions of the SPD were more and more determined by the politics of the trade unions.[270] In 1915, in the midst of the SPD's quarrels about the war credits, Paul Umbreit, the editor of the unions' journal *Correspondenzblatt*, wrote self-confidently: 'the trade unions are the party and the majority of the German working-class will follow their word.'[271] And Carl Legien in the same year called on trade union officials to participate actively in SPD organizations, in order to achieve a stronger 'trade unionization' of the party.[272]

The split in the German labour movement during the war forced the unions to declare their formal neutrality at their 1919 Nurenberg congress. After party unity had been lost the rifts between USPD and MSPD were also visible in the ADGB, and it remained the prime aim of the union leadership to maintain its unity. In their own interest the trade unions helped to bring about the reunification of the right wing of the USPD with the MSPD in 1922.[273] In the Weimar Republic the trade unions stressed their independence from the SPD more than ever, while simultaneously trying to increase their power within the party.[274] From 1923 to the Great Slump both organizations worked closely together. In the elections of 1924 the ADGB called on its members to vote for the reunited SPD.[275] In the economic depression relations soured. The financial programmes of ADGB and SPD differed, with the ADGB favouring quasi-Keynesian economics and the SPD more traditional deflationary policies. The trade unions were prepared to cut their ties to Social Democracy, in order to come to an agreement with the political right, notably with von Schleicher.[276]

In Britain socialist societies at the end of the nineteenth century had not managed to build up a mass membership of their own. Keir Hardie therefore turned to the unions for support. The prime task of the socialists, as he and most of his fellow ILPers perceived it, was to lure away the trade unions from their long-standing Liberal allies. In 1900 the socialist efforts were rewarded by the foundation of the LRC. The pre-war years were dominated by Labour's success in winning more trade union support

---

[269] Miller, *Burgfrieden und Klassenkampf*, 48 f.
[270] S. Neumann, *Die Parteien der Weimarer Republik* (Stuttgart, 1965), 32 f.
[271] Paul Umbreit, 'Die Gewerkschaften in der Arbeiterbewegung', *SM* 21 (1915), 1231.
[272] ZStA Potsdam, papers of Carl Legien, 90 Le 6, 35: printed speech of Legien, 27 Jan. 1915.
[273] Winkler, *Von der Revolution*, 486–9.
[274] Heinrich Potthoff, *Freie Gewerkschaften 1918–1933: Der ADGB in der Weimarer Republik* (Düsseldorf, 1987), 217–37.
[275] Winkler, *Der Schein der Normalität*, 216.
[276] Lothar Erdmann, 'Nation, Gewerkschaften und Sozialismus', *DA* 10 (1933), 129–61.

for independent labour representation.[277] The statutory powers of the trade unions over the Labour Party were substantial. Trade unions could affiliate to the Labour Party and therewith gain voting rights at the party conference according to the number of their members who paid the political levy. This ensured trade union dominance of the party conferences, as the bulk of the membership of the Labour Party remained affiliated through the trade unions. The so-called block vote at conferences meant that union officials voted for the whole of their membership which subscribed to the political levy of their union. Consequently, if some of the important union leaders raised their hands at conference, the rest of the delegates from the constituencies could only look on helplessly. Trade union delegates also formed a majority on the NEC of the party ever since 1902; most of the Labour Party's money and not a few of its activists came from the unions. As the trade unions, furthermore, rejected a financially independent party, they funded about four-fifths of the Labour Party's MPs directly.[278] The dependence of many local Labour Parties on trade union money led to a situation where the local party was left bereft, if the unions suddenly decided to withdraw their support from a parliamentary contest.[279]

In some localities the union branches in the form of the trades councils were the party. The establishment of local Labour Parties after 1918 was often 'managed' by the trades councils.[280] Even before 1914 politically active trades councils were trying to get Labour representatives elected nationally and locally.[281] Often unions and their officials were decisive in setting up Labour Party branches, as in Bedford, Wolverhampton, Doncaster, Wansbeck, and the Rhondda.[282] Trades council secretaries have been described as 'quiet men dedicated to organization ... They ... never

---

[277] Chris Wrigley, 'Labour and the Trade Unions', in Brown, *The First Labour Party*, 129–57.

[278] Clegg, *A History of British Trade Unions*, ii. 354. It should be noted here that according to Miller, *Electoral Dynamics*, 10 only 24 per cent of all Labour candidates were trade union sponsored. The high success rate of those candidates who were trade union sponsored shows the importance of trade union sponsorship. In most cases it was the only means of adequate sponsorhip available to Labour candidates.

[279] *Labour Organizer* (Jan. 1921), 19, and ibid. (Dec. 1921), 6.

[280] McKibbin, *Evolution*, 240.

[281] David Unger, 'The Roots of Red Clydeside: Economic and Social Relations and Working-Class Politics in the West of Scotland, 1900–1919' (University of Texas, Austin Ph.D. 1979), 271–275.

[282] *Bedford Politics, 1900–1924*, published by the Bedfordshire Record Office (Bedford, 1986), 4; Jones, *Borough Politics*, 123 f.; Teanby, ' "Not Equal to the Demand" ', 62; Celia Minoughan, 'The Rise of Labour in Northumberland: Wansbeck Labour Party, 1918–1950', in Callcott and Challinor, *Working-Class Politics in North-East England*, 80. Chris Williams, 'Democratic Rhondda: Politics and Society, 1885–1951' (University of Wales Ph.D. 1991), 251–271.

faltered in their work for independent working class representation.'[283] Even well-organized local Labour Parties, like the ones in Woolwich and Barrow, stressed the importance of close co-operation between party and local trade unions.[284] The financial scheme of the London Transport Workers and affiliation schemes of other unions were of vital significance for the LLP, despite Morrison's effort to bring the local parties to the forefront of organization.[285] It was only after the 1927 Trade Union Act and under pressure from both Labour Party and TUC, which had become distrustful of trades councils as hotbeds of left-wing radicalism, that the councils lost some of their local political significance and a clearer separation of industrial and electoral organization was achieved.[286]

As in Germany, the trade unions set the pace for the pro-war commitment of the majority of the Labour Party. Despite the fact, however, that the 1918 constitution made the trade unions within the Labour Party even more powerful, the following years up to 1931 saw the party struggling free from its trade union mentors. Especially on the national level, MacDonald achieved almost universal recognition of the autonomy of party decisions from trade union influence. Already in 1918 he stressed his belief that the alliance between trade unionists and socialists, constituting the Labour Party, could not be one of domination: 'The ILP wishes the Party to be controlled by its active political elements rather than by its cash paying sections.'[287] MacDonald's view was representative of the mood within the ILP at the time, as it was during the war itself.[288] After 1918 such a view was not restricted to MacDonald. Herbert Morrison tried to draw attention to the vital importance of local party organization for the fortunes of the party at large, and warned: 'it is highly desirable that the Labour Party should become more and more a political party and beware of the danger of being a mere aggregation of economic

---

[283] Bernard Barker, 'The Anatomy of Reformism: The Social and Political Ideas of the Labour Leadership in Yorkshire', *IRSH* 18 (1973), 7. For close personal links between trades councils and local Labour Parties see also: Robert Baxter, 'The Liverpool Labour Party', 41; Edmund and Ruth Frow, *'To Make that Future Now': A History of the Manchester and Salford Trades Council* (Manchester, 1976), 70; Boughton, 'Working-Class Politics in Birmingham and Sheffield', 155.

[284] *Twenty-Five Years History of the Woolwich Labour Party*, 27. *Report and Balance Sheet of Barrow-in-Furness LRC*, 1905–6, in Labour Party Archive, Local Labour Party Files.

[285] Herbert Morrison, *Labour Party Organization in London* (London, 1930), 11–13.

[286] Alan Clinton, *The Trade Union Rank and File: Trades Councils in Britain, 1900–1940* (Manchester, 1977), 170 f. estimates that by 1939 three-quarters of trades councils recognized by the General Council were distinct industrial organizations.

[287] James Ramsay MacDonald, 'Outlook', *SR* 15 (1918), 8.

[288] *Report of the Annual Conference of the ILP, 1916*, 95 f.; *Report of the Annual Conference of the ILP, 1917*, 27.

interests.'[289] Even the old trade unionist Arthur Henderson tried to strike a precarious balance between trade unions and socialist societies within the Labour Party structure:

The big unions have their share of power in the Labour Party, but no more than their share . . . it must not be forgotten that their support is absolutely necessary to the party's existence. They are the bankers of the movement . . . But we also recognize that the party derives much of its influence from the men and women with energy, enthusiasm and ideas who compose the political side of the movement.[290]

Leading trade unionists recognized this and up to 1931 tended to restrict themselves to trade union activity. Even at the early Labour Party conferences, some attempt had been made to differentiate the business of the trade unions from that of the Labour Party. In 1907, for example, a statement of the standing orders committee recommended the deletion of all resolutions of a purely trade character. In 1913 a conference resolution was carried which demanded that the Labour Party should concentrate on more urgent and direct political questions.[291] In 1926 the winding up of the Joint Departments of TUC and Labour Party for research, information, publicity, and various other services indicated a further separation between the political and industrial wings of the movement.[292] After 1918 no permanent union official could become a Labour Party MP. What is more, union MPs accepted the leading role of the party in politics and saw themselves primarily as representatives of the constituency, not the union.[293] Although there were seven trade unionists in MacDonald's first Cabinet,[294] double membership of NEC and the TUC's parliamentary committee was not permitted. As a consequence only second- and third-class trade unionists sat on the NEC. These were only too willing to follow the parliamentary leadership.[295] A bond of confidence had developed between the leaders of the big unions and the parliamentary leadership of the party up to 1931. It was only the union's disappointment about MacDonald's defection in 1931 and the behaviour of ministers generally during the 1931 crisis that led to a renewed tightening

[289] Herbert Morrison, in *Labour Organizer* (June 1921), 1 f.

[290] Arthur Henderson, 'Labour Looks Ahead', *Daily Herald* (12 Jan. 1918), 5.

[291] R. T. Spooner, 'The Evolution of the Official Programme of the Labour Party, 1918–1939' (University of Birmingham MA 1949), 17 f.

[292] Cole, *A History*, 217.

[293] Andrew Taylor, *The Politics of the Yorkshire Miners* (London, 1984), 103.

[294] Clegg, *A History* ii. 364.

[295] McKenzie, *British Political Parties*, 519.

of trade union domination over the party.[296] At a joint meeting with the NEC of the Labour Party the TUC General Council made clear its view of the party as ultimately subordinate to the trade unions: 'the primary purpose of the creation of the party should not be forgotten. It was created by the trade union movement to do those things in Parliament which the trade union movement found ineffectively performed by the two-party system.'[297] As the trade unions never abandoned their potential power to control party policy through their majority on the NEC, they could force their views on the party in situations where they deemed this necessary. The relationship between unions and Labour Party was different at different times in the twentieth century. The unions had more or less influence according to specific historical circumstances, but there were always limits to union interference in the affairs of the Labour Party.[298]

Institutions, devised as control instruments of the unions over the Labour Party, remained inefficient in fulfilling their task. One such example was the National Joint Council, set up in 1921. It consisted of an equal number of representatives from the National Executive of the Labour Party, the PLP, and the General Council of the TUC. Every important decision was to be placed before it. Yet, in the 1920s the importance of the National Joint Council remained limited. The formulation of policy before the war had rested largely with the ILP and after the war it was the PLP who decided Labour policy, with the trade unions in both cases acting as a filter. Only measures which would seem directly contradictory to the vital interests of trade unionism, like the 1931 decision of the Labour government to cut unemployment benefits, were rejected. It was only after the 1931 split that the National Joint Council looked as if it might become more important. Now half of its members were directly appointed by the trade unions. Henceforth it was to meet at least once a month and it should be summoned in every crisis. Its statements of policy were to be issued regularly and regarded as binding. Yet in practice even then the National Joint Council did not do these things. It remained ineffective as an instrument of trade union control over Labour Party policy.

The German unions never accepted the division of labour between

---

[296] For the development from party emancipation to renewed trade union control between 1918 and 1931 see Martin, *TUC*, 132–243.

[297] Churchill College, Bevin Collection, Bevin 1/5: Minutes of Joint Meeting of the TUC General Council and the NEC of the Labour Party at Transport House, 10 Nov. 1931.

[298] Lewis Minkin, *The Contentious Alliance: Trade Unions and the Labour Party* (Edinburgh, 1991), especially chs. 2–4, 9–11, 16 and pp. 619–27.

unions and party to the same degree as their British counterparts did. On the contrary, once they had emancipated themselves from party dominance they were quick to formulate their own ideas and programmes and they tried to force these onto a reluctant SPD. Bebel unsuccessfully tried to delineate a functional division between trade unions and party. In his view the political work should be monopolized by the party, whereas the trade unions should concentrate on the economic work.[299] Contemporary German socialist observers in Britain called upon the SPD to follow the British labour movement, where such a division could be found.[300] Instead of the German trade unions heeding such calls, the SPD became involved in workplace organization. Although this was a side-show and the main field of the party's electoral activity remained the constituency,[301] campaigning was carried out even before the First World War by publishing factory newspapers, like *AEG Sender* and by officials trying to recruit new members at the workplace.[302] The SPD strove to set up workshop cells, so called *Betriebszellen*, after standing orders had been changed in 1918 to permit them.[303] Had the Labour Party tried the same thing, the unions would have objected strongly—and successfully.

If the division of labour between trade unions and working-class party was less clear cut in Germany than in Britain, the socialist unions in Germany had far less statutory, formal powers over the party organization than their British counterparts. Unlike Britain, trade unions in Germany could not affiliate to the working-class party. Corporate membership was unknown. There were no direct trade union delegates to the SPD conferences, no block vote, and no trade union representative sat on the executive, council, or control commission of the party. Yet, as in the case of the Labour Party, a substantial number of MPs were from trade unions: in 1912 one-third of all SPD MPs were trade union officials,[304]

[299] August Bebel, *Gewerkschaftsbewegung und politische Parteien* (Stuttgart, 1900).

[300] Balthasar Weingartz, 'Auf dem Weg zum britischen Imperium', *SM* 36 (1930), 878.

[301] Fricke, *Die deutsche Arbeiterbewegung*, 232.

[302] IGA/ZPA, St. 22/16, nos. 2 and 3: police report about a delegate assembly of the SPD Potsdam-Spandau-Osthavelland, 9 Dec. 1906, in which the question of factory organization and *Agitation* was discussed for several hours. For factory newspapers see: IGA/ZPA, Handbill Collection, V, DF VII, 471.

[303] IGA/ZPA, St. 12/103, 59: anonymous report to the Bremen police, 19 Mar. 1925 about the setting up of workshop cells by the SPD. See also reports about the setting up of workshop cells in *Volksbote* (Stettin), 166 (18 July 1918) and *Vorwärts*, 196 (19 July 1918) and *Volksstimme* (Frankfurt am Main), 169 (22 July 1918).

[304] A. Herzig, 'Das Verhältnis zwischen Sozialdemokraten und freien Gewerkschaften (1868–1914)', in H. W. von der Dunk and Horst Lademacher (eds.), *Auf dem Weg zum modernen Parteienstaat: Zur Entstehung, Organisation und Struktur politischer Parteien in Deutschland und den Niederlanden* (Melsungen, 1986), 161.

and this group hovered around 20 per cent in the Weimar Republic.[305] Unlike the trade union MPs in the Labour Party, the trade union MPs in the SPD self-confidently formed a bloc which made strong policy demands on the party as a whole.[306] Channels of communication were mainly of an informal kind. Private meetings and unofficial consultation between trade union and party leaders were common. Trade unionists and the right-wing of the SPD came to co-ordinate their actions before 1914. In the 1920s the trade union leadership would meet regularly every fortnight with leading figures of the SPD to discuss policy matters.[307] In that sense—of an alliance between the reformist wing within the SPD and the trade union leadership—Schorske is right when he speaks of a 'pattern of trade union conquest' of the party, according to which the trade union congresses stated their views and presented the party with *faits accomplis* which the party executive could only support.[308] Many party leaders of the SPD, like Bauer, Braun, Ebert, and Severing, came from the trade union movement and this further facilitated informal contacts. Wels and Leipart were frequent guests at the conferences of both ADGB and SPD in the 1920s. The need for communication between party and trade unions was widely accepted and the press functioned as an important medium for that communication.[309] The party and trade union executives discussed all political questions long before 1914, in order to find common ground for their policies. In the Weimar Republic, trade union leadership and party executive corresponded about all important policy issues. Nevertheless it was only in the latter Weimar years that both organizations agreed on an exchange of representatives to the meetings of the Bundesausschuß of the ADGB and the Parteiausschuß of the SPD. From then on Wels and Graßmann, the deputy leader of the ADGB, took part in the meetings of the leading organs of party and trade union so that actions could be better co-ordinated and misunderstandings avoided.[310] In fact, as early as 1908, the trade unions served as a model for the SPD, as their centralized and streamlined structure came to be adopted by the party.[311]

The unions supported the SPD mainly by giving financial aid, helping

[305] Gerard Braunthal, *Socialist Labor and Politics in Weimar Germany: The General Federation of German Trade Unions* (Hamden, Conn. 1978), 137.

[306] Ibid. 139.

[307] IGA/ZPA, papers of Paul Löbe, 110/110, 60.

[308] Schorske, *German Social Democracy*, 108 f.

[309] Braunthal, *Socialist Labor and Politics*, 120 f. ,

[310] Potthoff, *Freie Gewerkschaften*, 224.

[311] Wilhelm Dittmann, 'Zur Neugestaltung unserer Parteiorganisation', *NZ*, 17 (1908–9), 430 f.

it in election campaigns and making their advertising facilities and their press available to the party.[312] From the turn of the century the unions formed a 'reservoir of labour' which became the main recruiting ground for the SPD.[313] Besides maintaining their own workers' educational organizations and institutions in various towns, trade unions and SPD also worked closely together in their educational efforts in the 1920s. These became centralized in the workers' cultural cartels.[314] At times, as with the case of the youth organizations of trade unions and party before 1914, cooperation was replaced by rivalry.[315] The membership of trade union and party was widely overlapping. Two-thirds of the SPD membership were unionists and union officers often had a post in the party. About 65 per cent of union members voted for the SPD and up to 95 per cent of local union officials were active party members.[316] Equally there was often a marked overlap in the leadership of local SPD and trade union institutions.[317]

In some places after 1905 the local political initiative came from the unions rather than the party.[318] Paul Umbreit had already stressed the political role of local trades councils: they should strive to become a force in communal politics and set the tone for the local union/party relationship.[319] The trades councils (*Ortskartelle*) had informal links with the local SPD, but they were not directly represented in the local SPD organization. Yet many full-time officials and voluntary workers worked for the party and the union at the same time. Even if local trades councils were not so vitally important as they were for the Labour Party, they did play a role for local SPD parties as well.[320]

---

[312] Braunthal, *Socialist Labor and Politics*, 127.

[313] Guttsman, *The Social Democratic Party*, 154.

[314] Fritz Fricke, *Zehn Jahre gewerkschaftlicher Bildungsarbeit in Berlin: Die Berliner Gewerkschaftsschule* (Berlin, 1932), 15.

[315] W. Sollmann, 'Jugendausschüsse und Jugendabteilung der Gewerkschaften', *NZ* 28 (1909–10), 933–5.

[316] Hunt, *German Social Democracy*, 170.

[317] Faulenbach and Högl (eds.), *Eine Partei in ihrer Region*, 163 ff., 170 ff. and 198 ff.

[318] Kandler, 'The Effects', 265; Müller, 'Die groß-hannoversche Sozialdemokratie', 156 f.; Zeitz, *Zur Geschichte*, 17.

[319] Paul Umbreit, *Die Bedeutung und Aufgaben der Gewerkschaftskartelle* (Berlin, 1903).

[320] Maja Christ-Gmelin, 'Die württembergische Sozialdemokratie, 1890–1914', in Jörg Schadt and Wolfgang Schmierer (eds.), *Die SPD in Baden-Württemberg und ihre Geschichte: Von den Anfängen der Arbeiterbewegung bis heute* (Stuttgart, 1979), 110. Also Adelheid von Saldern, 'Sozialdemokratische Kommunalpolitik bis 1914' in K. H. Naßmacher (ed.), *Kommunalpolitik und Sozialdemokratie: Der Beitrag des demokratischen Sozialismus zur kommunalen Selbstverwaltung* (Bonn, 1977), 36. The importance of local union organization for the success of the SPD is also mentioned by ZStA Merseburg, Rep. 77, S No. 656, I, 4: police report to the Prussian interior minister about the anarchistic and social democratic movement, 15 Jan. 1898, p. 9. See also Michels, 'Die deutsche Sozialdemokratie I', 489–92.

In marked contrast to countries like the USA and France, where links between trade unions and working-class parties were weak, close common bonds connected trade unions and working-class parties in Britain and Germany. Within the existing historiography, there is nevertheless a tendency to stress the dependency of the Labour Party on the British trade unions, and, conversely, to emphasize the relative independence of the SPD from the socialist trade unions in Germany.[321] As has been argued above such a view has some justification, as the statutory powers of unions over working-class parties were indeed very different. However, given the lack of correspondence between statutory and real powers, such a straightforward comparison is misleading. It has to be stressed that the German unions—without having any statutory powers over the SPD—were influencing SPD policies substantially already before 1914. This can be seen in the SPD's attitude to May Day strikes, to the General Strike and to its own youth movement.[322] British unions' formal power over the Labour Party was immense, but—far from dominating Labour Party policy—they came to accept a certain degree of party autonomy in the political sphere.

3.8. Conclusion

By comparing the organizations of the Labour Party and the SPD it has been possible to show striking similarities between the two: in the first three decades of the twentieth century both were involved in building up strong party organizations. The establishment of the large bureaucratic apparatus of the SPD was undertaken after 1905 and, although enlarged in the Weimar Republic, it did not undergo major changes after 1918. The process of organization-building was deeply interwoven with the process of growing centralization of power, especially at the regional party level. The Labour Party also underwent a process of bureaucratization and centralization especially after its reorganization in 1918. Both parties in 1905 and 1918 respectively tried to streamline the organization into a more effective piece of machinery developing party institutions with broadly similar functions and remits. In the course of this the party

---

[321] See, for example, Günther Lottes, 'Der industrielle Aufbruch und die gesellschaftliche Integration der Arbeiterschaft in Deutschland und England im viktorianischen Zeitalter', in A. M. Birke and Kurt Kluxen (eds.), *Viktorianisches England in deutscher Perspektive* (Munich, 1983), 77; Luebbert, *Liberalism*, 164; Hodge, 'The Trammels of Tradition', 50–68, 132, 149, 202.

[322] Schorske, *German Social Democracy*, 88–115.

leadership tightened its grip on the parties with the party conference losing much of its former control function.

Contributing to the formation of leadership élites was the lethargy of many of the rank and file which found expression at the local level of organization. The few enthusiasts who carried out the tasks, often over a considerable time, should not be accused of having done so out of self-interest. Local Labour Parties, as well as the Labour Party press, have been shown to be more similar to their SPD counterparts than is usually perceived. Each party tried to build up its individual membership as its financial and organizational backbone. Local organizations were split into smaller sections, efforts were undertaken to keep party members in constant touch with party affairs, fees were collected more systematically, a system of national and provincial newspapers was built up, and members were increasingly integrated into a kind of working-class party subculture. Furthermore, strong links connected trade unions and working-class parties in both countries and the relationship between the rank and file and the party's leadership has been characterized as a mixture of hero-worshipping on the part of the former and authoritarian behaviour on the part of the latter. The increase of executive power at all levels of organization, the removal of political decision-making from local to regional and district parties, the control of the party press and the suppression of intra-party discussions, if necessary by the use of disciplinary measures, reflected a diminished degree of intra-party democracy in both parties. However, it should equally be mentioned, that both parties remained organized according to democratic principles from the bottom upwards. Overall, the strong similarities of party organization call into doubt the wisdom of dividing both parties into different categories.

However, it has also been established that the two parties were by no means exactly the same. The greater bureaucratization and centralization of the SPD organization on the regional level allowed the party to expand at an extraordinary rate after 1905. It helped to make its campaigning more efficient and increased the channels of communication with its rank and file. At the same time, however, political debates about specific political aims took second place. Every effort was made to extend and nurture the organizational network of the party, such as increasing membership and dues, expanding the party press, developing a more effective election machine, and keeping thorough statistics. Consequently many of the party officials were less knowledgeable on party theory and on strategies of legislative reform at municipal or national level than on how to run an organization effectively. The world of party officials remained centred around the life of the party and its ancillary organizations. It was only towards the end of the Weimar Republic that criticism of such exclusive emphasis on organization-building was voiced. Alexander Schifrin and Carlo Mierendorff both stressed the danger of a depoliticization of the party.[323]

The Labour Party, whose bureaucratization and centralization took place on a smaller scale and never resulted in quite the same homogeneous, unified party structure, was less at risk from the negative consequences of organization-building. It was less threatened by depoliticization and it geared its efforts to a greater extent towards policy-making. Its local organizations, including their local papers, were far more difficult to control from the national centre and enjoyed greater levels of autonomy than their German counterparts. At the same time remaining organizational weaknesses of the Labour Party had their roots in the unwillingness to regionalize the party effectively and in the failure to become more independent from trade union funding. The deficiencies of the Labour Party organization were recognized by its leading 'would-be' centralizers, of which Henderson and Morrison were prime examples.[324] In their efforts to develop a strong party press, an individual mass membership, and a strong party machine generally, they looked to the German SPD as a 'model'. As Tom Fox in his presidential address to the 1914 Labour Party conference said, the prime cause for the Labour Party's failure to get to substantial social progress lay in 'the deplorable inefficiency of our methods of organization . . . Our German brethren have learned their lesson better and are using their experience to better purpose in spite of the greater political handicap they have to bear.'[325] What they failed to realize was the limits of the organizational successes of the SPD which should not be judged on the basis of its electoral strongholds alone. On the whole, then, it can be said that organization-building was important for the success of the Labour Party and the SPD in mobilizing and sustaining a large percentage of the working-class vote. As shall be seen in the next chapter, the Labour Party and the SPD not only built strong electoral machines, they both developed a 'milieu' in which feelings of community and solidarity amongst party members could thrive.

---

[323] Henryk Skrzypczak, 'Führungsprobleme der sozialistischen Arbeiterbewegung in der Endphase der Weimarer Republik', in *Herkunft und Mandat*, 128–47.

[324] Morgan, *Labour People*, 82: 'Throughout the party machine, he [Henderson] introduced a new generation of young organizers, including Jim Middleton, Arthur Greenwood, William Gillies and his son Willie Henderson.'

[325] *Report of the Annual Conference of the Labour Party in 1914*, 91.

4
The Labour Party and the SPD
as Communities of Solidarity

IN her study of the SPD in Düsseldorf, Mary Nolan has argued: 'Only by exploring the interaction among work, community and culture can we explain the character of social democracy.'[1] Such explorations are meaningful only within the confines of local studies. In section 4.1. local conditions which led to strong working-class party communities in Britain and Germany will be compared. The idea that SPD local parties can be seen as tight communities of solidarity has been well developed by now in numerous local and regional studies.[2] The prevailing view of the Labour Party on the other hand still is that it failed to build up such a community after the First World War.[3] It will be shown that there were at least exceptions to that rule, and that the Labour Party might be understood as a smaller version of that wider SPD community of solidarity. Section 4.2. will compare what constituted such communities of solidarity: what were their activities, and what ancillary organizations served the needs and wants of party members? How similar or different were the Labour Party and the SPD communities?

4.1. Organizational strength as basis for community feeling

The use of the concept of 'community' for the labour movement has been attacked by David Crew. He has rejected the effort to understand the

---

[1] Nolan, *Social Democracy and Society*, 4 f.

[2] For Imperial Germany see Roth, *The Social Democrats*, 204 f.; Stearns, 'Adaptation', 223 f.; Steenson, *'Not One Man'*, 141 f. For the Weimar Republic, when the SPD's community culture is held to have reached its high point see Peter Lösche and Franz Walter, 'Zur Organisationskultur der sozialdemokratischen Arbeiterbewegung in der Weimarer Republik: Niedergang der Klassenkultur oder solidargemeinschaftlicher Höhepunkt?', *GG* 15 (1989), 511–36. See also Richard Saage (ed.), *Solidargemeinschaft und Klassenkampf: Politische Konzeptionen der Sozialdemokratie zwischen den Weltkriegen* (Frankfurt am Main, 1986) and, more critical, Hartmut Wunderer, 'Noch einmal: Niedergang der Klassenkultur oder solidargemeinschaftlicher Höhepunkt?', *GG* 18 (1992), 88–93.

[3] Stephen Yeo, 'Towards "Making Form of More Moment Than Spirit": Further Thoughts on Labour, Socialism and the New Life from the Late 1890s to the Present', in Taylor and Jowitt, *Bradford, 1890–1914*, 73–88.

organization of the labour movement as a community because of the high geographic mobility of workers, the impersonal workings of the market-place, and the fact that sentiments of community did not necessarily lead to collective action. Crew has argued that parties and unions were part of a mechanism of association which made up for the loss of community.[4] No doubt, membership turnover within the SPD was high (for the Labour Party there are no corresponding statistics), yet there was a core of committed workers in many constituencies which often did not change over years and which kept the network of organizations constituting a community alive.[5] True, the market-place worked impersonally, but that is one of the reasons why workers might have been more likely—at least in some places—to form communities at neighbourhood level rather than at workshop level.[6] True also, collective action did not necessarily result from sentiments of community, but they could result from such sentiments. Eric Hobsbawm, for one, has stressed that labour movements in Europe were particularly strong in 'smallish towns' where a spirit of community was strongly developed.[7] The article by Crew is no doubt an important counterblast to any kind of sentimentalization of Labour history and indeed, the idea of 'community' in its idealized Tönniesian version, with its obvious emotional connotations can be a dangerous one. Despite this, there can be little doubt that among organized workers in Britain and Germany feelings of solidarity, of common aims and interests, were strong. For lack of a better word we shall call such feelings of belonging 'community'.

G. A. Ritter has stressed the difficulty of saying anything definite about the conditions which enhanced or hindered the formation of strong working-class parties in Germany.[8] The same can easily be said for Britain. It is a commonplace that economic, political, and social factors all played important roles in the formation of working-class parties in Britain and Germany, but exactly what that role was is difficult to define.[9] Widely

---

[4] David F. Crew, 'Kommunen, Klasse und Kultur. Class and Community: Local Research on Working-Class History in Four Countries', in Klaus Tenfelde (ed.), *Arbeiter und Arbeiterbewegung im Vergleich: Berichte zur internationalen historischen Forschung* (Munich, 1986), 279–84.

[5] Klaus Tenfelde, 'Großstadt und Industrieregion: Die Ausbreitung der deutschen Arbeiterbewegung in Grundzügen', in Sabine Weiss (ed.), *Historische Blickpunkte: Festschrift für Johann Rainer* (Innsbruck, 1988), 700 has spoken of a 'regional-local elite' of the SPD.

[6] For Upper Franconia this has been shown by Kandler, 'The Effects', 173–5. For Preston see Savage, *The Dynamics*.

[7] Eric Hobsbawm, 'Labour in the Great City', *NLR* 166 (Nov.–Dec. 1987), 40.

[8] Ritter, 'Die Sozialdemokratie', 320.

[9] For an excellent review of local research into the problem in Germany, see Hartmut Zwahr, 'Die deutsche Arbeiterbewegung im Länder- und Territorialvergleich 1875', *GG* 13 (1987), 448–507.

differing local conditions leave the historian with a bewildering number of factors which contributed to the making of strong working-class parties. Generalizations about traits of *the* local Labour or SPD party are therefore subject to the caveat that there has been as yet too little research into local working-class parties in either country to say anything final, and that, therefore, the following treatment speaks of tendencies rather than established facts. In a comparison between two nations, the danger of 'harmonizing' the outlook of local parties according to 'national' characteristics is great.

Strong working-class parties in both countries emerged with the processes of industrialization and urbanization. Industrialization meant to many craftsmen loss of income and pauperization. Forming party associations was one way of reacting against such changes.[10] Not only artisans, but workers generally shared a sense of their vulnerability to the vagaries of the labour markets. In the long run, however, industrialization brought greater prosperity to most workers, and in times of industrial growth, organized workers managed to win substantial gains in their living standards. In that respect, periods of economic boom also indicate periods of labour movement expansion.

Industrialization in both countries also brought more and more people to the new urban centres. These people found themselves uprooted from their traditional rural working and living surroundings. It is firmly established by now that the SPD found it extremely difficult to mobilize the rural, agricultural workers.[11] For the Labour Party a series of reports in the *Labour Organizer* points in the same direction: 'At the present time it is utterly impossible to get an avowed adherent to Socialism in many villages . . .'.[12] The methods used in the Labour Party to win a more substantial foothold in the countryside were remarkably similar to those used in the SPD. First, propaganda was almost always co-ordinated by a special committee from an urban party stronghold.[13] Then a system of correspondents or sympathizers were set up in the villages who were provided with the working-class parties' paper free. Sunday tours were organized, often by the youth organizations on their bicycles, to

---

[10] Breuilly, *Labour and Liberalism*, 80.
[11] Brandt and Rürup, *Volksbewegung*, 35 f.; Tenfelde, 'Großstadt', 689, Ritter, 'Die Sozialdemokratie', 344 f.
[12] *Labour Organizer* (Sept. 1925), 20.
[13] Karl-Ernst Moring, *Reformismus und Radikalismus in der Sozialdemokratischen Partei Bremens von 1890 bis 1914* (Hamburg, 1968), 50 f.; IGA/ZPA, St. 12/101, vol. ii, nos. 119–23: reports about the systematic *Agitation* amongst the population in the countryside in Franconia; *Labour Organizer* (Dec. 1925), 4–6; George Dallas, 'The Labour Party and the Rural Areas', *Labour Magazine*, 6 (1927–8), 172–4.

distribute propaganda leaflets. Sometimes the SPD would set up heavily subsidized countryside weeklies, for which the Labour Party lacked funds. Wherever a group of socialists had been converted, however small, an organization was set up and regular party and public meetings were held. However, ultimately, those successes remained transient in both the Labour Party and the SPD.[14] Even if rural workers moved to the industrial cities, the working-class parties did not necessarily find easy converts in them.[15] It was only the second or third generation of industrial urban workers who became the backbone of working-class party strongholds in Britain and Germany.[16] Often medium-sized industrial towns or certain quarters within a big city with stable populations and a developed sense of neighbourhood became centres of organizational strength of both the Labour Party and the SPD.

The nature of industry and the resulting occupational structure in a particular town was also important for the strength of the labour movement. Industrial centres with a dynamic and expanding economy often produced strong working-class parties. Sheffield, Glasgow, Barrow-in-Furness, Düsseldorf, Hamburg, Frankfurt am Main, and a number of smaller towns in textile, metal, and mining districts in Saxony, the Rhineland, or South Wales were prime examples of such a correlation.[17] Certain occupations, like printers, miners, building and metal workers in Germany had a particularly high organizational potential and towns like Leipzig, where printers were numerous amongst the work-force, developed strong local labour movements.[18] On the other hand, mono-

---

[14] Geary, *European Labour Politics*, 23

[15] The difficulties of the SPD in mobilizing the first generation of rural workers in the cities have been emphasized by Tenfelde, 'Großstadt', 689, Ritter, 'Die Sozialdemokratie', 321. Werner Berg, *Wirtschaft und Gesellschaft in Deutschland und Großbritannien im Übergang zum 'Organisierten Kapitalismus': Unternehmer, Angestellte, Arbeiter und Staat im Steinkohlebergbau des Ruhrgebiets und von Süd-Wales, 1850–1914* (Bielefeld, 1980), 810.

[16] For the SPD see Faulenbach and Högl (eds.), *Eine Partei in ihrer Region*, 78, Tenfelde, 'Großstadt', 698. For the Labour Party see Hobsbawm, 'Labour in the Great City'. Also David Howell, *British Workers and the ILP, 1888–1906* (Manchester, 1983), 278.

[17] Unger, 'The Roots of Red Clydeside', p. iv; Boughton, 'Working-Class Politics'; Hobsbawm, 'Labour in the Great City'; Williams, 'Democratic Rhondda'; Wickham, 'The Working-Class Movement in Frankfurt', 27; Nolan, *Social Democracy and Society*, 5; Tenfelde, 'Großstadt', 692; Helga Kutz-Bauer, 'Hamburg, "die Hauptstadt des deutschen Sozialismus" als Vorreiter und Experimentierfeld der Arbeiterbewegung (1873–1890)', in Arno Herzig and Günter Trautmann (ed.), *'Der kühnen Bahn nur folgen wir': Ursprünge, Erfolge und Grenzen der Arbeiterbewegung in Deutschland*, 2 vols. (Hamburg, 1989), ii. 72–96.

[18] Hartmut Zwahr, *Zur Konstituierung des Proletariats als Klasse: Strukturuntersuchung über das Leipziger Proletariat während der Industriellen Revolution* (Berlin, 1978). For a discussion of the different organizational potential of different occupations in Germany see also Ritter and Tenfelde, *Arbeiter*, 304 f.

industrial cities where the employers often exercised great power over their work-force were not beneficial for the development of strong labour movement organizations. Equally, big factories where the rate of fluctuation amongst workers was very high were unfavourable to the setting up of strong local labour movements.[19] In cities like Augsburg, Krefeld, and Chemnitz the strength of the labour movement grew with the diversification of industry.[20] Yet, conversely, a strongly diversified industry could also be inimical to working-class political mobilization. It could lead to a social fragmentation of the working class, whose upper end could find itself closer to the middle class than to the unskilled workers.[21]

Trends in British and German industry towards deskilling are sometimes held to have had a beneficial effect on the strength of the labour movement whilst any continued differentiation within the factory work-force is held to have had the opposite effect. There is considerable debate in the historiography of the British and the German labour movement as to the extent of deskilling.[22] There seems to be at least slightly more agreement as to the consequences of the First World War for the homogeneity of the working class and for class relationships in general. The war in both countries led to deskilling and a homogenization of the working class which, in turn, made efforts to organize the working class easier.[23]

Not only the nature of industry, but also the workplace experience of workers was important in determining the chances of independent working-class organizations. Christiane Eisenberg has argued that on the eve of the industrial revolution in Germany few occupational communities

[19] Ritter and Tenfelde, *Arbeiter*, 407 f.   [20] Tenfelde, 'Großstadt', 697.

[21] Karl Ditt, *Industrialisierung, Arbeiterschaft und Arbeiterbewegung in Bielefeld, 1850–1914* (Dortmund, 1982), 277. Boughton, 'Working-Class Politics', has claimed that Birmingham's small-scale industry produced a diversified, fragmented working class by which the development of working-class consciousness was impeded as inter-class relations were eased.

[22] For Germany Hartmut Zwahr, *Zur Konstituierung* and Ritter and Tenfelde, *Arbeiter*, 323 have argued that technical innovation led to substantial amounts of deskilling and the emergence of an increasingly unified work-force even before 1914. H. Schomerus, *Die Arbeiter der Maschinenfabrik Esslingen: Forschungen zur Lage der Arbeiterschaft im 19. Jahrhundert* (Stuttgart, 1977) and Breuilly, *Labour and Liberalism*, 46 have argued that the differentiation within the working class based on skill differentials remained substantial before the First World War. For the debate in Britain see Alastair Reid, 'The Division of Labour and Politics in Britain, 1880–1920', in W. J. Mommsen and H. G. Husung (eds.), *The Development of Trade Unionism in Great Britain and Germany, 1880–1914* (London, 1985), 150–65.

[23] Kocka, *Klassengesellschaft im Krieg*; Müller, 'Die groß-hannoversche Sozialdemokratie', 117–53; Waites, *A Class Society at War*.

and solidarities existed, whereas much evidence for such occupational solidarity can be found in Britain.[24] A working-class party in Germany could flourish in such a vacuum, whereas in Britain the party found it difficult to loosen existing occupational solidarities.

Industrial conflict and the existence of high trade union activity additionally stimulated support for working-class parties in Britain and Germany. In Woolwich, for example, the 1890s saw industrial conflict centred around the eight-hour working day in Woolwich arsenal. This was a prime factor in the establishment of a strong local Labour Party.[25] In Germany, for example, it was due to a strike wave in which party political bickering forestalled success that the two socialist parties finally decided to merge into one in Gotha in 1875. In the Thuringian town of Schmölln, the local SPD party could only be established in 1895 after a bitter and massive strike movement which lasted for several months.[26]

Associated with economic factors were political and social ones which contributed to the strength of local working-class parties in Britain and Germany. If local politics was organized around authoritarian, paternalist relationships and accompanied by massive discrimination against organized workers the solidarity of the latter helped to found working-class party communities.[27] As we have seen in section 2.1 both labour movements found themselves suffering under discrimination and from authoritarian paternalism at different times in their respective history. Other local political factors were of importance in determining the strength of the local working-class party. First, there was the question of the franchise. As we have seen in section 2.2. both parties suffered from

[24] Christiane Eisenberg, 'Artisans' Socialization at Work', conference paper, Lancaster 1988, 2. Published as 'Artisans' Socialization at Work: Workshop Life in Early Nineteenth-Century England and Germany', *Journal of Social History*, 24 (1991), 507–20.

[25] *Twenty-Five Years History of the Woolwich Labour Party, 1903–1928*, 9. Further examples in K. Laybourn, 'The Trade Unions and the ILP: The Manningham Experience', in Taylor and Jowitt, *Bradford, 1890–1914*, 31 f. Kenneth O. Fox, 'The Emergence of the Political Labour Movement in the Eastern Section of the South Wales Coalfield, 1894–1910' (University of Wales MA 1965), esp. 29–33, 69, 98–105, 119–25. For the connection between industrial conflict and the strength of working-class organizations in Germany see Wilhelm Heinz Schröder, *Arbeitergeschichte und Arbeiterbewegung: Industriearbeit und Organisationsverhalten im 19. und frühen 20. Jahrhundert* (Frankfurt am Main, 1978), 221.

[26] Friedhelm Boll, 'Changing Forms of Labour Conflict: Secular Development or Strike Waves', in L. Haimson and C. Tilly (eds.), *Strikes, Wars and Revolutions in an International Perspective: Strike Waves in the Late Nineteenth and Early Twentieth Centuries* (Cambridge, 1989), 71. For Schmölln see Franz Walter, Tobias Dürr, and Klaus Schmidtke, *Die SPD in Sachsen und Thüringen zwischen Hochburg und Diaspora: Untersuchungen auf lokaler Ebene vom Kaiserreich bis zur Gegenwart* (Bonn, 1993), 296.

[27] Nolan, *Social Democracy and Society*, 5. Dick Geary, 'Sectionalism in Britain and Germany Before the First World War', conference paper, Lancaster 1988, 8 f.

undemocratic local franchises which excluded substantial parts of the working class from the concept of citizenship. Furthermore, the decline of many local Liberal Parties in Britain in the decade before the outbreak of the First World War and in Germany in the 1870s left the path wide open for the development of strong working-class parties.

The existence of a tradition of radical working-class politics was also important for the development of strong working-class party communities. Where Chartism, radical working-class Liberalism or socialist societies had been strong in the nineteenth century, as in Sheffield, Merthyr, Manchester, London, or Glasgow, the Labour Party often became a vigorous force in local politics.[28] In 1884, for example, Chartist veterans carrying fifty-year-old Chartist banners led a demonstration of working men for electoral reform through Glasgow, thereby demonstrating the continuity between chartism and the labour movement of the late nineteenth century.[29] In Germany the working-class parties' communities were strongest where working-class radicalism could look back on a long tradition.[30]

There also was a correlation between the strength of social isolation of the working class and its readiness to organize. Many people who were excluded from or did not wish to participate in middle-class organizations found the SPD becoming the centre of their life after 1875.[31] Similarly, the separation of working-class from middle-class organizations happened in Britain in the 1830s and 1840s with Chartism.[32]

Workers had other choices besides the labour movement and middle-class associations as locations to spend their leisure time. Increasingly, they could choose from a growing variety of leisure activities offered by a commercial leisure industry. In Britain there is considerable evidence of a vibrant mass culture undermining the prospects of a labour movement culture already in the last quarter of the nineteenth century.[33] For Germany it can be said that the modern commercialized mass leisure culture began to develop strongly in the first decade of the twentieth

[28] J. Mendelson, W. Owen, S. Pollard, and V. M. Thornes, *The Sheffield Trades and Labour Council, 1858–1958* (Sheffield, 1958), 9–13; Glanmor Williams (ed.), *Merthyr Politics: The Making of a Working-Class Tradition* (Cardiff, 1966); Alan J. Kidd, 'The Social Democratic Federation and Popular Agitation amongst the Unemployed in Edwardian Manchester', *IRSH*, 29 (1984), 336–58; Thompson, *Socialists, Liberals and Labour*; Unger, 'The Roots of Red Clydeside', 278–315 and 357–72.
[29] Smith, 'Labour Tradition', 44.   [30] Nolan, *Social Democracy and Society*, 146–57.
[31] Rabe, *Der sozialdemokratische Charakter*, 3.
[32] Christiane Eisenberg, 'Arbeiter, Bürger und der "bürgerliche" Verein, 1820–1870', in Kocka, *Bürgertum im 19. Jahrhundert*, ii. 187–219.
[33] Cunningham, *Leisure in the Industrial Revolution*.

century—at a time when the SPD had already constituted itself.[34] Whereas
the Labour Party was founded only after the working class had already
found new ways of living, working, and 'enjoying' themselves participating
in the commercialized forms of mass culture on offer in the industrial
conurbations, the SPD in Germany could develop its own leisure associations without the same amount of competition by commercial providers.
As we shall see in the next section, this had serious implications for the
different scale of labour movement culture in both countries.

There were other working-class communities in Britain and Germany,
besides those constituted by party—for example, the community amongst
miners in mining areas. Franz-Josef Brüggemeier and Stephen Hickey
for the Ruhr area as well as Lawrence Schofer for Upper Silesia have
shown how forms of social cohesiveness amongst miners made the SPD
a negligible social force for a long time. The centre for all social relations
was the workplace. Here feelings of solidarity developed through the kind
of work as well as through common social background and education.
Within the community a union of small, often informal networks existed
which tried to ease the everyday hardship.[35]

In British mining towns the Miners' Hall was often the organizational
centre for the whole community.[36] Unionism and Methodism often formed
an organic relationship with a more traditional community mentality.[37]
The union lodge was of paramount importance in forming persisting
social relations which then came to be the basis of private 'social security
networks'.[38] The existence of such alternative working-class communities
made working-class party communities difficult to establish. This can
also be observed for locations where religious and/or ethnic divisions
were important. In places like Lancashire and the Ruhr, Catholicism and
nationality (for the Irish and Polish minorities respectively) remained
more central to the associational culture than the labour movement.[39]

[34] Lynn Abrams, 'From Control to Commercialisation: The Triumph of Mass Entertainment in Germany?', *German History*, 8 (1990), 278–93.
[35] Franz Josef Brüggemeier, *Leben vor Ort: Ruhrbergleute und Ruhrbergbau, 1889–1919*
(Munich, 1983); Stephen Hickey, *Workers in Imperial Germany: The Miners of the Ruhr*
(Oxford, 1985); Lawrence Schofer, 'Die Bergarbeiter in Oberschlesien', in Hans Mommsen
and Ulrich Borsdorf (eds.), *Glück auf, Kameraden* (Cologne, 1976), 132–49.
[36] See for example *The Onward March, 1924–1974*, ed. by the Tyldesley Trades Council
and Labour Party.
[37] Robert Colls, *The Collier's Rant: Song and Culture in the Industrial Village* (London,
1977), 163.
[38] For the minute description of the mining community of Ashton see N. Dennis,
F. Henriques, and C. Slaughter, *Coal is Our Life* (London, 1969).
[39] For the Ruhr see Karl Rohe, 'Political Alignments and Re-alignments in the Ruhr,
1867–1987: Continuity and Change of Political Traditions in an Industrial Region', in Karl

However, where such alternative communities were weak, party communities could flourish.

Memoirs of social democrats, such as those of Moritz Bromme, show how important and real the solidarity of comrades was to their everyday life.[40] This spirit was kept up right through the war. In 1915 a social democratic official wrote to party members in the trenches: 'Our organization is a powerful political construct that the war could not destroy and we hope that after the war has ended we will redevelop the party to its old glory . . . All letters that we get from members in the field show the spirit of ardent devotion and love for the organization . . .'.[41] It was not just state persecution and individual commitment that formed the basis of such feelings of solidarity, it was also the 'organizational patriotism' which put heavy emphasis on keeping the members in touch. The organization was the basis on which feelings of solidarity could develop. So, for example, the collector should not only collect fees, but try to look after the family of his comrade (e.g. make sure that they read the social democratic newspapers), introduce his children to the social democratic children's movement, and the comrade to his trade union if he was not already a member. For whole wards lists of houses were compiled which indicated sympathizers and enemies of the SPD, in order to make membership drives more successful.[42] In intra-party advice to officials it was repeatedly stressed that the weekly *Zahlabend* (pay evening) of the party should be used not just to collect the fees, but also to educate members politically and to draw them into the organization more closely.[43] For many proletarian families it became somewhat of a family tradition to support and belong to the SPD.[44] Acknowledging the existence of such elaborate SPD communities should not lead us to expect them everywhere in Germany.

Rohe (ed.), *Elections, Parties and Political Traditions: Social Foundations of German Parties and Party Systems, 1867–1987* (New York, 1990), 107–44. For Liverpool compare Baxter, 'The Liverpool Labour Party, 1918–1963'. For a separate discussion of local religious divisions of the working class which usually weakened the appeal of the working-class party in Britain and Germany see 5.3.

[40] Moritz Bromme, *Lebensgeschichte eines modernen Fabrikarbeiters* (Jena, 1905).

[41] IGA/ZPA, St. 10/228, nos. 67–70: letter from Hermann Kahmann to Social Democrats at the front, 8 Jan. 1915.

[42] Paul Sonnemann, 'Von der Kleinarbeit in der Partei', *Der Weg*, 2 (1928), 70 f. Also G. Unger, 'Zur Agitation', *NZ* 25/2 (1907), 175 f.; Heinrich Schulz, 'An die Arbeit', ibid., 744–50; Otto Rühle, 'Was ist zu tun', ibid. 750–3.

[43] IGA/ZPA, Handbill Collection, V/DF V/111, nos. 77 f. For the importance of party meetings for the close connection of its supporters see also James Wickham, 'Working-Class Movement and Working-Class Life', *Social History*, 8 (1983), 330 f.

[44] Stefan Bajohr, *Vom bitteren Los der kleinen Leute: Protokolle über den Alltag Braunschweiger Arbeiterinnen und Arbeiter 1900–1933* (Cologne, 1984), 76 f.

Lucas has shown that there were huge differences in local party organization between the SPD in Remscheid and the SPD in Hamborn. Only in the former case did the party match the above description. Even in the 'Red Vienna' of Saxony, Freital near Chemnitz, 90 per cent of workers remained unorganized by the SPD. Even here the party was not as firmly tied to the everyday lives of their members, let alone the workers at large, as a more sentimental and romantic view of the heroic time of the German labour movement would suggest.[45]

Such differences in the localities can also be found in Britain. Nationally and locally the 1900s saw a fervent debate about whether socialism found its proper expression in a social movement or in a party.[46] Neighbourhood institutions like working men's clubs, labour churches, and co-operative societies spread and in the 1890s a kind of socialist counter-culture emerged providing for leisure time and recreational activities.[47] The history of the Labour Party is usually written in terms of a failure to preserve such a distinct culture. For Leicester David Cox has shown that the ILP before 1914 created a remarkable community which the Labour Party after 1918 could not uphold.[48] In his study of the CIU and the ILP T. G. Ashplant has argued that educational and social activities became increasingly less important to local Labour Parties as they concentrated on winning elections.[49] Christopher Howard's essay comes to the conclusion that all attempts to mix politics and social life collapsed in the inter-war years.[50]

However, it has already been established in section 2.3. that many local Labour Parties after 1918 tried hard and were at least partially successful in building up viable organizational machines, resembling those of the SPD certainly in intention, but also in actual outlook. Furthermore, the distinction which is commonly made between a British party which was merely an electoral machine and a German community-oriented party[51] proves on inspection to have little basis in fact. The German SPD did not put community work before election work. In fact, the organizational machine was used to a great extent at election times to secure the success of the party:

---

[45] For Hamborn and Remscheid, see Lucas, *Zwei Formen*; for Freital see Walter, Dürr, and Schmidtke, *Die SPD in Sachsen und Thüringen*, 55 f.

[46] Bullock, 'Socialists and Democratic Form', 178.

[47] Yeo, 'The Religion of Socialism', 5–56.

[48] David Cox, 'The Labour Party in Leicester', *IRSH* 6 (1961), 210.

[49] Ashplant, 'The CIU and the ILP', 505 f.

[50] Howard, 'Expectations Born to Death', 65–81.

[51] For example Howell, *British Workers*, 392, Luebbert, *Liberalism*, 159.

In the cities and in all areas with a high percentage of industrial workers the factories became fields of *Agitation*. The men of confidence and the leaders of the organization, who were assisted by whole crowds of younger Social Democrats and also by social-democratic women, did *Agitation* and electoral work with extra-ordinary zeal. One electoral meeting followed the other . . .[52]

The London Labour Party (LLP), for example, saw ward meetings as 'becoming educational centres as well as a medium for establishing effec-tive electoral organization'[53] and the London Labour Choral Union would sing at victory demonstrations of the party.[54] Herbert Rogers, as agent for Bristol in the early 1930s, compiled lists of streets indicating sympathiz-ers and enemies of the Labour Party for all wards. These lists were used for election canvasses as well as for membership drives and they were the basis for a strong and vivid social life of the Bristol Labour Party.[55] It is not just rhetoric when party jubilee memorials start: 'it is gratifying to the older members to know that the same fraternity of spirit which was one of the chief characteristics of the earlier days, is still the mainspring of our party.'[56] It has been maintained for the SPD that the organization was the basis for the wide-spread community feelings amongst party mem-bers. What must now be considered is if an organizational boom of local Labour Parties did not also lead to similar feelings of community. Therefore the Labour Party's social life and its ancillary organizations (including organizations that co-operated with working-class parties) will be compared with the wider SPD community in the following section.

4.2. Activities of local working-class parties in Britain and Germany and their ancillary organizations

In the following a comparative overview of the educational, social, and other activities of the local party branches and their ancillary organizations in Britain and Germany is to be given. More research has so far been done on German than on British labour movement culture, since British historiography has concentrated far more on working-class culture, which

---

[52] ZStA Potsdam, 15.01, no. 13689, vol. iv, 7: police report to the Prussian Ministry of the Interior about the social democratic and anarchist movements, 1903–4, pp. 1 f.
[53] *Annual Report of the EC of the LLP, 1924/25* (London 1925), 8.
[54] *Programme of the Great Victory Demonstration to Celebrate Labour's Municipal Election and By-Election Victories* (London, 1934).
[55] Interview with Herbert Rogers of 30 Mar. 1990.
[56] *Twenty-Five Years of the Woolwich Labour Party*, 40.

often had little to do with labour movement culture.[57] Indeed, a clear gap between working-class life and labour movement culture has been observed by historians of German Labour history.[58] The labour movement culture did not appeal to the majority of the working class. The SPD campaigned against spreading consumerism, against new forms of popular entertainment, like cinema and spectator sports, and against alcohol consumption. In all those areas it came up against an existing working-class culture. Memoirs of local SPD officials like Otto Markert in Mannheim demonstrate the gulf that could exist between working-class and labour movement culture. Markert described fellow workers as 'primitive' people who became more civilized only under the influence of the social democratic party and trade union.[59]

In Britain a clear line between the working-class culture and the labour movement culture has been drawn by a number of historians, amongst them Gareth Stedman Jones, Ross McKibbin, Standish Meacham, and Richard Hoggart.[60] According to these authors the values of the labour movement were at odds with the individualism, the idea of self-help, the nationalism, and what is often termed the 'defensive class consciousness' of many British workers. Andrew Davies, in an article about the leisure activities of the Salford poor, does not even have to mention the labour movement.[61] Robert Tressell described the gulf that divided Labour Party culture from working-class culture in Britain in his *Ragged Trousered Philanthropists*: of Frank Owen, the socialist hero of the novel, he said: 'He was generally regarded as a bit of a crank: for it was felt that there must be something wrong about a man who took no interest in racing or football and was always talking a lot of rot about religion and politics.'[62]

However, this argument should not be taken to imply that the relationship between working-class culture and labour movement culture in Britain

---

[57] For the useful distinction between *Arbeiterkultur* (working-class culture) and *Arbeiterbewegungskultur* (labour movement culture) see Ritter, *Arbeiterkultur*, 19.

[58] See especially Lynn Abrams, *Workers' Culture in Imperial Germany: Leisure and Recreation in the Rhineland and Westphalia* (London, 1992), 192 f.; see also Evans, *Proletarians*, 79, Lidtke, *The Alternative Culture*, 19 f.

[59] 'Erzählte Lebensgeschichte eines Arbeiters und Sozialdemokraten: Otto Markert, Jg. 1891', in Lothar Steinbach, *Mannheim—Erinnerungen aus einem halben Jahrhundert: Sozialgeschichte einer Stadt in Lebensbildern* (Stuttgart, 1984), 129–54, esp. 132.

[60] Jones, *Languages of Class*, 235–8; McKibbin, *The Ideologies of Class*, chs. 2 and 3 and pp. 294 f.; Standish Meacham, *A Life Apart: The English Working Class, 1890–1914* (Cambridge, Mass. 1977), 200 f.; Richard Hoggart, *The Uses of Literacy* (London, 1957), 279 f.

[61] Andrew Davies, 'Leisure and Poverty in Salford', conference paper, Lancaster 1988.

[62] Robert Tressell, *The Ragged Trousered Philanthropists* (first pub. in 1914; London, 1965), 18.

was fixed. It could and did change with different local circumstances. At places like Burnley and Leicester, the labour movement was firmly located within the local working-class culture.[63] And Eric Hobsbawm, although allowing for a clear difference between labour movement culture and working-class culture, has maintained: 'the world and culture of the working classes is incomprehensible without the labour movement, which for long periods was its core.'[64] Willi Guttsman has recently argued for the existence of a similar link between working-class and labour movement culture in Germany. Far from being worlds apart, workers brought their everyday culture into the labour movement the moment they joined, whilst the labour movement culture, in turn, had important influences on the working-class culture.[65] Whilst Kirk, Hobsbawm, and Guttsman have a point in arguing for the existence of certain links between working-class and labour movement culture in Britain and Germany, for comparison's sake the two are best treated as separate categories. Otherwise, one is easily led astray by comparing the working-class culture of Britain with the labour movement culture of Germany. If, however, the two were not identical in either of the two countries, then any cross-national comparison of one with the other can only lead to an emphasis on differences.[66] The following comparison will limit itself strictly to the labour movement culture of Britain and Germany.

If the social life of the British and the German working-class parties is compared, it should not be forgotten that such a social life was also organized by other institutions and parties in both countries. In Germany most of the ancillary organizations developed out of, and often consciously or unconsciously copied, bourgeois social, musical, educational, or sports' associations. The *Verein* can be understood as a specifically bourgeois (*bürgerlich*) form,[67] which Social Democrats inherited. Although it is true that apart from the Catholic Centre Party no other German party set up a comparable network of social institutions, the non-party *bürgerlich* clubs often served as social outlets for the *bürgerlich* parties. In

---

[63] Neville Kirk, ' "Traditional" Working-Class Culture and the "Rise of Labour": Some Preliminary Questions and Observations', *Social History*, 16 (1991), 203–16.

[64] Hobsbawm, *Worlds of Labour*, 178. See also ibid. 209.

[65] Guttsman, *Workers' Culture in Weimar Germany*, 1–19, esp. 11.

[66] For an example of such a comparison see Dick Geary, 'Arbeiterkultur in Deutschland und Großbritannien im Vergleich', in Dietmar Petzina (ed.), *Fahnen, Fäuste, Körper: Symbolik und Kultur der Arbeiterbewegung* (Essen, 1986), 91–9.

[67] Thomas Nipperdey, 'Verein als soziale Struktur in Deutschland im späten 18. und frühen 19. Jahrhundert: Eine Fallstudie zur Modernisierung', in id., *Gesellschaft, Kultur, Theorie: Gesammelte Aufsätze zur neueren Geschichte* (Göttingen, 1976), 175–205.

many localities they outnumbered by far the social democratic clubs. In the town of Lahr, for example, there were twelve social democratic clubs as against ninety *bürgerlich* clubs.[68]

In Britain, a strong non-political associational culture, for example in the area of music and choir-singing, was not unknown. As in Germany, it also acted as a counterbalance to the expansion of any labour movement culture. Additionally, the Conservative and the Liberal Party were both engaged in social activities. Martin Pugh has drawn attention to Conservative workingmen's clubs and the Primrose League, which—with its rich masonic symbolism—had the task of integrating the working class socially into the Conservative Party. Branches were set up in nearly every town. They organized a regular programme of social events as well as sports, women, and youth organizations.[69] Furthermore, the leisure industry in Britain proved to be an earlier and stronger competitor for the social activities of Labour than of the SPD.[70] Finally, from the second half of the nineteenth century onwards parks, monuments, museums, and libraries were made public in Britain and Germany as a means of providing rational recreation facilities for the working class. In this way, the municipal/state authorities hoped to make an independent labour movement culture less attractive to workers. As we shall see below, in both countries such efforts only met with limited success.

The working-class parties and education

In the big industrial cities, like Leipzig, Berlin, and Hamburg, the educational facilities provided by SPD and free trade unions were no doubt impressive.[71] A study of Hamburg attempts to show that the labour movement was at heart a broad cultural movement whose aim was the education of the working class.[72] Yet this was not a German peculiarity. Much like the leaders of the SPD's educational associations, the Principal

---

[68] Walter Caroli and Robert Stimpel, *Geschichte der Lahrer SPD* (Lahr, 1979), 93.

[69] Pugh, *The Tories and the People*, 21–58. The importance of Liberal Clubs for the organization of leisure activities is stressed by Roy Douglas, *The History of the Liberal Party, 1895–1970* (London, 1971), 17.

[70] See 4.1. above.

[71] Gerhard Beier, 'Arbeiterbildung als Bildungsarbeit', in P. von Rüden (ed.), *Beiträge zur Kulturgeschichte der deutschen Arbeiterbewegung, 1848–1918* (Frankfurt am Main, 1979), 43–61. Also Dieter Langewiesche, 'Arbeiterbildung in Deutschland und Österreich, Konzeption, Praxis, Funktionen', in Werner Conze and Ulrich Engelhardt (eds.), *Arbeiter im Industrialisierungsprozeß: Herkunft, Lage und Verhalten* (Stuttgart, 1979), 439–67.

[72] Johannes Schult, *Die Hamburger Arbeiterbewegung als Kulturfaktor* (Hamburg, 1955), 30–118. For Leipzig as a stronghold of workers' education, see Fritz Borinski, 'Arbeiterbildung im Leipzig der 20er Jahre', in *Arbeiterbildung, Erwachsenenbildung, Presse: Festschrift für Walter Fabian zum 75. Geburtstag* (Cologne, 1977), 11–25.

of Ruskin College, H. Sanderson Furniss, expressed his belief 'that working-class education must be under working-class control . . . [and] that working-class education must help to fit the workers for service in the working-class movement . . .'.[73]

From the 1860s onwards the SPD and the trade unions were committed to building up their own institutional network to cater for the educational and cultural needs of the working class. In Britain Chartism and the early nineteenth-century labour movement already provided cultural institutions for the working class.[74] Later on the ILP, SDF, and the Clarion movement all saw themselves as educational movements, bringing this conviction into the Labour Party from the start.[75] The importance of education was realized in the British Labour Party and activities were undertaken within the movement to provide for education. Local Labour Parties organized public lectures, ward lectures, study circles, outdoor summer and indoor winter lectures.[76] In 1928 a panel of forty-seven speakers was compiled by the LLP for local education work in London.[77] The LLP also bought two vans from the Clarion movement in the 1920s which it lent out to local parties in order to increase the amount of education work.[78] At some places, for instance Coventry, an educational officer was appointed whose task lay in the planning and co-ordination of the various educational and cultural activities.[79]

Besides the general education of party members, a specific concern for both the Labour Party and the SPD was the education of officials. The Leipzig SPD's speakers' classes, for example, were meant 'to give the gifted comrades the chance and turn themselves into orators'.[80] Speakers' classes were held in local Labour Parties 'and it is hoped that by this

[73] H. Sanderson Furniss, 'A New Renaissance', *Labour Magazine*, 3 (1924–5), 208.

[74] E. Yeo, 'Robert Owen and Radical Culture', in S. Pollard and J. Salt (eds.), *Robert Owen, Prophet of the Poor* (London, 1971), 84–114 and J. Epstein, 'Some Organizational and Cultural Aspects of the Chartist Movement in Nottingham', in J. Epstein and D. Thompson (eds.), *The Chartist Experience: Studies in Working-Class Radicalism and Culture, 1830–1860* (London, 1982), 221–68.

[75] For the SDF see Pierson, *British Socialists*, 82, for the ILP see Frank Hodges, *My Adventures as a Labour Leader* (London, 1925), 24. For the Clarion movement see Fincher, 'The Clarion Movement'.

[76] The *Labour Organizer* and the *Labour Leader* reported regularly on these events. For the stress on the importance of educational work see also Herbert Morrison, *Labour Party Propaganda and Education in London: A Memorandum for the Consideration of Local Labour Parties, etc.* (London, 1932).

[77] *Annual Report of the EC of the LLP* (1928–9), 7.

[78] For the activity of the LLP vans see: *Annual Report of the EC of the LLP* (1924–5), 6 and *Labour Organizer* (July 1924), 2.

[79] *Labour Organizer* (Sept. 1925), 9 f.

[80] *Arbeiterführer für Leipzig und Umgebung: Nachschlagewerk*, xi, ed. R. Lipinski (Leipzig, 1909), 70.

means an appreciable number of capable party propagandists may be produced'.[81] The increasing demand for party organizers in the 1920s made it absolutely necessary that party activists were taught the essentials of organization and propaganda. Within local SPD parties, the teaching of officials became increasingly important with the bureaucratization of the organization.

The educational work of the local SPD parties was often directed by the local Agitationskommission. It co-ordinated lectures, mass demonstrations, press campaigns, and other programmes of an educational nature. The national educational council (Zentralbildungsausschuß), set up in 1906, was a kind of advisory body for the local SPD parties and their ancillary organizations. It held conferences for the training of officials and, published model programmes for educational and cultural activities and model guides to plays and music. By 1911 244 local educational councils were organizing the educational work of the German labour movement in the country.[82] The local social democratic teachers' association often organized lecture series, proletarian festivities (*proletarische Feierstunden*), and drama groups.[83] The Labour Party set up a National Association of Labour Teachers in 1932, but little can be ascertained about the scope and nature of its activities.[84] SPD *Wanderlehrer* (itinerant teachers) travelled throughout the country to bring enlightenment even to the remotest spots. Their numbers increased steadily from two in 1907 to thirteen in 1914. Itinerant teachers who brought the gospel of socialism to the people could also be found in the British Labour Party. Bruce and Katherine Glasier, for example, spent most of their lives travelling up and down the country preaching socialism. In the late 1920s and early 1930s the Labour Party engaged two national propagandists, Tom Myers and W. F. Toynbe, who undertook campaign tours from five to ten days' duration up and down the country.[85]

Both parties came to rely increasingly on the local party press which served as the most important channel of communication between the

---

[81] *Annual Report of the EC of the LLP* (1931–2), 12. Also William Howard, 'How to Run a Speakers' Class', *Labour Organizer* (Apr. 1925), 10 f.

[82] Lidtke, *The Alternative Culture*, 176, 225 f., Guttmann, *Workers' Culture*, 64–7. For the extensive network of associations offering educational and cultural facilities to the workers in Frankfurt at the time of the Weimar Republic see Stübling, *Kultur und Massen*.

[83] Faulenbach and Högl, *Eine Partei in ihrer Region*, 106.

[84] See Labour Party Archive, Organization Subcommittee Minutes, 27 Jan. 1932, p. 1.

[85] For the Glasiers see: L. V. Thompson, *The Enthusiasts: A Biography of J. and K. B. Glasier* (London, 1971), 91–4; for Myers and Toynbe see *Report of the Annual Conference of the Labour Party, 1930* (London, 1930), 6 f.

various educational and cultural organizations of the labour movement and the rank and file. At the same time the press became the most important instrument of education itself.[86] It advertised the activities of local workers' educational institutions, party lectures, ward and public meetings, and generally reported the activities of the local labour movement. There were also extensive reports of the local municipal council and the work of the party's councillors. Alongside the party press, libraries and party bookshops were thought vital for the task of educating the rank and file. As Heinrich Peus wrote in 1925 of the SPD: 'Besides the newspaper the party bookshop has to become a powerful *Agitator* for our world view.'[87] The *Dietz Verlag* and the *Vorwärts Verlag* published several series of cheap socialist handbooks from the 1880s onwards.[88] The Independent Labour Party published the *Socialist Library* from 1905 onwards and it ran its own bookshops.[89] Furthermore, encouraged by the NEC, a number of local Labour Parties promoted the appointment of literature secretaries.[90]

In 1929 about 2,500 workers' libraries existed in Germany with about one and a half million books.[91] The workers' library in Leipzig was a model example: in 1911 there were 16,874 readers who could choose from 53,000 books in fifty-nine workers' libraries. Seventeen of the Leipzig libraries had their own buildings.[92] The importance of careful guidance provided by the librarians to the workers was stressed by party officials. The library should have a pedagogic, educational function.[93]

Nothing of similar scope to Leipzig existed within the British labour movement. However, on the one hand Leipzig was extraordinary even

---

[86] See above, 2.5. Also Loreck, *Wie man früher Sozialdemokrat wurde*, 36 and 77. Herbert Drinkwater, 'The Organization of Propaganda', *Labour Organizer*, (July 1924), 11.

[87] Heinrich Peus, 'Die Parteibuchhandlung', *SM*, 31 (1925), 89.

[88] Fricke, *Handbuch*, i. 665 f.

[89] 'The Socialist Library: Prospectus', in no. 7 of the Socialist Library: Eduard Bernstein, *Evolutionary Socialism* (London, 1909). Also G. B. Woolven, *Publications of the ILP* (Warwick, 1977), vii–x.

[90] Labour Party Archive, Organization Sub-Committee Minutes, 23 Mar. 1932: 'Some parties have literature secretaries. . . . they should all be urged to appoint such an official.' *Annual Report of the EC of the LLP* (1925–6), 11. Also Report of the Literature Secretary to the Annual General Meeting of the Faversham Divisional Labour Party, Dec. 1939, in Labour Party Archive, Local Labour Party Files.

[91] *Jahrbuch der SPD* (1929), 208 f. See generally on the topic of workers' libraries in Germany: Dieter Langewiesche and Klaus Schönhoven, 'Arbeiterbibliotheken und Arbeiterlektüre im Wilhelminischen Deutschland', *AfS* 16 (1976), 135–204.

[92] *Bericht über die Tätigkeit des Bezirksvorstands der SPD Leipzig für das Jahr 1911/12*, 78 f.

[93] Rudolf Waclawiak, 'Das Bibliothekswesen der Gewerkschaften und der Parteien', *NZ* 17 (1908–9), 478 f.

within Germany, and on the other hand the idea of workers' libraries for workers' education was far from alien to the British labour movement. In an address to the American Federation of Labour on 29 July 1919 Margaret Bondfield praised the Fabian libraries as a major educational facility from which many of the leaders of the ILP had received their training.[94] Many trades councils and Labour Halls kept libraries for the entertainment and education of their members. Some of the finest workers' libraries in Britain were those of the miners' unions.[95] The Sheerness Labour Party reported in 1926 'a steady demand for books from the lending library . . .'[96] In 1924 a central lending library was set up at head office for the use of local party agents.[97] Reading clubs and study circles could be found in both Labour Party and SPD.[98] The Lewisham Labour Party organized a Pamphlet Club. Any member who was willing to pay an annual subscription, could receive all pamphlets published throughout the year by the National Labour Party. Thereby the party member could automatically obtain the party's literature which 'should considerably help in the very necessary work of education amongst our own party'.[99]

The local SPD's educational efforts were enriched by a number of educational facilities, designed mainly for the training of future officials of the movement. The Workers' Educational School (Arbeiter-bildungsschule) was founded in Berlin in 1891. It taught a wide range of subjects with special emphasis on politics, political economy, and history. In 1930, for example, there were sixty-four classes with 1,492 pupils. The Berlin Party School (*Parteischule*) was set up in 1906. There were about 20–30 classes a year with about 15–52 participants in the mid-1920s. The subjects dealt with ranged from history and sociology to economy and capitalism. Additionally there were one-week summer schools.[100] The Socialist Workers' College (Hochschule der sozialistischen Arbeiterschaft) in Hamburg and the Workers' Academy (Arbeiterakademie) in Frankfurt worked on similar lines.[101] After the First World War the SPD built up

[94] Marius Hansome, *World Workers' Educational Movement* (New York, 1931), 30.
[95] Hywel Francis, 'The South Wales Miners' Library', *HWJ* 2 (1976), 183–205.
[96] *Annual Report of the Sheerness Trades Council and Labour Party, 1926.*
[97] *Labour Organizer* (July 1924), 3.
[98] Marga Beyer, 'Die Berliner Sozialdemokratie um die Wende vom 19. zum 20. Jahrhundert', *Geschichtsunterricht und Staatsbürgerkunde*, 29 (1987), 438. Labour Party Archive, Local Labour Party Files: files of the LLP: 'Labour Party Propaganda and Education in London: A Memorandum for the Consideration of Local Labour Parties etc.' (London, 1932).
[99] *Labour Organizer* (June 1924), 1.   [100] Lidtke, *The Alternative Culture*, 162–79.
[101] See Johannes Schult, *Geschichte der Hamburger Arbeiter*, 208–21, and Hans Marckwald, 'Eine Frankfurter Arbeiterakademie', *NZ* (1919–20), 352–6.

a residential college for workers at Schloß Tinz, the socialist trade unions widened their own educational facilities substantially, and in 1925 the Socialist Culture League (Sozialistischer Kulturbund) was set up. It tried to concentrate all allied organizations within the German labour movement into a great culture alliance, so as to co-ordinate their actions. The SPD's National Committee on Education, the Socialist Teachers' Association, the Kinderfreunde (the children's organization of the SPD), the Youth Organization, the National Committee for Workers' Welfare, the Choral Union, the Society for Labour Sport, the Federation of People's Theatres, and the trade unions were all united in this *Kulturbund*.[102]

In Britain the Labour Party Scheme of Study and Examination of Party Agents enrolled 300 students including 105 party agents in 1930. Besides, the classes and lectures of the Workers' Educational Association (WEA) reached a mass audience. The WEA was founded in 1903 by Albert Mansbridge as a non-party-political and non-sectarian organization. Yet, by the 1920s it was justifiably said: 'The WEA regards itself as an educational expression of the working-class movement.'[103] Many Labour Party activists, like R. H. Tawney who was one of the first tutors of the organization, worked for the WEA. Its main activities lay in the organization of one-year tutorial classes. Yet active local WEA branches also organized rambles in the summer, socials in the winter, and dramatic and musical societies.[104] The aim of the WEA was to bring 'cultural education of high standard to those who had never had a chance of it in their youth'.[105] In 1919 the trade unions founded the Workers' Educational Trade Union Committee (WETUC) which set up education schemes under the sponsorship of the WEA.[106] Such schemes included special day schools and courses for members of the labour movement, remission of class fees, provision of scholarships, and provision of books and tuition by correspondence.[107]

Quite apart from the WEA, Ruskin College was set up as a residential college for working men in 1899. Right from the start it also arranged correspondence classes which quickly became extremely popular in

[102] Guttsman, *Workers' Culture*, 67–71.
[103] J. M. MacTavish, 'The WEA', *Labour Magazine*, 1 (1922–3), 220. For the Labour Party Scheme which had been approved at the 1926 Margate conference of the Labour Party see *Report of the Annual Conference of the Labour Party, 1930* (London, 1930), 7.
[104] Michael Turner, *A History of the Workers' Educational Association: Western District, 1911–1986* (Bristol, 1986), 17 and 40 f.
[105] Margaret Cole, *Growing Up into Revolution* (London, 1949), 114.
[106] J. P. M. Millar, *The Labour College Movement* (London, 1979), 25.
[107] Turner, *A History of the WEA*, 26.

Labour strongholds. By 1902 a total of ninety-six classes operated in various parts of the country.[108] Ruskin's main task, however, remained the teaching of trade unionists in the social sciences in one- or two-year courses. Many of those who came to Ruskin later became union or party officials. In 1909 a couple of students who deplored the absence of socialism and industrial matters from the curriculum of Ruskin College set up the Central Labour College (CLC) in London, which always remained a small institution, having only fourteen students in 1914. Despite this inability to attract and finance greater numbers, the CLC's students included men such as Aneurin Bevan and James Griffiths who were to become important Labour leaders. Therefore its influence on the British labour movement far exceeded its actual size. Possibly even more influential than the CLC itself was the decision of the CLC activists to set up branches in local communities under the name of Plebs Leagues from 1909 onwards. South Wales, Scotland, Lancashire, the North East, and the West Riding became centres of Plebs League strength in the following years, and especially in and after the First World War.[109] In Scotland there were 2,854 students attending fifty-one classes by 1920. In 1921 these regional activities could no longer be directed from London, so the National Council of Labour Colleges (NCLC) was set up. It continued running classes, correspondence courses, day and week-end schools, branch lectures, and the publication of the magazine *Plebs*. Their subjects lay mainly in the social sciences and its orientation was specifically Marxist. Local Labour Parties, trade unions, or co-operatives had to affiliate to the local NCLC, so that their members could attend the lectures and events free of charge.

In 1925 the foundation of a residential working-class education centre at Easton Lodge, whose principal was to be G. D. H. Cole, was discussed by the labour movement. It was to take over the tasks of Ruskin, the CLC, and the Co-operative residential college. The Countess of Warwick was prepared to give her house and grounds at Easton Lodge for the purpose, and the TUC Education Committee, Ruskin College, and WEA representatives sponsored a £50,000 Easton Lodge scheme (approximately £1.5 million in 1991). The 1926 TUC congress, however, voted against it. The decision was taken only four months after the General Strike had practically wiped out trade union funds and the miners were still on

---

[108] Harold Pollins, *The History of Ruskin College* (Oxford, 1984), 14.
[109] Millar, *The Labour College Movement*, 21.

strike at the time. The timing of the Easton Lodge scheme can only be called unfortunate.[110]

Socialist Sunday Schools (SSS) were active on behalf of the Labour Party as well. As can be seen from the correspondence between Middleton and the National Secretary of the SSS, Jim Simmons, at the beginning of the 1930s Labour speakers and candidates were to make propaganda for the SSS, and an advertisement campaign for the SSS was to start in all national and local Labour newspapers.[111] In a circular to all local Labour Parties' Leagues of Youth of 12 June 1934, Middleton further stressed the necessity of working with the SSS and forming SSS in all constituencies.[112] The first SSS was founded in Manchester in 1892. The years before the First World War saw a remarkable expansion of the movement. SSS in the same district joined to form district unions and in 1909 the National Council of British Socialist Sunday School Unions was founded. Its central task was the setting up of classes for children, although it also ran adult courses. In the mid-1920s the SSS ran 110 schools in Britain which catered for 6,000 children.[113] The SSS sought to create a socialist atmosphere in which children would be free of the restraints of 'capitalist' education. Their prime ideal was to develop the feeling of fellowship in the children. Their activities included not only Sunday school lessons, but also drama, needlecraft, political campaigns such as the 'citizen peace crusade', Morris dancing, singing, nature studies, rambling, correspondence in esperanto, and the monthly publication of the *Young Socialist*.[114] The Glasgow SSS even started a socialist comedy school in 1906.[115] Another youth organization, having connections to the labour movement, which tried to cater for the education of the young was the so-called Woodcraft Folk, set up in 1925.[116] It was co-educational, non-religious, and non-military and it tried to combine naturalism with the teaching of socialism. It had an active membership of about 3,000 in

[110] G. D. H. Cole, 'Easton Lodge: The Plea of an Enthusiast', *Labour Magazine*, 5 (1926–7), 207–9.
[111] Labour Party Archive, Middleton Papers, JSM/SU, 3.
[112] Ibid., JSM/SU, 19.   [113] Ibid., JSM/SU, 8.
[114] *Labour Organizer* (Jan. 1927), 12. Also F. Reid, 'Socialist Sunday Schools in Britain, 1892–1939', *IRSH*, 14 (1966), 18–47.
[115] *Labour Leader* (23 Feb. 1906).
[116] For the English left-wing woodcraft groups of the 1920s, the Order of Woodcraft Chivalry, the Kibbo Kift, and the Woodcraft Folk see John Springhall, *Youth, Empire and Society* (London, 1977), 110–20. Also D. L. Prynn, 'The Socialist Sunday Schools, the Woodcraft Folk and Allied Movements' (University of Sheffield M.A. 1972).

the mid-1930s and constituted 'a determined attempt to provide a sub-stitute for the Scout movement'[117] with its imperialist and militaristic leanings.

Drama, music and sports within the British and the German working-class parties

In 1890 the *Freie Volksbühne* was founded in Berlin by liberal bourgeois writers with the aim of winning the social democratic workers for the arts. The SPD soon won a dominating influence within the society and it was imitated in Hamburg and other big cities.[118] In the 1920s the People's Theatre Movement had an overall membership of 600,000.[119] Lay groups could often be found in local SPD parties. In 1908 the Federation of Workers' Theatrical Clubs was set up. By 1913 it had sixty-six member clubs with a total membership of 985.[120] Often local SPD parties addition-ally organized visits to big city theatres, distributing tickets at reduced prices.

Socialist theatre also existed in Britain, and when the Labour Party took up the idea in the 1920s and 1930s, it could already look back on a long tradition and co-operate with a number of existing theatres.[121] The National Association of Clarion Dramatic Clubs, the SSS, Woodcraft Folk, and the Co-op Guilds all sponsored drama classes, prepared dra-matic tableaux for May Day, and formed theatrical troupes. In 1924–5 the LLP Dramatic Federation was established on the basis of constitu-ency dramatic activity: seventeen constituency Labour Parties had established drama societies in London.[122] After the war the Arts League of Service was established as a travelling company. Local Labour Parties could hire the services of the company and Herbert Morrison warmly

---

[117] Springhall, *Youth, Empire and Society*, 118.

[118] Hyun-Back Chung, *Die Kunst dem Volke oder dem Proletariat? Die Geschichte der Freien Volksbühnenbewegung in Berlin, 1890–1914* (Frankfurt am Main, 1989). For Ham-burg's *Volksbühne* see Schult, *Geschichte der Hamburger Arbeiter*, 94 f. For the period of the Weimar Republic see Dietmar Klenke, Peter Lilje, and Franz Walter, *Arbeitersänger und Volksbühnen in der Weimarer Republik* (Bonn, 1992).

[119] Guttsman, *Workers' Culture*, 212.

[120] Lidtke, *The Alternative Culture*, 136 f.

[121] For the Workers' Theatre Movement, the Left Theatre, the Unity Theatre Club, and the Left Book Club Theatre Guild see Reiner Lehberger, 'Internationale Verbindungen und Beeinflussungen des sozialistischen Theaters in England der dreißiger Jahre', *Das Argument*, special vol. 29 (1978), 67–79. For the Workers' Theatre Movement and the tradition of labour movement theatre see also Tom Thomas, 'The WTM: Memoirs and Documents', with an editorial introduction by Raphael Samuel, *HWJ* 4 (1977), 102–42.

[122] *Annual Report of the EC of the LLP* (1924–5), 14, ibid. (1925–6), 18, ibid. (1926–7) 21 f. Also *London News* (May 1925), 4 and (July 1925), 3.

recommended the Arts League in a circular of 4 August 1921. After the war the Leeds Industrial Theatre was set up, consciously referring to the German SPD's ancillary organization as a model.[123] In Birmingham the 1920s saw the foundation of several drama groups in various wards. In 1924 a People's Theatre Movement was founded in Birmingham, and earlier, in 1921, a Workers' Poetry and Art Union had been set up.[124] In Newcastle upon Tyne a People's Theatre had already existed in 1911. It was to become a most successful venture, which was promoted by G. B. Shaw. The Gateshead ILP set up a dramatic club which, for example, successfully staged *The Pitman's Pay*, a play by the miner Thomas Wilson dating from 1826 celebrating the communal aspects of everyday life in a mining community.[125] In an article in the *Labour Magazine* M. H. Dodds suggested

that the artistic expression [of the Labour and Socialist movement] exists, but that it is not widely recognised. . . . In Newcastle the professional theatre has its regular two paragraphs a week, . . . but the People's Theatre gets no more than one a year. . . . Yet, without money, without influence, without press notices or advertisement, the work goes on.[126]

Within the SPD the foundation of choirs and musical associations (usually single-sex up to 1918) experienced rapid expansion from the 1890s onwards.[127] Not all members were active singers; a large percentage were passive members, who enjoyed listening to music and attending the social functions of the clubs. In the district of middle Germany (Gau Mitteldeutschland), for example, only 3,712 out of 5,091 members were active members in 1911.[128] The labour movement choirs developed their own tradition of songs fixed in the publication of songbooks. They were an integral part of social democratic festivities and performed regularly in May Day, Revolution Day, and Day of the Republic festivities.[129] The

---

[123] John Amott, 'Factories and Footlights. Leeds Industrial Theatre', *Labour Magazine*, 1 (1922–3), 489–91.

[124] Boughton, 'Working-Class Politics', 300–3.

[125] For the 19th-century miners' literature see H. G. Klaus, *The Literature of Labour: Two Hundred Years of Working-Class Writing* (Brighton, 1985), 62–88.

[126] M. H. Dodds, 'Socialists and the Drama', *Labour Magazine*, 2 (1923–4), 109 f.

[127] Dieter Dowe, 'The Workingmen's Choral Movement in Germany before the First World War', *Journal of Contemporary History*, 13 (1978), 269–96. For the Weimar Republic see Klenke, Lilje, and Walter, *Abeitersänger*.

[128] Siegfried Flügel, 'Die Entwicklung des Arbeitergesangs im Raum Halle, Weißenfels und Zeitz zwischen 1890 und 1933' (University of Halle Ph.D. 1965), 151.

[129] *Vorwärts und nicht vergessen: Arbeiterkultur in Hamburg um 1930* (Hamburg, 1982), 207–20.

SPD's choirs performed four functions: they were used for mass singing, for propaganda, for hall concerts, and for first-rate competitive concerts (*Spitzenkonzerte*). Overall there was a bias to bourgeois classical music and a reluctance to see their tasks as 'merely' political.[130]

The view of the SPD's Workers' Singing Association (DAS) that the workers' choir movement was 'completely insignificant' in England seems unfair.[131] No doubt, it never reached the numbers it reached in Germany, but it was there and followed much the same path as its German counterpart. In the first decades of the twentieth century it was an important part of the labour movement culture in Britain. Developing mainly out of local initiatives, dating back to ILP, SDF, or Clarion activity of the 1880s and 1890s, Labour Choirs flourished in the 1920s.[132] The LLP Choral Union in 1925 had fifteen choirs with 500 members and the party organized musical festivals and choir contests throughout the 1920s. It even organized weekend schools for choirs in 1925–6. In 1930 the London Labour Choral Union affiliated to the Singers International.[133] In some London constituencies even symphony orchestras were set up.[134] Many choirs stressed the quality of the music performed rather than the political function, much as their German counterparts did: 'In the first place, the music we attempt is of the best. While always prepared to lead the audiences at meetings with the well-known Labour songs we are keeping abreast of the times by studying the unrivalled music of the Elizabethan period.'[135] Apart from the Labour choirs, there were, of course, the miners' brass bands. Eric Hobsbawm has impressively described the miners' gala as

highly elaborate, with each lodge gathering at an allotted billet—generally a pub—from where they formed up—four abreast, as the rules insisted—to take their place in the procession, . . . At their peak each lodge . . . probably had three to four large banners and Niagara of brass bands demonstrated the power of labour to all.[136]

---

[130] Burns and van der Will, *Arbeiterkulturbewegung*, 107 f.

[131] ZStA Potsdam, 15.01, no. 25830, 13: letter from Dr Alfred Guttmann (DAS) to the German foreign office, 1 June 1927.

[132] Stephen G. Jones, 'The British Labour Movement and Working-Class Leisure, 1918–1939' (University of Manchester Ph.D. 1983), 276 f. See also Ian Watson, 'Alan Bush and Left Music in the Thirties', *Das Argument*, special vol. 29 (1978), 80–9.

[133] *Annual Report of the EC of the LLP* (1930–1), 7.

[134] *Annual Report of the EC of the LLP* (1925–6), 18; ibid. (1926–7), 22.

[135] Sidney A. Court, 'Music and the People: A Message to the Labour Movement', *Labour Magazine*, 2 (1923–4), 445.

[136] Hobsbawm, *Worlds of Labour*, 73.

Workers' sports and athletics clubs in most localities were the most popular and numerous of the various SPD ancillary organizations in existence. They catered for almost every sport; especially popular were cycling, acrobatics, gymnastics, athletics, and football. By the end of the 1920s, they owned 249 gymnasia, 1,265 sports and playing fields, 100 bathing places, forty-eight boat houses, two ski-jumps, four regional residential homes, and a bicycle factory.[137] They were different from the 'bourgeois' sports' clubs in that they rejected the competitive nature of bourgeois sport with its achievement principle.[138]

The various local sports organizations within the Labour Party were finally brought together in the British Workers' Sports Association (BWSA) in 1930. The BWSA consciously copied the continental example of workers' sports organizations. In the first of his monthly columns about the BWSA in the *Labour Organizer*, George H. Elvin, the General Secretary of the BWSA claimed that 'there is no reason at all why this country should not organize as successful and enthusiastic a Worker's Sports Movement as our Continental comrades have done.'[139] The interest of the British labour movement in sports can be seen from the fact that British representatives were present at all international meetings arranging for a Workers' Sport International.[140] It was the declared aim of the BWSA to organize national competitions in several different sports, and on 30 June 1931 the first National Workers' Sports Day took place at Crystal Palace.[141] The LLP established a LLP Sports Association in July 1928. It established a football league and held Labour Sports meetings and festivals. It also catered for cricket, tennis, darts, billiards, and swimming clubs.[142] The LLP football team maintained relations with the German Workers' Sports Association:

An invitation to the Leipzig *Arbeiter Sportsbund* to send a workers' football team resulted in a visit to London at Easter of a team which turned out to be a German National Representative team. . . . the London team were rather badly beaten in

---

[137] This impressive list can be found in Guttsman, *Workers' Culture*, 137.

[138] Horst Überhorst, *Frisch, Frei, Stark und Treu: Die Arbeitersportbewegung in Deutschland, 1893–1933* (Düsseldorf, 1973).

[139] *Labour Organizer* (Oct. 1930), 189.

[140] Überhorst, *Frisch, Frei, Stark*, 162 f. See also F. O. Roberts, 'Impressions of the Workers' Olympiad', *Labour Magazine*, 6 (1927–8), 152 f. For the numerous contacts between the British and the continental labour movement sports' movement see also Stephen G. Jones, 'The European Workers' Sport Movement and Organized Labour in Britain between the Wars', *EHQ* 18 (1988), 3–32.

[141] *Labour Organizer* (Nov. 1930), 212.

[142] *Annual Reports of the EC of the LLP* from 1927–8 onwards.

each of the two games played. A return visit by a splendid workers' team . . . was made in July to Hamburg, Magdeburg, Leipzig and other towns, and our team more than held their own, and in addition were given a right royal reception by their German comrades.[143]

The BWSA had particularly strong sections in London, Birmingham, Reading, Bath, Swindon, and Bristol. Of course, the British labour movement sports clubs did not organize the hundreds of thousands that its German counterparts organized. The Clarion Cycling Clubs had a membership of 8,000 in 1914, and the membership of all British labour movement sports clubs, including the communist ones, has been estimated at 15,000 in the first half of the 1930s.[144] Yet Elvin stated in 1930 that there were a 'surprisingly large number' of workers' sports clubs to be found throughout the country, thereby indicating that here as elsewhere, Labour was creating a smaller version of that wider SPD culture.[145] The BWSA finally even became the instigator of a revival of workers' sport after the Second World War.[146]

Women's and youth organizations in the working-class parties of Britain and Germany

Within the SPD the organization of women was carried out separately at first, as the restrictive Prussian law of assembly prevented the integration of women into the party structure until 1908. From 1908 to 1911 a special central women's bureau of the SPD co-ordinated local efforts. When it was dissolved it was replaced by a women's secretary within the party executive.[147] In the SPD special women's *Agitation* committees and women's reading and discussion clubs either continued to exist or were set up in the localities after 1908. The women's sections of the Berlin party, for example, were extremely lively in various forms. The number of women's evenings progressed rapidly from the mid-1920s onwards (from 65 in 1925 to 999 in 1931) and special women's classes and trips to the countryside were organized. There were regular lectures and yearly district

[143] *Annual Report of the EC of the LLP* (1928–9), 10.
[144] Jones, 'The European Workers' Sport Movement', 7 f.
[145] *Labour Organizer* (Oct. 1930), 191.
[146] Stephen Bird, 'History of the BWSA', *SSLH*, 50 (1985), 9.
[147] For the development of the social democratic women's movement see generally: Fricke, *Handbuch*, i. 409–53; Jean Helen Quataert, 'The German Socialist Women's Movement, 1890–1918: Issues, Internal Conflicts and the Main Personages' (University of Los Angeles Ph.D. 1974) and her book *Reluctant Feminists in German Social Democracy 1845–1917* (Princeton, NJ, 1979); Renate E. Pore, 'The German Social Democratic Women's Movement, 1919–1933' (University of Morgantown Ph.D. 1977); Sabine Richebächer, *Uns fehlt nur eine Kleinigkeit: Deutsche proletarische Frauenbewegung 1890–1914* (Frankfurt am Main, 1982).

conferences as well as more frequent special conferences. *Agitation* weeks whose aim was the winning of new women members were also held every year. Before the war the women's sections were very active in campaigning for women's suffrage by organizing special *Frauenwahlrechtstage* (women's suffrage days). Two weekly papers were published for Berlin women, the *Frauenstimme* and the *Frauenwelt*. Tours through Berlin museums as well as through Berlin workshops were organized. At the end of the 1920s membership of the Berlin women's sections was an impressive 19,062, followed by the Hamburg women sections which numbered 17,909. In Berlin in 1930, 428 women functionaries were active in organizing the women's activities.[148]

In Britain the 1890s saw the establishment of local ILP women's sections and guilds as well as a Co-operative Women's Guild. In 1906 the Women's Labour League was founded in defiance of the Labour Party's opposition to such organizational separatism.[149] Locally the League's sections sent delegates to party meetings, arranged joint events, shared platforms at public meetings and helped to fight election campaigns. The local branches of the League remained relatively autonomous and it was only after the war that the women became firmly integrated into the Labour Party's structure. A National Women's Organizer, Marion Philipps, was appointed in 1918. Sixty-two Advisory Councils were set up in order to enable representatives of women's sections to meet and keep in touch. Nine district organizers tried to encourage the growth of the women's sections locally. Labour women had their own paper, the *Labour Woman*, as the SPD women had their paper, *Die Gleichheit*.

Throughout the 1920s the women's sections grew strongly and by 1932 there were 1,705 sections in the country.[150] By 1926 the women's sections had 250,000 individual members.[151] By comparison the SPD in the same year only had 165,492 women members.[152] Marion Philipps placed special emphasis on the training of women's speakers and the appointment of women's organizers in the local parties.[153] A party paper on women's organization described the tasks of the sections as follows: 'a) meetings held partly for business and partly for education. b) a limited

---

[148] *Jahresbericht des Bezirksverbands der SPD Berlin* (1930), 102.
[149] Christine Collette, *For Labour and for Women: The Women's Labour League, 1906–1918* (Manchester, 1989), 38.
[150] Labour Party Archive, Organization Subcommittee Minutes, 1932: therein paper on women's organization, p. 3.
[151] *Labour Magazine*, 5 (1926–7), 266.
[152] Winkler, *Der Schein der Normalität*, 350.
[153] Marion Philipps, 'Organizing the Women Electors', *Labour Organizer* (May 1922), 12 and (Oct. 1922), 22.

number of public meetings. c) social activities, d) money raising efforts for the section or for the party to which they are attached.'[154] The LLP set up a Women's Advisory Committee after the First World War, which encouraged local women's organization. Herbert Morrison stressed in 1921 'the profound importance of securing the support of the women electors'.[155] Conferences, mass demonstrations, weekend and summer schools were organized, with the result that by 1927–8 seventy women's sections were active in the London area. Their growing strength and importance was illustrated by the growing numbers of female LCC candidates, and by the fact that there were eleven Labour women on the LCC by that time. Amongst the five officers of the LLP two were women. They celebrated 'women's month' 'by a big and most successful combined picnic in the Co-operative Woods at Woolwich and by various other social functions, in addition to a series of visits to the Houses of Parliament, County Hall and the LCC Fire Brigade Headquarters'.[156]

In Stockport[157]—another example of a lively women's section—women ward secretaries were appointed in 1925, women were responsible for the women's column and the children's corner in the local Stockport Labour newspaper, yearly winter programmes were set up, which consisted of lectures given to the women by invited speakers, and visits to neighbouring Labour Parties were organized. Although the women of Stockport also organized whist drives and socials, they put up their own women candidates for the Board of Guardians elections, they organized a scheme to help the miners in 1926 and they put specific policy proposals concerning the municipality to the male-dominated EC of the Stockport party.

Women's organizations in both the Labour Party and the SPD often found it difficult to come to terms with hostility from their male comrades. Undeniably, Bebel and Keir Hardie amongst others were in the forefront of those socialists fighting for women's liberation. There is also some evidence that the official pro-emancipation stance of the SPD had some bearing on the party's rank and file.[158] However, women remained

---

[154] Labour Party Archive, Organizational Subcommittee Minutes, 1932: therein paper on women's organization, 3.

[155] Labour Party Archive, Local Labour Party Files: files of the LLP, 'Organization Points', no. 17, 11 July 1921.

[156] *Annual Report of the EC of the LLP* (1926–7), 6. For the extraordinary activity of the London Labour women see also *London News* (June 1925), 2 and (July 1925), 2.

[157] Minutes of the meeting of the women's section of the Stockport Labour Party, 13 Jan. 1925 to 3 May 1927, in Stockport Labour Party files, in *Origins*, ed. Clark.

[158] Evans, *Proletarians*, 163–7.

heavily underrepresented in SPD organizations. Male Social Democrats—not to speak of male trade unionists[159]—often neglected *Agitation* amongst women; they remained sceptical of organized women and put up massive resistance to demands for more autonomy from the women's sections.[160] In the male-dominated cultural organizations of the SPD, prejudices against women were widespread[161] and the police reported to the Prussian Minister of the Interior in 1898: 'even men in the SPD are critical of women's liberation and equal rights for women'.[162] In 1913 the male-dominated executive of the SPD tried to abandon women's day, as they felt uneasy about women demonstrating in the streets, and in 1918 the SPD leaders in coalition talks with the liberals were even willing to abandon their demand for female suffrage in return for full manhood suffrage.[163] Contrary to all programmatic statements of the party in the 1920s, the position of women in the SPD was still a subordinate one and the policy-making organs of the party at all levels remained dominated by men.[164]

Women experienced similar difficulties in the Labour Party. Even the revered Keir Hardie was criticized within the PLP because of his 'obsession' with feminism.[165] The trade union wing, particularly, was anti-women. In Preston, for example, the local Labour Party after 1918 actively attempted to prevent the organization of women in the party, and the party throughout the 1920s was not concerned with women's issues in its political campaigns.[166] In 1932 the Acting Chief Women's Officer, Barbara Ayrton Gould spoke of a difficult relationship between many local parties and the women's sections: 'In a good many areas there is trouble in various women's sections because the local Labour Party will not allow the members to retain any of their 1 d. per week and the women have to pay the rent of a room for their meetings . . .'.[167]

Women's organizations were not alone in enriching the community

---

[159] For the anti-emancipation stance of many trade unions in Germany see Gisela Losseff-Tillmanns, *Frauenemanzipation und Gewerkschaften* (Wuppertal, 1978), 107 f.

[160] Friedhelm Boll, *Massenbewegungen in Niedersachsen, 1906–1920* (Bonn, 1981), 106 f.

[161] Lidtke, *The Alternative Culture*, 37.

[162] ZStA Merseburg, Rep. 77, no. 656, I, 4: police report to the Prussian Ministry of the Interior about the social democratic and anarchistic movement, 15 Jan. 1898, p. 9.

[163] Richard J. Evans, *Comrades and Sisters: Feminism, Socialism and Pacifism in Europe, 1870–1945* (New York, 1987), 70–3 and 85 f.

[164] Karen Hagemann, *Frauenalltag und Männerpolitik: Alltagsleben und gesellschaftliches Handeln von Arbeiterfrauen in der Weimarer Republik* (Bonn, 1990), 630–8.

[165] Morgan, *Keir Hardie*, 166 f.   [166] Savage, *The Dynamics*, 167–9.

[167] Labour Party Archive, Organization Subcommittee Minutes, 1932: letter from Barbara Ayrton Gould to Miss Tavener, 8 Mar. 1932.

character of the working-class parties in Britain and Germany: the same can be said about their youth organizations. In Germany local efforts to form youth organizations go back to the 1870s. As with women, there were legal difficulties in some German states, notably Prussia, yet in 1908 the youth organization was successfully integrated into the party machine. Local *Jugendausschüsse* (youth sections) were supported and encouraged by a Zentralstelle für die arbeitende Jugend Deutschlands (Central Bureau for the Working Youth of Germany). In 1914 there were 837 youth sections in local party organizations. There were yearly Whitsun meetings where many sections were represented and the work of the local sections was various. In bigger towns they had their own *Jugendheime* (youth centres) which served as centres for the educational and social activities of the youth sections.[168] In Altenburg, for example, the activities of the youth sections comprised visits to museums, reading and discussion evenings, rambling, handicraft work, and the organization of parties at Christmas and on other occasions.[169] The *Kinderfreundebewegung* formed an institutional framework for the six- to fourteen-year-olds. It organized 'children's republics' in the 1920s and local groups provided ample opportunities for play and early experience of a 'socialist way of life'.[170]

The ILP and the Clarionettes had formed youth organizations long before the Labour Party came into existence. The Labour Party itself was not always energetic in the promotion of its own youth sections, as a letter from William Gillies to Erich Ollenhauer in 1922 indicates:

I may say that, in general, our ideas about the organization of the Youth in the labour movement are of a tendency quite opposite to those of continental socialists. We do not believe in the separate organization of sympathizers below or above a certain age limit.[171]

Yet, the first local Junior Labour League was founded by the Barrow Labour Party in 1905.[172] People within the Labour Party who tried

---

[168] Rudolf Waclawiak, 'Jugendbildungsstätten', *SM* 14 (1910), 378–81. For the structure and organization of the German youth movement as a whole see Fricke, *Handbuch*, i. 454–94.

[169] Müller, *Zur Geschichte der Arbeiterbewegung in Sachsen-Altenburg*, 79. For the extensive activities of the Frankfurt youth sections see: *Arbeiterjugendbewegung in Frankfurt, 1904–1945: Material zu einer verschütteten Kulturgeschichte* (Lahn, 1978).

[170] Kurt Löwenstein, 'Die Aufgaben der Kinderfreundebewegung', *SM* 35 (1929), 1116–120.

[171] IISG, files of the Socialist Youth International: correspondence between Ollenhauer and Gillies in 1922–3, no. 24g.

[172] *Our Struggle for Socialism in Barrow: Fifty Years Anniversary*, ed. by the Barrow Labour Party (Barrow, 1950), 16.

to promote the setting up of Young People's Sections in local Labour Parties in the 1920s, like W. A. Peacock, argued that such youth organizations would be 'training centres for the movement of tomorrow'.[173] For them, the SPD's youth organization became a model and they sought to learn from the SPD how to build up a socialist youth culture.[174] The *Labour Organizer* in the 1920s continually promoted the establishment of youth sections in local Labour Parties and by 1929 300 branches had been set up.[175] They mainly organized the sons and daughters of Labour Party members up to the age of 18, and they held educational classes and meetings and 'provided the means of social intercourse, mutual assistance, mental and moral improvement, and rational recreation'.[176] Rambles were organized, camping sites erected. Cycling was a popular activity and a means to combine pleasure with propaganda. Visits were arranged to museums, the Houses of Parliament, and to local factories and public institutions and mock parliaments, discussion clubs, and local youth papers were set up.[177] Youth sections saw their tasks as being wider than the political sphere: 'Socialism has more than a political expression, and therefore there should undoubtedly be more than purely political activities.'[178]

Club life and festival culture in the working-class parties of Britain and Germany

Central to the social life of the Labour Party and the SPD were the Labour Clubs and *Gewerkschafts-/Parteihäuser* respectively. Both institutions usually had a bar and a hall for large public meetings, as well as offices for party officials. Many *Gewerkschaftshäuser* would also run a hostel for travelling trade unionists as well as a workers' library. Often the *Gewerkschafts-/Parteihäuser* could be understood as educational and cultural centres of the local SPD organization.[179] Having returned from a

---

[173] W. A. Peacock, 'Labour and the Coming Nation', *Labour Magazine*, 5 (1926–7), 307.

[174] See correspondence between Peacock and others involved in the League of Youth with Ollenhauer, in IISG, Amsterdam, files of the Socialist Youth International. The model character of 'the Youth Movement on the continent' is also mentioned by Egerton Wake at the 1924 Labour Party Conference. See *Report of the Annual Conference of the Labour Party, 1924* (London, 1924), 118.

[175] *Labour Organizer* (Dec. 1929), 235 f.   [176] *Labour Organizer* (Aug. 1923), 11.

[177] See *The League of Youth Bulletins* published in the *Labour Organizer* from May 1930 onwards.

[178] Paul Williams, 'Give Young Britain its Chance', *Labour Magazine*, 10 (1931–2), 509. He cited the ancillary organizations of continental working-class parties as models for the Labour Party.

[179] Werner Piechocki, *Der Volkspark als Kultur- und Bildungsstätte der halleschen Arbeiter (1907–1914)* (Halle, 1968).

visit to the German SPD, Arthur Henderson began to campaign fervently for the establishment of a Labour Club in London 'after the style of these in Germany'. Yet, according to J. Sassenbach, most German *Gewerkschafts-/Parteihäuser* experienced financial difficulties. He advised the creation of such houses only in those cases where it was not otherwise possible to solve the problem of hiring a meeting-place.[180] Difficulties in obtaining a decent meeting-place was often also the reason for a foundation of a Labour Club in Britain.[181] In towns where there was no hall, British as well as German party members would mostly choose a pub as party and social meeting-place.[182]

The booming number of Labour Clubs after 1918 met with a mixed reaction from many official party organizers. As signs of growth the setting up of Labour clubs was welcomed.[183] Soon critical voices could be heard. In 1925 the *Labour Organizer* warned: 'in a great number of cases the facilities [bars] become the attraction and Labour activity takes second place or even fifth place.'[184] This, however, does not mean that all Labour Clubs primarily were 'drinking dens'.[185] Paul Thompson, for example, has pointed to the vital political role the Labour Club had for the foundation of the Woolwich Labour Party in London.[186] In the Rhondda Valley, Labour Clubs were places of learning and discussion. They had their own libraries, discussion clubs, and educational classes.[187] David Clark has called the Colne Valley Labour Clubs 'oases of socialism where a counterculture to the materialism of Victorian capitalism evolved. Reading rooms and discussion groups flourished . . .'.[188]

The community character of both working-class parties on the local level was further emphasized by annual festivities. May Day demonstrations

---

[180] Historische Kommission, papers of the ADGB, NB 543: trade union houses, no. 3 and NB 461: SPD local parties, no. 10. For Henderson's efforts see Chris Wrigley, *Arthur Henderson* (Swansea, 1990), 64 and 74.

[181] *History of the Colne Valley Labour Party*, 8; Ashplant, 'The CIU and the ILP', 87.

[182] For Germany see Evans, *Proletarians*, 124–91. For Britain see: McKibbin, *Evolution*, 215 and Cunningham, *Leisure*, 84.

[183] *Labour Organizer* (Apr. 1921), 4.   [184] *Labour Organizer* (Aug. 1925), 3.

[185] As maintained by Elisabeth Domansky, 'Repräsentationsbauten der Arbeiterbewegung: Gewerkschaftshäuser in Westeuropa vor dem ersten Weltkrieg', in *Gewerkschaftsbewegung im 20. Jahrhundert im Vergleich: Forschungskolloquium Wintersemester 1984/1985*, ed. by the Institut zur Geschichte der Arbeiterbewegung an der Ruhr-Universität Bochum (Bochum, 1985), 18.

[186] Thompson, 'London Working-Class Politics', 438.

[187] Williams, 'Democratic Rhondda', 277 f.

[188] Clark, *Labour's Lost Leader*, 15.

were important yearly events in both countries.[189] Robert Schmidt's suggestion to the Cologne conference of the free trade unions in 1905 that there were almost no May Day celebrations in England was clearly overstating the case.[190] The Labour Party readily admitted that May Day celebrations on the continent were grander events than they were in Britain, but—once again—the continental labour movement became a model in the 1920s.[191] In both countries the form the May Day celebration took differed from place to place. Often there were May Day journals with articles describing the central demands of the labour movement. They were richly decorated by artists such as Walter Crane or Max Slevogt. Participants in May Day demonstrations wore a red flower or a red handkerchief, poems were read and songs sung. Some May Day celebrations had the character of garden parties, others, especially those accompanied by strike actions, carried notions of militant class war and were powerful assertions of the working-class party's claim to overthrow the state.

When Engels in 1890 witnessed the massive May Day celebration in London, when 300,000 people participated, he wrote that the first place in the May Day movement of 1890 belonged to the British proletariat.[192] Although this momentum could not be upheld, Julius Motteler in 1898 still counted 20,000 people at a central London demonstration including 35 musical bands, 53 wagons, and 186 banners.[193] In Glasgow in the years preceding the First World War as well as in Birmingham in the mid-1920s, tens of thousands of workers regularly participated in May Day rallies.[194] Even if many of the demonstrations did not meet the size of the big May Day marches of the SPD, the feeling of community amongst those participating in the march was just as high, as E. Muir remembered:

I can remember the banners floating heavily in the windless air, their folds sometimes touching like a caress the heads and faces of the people marching

---

[189] Janos Jemnitz, 'A Comparative Historical Sketch of the Early European May I Celebrations', in Andrea Panaccione (ed.), *May Day Celebration* (Venice, 1988), 191–206. Also Udo Achten (ed.), *Mein Vaterland ist international: Internationale Geschichte des 1. Mai* (Oberhausen, 1986).

[190] Robert Schmidt cited by Udo Achten, *Illustrierte Geschichte*, 110.

[191] *The Meaning of May Day*, ed. by the Labour Research Department, Labour White Papers, no. 42 (London, 1929), 4–7.

[192] Fricke, *Kleine Geschichte*, 27 f.

[193] FES, papers of Julius Motteler, 1823/10.

[194] Smith, 'Labour Tradition', 38, Boughton, 'Working Class Politics', 177 f.

behind them. . . . what I am most conscious of is the feeling that all distinction had fallen away like a burden carried in some other place, and that all substance had been transmuted.[195]

Certainly the May Day demonstrations in Nottingham in the 1920s were impressive by any standard:

The demonstration was imagined as a whole and deliberately planned in detail to preserve wholeness. Form and rhythm were secured by due alternation of cars and walking contingents. A colour scheme was settled from one end to the other by the use of specially designed cars; to secure 'largeness', interest was excited in the ward organizations and trade union branches . . . A single idea was attempted to be impressed on the onlooker . . . that the wage labour of today is . . . a passing phase of history . . . This was suggested in a series of tableaux. . . . The debasement of colour in social and industrial life was suggested by the declension from the rich hues of the Middle Ages to the drabs of today, both in the costumes and designs of the car . . . the five acres of the Great Market presented a great spectacle as the procession assembled and marshalled . . . Red flowers and programmes sold and collections during the two hours of the pageant brought in between £50 and £60, despite the widespread distress in Nottingham.[196]

Additionally the Nottingham Labour Party would organize competitions like 'Best Decorated Car', 'Best Fancy Dress', or 'May Queen', in order to raise interest in the demonstration as a social event, involving the whole community of Labour.[197]

The SPD and its ancillary clubs and organizations offered a whole way of life to its members who laughed, socialized, practised sport, made music, and discussed politics within the confines of the labour movement.[198] Nowhere does the community character of the SPD become clearer than in the pages of *Sozialistische Lebensgestaltung*, edited by Karl Mennicke from 1921 to 1923. Here, SPD clubs, circles, communities reported regularly about their activities up and down the country. Associations for a Socialist Way of Life (Vereinigungen für sozialistische Lebensgestaltung) were set up which aimed at making it possible for the individual to live as a socialist under capitalism. In a programmatic article, the editor compared the associations with the churches of old,[199] and Georg Braun of the Berlin association stressed the importance of communitarianism for the associations: 'the idea of community is the basis [for

---

[195] E. Muir, *An Autobiography* (London, 1964), 114.
[196] *Labour Organizer* (May 1921), 12 f.   [197] *Labour Organizer* (Apr. 1925), 16 f.
[198] For the festival culture of the SPD see also Guttsman, *Workers' Culture*, 233–53.
[199] *Sozialistische Lebensgestaltung*, 2 (Feb. 1921), 5.

our associations] . . . we learn to live in a community, to produce the things we need for ourselves and exchange them amongst us, so that we may become one people, one model.'[200] The Associations were part and parcel of a wider movement for the 'reform of life' (*Lebensreform*) in the SPD after 1918.[201] The Associations for a Socialist Way of Life certainly characterized an extreme form of communitarianism even within the SPD, but there was a spark of such feelings in many local parties and SPD ancillary organizations. The frequency of events within the community varied widely; usually recreational clubs would meet on a weekly basis, mixing exercise with sociability. A specific club language, and specific banners and symbols were created. Nearly every club held its own festival once or twice a year. In addition, each local SPD party had at least four big central festivities a year: the March, May Day, Lasalle, and Foundation Festival. In the 1920s the SPD even published little festival handbooks (*Feste der Arbeiter*) for their members which included suitable songs, poems, and texts for the occasion.[202] Festivals usually took the form of Sunday family outings and a whole range of social democratic clubs and organizations participated. At the foundation festival of the sixth Berlin SPD constituency party there was a concert, singing, declamations of short texts and poems, and an athletics demonstration. To close, Karl Liebknecht gave a lecture. Afterwards the comrades danced till the early morning hours.[203]

Many local Labour Parties in Britain were also characterized by efforts to combine their political work with a form of sociability that would bring party members closer together. Once again the Labour Party followed a tradition laid out by the smaller socialist organizations of the 1880s and 1890s, the SDF, ILP, and the Clarion. The local Clarion Fellowships were typical social institutions. Their main activity was the organization

---

[200] Georg Braun, 'Lebensgemeinschaft', *Sozialistische Lebensgestaltung*, 1 (Jan. 1921), 2.

[201] Guttsman, *Workers' Culture*, 288–90. Many of the associations who were central to the socialist 'reform of life' movement are at present being thoroughly researched in a four-volume project. See Peter Lösche, (ed.) *Sozialistische Kultur- und Freizeitorganisationen in der Weimarer Republik* (Bonn 1990–1993). The second volume in particular deals with health and 'reform of life' associations. See Franz Walter, Viola Denecke, and Cornelia Regin, *Sozialistische Gesundheits- und Lebensreformverbände* (Bonn, 1991).

[202] See for example Erich Altenberger (ed.), *Arbeiters Weihnachten: Ein Haus- und Handbuch für freie Menschen* (Waldenburg im Schlern, 1927); id. (ed.), *Herbst- und Jahreswende* (Waldenburg im Schlern, 1929); id. (ed.), *Revolution und Nie Wieder Krieg* (Waldenburg im Schlern, 1929).

[203] IGA/ZPA, St. 22/37: police report about the foundation festival of the social democratic constituency party of the 6th Berlin constituency, 11 Mar. 1911.

of dinner parties and the provision of social intercourse between like-minded persons of one locality.[204] The pages of the ILP's *Labour Leader* were full of reports about carol singing, teas and musical programmes, dances, rambling, member's nights, and so on. Annual socials were a common feature of many local Labour Parties.[205] In relation to Labour's symbolism, festivals and demonstrations, Eric Hobsbawm has spoken of the 'wealth of this British iconographical tradition'.[206]

The LLP organized 'an annual social gathering of Labour People from all parts of London' from 1921 onwards.[207] Besides there was the triennial London Labour Fair, where thousands of people were attracted by the numerous bazaar stalls, concerts, side shows, and dramatic entertainments. Organizers felt that those fairs had a strong activating effect on the membership of the LLP. In the words of one, doubtless partisan, observer: 'everyone is drawn into the net of the activities of one or more of the subcommittees . . . the 'Labour Fair' is on everyone's lips. . . . Everywhere activity both of group and individual; everywhere recruitment of new workers, and a more widespread publicity of tongue and pen.'[208] Apart from the regular, mostly annual socials, many local Labour Parties organized occasional events like flower shows, bazaars, 'sales of work'. The Coventry Labour Party, for example, held an annual bazaar from 1923 onwards for fifteen consecutive years.[209] Many local Labour Parties set up Social Committees and social secretaries were appointed. In Darlington, for example, its activities ranged from arranging dances to organizing annual trips to Blackpool.[210] The Stourbridge DLP, for example, organized four excursions between 1928 and 1930. The most popular one was a trip to London, where the party had to hire two trains to take about 1,000 people.[211] The Glasgow Labour Party advertised rambles into the countryside in *Forward* each week in the summer from a suitable tram

[204] Lawrence Thompson, *Robert Blatchford: Portrait of an Englishman* (London, 1951), 158–60.

[205] See for example the report about the annual 'At Home' of the Blackburn Labour Party in *Labour Organizer* (Jan. 1921), 17.

[206] Hobsbawm, *Worlds of Labour*, 72. For an interesting collection of Labour's badges, banners, ceramics, certificates, emblems, leaflets, membership cards, paintings, prints, sashes, photographs, and other objects testifying to the existence of Labour Party community culture, see John Gorman, *Images of Labour: Selected Memorabilia from the National Museum of Labour History* (London, 1985).

[207] *Annual Report of the EC of the LLP* (1929–30), 20.

[208] Mary B. Colebrook (Assistant Secretary of the London Labour Fair), 'London's Labour Fair', in *Labour Organizer* (Oct./Nov. 1924), 8. For a description of the fair see also Mary B. Colebrook, 'Great Success of London's Labour Fair', *London News* (Jan. 1925), 3.

[209] Hodgkinson, *Sent to Coventry*, 83.

[210] Labour Party Archive, Darlington Labour Party Minutes.

[211] *Labour Organizer* (Nov. 1930), 202 f.

terminus.[212] Efforts to increase the *Daily Herald*'s circulation after October 1912 led to the foundation of *Herald* Leagues in many localities.[213] The Leagues also performed wider political and social functions and became part of a vigorous Labour subculture in some of the party's strongholds. They became centres for political discussion and debate. Its members were to 'try to develop and extend to teach and propagate their desires as fully and widely as possible, [thereby] they might accomplish small miracles of missioning amongst our people.'[214]

Furthermore travel clubs, working in close association with the labour movement, existed in both Britain and Germany. The tourist club Die Naturfreunde was set up in Austria in 1893. Its first German association was founded in Munich in 1905. In Germany it never became a mass membership organization. Before 1914 local associations often only had 50–100 members, and its total membership peaked in 1923 with 116,124 members. Its main activity lay in the organization of rambling holidays and in the foundation of holiday homes for members, of which there existed 230 in 1933. Furthermore it published various rambling journals and organized lecture tours.[215] In addition, the party ran a national travel service, organizing tours to foreign countries and within Germany. In 1927–8 717 comrades participated in tours to London, Vienna, Copenhagen, Brussels and Paris, Tyrol, the Rhine, Hamburg, the Riviera, and Switzerland.[216]

The British Workers' Travel Association in Britain (WTA) was founded in 1921 in order to encourage organized workers to travel abroad. It was to become one of the major holiday providers in Britain in the inter-war years.[217] Contact between the local groups and head office was maintained through the *Travel Log*, the newsletter of the association published quarterly from 1926. The WTA organized reunions in a number of towns and it supplied local Labour Parties with travel lectures. As Harry Gosling, MP pointed out:

The WTA, the latest great venture of the Labour Movement, has wonderful possibilities in it. It gives the rank and file of the working class movements, Trade

[212] Ian McLean, *The Legend of Red Clydeside* (New York, 1983), 233.

[213] R. J. Holton, 'Daily Herald vs. Daily Citizen', *IRSH* 19 (1974), 368–70 about the *Herald* Leagues.

[214] *Daily Herald* (5 Jan. 1918), 11.

[215] Hartmut Wunderer, *Arbeitervereine und Arbeiterparteien: Kultur- und Massenorganisationen in der Arbeiterbewegung, 1890–1933* (Frankfurt am Main, 1987), 67–74. More detailed is Cornelia Regin, 'Der Touristenverein "Die Naturfreunde" ', in Walter, Denecke, and Regin, *Sozialistische Gesundheits- und Lebensreformverbände*, 241–92.

[216] Hansome, *World Workers' Educational Movements*, 251 f.

[217] Helen Walker, 'The Workers' Travel Association, 1921–1939', *SSLH* 50 (1985), 9.

Union, Co-operative, political Labour alike, the opportunity of making very real the Internationals of their respective bodies. . . . Conferences between leaders of organizations in different countries are of small avail if the excellent resolutions they adopt are turned down by the rank and file in the day of their proposed application.[218]

The WTA was the most successful ancillary organization of the British labour movement providing for holidays and excursions. It was, however, by no means the only one: rambling organizations like the Sheffield Clarion Ramblers and holiday organizations like the Holiday Fellowship served the same purpose. Some of these organizations' officials, like Arthur Leonhard of the Holiday Fellowship, were directly inspired by the German SPD and its ancillary organizations.[219]

The officials of both parties developed a rather ambiguous attitude towards these local social activities and towards the ancillary organizations. German Social Democrats argued that they would divert members' attention from political tasks and would carry sectional interests into the party: 'If the comrades were to direct their attention more towards political work, they would be more useful for the party than if they took an interest in Esperanto, short-hand and other such things.'[220] Equally Keir Hardie warned against any one-sided concentration on social activities in Labour Clubs. Those who did, he claimed, were in danger of turning the party into a 'lounge for loafers'.[221] In 1930 the *Labour Organizer* warned yet again: 'Members of clubs are in danger of stressing the social side too much.'[222]

4.3. Conclusion

The German clubs certainly organized many more party members than the Labour Party and appeared to be different from their British counterparts simply by their sheer size and scope. Even in the first decade of the twentieth century, membership in the three big ancillary organizations was around 100,000: the Workers' Singing Association (Arbeitersängerbund) had 90,000 members in 1907, the Workers' Cycling Clubs

---

[218] Harry Gosling, 'Foreign Travel for Workers', *Labour Magazine*, 2 (1923–4), 124.

[219] H. J. Walker, 'The Outdoor Movement in England and Wales, 1900–1939' (University of Sussex Ph.D. 1987), 117–224.

[220] *Bericht über die Tätigkeit des Bezirksvorstands der sozialdemokratischen Partei Leipzigs, 1913/14*, 137. For similar statements see: W. Dittmann, 'Zum Ausbau unserer Organisation', *NZ* 21 (1902–3), 262; F. Unger, 'Zur Agitation', *NZ* 25 (1907), 176.

[221] *Labour Leader* (2 June 1894).   [222] *Labour Organizer* (Oct. 1930), 184 f.

(Arbeiterradfahrvereine) had 130,000 members in 1910, and the Workers' Gymnastic Federation (Freier Arbeiterturnbund) had 140,000 members in 1910. Minor clubs such as the workers' rambling, sailing, or chess clubs still numbered their members in thousands. In the Weimar Republic, the membership of the SPD's ancillary organizations peaked in 1928, when they finally split into a social democratic and a communist wing. At that time membership of the Workers' Gymnastic Federation, for example, stood at 770,000 and the Cycling Clubs had a membership of over 220,000.[223]

Many visitors from the British labour movement, such as John Paton, expressed admiration for the scale of the SPD's educational, cultural, and leisure operations.[224] The sheer scope of SPD cultural organizations in some of their strongholds, like Leipzig, Berlin, or Hamburg made it appear to observers as though the German Social Democrats were in a different league from their Labour Party brothers. However, seen in a qualitative light, and taking account of the fact that elaborate SPD organizations were concentrated in its electoral strongholds,[225] the two parties' efforts to provide cultural recreation and education for its members appear to be much more similar. If numerically the SPD ancillary organizations were certainly more important than their British labour movement's counterparts,[226] in outlook and mentality the organizations have been shown as similar in every area of labour movement culture: education, theatre, music, sports, festival culture and travel, women's and youth organizations. They seem to have been more like a smaller version of the SPD's organizational network. More recently Chris Waters and Stephen Jones have uncovered a wealth of evidence for the existence of a rich community culture in the Labour Party throughout the period under discussion here.[227] Feelings of solidarity and common belonging were strong. The organizers of the Nuneaton League of Youth in the 1920s, Harry and Kitty Grey emphasized the fact that members have kept in touch all the time, even a whole life time: 'we have always mixed with

---

[223] Wunderer, *Arbeitervereine und Arbeiterparteien*, 29–76.

[224] John Paton, *Left Turn* (London, 1936), 350.

[225] Lidtke, *The Alternative Culture*, 168 has argued that labour movement culture was by and large a phenonomenon to be encountered in the big cities and other strongholds of the party only.

[226] In Britain overall membership of the party's ancillary organizations certainly numbered in thousands, but never in hundreds of thousands.

[227] Chris Waters, *British Socialists and the Politics of Popular Culture, 1884–1914* (Manchester, 1990) and Stephen G. Jones, *Workers at Play: A Social and Economic History of Leisure 1918–1939* (London, 1986), esp. 133–63.

socialists, all our life'.[228] Theirs is by no means a single voice: '[Labour] was something that informed your whole life . . . We lived for the party. We used to give to it, our time, our money, our love and faith . . . The Labour Party was our social life . . .'[229]

In cities under Labour rule, like Coventry in the 1930s, and Bermondsey in the 1920s, the Labour Party preferred to extend municipal social and recreational amenities rather than set up party recreational organizations. Nationally the Labour Party fought for paid holidays and for leisure-oriented solutions to unemployment.[230] If this attitude prevented any one-sided concentration on the development of the Labour Party's own leisure institutions, it should be pointed out that the SPD proved itself equally ready to co-operate with the state in providing better leisure facilities for the working class after 1918. The best example is the SPD's acceptance of and co-operation with the *Volkshochschulen* after 1918. The party used its own educational institutions increasingly for the training of party officials and left the education of the wider working-class public to the state-funded *Volkshochschulen*.[231] Another example is to be found in the many workers' libraries which were dissolved after 1918 and taken over by city public libraries.[232] Apart from such common efforts of the Labour Party and the SPD to improve the municipal/state provisions of culture and leisure for the working classes, it remains the case that the SPD's efforts of building up a separate sub-culture were more successful than the Labour Party's efforts, yet such a difference, it has been argued, was one of degree rather than substance.

---

[228] Interview with Harry and Kitty Grey, Nuneaton 30 Apr. 1990.

[229] Jeremy Seabrook, *What Went Wrong? Working People and the Ideals of the Labour Movement* (London, 1978), 89 f.

[230] Jones, 'The British Labour Movement', 137–202 and 382–435.

[231] Dieter Langewiesche, 'Freizeit und Massenbildung: Zur Ideologie und Praxis der Volksbildung in der Weimarer Republik', in Gerhard Huck (ed.), *Sozialgeschichte der Freizeit* (Wuppertal, 1980), 223–48. For the SPD's positive view on the *Volkshochschulen* after 1918 see also Konrad Haenisch, *Neue Bahnen der Kulturpolitik: Aus der Regierungspraxis der deutschen Republik* (Berlin, 1921), 108–18.

[232] Adelheid von Saldern, 'Arbeiterkulturbewegung in Deutschland in der Zwischenkriegszeit', in Friedhelm Boll (ed.), *Arbeiterkulturen zwischen Alltag und Politik* (Munich, 1986), 46.

5
The Working-Class Parties and Ideology

THE main thrust of this book has so far dealt with the organization of the British and German working-class parties. It has been argued that structurally both parties were more similar than is often perceived. In this chapter the ideology of the Labour Party and the SPD will be discussed. Whereas books about the Labour Party's ideology are rare, the SPD's ideology is one of the best-examined parts of SPD historiography. This does not make the comparison easier. What strikes the scholar when reading about both working-class parties' ideologies is the attributed difference in intensity and content of ideological debates in the two parties. The SPD is held to have been constantly engaged in discussions about Marxism and its consequences for a revolutionary party's policy, whereas the labourism of the Labour Party is seen as representing more of an underlying consensus—seldom discussed—holding the diverse elements of the reformist Labour coalition together. Geoffrey Foote, for example, has written: 'British socialism had an ethic and political outlook of its own, stamped with peculiarly British characteristics and separate from the socialist parties elsewhere in Europe. In other countries, a dogmatic form of Marxism prevailed, as in Germany . . .'.[1] G. D. H. Cole has argued: 'Socialism [in Britain was] essentially different from the 'scientific' Marxism of the continental Social Democrats'.[2] Ross McKibbin has written an influential article on the absence of Marxism from the British political scene.[3] And Kirk Willis has held the Labour Party's firm belief in the existing political institutions mixed with a peculiarly British spirit of pragmatism responsible for its unique ideological stance amongst the European working-class parties.[4] Without discussing subtle differences of political theory here, it shall be argued in the first section that any simple

---

[1] Geoffrey Foote, *The Labour Party's Political Thought: A History* (2nd edn., Beckenham, 1986), 17.
[2] G. D. H. Cole, *A History of Socialist Thought, 1789–1939* iii/1 (London, 1968), 143.
[3] McKibbin, 'Why was there no Marxism in Great Britain?', 297–331.
[4] Kirk Willis, 'The Introduction and Critical Reception of Marxist Thought in Britain 1850–1900', *Historical Journal*, 20 (1977), 417–59.

differentiation between a Marxist, revolutionary SPD and a Labourist, evolutionary Labour Party cannot be sustained. By slightly shifting the focus away from the official ideology in the second section the hopes and desires that motivated many of the rank and file will be discussed. It will be suggested that on the level of ideology from below both movements were closely related. Most surprisingly, such similarities can also be found when comparing both parties' relationship towards religion and the churches in the third section.

5.1. The official ideology

At the level of the official ideology differences between the Labour Party and the SPD seem to be indisputable, at least on the surface. The SPD not only devoted a greater part of its resources to theory, it also had internationally renowned theorists amongst its ranks: first of all there was the towering personality of Friedrich Engels, who gave advice to the party leaders and kept in constant touch with events in Germany. Names like Karl Kautsky, Eduard Bernstein, and Rudolf Hilferding won recognition beyond German borders. It is difficult to find any real counterparts in Britain. The Webbs, empiricists to the bone, were not really interested in political theory, Bertrand Russell was never deeply involved with the party, MacDonald was more of a popularizer of ideas, and in that, comparable to Bebel. The first important figures that spring to mind are G. D. H. Cole and Harold Laski in the 1920s and 1930s,[5] at a time when the Labour Party had long come of age. In 1908 Friedrich Naumann compared the 'intellectual poverty' of the British labour movement with the 'scientific quality' of its German counterpart,[6] indicating the difference in the weight that both parties attached to questions of theory. At the turn of the century Max Beer testified to the difference between a 'scientific socialism' in Germany and an 'empirical socialism' in Britain. Portraying the socialist conceptions of Keir Hardie, Beer stated: 'Keir Hardie . . . has no theories.'[7]

Theoretical debates within the circle of party intellectuals and party leaders apparently played a larger role in the SPD. The intellectual background of Labour Party leaders was often narrow. In a survey on reading habits of Labour leaders, W. T. Stead found out that most of the

[5] Kingsley Martin, *Harold Laski: A Biographical Memoir* (London, 1953); L. P. Carpenter, *G. D. H. Cole: An Intellectual Biography* (Cambridge, 1973); A. W. Wright, *G. D. H. Cole and Socialist Democracy* (Oxford, 1979).

[6] *Neue Rundschau*, Oc. 1908, quoted from *Die Sozialdemokratie im Urteile ihrer Gegner* (Berlin, 1911), 12.

[7] Max Beer, 'Parteipolitische Projekte in England', *NZ* 3 (1900–1), 434.

movement's leaders read little socialist literature, let alone Marxist philosophy. If they read anything at all, and often day-to-day experience seemed more important for their intellectual development than reading habits, it was mostly religious literature.[8] Therefore it is hardly surprising that Labourism has been described as a conglomerate of ideas, often of an ethical nature.[9] A pluralism of beliefs was accepted in the Labour Party. Bruce Glasier wrote in 1919: 'There is, and can be, no authoritative statement of Socialism.'[10] Labourism included the belief that the wealth of the nation had to be distributed more justly, that the 'capitalist' unjustly pocketed the 'surplus' produced by labour, and that strong and independent working-class organizations were necessary gradually to reduce the profits of the capitalists. More precise ideologies, like the Marxism of the SDF, the Fabianism of the Webbs, or the ethical/religious socialism of the ILP (those three constitute the main traditions of British socialism) were all acceptable to the extent that they were compatible with Labourist beliefs.

Whilst it shall not be denied that these arguments are based on some very real differences between the Labour Party and the SPD, the following discussion is meant to draw attention to some much-neglected similarities between the ideologies of the two working-class parties. The German party was by no means originally a Marxist party; it only adopted Marxism in the period of intense persecution under the Anti-Socialist Law, 1878–1890, and it was not before the 1891 Erfurt programme that Marxism was officially declared the basic philosophy of the party. Despite Erfurt, substantial numbers of Social Democrats always remained little influenced by the writings of Karl Marx.[11] If anything, it was Kautsky's particular brand of popular Marxism which made some headway amongst the party's rank and file.[12] SPD leaders like Hermann Müller, Friedrich Ebert, Otto Wels, Otto Braun, and many SPD officials were almost certainly more influenced by the day-to-day organizational routine

---

[8] See David Martin, 'Ideology and Composition', in Brown, *The First Labour Party*, 20–3.

[9] For labourism, its main components and development see Foote, *The Labour Party's Political Thought*; also Adam B. Ulam, *Philosophical Foundations of English Socialism* (Cambridge, Mass., 1951).

[10] J. Bruce Glasier, *The Meaning of Socialism* (Manchester, 1919), p. vii.

[11] H. J. Steinberg, *Sozialismus und deutsche Sozialdemokratie: Zur Ideologie der Partei vor dem 1. Weltkrieg* (5th edn., Berlin, 1979), 1–24 and 43 f. Also Roger Fletcher, *Revisionism and Empire: Socialist Imperialism in Germany 1897–1914* (London, 1984), 26 f.

[12] Evans, *Proletarians*, 144 f. For the influence of Kautskyanism on social democratic workers see Adolf Levenstein, *Die Arbeiterfrage: Mit besonderer Berücksichtigung der sozialpsychologischen Seite des moderen Großbetriebes und der psycho-physischen Einwirkungen auf die Arbeiter* (Munich, 1912). Also Jörg Schadt (ed.), *Wie wir den Weg zum Sozialismus fanden* (Cologne, 1981).

of party life than they were by party philosophy.[13] Long before 1914, Bernstein's reformism, influenced by, though not resulting from Fabianism,[14] made great inroads into the party's official theory. Reformism as a practice had been established after 1900 independently of Bernstein's *Voraussetzungen*. Various factions within the SPD were successful in making the pre-war SPD primarily a democratic reform party.[15] From the turn of the century outspoken anti-Marxists, like Leo Arons, Albert Südekum, Josef Bloch, and Wilhelm Kolb, amongst others, held influential positions in the party.[16]

The heterodox and amorphous coalition of those critical of Marx rejected the phraseology of a radical transformation of society. In February 1912 Ludwig Frank wrote to Paul Löbe: 'The emancipation of the working class has to begin with the emancipation from phraseology . . .'[17] In the same year Paul Kampffmeyer stressed the necessity of subordinating theory to the fighting of elections. The SPD should concentrate on *realpolitik*, not on ideology.[18] Eduard Bernstein's commitment to non-violent methods of reform and to parliamentary democracy only reflected beliefs and practices widespread in the SPD long before 1914.[19] Democratic convictions and non-revolutionary attitudes were not only found amongst revisionists. The Marxist keeper of the grail Karl Kautsky can be seen as a proponent of a kind of 'democratic Marxism'.[20] Kautsky was convinced that socialism could be achieved without a violent overthrow of the political system. In contrast to Lenin he advocated the conquest of a parliamentary majority and emphasized the importance of freedom of speech and toleration of dissent.[21]

[13] For Braun's disinterest in political theory see: Hagen Schulze, *Otto Braun oder Preußens demokratische Sendung: Eine Biographie* (Frankfurt am Main, 1977), 145 f.

[14] Herbert Frei, *Fabianismus und Bernsteinscher Revisionismus, 1884–1990: Eine ideologie-komparatistische Studie über wissenschaftstheoretische, philosophische, ökonomische, staatstheoretische und revolutionstheoretische Aspekte der Marxschen, Fabischen und Bernsteinschen Theorie* (Berlin, 1979).

[15] Emil Lederer, *Die wirtschaftlichen Organisationen und die Reichstagswahl* (Tübingen, 1912) Also Brandt and Rürup, *Volksbewegung*, 57.

[16] Fricke, *Die deutsche Arbeiterbewegung*, 228 f.

[17] IGA/ZPA, papers of Paul Löbe, NL 110/48, 3: letter from Ludwig Frank to Paul Löbe, 20 Feb. 1912.

[18] Paul Kampffmeyer, 'Ziele und Mittel der sozialdemokratischen Agitation', *SM* 16 (1912), 234–9.

[19] For Bernstein's commitment to democratic theory see Eduard Bernstein, *Die Voraussetzungen des Sozialismus und die Aufgaben der Sozialdemokratie* (repr. of the 1921 edn., Bonn, 1977), 170–98.

[20] Dick Geary, *Karl Kautsky* (Manchester, 1987), 126.

[21] Massimo L. Salvadori, *Karl Kautsky and the Socialist Revolution, 1880–1938* (London, 1979), 153 and Gary P. Steenson, *Karl Kautsky, 1854–1938: Marxism in the Classical Years* (Pittsburgh, 1978), 6 f.

In the Weimar Republic the party's theory became increasingly 'democratic', although Marxism was officially retained and a vociferous Marxist left-wing, demanding the socialization of all the means of production and a return to the rhetoric of the class war, remained in the party, giving it a Janus-faced appearance. Hilferding's theory of organized capitalism, which became the official theory of the SPD in the Weimar Republic, emphasized the evolutionary character of the transformation from capitalism to socialism. The Marxist idea of the state as an instrument of class repression was effectively countered by the views of Hermann Heller who, in the 1920s, positioned himself and the party within a tradition which could hardly deny its closeness to liberal English political theory of the seventeenth and eighteenth century. Furthermore, in the Great Slump at the end of the 1920s the SPD pinned their hopes on liberal ideas of the automatic self-regulation of market forces and rejected any ideas of deficit spending.[22] The SPD conferences right through from 1919 to 1931 reflected the commitment of the party to the republic and to democracy.[23] In fact the Social Democrats were the strongest supporters of the Weimar Republic.[24] Susanne Miller, in an effort to define the major values of Social Democracy, identified (1) the rights of democratic freedom, (2) the demands for social justice, and (3) the idea of solidarity.[25] None of those values was necessarily connected with Marxism (although they were not opposed to Marxism either).

One should be cautious not to emphasize the difference in ideological content too much. Duncan Tanner has recently observed that the ideological debates within the Edwardian Labour Party were similar to the ideological debates within continental socialist parties.[26] Apart from what Ludwig Frank called 'phraseology', the core beliefs of both parties as embodied in Miller's definition and the 'Labourist' principles were not worlds apart. If one should not overemphasize the importance of Marxism for the SPD, one should also not simply discard any influence of Marxism upon the British Labour Party. E. P. Thompson, in a now

---

[22] For the SPD's ideology in the Weimar Republic see generally Franz Ritter, *Theorie und Praxis des demokratischen Sozialismus in der Weimarer Republik* (Frankfurt am Main, 1981). For the development of a liberal democratic constitutional theory within the SPD see also Steinbach, *Sozialdemokratie und Verfassungsverständnis.*

[23] See for example *Protokoll des SPD Parteitags 1919*, 238 f. and *Protokoll des SPD Parteitags 1931*, 234.

[24] Breitmann, *German Socialism and Weimar Democracy*, esp. ch. 1: 'Parliamentarism and Progress', 9–21. Also an underlying topic in. Maehl, *The German Socialist Party.*

[25] Susanne Miller, 'Grundwerte in der Geschichte der deutschen Sozialdemokratie', *aus politik und zeitgeschichte*, 11 (1976), 16–31.

[26] Duncan Tanner, 'Ideological Debate in Edwardian Labour Politics: Radicalism, Revisionism and Socialism', in Biagini and Reid, *Currents of Radicalism*, 271–93.

famous debate with Nairn/Anderson almost thirty years ago, warned against any simple notion of an English *Sonderweg* in socialist political thought. A mere statement of the fact that the British left was without a structured ideology would flatten, stretch, and condense the history of the movement and deny the existence of a substantial minority movement which was not 'Labourist'.[27] The enormously popular novelist H. G. Wells, for example, revealed an admiration for Karl Marx that may well have been shared by many of the rank and file in British Labour: 'He opened out socialism . . . One may quibble about the greatness of Marx as one may quibble about the greatness of Darwin; he remains great and cardinal.'[28] Amongst the organized miners of South Wales, the writings of Marx and Joseph Dietzgen as a popularizer of Marxist ideas were certainly widely read, and Karl Marx Centenary Celebrations like the ones in Tonypandy on 5 May 1918 also testify to the popularity of Marxism in Britain at certain times and places.[29]

Any kind of Marxist or Labourist homogeneity of SPD and Labour Party should not be too easily taken for granted. It has been stressed, for example, that the SPD had difficulties in developing a positive attitude towards political power in the Weimar Republic, because of its inability to come to terms with its radical Marxism.[30] Such a narrowly ideological explanation becomes less plausible when weighed against the attitudes of the Labour Party to political power, because here the same apprehensive attitude can be found. Between 1924 and 1929 successive demands not to take office as a minority government could be heard in the Labour Party and although those voices were eventually overruled, they made life difficult for the Labour governments. It therefore seems to be more sensible to conclude that both working-class parties included strong minorities, Marxist or not, which were against taking political responsibility within a society that they wanted to overcome. Yet more importantly the majority within both parties, who had forgotten or lost earlier transformatory aims, remained ambivalent about what they regarded as the 'immorality

[27] Edward P. Thompson, 'The Peculiarities of the English', *Socialist Register* (1965), 337 f. For the influence of Marxism on the British labour movement before 1900 see Stanley Pierson, *Marxism and the Origins of British Socialism: The Struggle for a New Consciousness* (New York, 1973). For the particularly strong influence of Marxism between 1917 and 1921 see Stuart Macintyre, *A Proletarian Science: Marxism in Britain 1917–1933* (Cambridge, 1980). For examples of more specific influence on the Labour Party see ibid. 33–5.

[28] H. G. Wells, *New Worlds for Old* (London, 1908), 240.

[29] Francis and Smith, *The Fed*, 54, Williams, 'Democratic Rhondda', 273.

[30] Winkler, *Von der Revolution*, 12 f. *Id., Der Schein der Normalität*, 263 f., 636–9, 821.

of capitalism': '[The Labour Party] suffered from a split personality: . . . It was a parliamentary party with a Utopian ethic . . .'.[31] Additionally the labour movement culture in both countries, tending to see the world in a 'them and us' dichotomy, made full integration of both parties into their political systems problematic. Whether this culture was Marxist or ethical socialist mattered comparatively little.

A minority within both parties finally seceded from the Labour Party as well as the SPD at the beginning of the 1930s because of 'ideological impurity'. Neither the ILP nor the SAP[32] could believe in the possibility of making 'capitalist' society more just by working through its institutions. Fenner Brockway, MP, recalled in his autobiography how John Wheatley, MP, expressed the fears of the whole left wing of the Labour Party when in 1929 he warned the Labour Party that it would fail should it choose to administer capitalism rather than transform it.[33] John Paton, MP, argued that the failure of the Labour Party in 1931 and the disaster of the SPD in 1933 both lay in the 'lack of revolutionary determination' of the working-class parties.[34]

Yet German scholars like Heinrich August Winkler and Susanne Miller have not only blamed Marxism for the SPD's fear of power, they have also argued that the adoption of a more or less rigid Marxism encouraged the party not to work out any definite policy proposals. Thus in 1918, the party which had prophesied the revolution for so long stood without any detailed plans, confused and too willing to surrender power when it had acquired it.[35] In the comparative light this hypothesis becomes less plausible. It hardly needs Marxism to explain why the Social Democrats in 1918 failed to make more use of the revolution. It is quite sufficient to refer to the SPD's acute sense of patriotism, their urge to help 'the fatherland in the hour of need', and their sense of democracy which made them hesitant to reform German society structurally without a democratic mandate. What is more, the non-Marxist Labour Party suffered from the same defect. When in power, both parties lacked concrete 'socialist' policies. Indeed, R. H. Tawney argued after the 1931 débâcle that the party lacked any specific socialist policy, because it lacked an ideology, a unifying creed. This hindered the development of 'a common

---

[31] Robert Skidelsky, *Politicians and the Slump* (London, 1967), p. xii.
[32] Robert E. Dowse, *Left in the Centre: The ILP, 1893–1940* (London, 1966), 173–200. Heinz Niemann, 'Entstehung und Rolle der SAP in der Endphase der Weimarer Republik', *BZG* 29 (1987), 745–52.
[33] Brockway, *Inside the Left*, 197.   [34] Paton, *Left Turn*, 395.
[35] Winkler, *Von der Revolution*, 48, 83, 146–9. Also Miller, *Die Bürde*, 446 f.

conception of the ends of political action and of the means of achieving them'.[36] Tawney simply turned round Winkler's and Miller's argument about the relationship between ideology and concrete policy proposals. Both views put too much importance on questions of official ideology. The Labour Party and SPD partly lacked concrete policy proposals because both originated as protest movements against basic injustices. As such they had been concerned with a moral crusade more than with specific policies. Furthermore arguments about their lack of policies often fail to remember that both parties in the 1920s never had a chance to implement their policies without constraint. In Britain the Labour Party came to power as a majority party only in 1945 (and few would doubt the impact the Attlee government had on post-war Britain), whereas in Germany the coalition governments before 1933 did not allow the SPD to implement their policies uninhibitedly.

So far, only the official ideology of both parties has been discussed. Certain differences have been mentioned, but it has also been argued that those differences should not be overemphasized in their importance. The viciousness and subtlety of doctrinal debates escaped most of the rank and file in the Labour Party and the SPD. Local studies in both countries have revealed that local parties were most interested in municipal and social policies, and there is little support for the assumption that they were intensely interested in questions of political theory.[37] Organized German workers who used the party's libraries seldom chose to borrow party philosophy,[38] and the 1901 police report into Social Democracy stressed that the contradiction between the stability of the party and the raging ideological infighting could only be explained in terms of widespread indifference of the rank and file: 'the political controversies, which inflame passions amongst the leaders of the party for years, leave the great mass of party members completely indifferent.'[39] Therefore it makes more sense to look at those ideological efforts which were more popular with the rank and file.

---

[36] R. H. Tawney, 'The Choice before the Labour Party', *Political Quarterly*, 3 (1932), 327.

[37] Von Saldern, *Vom Einwohner*, 132, 139 f., 145, 222–6. Georg Fülberth, 'Zur Genese des Revisionismus in der deutschen Sozialdemokratie vor 1914', in *Das Argument*, 63 (1971), 1–21. D. James, 'The Keighley ILP, 1892–1900', Taylor and Jowitt, *Bradford 1890–1914*, 64 f. Barker, 'The Anatomy of Reformism', 1–27.

[38] Josef Klicke, 'Arbeiterlektüre', *NZ* 15 (1911), 317–19.

[39] ZStA Potsdam, 15.01: Reichsministerium des Inneren, Interior Ministry, no. 13688/1, vol. iii, 47, p. 1.

5.2. The need for utopia in the British and German working-class parties

For the socialists of both Britain and Germany the vision of the future socialist society was of great importance. The popularity of that issue decreased somewhat in time, being more popular before 1914 than thereafter.[40] In the 1920s party technocrats like Wels, Ollenhauer, Henderson, and Morrison succeeded the earlier prophets like Bebel and Keir Hardie. As one biographer wrote of Ollenhauer: 'A utopian concept [*Prinzip Zukunft*] he knew not; in his daily work . . . it would have found no space.'[41] Yet there was no clear break between the need for utopia before 1914 and an orientation towards pragmatic policy-making thereafter.[42] The two always coexisted, just as socialist utopianism coexisted with the persistence of the traditional value system amongst many professed socialists.[43]

In the following the efforts of popular socialist writers to outline the future socialist society in Britain and Germany shall be compared. Thereby it will be possible to reconstruct some of the basic beliefs of the rank and file, for whom those often propagandistic outlines constituted much of their ideology. For many leaders of the British as well as for the German labour movement those socialist utopias were their first encounter with socialism. Walter Citrine's and Ellen Wilkinson's first introduction to socialism was provided by Blatchford's *Merrie England* (1893) and *Britain for the British* (1902).[44] *Merrie England*, which had sold 700, 000 copies when the 1895 edition appeared, became so popular within the British labour movement that Labour churches and other socialist groups held *Merrie England* study classes and *Merrie England* fund-raising fairs, sometimes staged in specially constructed model villages.[45] Herbert Morrison turned to socialism by reading cheap historical and political pamphlets on 'the ideas of those who wanted to create a new society'.[46] G. D. H. Cole

---

[40] Pierson, *British Socialists*, 192; Helga Grebing, *Der 'deutsche Sonderweg' in Europa, 1806–1945: Eine Kritik* (Stuttgart, 1986), 132.

[41] Seebacher-Brandt, *Erich Ollenhauer*, 38.

[42] Susanne Miller, *Das Problem der Freiheit im Sozialismus: Freiheit, Staat und Revolution in der Programmatik der Sozialdemokratie von Lasalle bis zum Revisionismusstreit* (Frankfurt am Main, 1964), 291 for the simultaneity of utopian aspirations and constructive policy-making. Also White, 'Reconsidering European Socialism', 256.

[43] Loreck, *Wie man früher Sozialdemokrat wurde*, 100 f.

[44] Walter Citrine, *Men at Work: An Autobiography* (London, 1964), 62. Betty Vernon, *Ellen Wilkinson* (London, 1982), 9.

[45] Fincher, 'The Clarion Movement', 95.

[46] Morrison, *An Autobiography*, 24.

was converted to socialism by the writings of William Morris.[47] Friedrich Stampfer of the SPD confessed in his memoirs that it was Bellamy's *Looking Backward* which made him turn to socialism.[48]

Edward Bellamy's *Looking Backward—2000* became a bestseller in both Britain and Germany around the end of the nineteenth century. The book introduced a technocratic vision of a well-planned and co-ordinated future society in which there was neither waste of resources nor social misery. It was serialized in major social democratic and Labour newspapers, at a time when the serialization of utopian novels became a habit in both the British and the German labour movement press. Many British and German socialists were critical of Bellamy's simplistic equation of technocratic progress with ultimate happiness. Thus William Morris's *News from Nowhere* was directly inspired by Bellamy's book and was meant as a counter-vision in which the key notion was not scientific technological progress but human fellowship and brotherhood. August Bebel in the foreword to the ninth edition of *Die Frau* criticized Bellamy's book. According to him Bellamy's vision was that of a moralistic bourgeois social reformer who had heard or understood nothing about class war and the class antagonisms which lie at the basis of all human progress.[49] Clara Zetkin, who had translated Bellamy's book into German in 1890, agreed with Bebel as to the unscientific nature of Bellamy's socialism, yet she issued a second edition in 1914 arguing that the book pointedly answered some of the questions regarding the socialist state-to-come.[50]

There were other utopian novels, like Karl Ballod's *Der Zukunfisstaat* (1898), Michael Flürscheim's *Deutschland in 100 Jahren oder: Die Galoschen des Glücks. Ein soziales Märchen* (first serialized 1886) and Theodor Hertzka's *Freiland* (1890) in Germany[51] and William Thompson's *A Prospectus of Socialism, or, a Glimpse of the Millennium*, Philipp Frankford's *The Coming Day: Some Scenes from Life under Socialism*, and Jane Hume

---

[47] Foote, *The Labour Party's Political Thought*, 107.

[48] Friedrich Stampfer, *Erfahrungen und Erkenntnisse: Aufzeichnungen aus meinem Leben* (Cologne, 1957), 12.

[49] August Bebel, *Die Frau und der Sozialismus*, (10th edn., Stuttgart, 1891), pp. v–vii. The first edition of Bebel's book was published in 1879 and was one of the first victims of the anti-socialist law. The second edition in 1883 had to be distributed illegally.

[50] Edward Bellamy, *Ein Rückblick aus dem Jahre 2000 auf das Jahr 1887*, trans. and ed. Klara Zetkin (Stuttgart, 1914), 3 f.

[51] For a bibliography of German utopian socialist novels see Lucian Hölscher, *Weltgericht oder Revolution: Protestantische und sozialistische Zukunftsvorstellungen im deutschen Kaiserreich* (Stuttgart, 1989), 446 f.

Clapperton's *A Vision of the Future* (1904) in Britain.[52] Socialist utopias provoked anti-socialist utopias. Anti-socialist novels included Edward Herbert's *New Era: A Socialist Romance* and Ernest Bramah's *The Secret of the League* in Britain and Eugen Richter's *Pictures of the Socialist Future* in Germany. They usually concentrated on themes like the loss of individual freedom and the creation of an omnipresent state under socialism.

Frank Bealey's claim that 'the socialist society of the future was not a keen matter of debate at official levels of the Labour Party before 1914'[53] has to be juxtaposed with the great popularity of utopian literature amongst members of the British working-class parties. Maybe the leaders of the emerging Labour Party did not emphasize a socialist utopia in their efforts to convince Liberal trade union leaders to affiliate to the Labour Party, but the writings of nearly all prominent socialists, of those who wrote at all, were littered with references to the future socialist state.[54] Ramsay MacDonald developed an outline of the socialist state to come in his 1911 book *The Socialist Movement*, even though, by then, MacDonald had come a long way from his early involvement in the Fellowship of the New Life, when his writings were of an even dreamier utopianism.[55] Although he admitted in 1911 that certain questions of the socialist state 'cannot be discussed profitably except as a speculative exercise'[56] he went on to describe society as a machine that has to be properly studied. From such an investigation 'the Socialist rises with a clear conception of the social will . . . he carries on in idea the tendency which he sees beginning to operate now; from the walls of the temple so far built, he can anticipate the architect's idea, continue his lines, and form some conception of the completed fabric.'[57] In that interpretation the socialist comes close to the discoverer of natural laws, who can identify the forces which will shape the future. The underlying basis of many utopias, the belief in a constant drift towards progress via science, is unmistakably present in MacDonald's thought. The socialist 'can map the drift of progress; [he] . . . can trace the course of history through some part of the misty

---

[52] For a discussion of a number of other utopian novels serialized in the London socialist press see Jack Mitchell, 'Tendencies in Narrative Fiction in the London-Based Socialist Press of the 1880s and 1890s', in H. Gustav Klaus (ed.), *The Rise of Socialist Fiction 1880–1914* (New York 1987), 49–72.

[53] Frank Bealey, *The Social and Political Thought of the Labour Party* (London, 1970), 11 f.

[54] Waters, *British Socialists and the Politics of Popular Culture*, 45 makes a similar point about the importance of utopian thought in the pre-war Labour Party.

[55] Morgan, *Labour People*, 42 f.   [56] MacDonald, *The Socialist Movement*, 113.

[57] Ibid. 118.

future; by discovering the dream cities which men have built in their hearts as abiding places for their souls, can tell what social fabrics they are to raise . . .'.[58]

Arthur Henderson's 1918 *The Aims of Labour* is another effort to outline the future socialist state after the transformation of society towards the common ownership of production. 'The coming era of revolutionary change'[59] would then lead towards world democracy and towards a new mankind of highest moral standards. Characteristically his publication starts off with a poem by John Addington Symonds, reflecting the general mood of the booklet:

> These things shall be! a loftier race
> Than ere the world hath known shall rise,
> With flame of freedom in their souls,
> And light of knowledge in their eyes. . . .
> New arts shall bloom of loftier mould
> And mightier music fill the skies,
> And every life shall be a song,
> When all the earth is paradise.

Nobody embodied the utopian, somewhat nebulous character of British socialism more than Bruce Glasier: preferring to hold talks about subjects like 'Socialism, the Light and the World' or 'The Promise and Prophecy of Socialism', 'he saw himself . . . as a wandering wise man, pilgrim's wallet slung from his shoulders, pilgrim's staff in hand.'[60] In his visionary 1919 book *The Meaning of Socialism* he foresees the triumph of socialism:

The millionaire rolls his monster coils about the nation and fouls our cities with his wealth, but the young Perseus is preparing his spear, and soon will flash as from the sun the annihilating stroke . . . Not one but ten thousand dragons devouring and fouling the earth there maybe, but Socialism, lo!, its light is in the world and its triumph is heralded in every wind. It is the advent of peace, the epoch of man released from the brute, the reign of equality.[61]

Glasier, like MacDonald, felt history on the side of socialism: 'I believe Socialism is inevitable not simply because of the economic and material factors of modern civilisation, but because also of the spiritual factors of social evolution.'[62] According to G. B. Shaw it was exactly this crusading

---

[58] MacDonald, *The Socialist Movement*, 121.
[59] Arthur Henderson, *The Aims of Labour* (London, 1918), 12.
[60] Thompson, *The Enthusiasts*, 92.   [61] Glasier, *The Meaning of Socialism*, 18 f.
[62] J. Bruce Glasier, 'The Meaning of Socialism', *Socialist Review*, 16 (1919), 333.

zeal of socialism which 'wins its disciples by presenting civilisation as popular melodrama, or as a Pilgrim's Progress through suffering trial and combat against the powers of evil to the bar of poetic justice with paradise beyond'.[63] Even after 1918 men like MacDonald and Sidney Webb remained convinced that Britain was moving inevitably towards a system of public ownership, economic equality, and democratic control.[64] The idea of the pilgrimage remained strong. When the second Labour government came to power in 1929 Frank Smith wrote: 'It was a pilgrimage of forty years which the children of Israel endured before they got within reach of the promised land. They did not have exactly a joy march all the way. . . . May 30, 1929, did not bring in the Socialist millennium, but it has brought us to Westminster as a preliminary.'[65]

In Germany both revisionists and Marxists were prone to create similarly prophetic pictures of a socialist society. Bernstein was one of the few to reject such visions: 'I am not concerned with what is going to happen in the distant future, but with what happens in the present and what can and should be done in the near future.'[66] This did not prevent fellow revisionists from using the language of the millennium. In a speech to the ILP on his visit to Britain in 1906 Albert Südekum declared:

We are going on. Our movement is towards a better, fairer organization of society; and our faith is strong and high that the time will surely come . . . when the dull, grey clouds under which millions of our workmen are monotonously toiling will break and melt, and vanish forever in the sunshine of a new and noble age.[67]

In an essay in 1903 Wolfgang Heine praised efforts to describe the future socialist state as aesthetically pleasing as well as one factor in the politicization of workers. According to him, such utopias would support the assumption that socialism was economically and historically possible as well as psychologically thinkable.[68] According to Heine's memoirs he, himself, tried to write about the socialist utopia and used William Morris as his guide.[69] In the war L. Radlof remembered: 'In my youth nothing

[63] G. B. Shaw, 'The Illusions of Socialism', in E. Carpenter (ed.), *Forecasts of the Coming Century* (London, 1897), 171.

[64] Richard Price, 'Labour, State and Society in Britain before 1914', paper held at the International Colloquium Graz, 5–9 June 1989, p. 13; Pierson, *British Socialists*, 342.

[65] Frank Smith, 'Forty Years of Pilgrimage: Has Labour Arrived', in *Labour Magazine*, 7 (1928–9), 99.

[66] Bernstein, *Die Voraussetzungen des Sozialismus*, 196.

[67] BA Koblenz, Papers of Albert Südekum, NL 190, 91/41.

[68] Wolfgang Heine, 'Utopien', *SM* 7 (1903), 649 f. and 654.

[69] For a recollection of Heine's novelette in his memoirs see Wolfgang Heine, 'Erinnerungen', in BA Koblenz, Papers of Wolfgang Heine, Kl. Erw, no. 371–15, pp. 384–8.

was more interesting than a debate about the final goal . . . We all dreamt
more or less of a breakdown of capitalist society . . .'[70] Karl Kautsky, in
1909 wrote a whole book about the transformation from capitalism to
socialism. This book was explicitly meant as socialist prophecy: 'In politics
nothing goes without prophecies.'[71] Kautsky started off by demonstrating
the qualities of Marx and Engels as prophets and went on to prophesy
'a new age of revolutions'.[72] There is no shortage in social democratic
propaganda material which described the 'new age'.[73]

The vocabulary of those 'utopian' publications was strikingly similar in
both countries. Nationalization or socialization of all means of production
and of the land would have to precede any change towards socialism.
Often the wage system would be swept away, exploitation would cease. In
British publications nationalization was more often seen as municipal
rather than state, which reflected the stronger current of municipal socialism in Britain. Key words used in socialist utopias included 'Freedom', 'Community', 'Cooperation', and 'Fellowship'.

The physical as well as the mental needs of the whole population
would be satisfied by a new kind of economic system and a new attitude
of man towards man. Everyone would have access to education and could
fulfil his or her potentials. Communal restaurants and leisure facilities
would exist for the enjoyment of all. Crime would have disappeared as all
source of crime, namely a criminal society, would also have disappeared.
Under a competitive commercial system men had lived in a state of war,
but under a system in which solidarity had replaced competition the
natural goodness of men would be allowed to emerge. The spirit of gain
would be overcome by the spirit of service. The age of individualism
would be overcome by the age of solidarity. Work would be a pleasure
through shorter working hours and the extensive use of machinery and
electricity. Science and the arts would bloom under their new freedom
and everybody would enjoy their fruits. Parties and politicians would
cease to exist, as the age of socialism would not be the age of conflicting
interests, but the age of harmony and goodwill.

Some of the key words of British and German ideology from below
shall be further examined: the perception of the state, the moralistic idea

[70] Ludwig Radlof, *Vaterland und Sozialdemokratie* (Munich, 1915), 70.
[71] Karl Kautsky, *Der Weg zur Macht: Politische Betrachtungen über das Hineinwachsen in die Revolution* (Berlin, 1909), 23.
[72] Ibid. 14–22 and 89–104.
[73] See for example J. Stern, *Der Zukunftsstaat* (5th edn., Berlin, 1906). Also Kenneth R. Calkins, 'The Uses of Utopianism: The Millenarian Dream in Central European Social Democracy Before 1914', *Central European History*, 15 (1982), 128–33.

of a 'new man', the historical determinism, the preoccupation with the scientific nature of socialism, the attitude to revolution of both working-class parties and the backward looking character of British socialism.

Bruce Glasier saw an increased role of the state as a positive necessity of any future socialist society. This idea he shared with German socialists like Rudolf Hilferding. For Glasier 'the state always is for the time being very largely the instrument of the self-interest of the dominant person, faction or class in the community, whosoever they may be'.[74] Hilferding's theory of organized capitalism also saw the state as a neutral instrument of change in the hands of whoever commanded political authority.[75] The state orientation of German socialists was not only shared by Glasier. John Ruskin, whose book *Unto this Last* became influential amongst the labour movement in Britain, had already stressed the fact that a more just society needed more state action, especially in areas like education, unemployment, provision for old age and sickness. State workshops should manufacture 'for the production and sale of every necessary of life', competing with private enterprise.[76] Hardie believed that 'the state . . . is what its people make it'.[77] Already before 1914 the Labour Party developed a theory of collectivism in which decentralized state provision in the form of 'municipal socialism' would form the remedy against social misery.[78] It has been shown that the Labour Party, under Fabian influence after 1918, increasingly looked towards the state to provide not only social welfare but also 'rational' recreation. It was the state which should encourage working-class access to the cultural inheritance of the nation.[79] German Marxists as well as British 'Labourists' came to regard the state as the major instrument for improving the conditions of the working class.

There was a form of ethical or cultural socialism in both Britain and Germany which developed another utopia, not that of the state, but that of man. A 'new mankind' was to be created through socialism. In Britain the main proponent of such a form of socialism was R. H. Tawney. In his 1921 *The Acquisitive Society* he described capitalism as a society which

[74] Glasier, *The Meaning of Socialism*, 183.

[75] Rudolf Hilferding, 'Die Aufgaben der Sozialdemokratie in der Republik', in *Protokoll des SPD Parteitags, 1927*, 165–84.

[76] John Ruskin, *Unto this Last: Four Essays on the First Principles of Political Economy* (7th edn., London, 1890), p. xvi.

[77] Keir Hardie, *From Serfdom to Socialism* (London, 1907), 23.

[78] Pat Thane, 'Labour and Local Politics: Radicalism, Democracy and Social Reform 1880–1914', in Biagini and Reid, *Currents of Radicalism*, 244–70.

[79] Waters, *British Socialism*, 192 f.

'makes the individual the centre of his own universe, and dissolves moral principles into a choice of expediencies'.[80] Tawney then developed his idea of the need for a 'functional society', in which the social organization would be based on moral principles and the purpose of industry would be to provide the material foundations of a 'good life' rather than the enrichment of a few. Society as a whole would be organized for the performance of duties rather than for the maintenance of rights and a new morality would govern mankind. In the 1928 Labour Party programme, written by Tawney, socialism was defined as 'the practical recognition of the familiar commonplace that "morality is in the nature of things", and that men are all, in very truth, members of one another'.[81] For Keir Hardie 'socialism . . . is at bottom a question of ethics'[82] and a local study of the Colne Valley Labour Party supports the conclusion that the appeal of socialism was largely ethical—a desire for a new moral order based on a drastic restructuring of the economic system.[83]

In his 1929 book *Der Sozialismus als Kulturbewegung* Hendrik de Man similarly argued that bourgeois culture was dominated by the government of money, egoism, and the lack of truthfulness.[84] He attacked Marxist tendencies within the SPD which declared that a change of economic conditions would mean an automatic change of man,[85] whereas it was—according to de Man—exactly vice versa: 'new conditions can only be the work of new men'.[86] Any 'new man' would only develop if he changed his life-style, if he took the highest standards of morality and tried to live them. He saw the contradiction between the longing of many socialists for the transformation of capitalist society and the continuity of capitalist values within the very same persons: 'one can very well be an organized class warrior and at the same time—at heart—a petty-bourgeois.'[87] In the party's youth movement de Man's ideas were very popular.[88] Willy Brandt who belonged to the socialist youth movement in the Weimar Republic recalled that 'the kind of socialism with which a young German of my age grew up was less scientifically and more morally motivated. For us socialism was the fight against injustice and exploitation, suppression and war: the left, where the heart beats . . .'[89] Forms of ethical socialism proved to be popular not only in the SPD of the Weimar Republic. In fact, they had

[80] R. H. Tawney, *The Acquisitive Society* (London, 1921), 33.
[81] *Labour and the Nation* (London, 1928), 6.
[82] Hardie, *Serfdom*, 35.   [83] Clark, *Colne Valley*, 145 and 186.
[84] Hendrik de Man, *Der Sozialismus als Kulturbewegung* (Berlin, 1929), 17.
[85] Ibid. 6.   [86] Ibid. 19.   [87] Ibid. 26.
[88] Victor Engelhardt, *An der Wende des Zeitalters* (Berlin, 1924), 108 and 123–6. Engelhardt's book was published by the SPD's youth movement.
[89] Willy Brandt, *Links und Frei: Mein Weg, 1930–1950* (Hamburg, 1982), 58.

been represented within the SPD from very early on. Neo-Kantian Social Democrats like Staudinger, Vorländer, David, Eisner, or Stammler before the First World War and Willi Eichler thereafter tried to justify socialism from an ethical position, not from a 'scientific law'.[90] After 1945, on its way to Godesberg, those ethical socialist positions were taken up by the SPD once again and practically replaced all notions of 'scientific socialism'.[91]

As has been argued above, a belief in the historical inevitability of socialism can be found in MacDonald and Glasier. It is also present in this most popular of socialist authors, H. G. Wells. According to G. D. H. Cole, H. G. Wells's *New Worlds for Old* (1908) was 'the most influential piece of Socialist propaganda in Britain since *Merrie England*'.[92] It reveals a staunch belief in science, especially in Darwin, as well as in the inevitable progress of history towards socialism. The latter was also a major theme in Wells's *The Outline of History* (revised edition, 1923), in which he aimed to discover the 'general laws' of world history. His 'futurology' he first elaborated in *The Discovery of the Future* (1913, republished 1924), in which he suggested 'that along certain lines and with certain qualifications and limitations a working knowledge of things in the future is a possible and practicable thing.'[93] The book ended with a prophecy *par excellence*: 'We are in the beginning of the greatest change that humanity has ever undergone . . . all the past is but the beginning of a beginning, and . . . all that is and has been is but the twilight of dawn.'[94]

A belief in the inevitability of socialism can equally be found in the writings of German socialists. In the debate about the social democratic *Zukunftsstaat* in the German Reichstag in 1893 Bebel finished his outline of the state-to-come with the words: 'the future belongs to us and to us only.'[95] Such historical determinism also formed the basis of *Die Frau und der Sozialismus*, where he described the realization of socialism as a 'developing natural law'. Socialists could be content in the certainty that history was on their side: 'the dawn of a beautiful day is coming. Let us

[90] Steinberg, *Sozialismus*, 96–106.

[91] Kurt Klotzbach, *Der Weg zur Staatspartei: Programmatik, praktische Politik und Organisation der deutschen Sozialdemokratie, 1945–1965* (Berlin, 1982), 181–7.

[92] Cole, *A History of Socialist Thought*, iii/1. 204 f.

[93] H. G. Wells, *The Discovery of the Future* (London, 1913, repub. 1924), 24.

[94] Ibid. 58 f.

[95] *Der sozialdemokratische Zukunftsstaat: Verhandlungen des deutschen Reichstags am 31. Januar, 3., 4., 6. und 7. Februar 1893* (Berlin, 1893), 21. On this debate and its implications for social democratic millenarianism see also Hölscher, *Weltgericht*, 378–435. For the widespread 'history-on-our-side' belief amongst Social Democrats see also Thomas Nipperdey, 'Sozialdemokratie und Geschichte', in H. Horn, A. Schwan, I. Weingartner (eds.), *Sozialismus in Theorie und Praxis: Festschrift für Richard Löwenthal* (Berlin, 1978), 493–517.

fight and struggle forward . . . If we fall in that great fight for the freedom
of humanity those who emulate us will continue the battle.'[96] According
to a popular SPD pamphlet it was 'progress itself, which forces mankind
to want this aim [socialism].'[97]

Both working-class parties were obsessed with the idea that the socialism they strove for was scientific and that a reorganization of society was
the most reasonable solution to what they saw as the continuous waste
and crisis of the capitalist system. In the British Labour Party an overwhelming belief in science has already been discussed in the writings
of MacDonald and Wells. Blatchford and with him the Clarionettes
'assumed that society was evolving towards a higher state and that a new
society organized more rationally and humanely would appear in time.'[98]
Labour and the New Social Order, the 1918 programme of the Labour
Party, reads: 'The Labour Party stands for increased study, for the scientific investigation of each succeeding problem, for the deliberate organization of research and for a much more rapid dissemination among the
whole people of all the science that exists.'[99] Sidney Webb, who had
written the programme, was among the most vociferous representatives
of the scientific optimism preceding the two World Wars in the twentieth
century.[100]

In Germany the word 'scientific' was regularly attached to the word
'socialism' so as to differentiate the right form of socialism from the
merely 'utopian' socialism of pre-Marxian thinkers. Books about the
future socialist state in Germany regularly took refuge in the image of
science. Bebel wrote: 'Human progress and the true, pure science will be
the watchwords of the new society.'[101] It was stressed by some that the
problems of production and consumption in a future socialist state could
be scientifically predicted[102] and others maintained that their literary
visions of the society-to-come were based on sound scientific research.[103]

The prophecy of revolution was the central motive of pre-First World

[96] Bebel, *Die Frau und der Sozialismus*, 373, 381.
[97] *Was ist, was will der Sozialismus?*, ed. by the party executive of the SPD (Berlin, 1919),
5.
[98] Fincher, 'The Clarion Movement', 87.
[99] *Labour and the New Social Order* (London, 1918), 21.
[100] Leonard Woolf, 'Political Thought and the Webbs', in Margaret Cole (ed.), *The Webbs and their Work* (London, 1949), 255 f.
[101] Bebel, *Die Frau und der Sozialismus*, 315.
[102] Karl Ballod, *Der Zukunftsstaat: Produktion und Konsumtion im Sozialstaat* (2nd edn., Stuttgart, 1919), 1, 6, 44 f.
[103] Theodor Hertzka, *Freiland: Ein soziales Zukunftsbild* (10th edn., Dresden, 1896), pp. xiv f.

War Social Democracy in Germany.[104] Yet the prophecy did not corre-
spond with the reality of the basic acceptance of the parliamentary system
and the integration into an existing political system. As Kautsky's famous
phrase went: the Social Democrats were a revolutionary, but not a
revolution-making party.[105] There is some evidence that the party's rank
and file agreed with Kautsky: their hopes were pinned on a peaceful,
orderly transition from capitalism to socialism, not on violent tactics.[106] In
Britain there was no scarcity of the use of the word 'revolution' or
'revolutionary' either, but it was seldom used to suggest a violent and
sudden transformation of society. The change of society would be revolutionary, but it would all happen constitutionally and without any use of
force. Such at least was the essence of much of the Labour Party's official
propaganda and programmatic statements. When the Labour Party's aim
in 1918 was 'to do our utmost to see that the individualist system of
capitalist production is buried with the millions whom it has done to
death'[107] the programme as well as the actions of the party in the following
years left little doubt that the death blow would have to come from the
ballot box.[108] Yet, popular novels amongst socialists included William
Morris's *News from Nowhere*, where the transition from capitalism to
socialism only comes after prolonged and bloody civil war. Chapter 17 of
his book 'How the change came?' is fully devoted to a lengthy description
of that war.[109] Utopian socialist writing in both Britain and Germany
included the notion of revolution as violent upheaval, even when both
parties were not acting as revolutionary parties.

The millennium of the British socialists was more backward-looking
than that of their German comrades. Themes such as the myth of a
golden, pre-commercial age, pastoral fantasies and the pre-Norman
freedoms were dominant in much socialist literature in Britain at the
time. William Morris, for example, wrote:

More akin to our way of looking at life was the spirit of the Middle Ages, to
whom heaven and the life of the next world was such a reality, that it became to
them a part of the life upon the earth; which accordingly they loved and adorned, in
spite of the ascetic doctrines of their formal creed, which bade them condemn it.[110]

---

[104] Hölscher, *Weltgericht* 199–281. Also Rudolf Walter, '*Aber nach der Sintflut kommen
wir und nur wir*' (Frankfurt am Main, 1979).
[105] Geary, *Karl Kautsky*, 73–85.   [106] Evans, *Proletarians*, 131–5.
[107] *Labour and the New Social Order*, 4.
[108] For Keir Hardie's clear rejection of revolution see Morgan, *Keir Hardie*, 203.
[109] William Morris, *News from Nowhere and Selected Writings and Designs* (Harmondsworth,
1962), 272–96.
[110] Ibid. 298.

It was not only Morris who wished for the good old times. In part three of his *The Meaning of Socialism*, entitled 'Socialism in Existing Society', Bruce Glasier described the revival of village life in the socialist society-to-come.[111] Keir Hardie shared such medievalism: 'the golden age of the English workman was the 15th century . . . there were neither million-aires nor paupers in those days, but a rude abundance for all . . . ; a strong element of Communism . . . characterized town and village life.'[112] Tawney as well as the guild socialists around A. J. Penty, much like Morris, looked to the Christianity of the pre-eighteenth century for a more famil-iar, human, and loving community.[113] This argument about the backward-looking nature of British socialism should, however, not be carried too far. First, the Labour Party's ultimate aim was forward-looking: the nationalization of all means of production, as laid down by Clause Four of the party constitution, had little of a medieval project. And secondly, backward-looking utopias were not unknown in those national labour movements which included substantial parts of artisans or craftsmen whose traditional life-style was threatened by industrialization.[114]

Apart from the written word, the festivities of the working-class parties were testimony to the hopes and beliefs connected with the future. No festivity was more devoted to a commemoration of the society-to-come than that of May Day. The German May Day journals particularly with their rich symbolism (the coming to life of nature, the rising sun, 'free-dom' as allegory, blacksmith of the 'New Age', etc.) designed pictures and images which demonstrated the Social Democrats' hope for a better future.[115] Many social democratic and Labour songs sung on occasions like May Day were millenarian in outlook.[116] Theatre plays, like the ones staged by the Frankfurt am Main culture cartel in the 1920s, mirrored the longing for the transformation of society. They tried to give a glimpse of the 'new society' and the 'new man'. Such was the aim of the plays of Ernst Toller which belonged to the most popular plays of socialist theatre in Germany and Britain alike.[117] Keir Hardie echoed those sentiments in his 1909 May Day greeting:

---

[111] Glasier, *The Meaning of Socialism*, 133–92.   [112] Hardie, *Serfdom*, 45–8.

[113] Foote, *The Labour Party's Political Thought*, 74 f., 104.

[114] Breuilly, *Labour and Liberalism*, 97, 101.

[115] Wolfgang Ruppert, 'Heute soll Sonne sein: Heute soll ruhen die Hand', in id. (ed.), *Die Arbeiter: Lebensformen, Alltag und Kultur von der Frühindustrialisierung bis zum Wirtschaftswunder* (Munich, 1986), 238–50.

[116] Lidtke, *The Alternative Culture*, 119. Waters, *British Socialists and the Politics of Popular Culture*, 111.

[117] Stübling, *Kultur und Massen*, 35–42; Thomas, 'The WTM', 105.

The springtime is the season which best symbolizes our Socialist hope. The land is then filled with beauty, and everywhere there is the promise of a coming fullness of life . . . all the world seems young and filled with a newness of life and joy. And that typifies our Socialist hope. It is a wonderful testimony to the power of altruism as a factor in life that in every corner of the earth comrades holding a common faith with ourselves are at work building a City Beautiful which they cannot hope to inhabit . . .[118]

Some socialists in Britain, in their longing for the coming millennium, joined spiritualist societies, where they could already converse with the spirits of 'Summerland', an anticipation of future socialism.[119] In Germany Theodor Hertzka's novel *Freiland*—which was also serialized in the British Labour press, for example in the *Huddersfield Worker* or the *Halifax and District Labour News*[120]—inspired efforts to construct the future socialist society in Africa. *Freiland* societies were founded in many German cities and an expedition of socialists even set sail to Africa in 1893–4 to set up the promised land.[121]

The common preoccupation with utopianism and millenarianism no doubt functioned as a necessary source of hope, enjoyment, and encouragement for socialists in both countries. What is more, it politicized those who had been indifferent as well as those whose imagination could not reach beyond the fabric of contemporary society. The belief in the historical inevitability of socialism also gave organized workers strength in times of persecution. Those positive consequences of utopianism have to be contrasted with the negative ones. The firm belief in the society-to-come made them less conciliatory towards other parties and social interests.[122] As they were convinced that the coming of the socialist society was inevitable, why bother about building day-to-day compromises with 'bourgeois' parties, why bother with coalition-building or minority government? Both working-class parties found themselves trapped between utopianism and pragmatism, inheriting the worst of both worlds: they could not decide upon a working coalition with representatives of a

---

[118] *Labour Leader* (30 Apr. 1909), 281.

[119] Logie Barrow, 'Socialism in Eternity: The Ideology of Plebeian Spiritualists, 1853–1913', *HWJ* 9 (1980), 37–69.

[120] Waters, *British Socialists and the Politics of Popular Culture* , 51.

[121] About this effort and its failure see: Hertzka, *Freiland,* 10th edn., p. xxiii. According to Cole, *A History of Socialist Thought,* iii/z. 565, there were a substantial number of Freiland societies in Britain.

[122] Lösche and Walter, 'Auf dem Weg zur Volkspartei?', 75–136 have demonstrated how the SPD was caught between the wish to participate constructively in the political system of the Weimar Republic and the utopian ethic of the party, which made such participation difficult.

'capitalist' state and they were afraid to campaign forcefully for a socialist government. As Lucian Hölscher, who interpreted some of the early
socialist utopias in Germany, rightly noted, none of those visions—and
the same is true for their British equivalents—took into account certain
set factors which limit the actions of human beings in any historical
situation. Many just assumed that human planning and free decision-
making would be the basis of the coming change.[123] Any realistic development of policy strategies could not proceed within such a utopian
ethic. Stanley Pierson has pointed out that the development of the idea of
a new life, of a new utopian state seemed to have been the result of 'the
divided consciousness' in nineteenth- and twentieth-century Europe.[124]
The personal ideals of the socialists did not coincide with the workings of
the countries' social institutions and out of such division developed the
longing for 'regeneration', 'culture', 'wholeness', and an 'undivided existence'. Such longing for the society-to-come, if it became too dominant,
could lead to a failure to accommodate to the political and social reality of
the existing societies and their political systems. As has been argued
above, large minorities within both working-class parties had exactly
these problems, and some of them finally decided to quit a party which
seemed to deviate too much from the path towards their utopia.

Marxism and Labourism usually describe the ideologically incompatible systems of belief of SPD and Labour Party, yet, as has been argued,
both parties were not ideologically homogeneous and substantial minority
positions within the official ideologies could be found. The official ideology, embodied in the term Marxism in Germany, had little influence
on the direct policy-making of the SPD. Theoretical debates remained
rare in the Labour Party, but its ethos was no less ambiguous about
participation in an existing economic, social, and political system that was
perceived as unjust. Many of the British and the German organized
working class were not interested in the subtleties of political philosophy,
but preferred the visualization of the society-to-come in the vivid description of utopian novels or the drastic symbolism of the labour movement's festival culture.

An examination of fiction and non-fiction which was largely published
by the working-class parties themselves or serialized within their newspapers, reflected discussions about the future socialist state. Both parties
were state-oriented and often the motivation for any socialist transformation was justified morally: the immoral capitalist system was set against

---

[123] Hölscher, *Weltgericht*, 294.   [124] Pierson, *British Socialists*, 17.

the new morality of the future socialist system. If the concept of revolution was more prevalent amongst German socialists, the notion of an abrupt and violent transformation of society was by no means unknown to the socialists of Britain. Both parties perceived themselves as 'progressive agents' of history and both were convinced of the scientific nature of their belief. They were convinced that the future would inevitably belong to them, and therefore socialists in both Britain and Germany were liable to form sectarian ghettos of the elect, the enlightened, those who held the key to the future in their hands. Such a belief was, as has been argued, ambivalent in its consequences. On the one hand, it increased the unwillingness of both movements to become integrated into the political system. On the other, it served to politicize many workers who had not seen any other way out of the squalor and misery they were living in, apart from the fact that such utopias brought hope and bright expectation to many otherwise sullen and grey lives. In Robert Tressell's *Philanthropists* the socialist hero Owen, for example, is faced with depressing thoughts about his family's future: 'The story of the past would continue to repeat itself for a few years longer. He would continue to work and they would all three continue to do without most of the necessaries of life. When there was no work they would starve.'[125] It was for men like Owen that socialist utopianism was important.[126]

5.3. Religion and the working-class parties

The argument that both working-class parties were largely utopian, sometimes millenarian in character, leads to the question: how did they see their relationship to organized religion, which also held out promises of a millennium—if not of this, then of another world? The attitudes of the working-class parties in Britain and Germany towards religion can best be described as ambivalent. On the one hand, there was a confrontation between the two systems of belief, on the other, socialists imitated certain religious modes of thought and some of them even tried to reconcile religion and socialism. In the following the relationship of the working-class parties towards the churches, the use of religious vocabulary by the

---

[125] Tressell, *The Ragged Trousered Philanthropists*, 87.

[126] For the importance of utopianism for working-class movements see also Zygmunt Baumann, *Socialism: the Active Utopia* (London, 1976), 13–17. The utopian impetus seems nowhere better expressed than in Ernst Bloch, *The Principle of Hope* (Oxford, 1986), 42: 'The obsession with what is better remains, even when what is better has been prevented for so long.'

working-class parties, and the understanding of the labour movement as a 'new religion' in both the British and the German working-class parties will be examined.

Hugh McLeod has argued that socialists in Germany were largely irreligious, whereas in Britain socialists comprised a peculiar mixture of Christians, secularists, and the religiously neutral. In Germany after 1848 the attack by enlightened opinion on religion trickled down from the bourgeoisie to the labour movement, which came to identify itself strongly with left-wing, secular Jacobinism. In Britain there was a strong tradition of political religious dissent reaching back to Elizabethan England which formed a line of tradition in the British labour movement hardly known in Germany. Liberalism—from which socialism in both countries descended—was more associated with religion in Britain than in Germany and consequently the formative influence of Christianity on many British Labour leaders was much bigger than in Germany.[127]

The hostility of German socialism to religion was most prominently publicized by the 1874 polemic *Christentum und Sozialismus*, in which Bebel anonymously spoke out against Christianity. The famous phrase: 'Christianity and socialism are like fire and water' was to be coined here and its indictments of the Christian religion were numerous. It was the enemy of culture and freedom, the Bible was the most confusing book that ever existed, and the church had always been servile to the authorities.[128] Bebel's polemic was followed up by numerous anti-religious, anti-church booklets and pamphlets published by the SPD.[129] In a letter to Gehieb, Bebel wrote in 1891 that atheism would be a consequence of socialism.[130] In 1907 Hermann Wendel wrote: 'For the first time in history atheism becomes a mass phenomenon with the appearance of the working class, because the working class lacks any basis on which religious ideologies could grow. The working class dispenses with religion, because it has knowledge.'[131] Furthermore one of the most popular books in the workers'

---

[127] Hugh McLeod, 'Religion in the British and German Labour Movements, c.1890–1914: A Comparison,' *SSLH* 55 (1986), 25–35.

[128] *Christentum und Sozialismus: Eine religiöse Polemik zwischen Herrn Kaplan Hohoff in Hüsse und dem Verfasser der Schrift 'Die parlamentarische Tätigkeit des deutschen Reichstages'* (Leipzig, 1874).

[129] See for example Kurt Falk, *Die christliche Kirche und der Sozialismus: Eine sozialdemokratische Antwort auf die Enzyklika Leos des XIII.* (Nuremberg, 1891). 'Thron, Altar und Geldsack', *Vorwärts*, 127 (2 June 1895). 'Die Kirche als Bollwerk des Staates', *Vorwärts*, 138 (17 June 1906).

[130] IGA/ZPA, papers of August Bebel, NL 22/127, 6: letter from Bebel to Gehieb, 12 Dec. 1891.

[131] Hermann Wendel, *Sozialdemokratie und anti-kirchliche Propaganda* (Leipzig, 1907), 24.

libraries of SPD and free trade unions up to 1914 was Corvin's *Pfaffenspiegel*, strongly anti-Christian and anti-clerical in character.[132]

Certainly the strong orientation of the Protestant Church in Imperial Germany towards the anti-socialist state and the equally strong anti-socialism of the Catholic Church in Germany tended to alienate the organized working class. Before 1914 only three Protestant pastors joined the Social Democrats. They were promptly discharged from their pastoral jobs by the Protestant hierarchy. No Catholic priest was a social democrat. Social Democracy was left in no doubt that it had no place in the church and therefore found it easy to break with traditional religion.

In Britain the churches were on the whole more sensitive to the social problems of the working class. Particular churches in Britain helped socialist organizations in the latter's organizational efforts in certain localities. The Christian Socialist League, an Anglican foundation of the 1890s, contributed significantly to the socialist cause, as did the non-conformist League of Progressive Religious and Social Thought, founded in 1908 by the Revd. R. J. Campbell.[133] In 1906 Father Adderley lent his support to Bruce Glasier's election campaign, calling Glasier 'a true shepherd who acts from love of his flock—not from deference to the wolves and foxes'.[134] In 1910 several young ministers of Merthyr's nonconformist churches served on Keir Hardie's election platform.[135] In 1923 a memorial signed by over 400 ordained members of the Church of England and the Episcopal Church of Scotland pledged the memorialists actively to support the efforts of the Labour Party. The Revd. Gordon Lang, who believed 'that the ideals of the modern Labour Movement are ideals which are inherent in the religion professed by all churches', called that memorial 'the first fruits of a real revival of religion and one of the most significant events in post-war history'.[136] Undoubtedly, religion was a strong influence on some Labour activists and sometimes even on whole local Labour Parties.[137]

Many socialist symbols were rooted in the chiliastic utopianism of

---

[132] Hans-Josef Steinberg, 'Workers' Libraries in Germany Before 1914' *HWJ*, 1 (1976), 175.

[133] R. J. Campbell, *Socialism* (London, 1909); also Pierson, *British Socialists*, 138–47.

[134] Father Adderley, 'A True Shepherd', *Labour Leader* (12 Jan. 1906), 491.

[135] Kenneth O. Morgan, 'The Merthyr of Keir Hardie', in Glanmor Williams (ed.), *Merthyr Politics: The Making of a Working Class Tradition* (Cardiff, 1966), 77.

[136] Revd. Gordon Lang, 'Labour's Challenge to the Churches', *Labour Magazine*, 1 (1922–3), 539 f.

[137] Duncan Tanner, 'Ideological Debate', in Biagini and Reid, *Currents of Radicalism* 289 f., Rose, 'Locality', 295.

Protestant sects[138] and the experience of Protestant revivals was crucial
for many later Labour leaders. As Frank Hodges recalled the effects of
the Welsh revival on him: 'I was shot straight out of agnosticism into the
waiting arms of religion.'[139] In fact many Labour leaders started their
careers as preachers in the local chapel. Fred Jowett, the first Labour MP
for Bradford in 1906, was a member of Horton Lane Congregational
Church in the 1890s. Ben Tillett, who stood for Bradford West in 1892
and 1895, came from a Congregationalist background. Both the *Daily
Citizen* and the *Daily Herald* carried many positive articles about religion
and showed a considerable interest in Christianity. Socialists writing in
both papers generally expected the churches to help Labour to improve
society.[140] Some historians have stressed the Christian roots of Labour
Party ideology and the interest of Labour Party activists in religion and
church/chapel.[141]

Yet it should not be forgotten that those tensions which characterized
the relations between the churches and the labour movement in Germany, also existed in Britain. The traditional churches all had political
ties to the older parties: nonconformists strongly identified with the Liberal Party, whereas the Anglican Church was often described as 'the Tory
party at prayer'. In South Wales, for example, nonconformism largely
rejected the ILP because the party was perceived as essentially Darwinian
and irreligious.[142] Even if one concedes that the Welsh labour movement
went through a religious phase between 1906 and 1914, it has been
observed that this phase was only the 'stepping off point to complete
religious alienation' for many.[143] In Bradford the nonconformist ministers
largely ignored social conditions and remained wedded to the Liberal
Party.[144] Liberals as well as Tories attacked the 'atheism' of the Labour
Party, despite the number of Labour politicians who were active

---

[138] R. F. Wearmouth, *Methodism and the Working-Class Movements of England, 1800–
1850* (London, 1937) overemphasized the importance of Methodism for the British labour
movement, yet he was the first systematically to draw attention to the strong connection
between the two. For Yorkshire it has been stressed that Congregationalism rather than
Methodism was an important influence on the development of the Labour Party. See K.
Laybourn and J. Reynolds, *Liberalism and the Rise of Labour 1890–1918* (London, 1984).

[139] Hodges, *My Adventures as a Labour Leader*, 18.

[140] Ichikawa, 'The Daily Citizen', 68–71.

[141] Stephen Mayor, *The Churches and the Labour Movement* (London, 1967), 339.

[142] Fox, 'The Emergence', 11.

[143] C. B. Turner, 'Conflicts of Faith? Religion and Labour in Wales 1890–1914', in D.
R. Hopkin and G. S. Kealey (eds.), *Class, Community and the Labour Movement* (n.p., 1989),
81 f.

[144] J. A. Jowitt, 'Late Victorian and Edwardian Bradford', in Taylor and Jowitt, *Bradford, 1890–1914*, 14.

Christians. In local elections in Stockport in 1908 the tactics of the opponents relied on 'the lying statements . . . to the uneducated that we were atheist'. It resulted in a complete loss of the Irish vote, as Catholic priests advised against voting Labour.[145] In Liverpool, another city with a sizeable Catholic minority, the Labour Party suffered from the lack of any religious base in a community which largely defined itself by its religious affiliations. The Irish Nationalists were supported by the Catholics (up to 1923, thereafter most Catholics began to support the Labour Party), and the Tories commanded the Protestant vote.[146] Some emerging working-class religious sects in Britain, the Salvation Army for example, were hostile to the labour movement from the start.[147]

Just as large sections of the churches remained hostile to the labour movement, so the secular wing of British socialism came to see socialism and organized Christianity as incompatible systems of belief.[148] Socialist plays like G. B. Shaw's *Major Barbara* and propaganda literature were highly critical of the churches: 'It is difficult to imagine how any great human good can come from a source that is so chaotic and respectable.'[149] *Reynolds' Newspaper*, one of the more important working-class papers with links to the labour movement, had a long tradition of being hostile towards the churches.[150] One of the great popularizers of socialist ideas, Robert Blatchford savagely attacked what he saw as the superstition, ignorance, self-righteousness, and cruelty of religion. In 1903 he proudly called himself an infidel and proclaimed: 'I oppose Christianity because it is not true . . .'.[151] Three years later he attacked Christianity even more vehemently: 'the religions of the world are childish dreams or nightmares . . . [and] our most cherished and venerable ideas of our relations with God and to each other are illogical and savage.'[152] For Blatchford God was a human invention.

[145] Letter from the Stockport Labour Party to the Labour Party head office, 26 Nov. 1908, LP/EL/08/1/156, in: files of the Stockport Labour Party, in *Origins*, ed. Clark.
[146] Baxter, 'The Liverpool Labour Party', 16–28. Miller, *Electoral Dynamics*, 227 has also established a clear link between religiosity and anti-Labour voting.
[147] Victor Bailey, ' "In Darkest England and the Way Out": The Salvation Army, Social Reform and the Labour Movement, 1885–1910', *IRSH* 29 (1984), 133–71.
[148] Eric Hobsbawm, *Primitive Rebels: Studies in Archaic Forms of Social Movement in the 19th and 20th Centuries* (Manchester, 1959), 128.
[149] Dan Griffiths, 'Socialism and Religion', in *id.*, *The Real Enemy and Other Socialist Essays*, 77.
[150] V. S. Berridge, 'Popular Journalism and Working-Class Attitudes 1859–1886: A Study of Reynolds' Newspaper, Lloyd's Weekly Newspaper, and the Weekly Times' (University of London Ph.D. 1976), 353–5.
[151] Robert Blatchford, *God and My Neighbour* (London, 1903), pp. vii and 7.
[152] Robert Blatchford, *Not Guilty: A Defence of the Bottom Dog* (London, 1906), 8 f.

As E. P. Thompson has observed, the religious phraseology of Labour in Britain did not necessarily mean that its relationship with the organized churches was unproblematic: 'the Biblical echoes, the references to the Sermon of the Mount . . . [are] not a question of creed, belief, or church, but a question of language, a question of moral texture. It was as much a revolt against organized Christianity as a form of Christian expression.'[153] This was largely true for Keir Hardie whose 'Christianity was highly flexible, a religion of humanity with little doctrinal content, utopian, romantic . . .'.[154] The issue of religion was dividing many Labour communities in Britain. In the meetings of the Colne Valley Labour Party, for example, hymns were usually sung and many lectures had religious overtones. When Blatchford's *God and my Neighbour* was published, a debate about this book continued for years in the columns of the *Slaithwaite Guardian* and in local socialist meetings revealing the deep divisions in the movement regarding the issue of religion.[155]

Those few Christian priests in Germany who had openly declared their sympathies for Social Democracy became within the party symbolic figures of a possible alignment of Christians to the SPD.[156] Paul Göhre's *How a Parson Became a Social Democrat* became an extremely successful SPD pamphlet which sought to link socialism and Christianity.[157] In Düsseldorf, for example, the SPD appealed to the Catholic voters, in order to compete with the Centre Party.[158] In many rural areas of Germany the population could only be won by appealing to their still strong religious sentiments.[159] Therefore the party recruited theologically trained propagandists for rural areas.[160] The revisionist journal *Sozialistische Monatshefte* campaigned for an alliance between church and socialism from 1910–11 onwards. Lucian Hölscher has written about the relations between Social Democracy and religion in Imperial Germany: 'The separation of religious from secular expectations was . . . by no means common nor radical

---

[153] E. P. Thompson, 'Homage to Tom Maguire', Briggs and Saville, *Essays*, 290.

[154] Morgan, *Keir Hardie*, 9.

[155] Clark, *Colne Valley*, 50 and 146–9. For similar divisions between a secular and a religious wing within one local Labour Party see Smith, 'Labour Tradition', 36 f.

[156] For Christoph Blumhardt see Maja Christ-Gmelin, 'Die württembergische Sozialdemokratie, 1890–1914', in Schadt and Schmierer (ed.), *Die SPD in Baden-Württemberg*, 113 f. For Paul Göhre see Ernst Heilmann, *Geschichte der Arbeiterbewegung in Chemnitz*, 283–6.

[157] Paul Göhre, *Wie ein Pfarrer Sozialdemokrat wurde* (Berlin, 1909). Also by an anonymous author: *Ein katholischer Pfarrer als Sozialdemokrat*, ed. by *Vorwärts* (Berlin, 1906).

[158] Mary Nolan, *Social Democracy and Society*, 164 f.

[159] Paul Kampffmeyer, 'Bauer und Sozialdemokratie', *SM* 33 (1927), 276–80.

[160] Ditt, *Industrialisierung*, 267 f.

nor irreversible.'[161] Even the anti-religious Bebel stressed in his *Die Frau* that under socialism 'Religion will not be abolished . . . If anyone feels religious needs, he can satisfy them with his fellow believers.'[162]

It is well known that many British Labour leaders had staunch Christian convictions. In a publication of brief definitions of socialism by well over 100 Labour affiliates or sympathizers, Charles Ammon, MP, for example, said: 'Socialism is the practical expression of Christ's teaching.'[163] Katharine Bruce Glasier put it: 'International socialism is the only possible political and economic expression of the aspirations of the Lord's Prayer.'[164] What is probably more surprising is the fact that those statements can also be found in the SPD's propaganda. It was stressed that 'the whole activity of Social Democracy corresponds with the spirituality of true Christianity'.[165] At the international Socialist Congress in Basle in 1912 it was Bebel who stressed: 'I am convinced that—if the Christian saviour would come again today— . . . he would not stand amongst those who call themselves Christians only in name, but that he would stand in the midst of our army.'[166] A social democratic pamphlet against the Reichsverband, entitled 'Was Christ a Social Democrat?', simply argued: 'Who really wants to fight for better, more just and more Christian conditions has to affiliate to the party which alone has written the struggle for such better conditions on its banners . . . It is in that party, that Christ—were he to live today—would stand in the front ranks. This party is Social Democracy.'[167] Bernstein at the 1912 party conference at Chemnitz described Jesus as 'the greatest social reformer of all times'.[168] In 1913 a Social Democrat was sentenced to one month imprisonment because she had dressed as Christ on a mask ball, wearing a sign that read: 'The first Social Democrat'.[169] In 1905–6 the Marxist *Neue Zeit* ran

---

[161] Hölscher, *Weltgericht*, 139. Hölscher has systematically researched the similarity between religious and social democratic eschatological beliefs in Imperial Germany for the first time, pointing to the widespread use of religious symbolism and topics within the SPD. See also H. Grote, *Sozialdemokratie und Religion* (Frankfurt am Main, 1968).

[162] Bebel, *Die Frau*, 313–15.

[163] Dan Griffiths (ed.), *What is Socialism? A Symposium* (London, 1924), 13.

[164] Ibid. 35.

[165] *Christentum, Zentrum und Sozialdemokratie* (n.p., n.d.), 5.

[166] *Außerordentlicher Internationaler Sozialistenkongreß zu Basel am 24. und 25. November 1912* (Berlin, 1912), 40 f.

[167] *War Christus Sozialdemokrat?*, no. 2 of the series: *Sozialdemokratische Antworten auf Flugblätter des Reichsverbandes*, ed. by the Party Executive (without location and year). See also the similarity of arguments in no. 6 *Sozialdemokratie und Christentum* and no. 10 *Wie Geistliche über die Sozialdemokratie urteilen* of this series.

[168] *Protokoll des SPD Parteitags 1912*, 421.

[169] ZStA Potsdam, 07.01, nos. 1395/8/230–4.

two articles on the topic of 'Jesus as the first socialist' and the possibility of Christians supporting the SPD.[170] Johannes Kleinspehn, religious socialist and SPD activist from Nordhausen in Saxony, frequently argued that the 'proletarian babe' from Bethlehem and his message mattered for modern socialists. In Adolf Levenstein's collection of proletarian biographies, Christian belief can be found standing side by side with socialist convictions. One social democratic miner even attributed a Christian mission to Social Democracy:

My parents as well as my wife's parents were pious people. Myself and my wife and children are also pious. We have never deceived other people. In 1892 I became a Social Democrat, because most people do not know that they persecute and harm their fellow human beings and therefore I wish that the comrades will act against the way things go so that no unjust punishment will come upon those who acted loyally and faithfully.[171]

Male SPD activists and supporters—unlike their wives—may have rejected the churches as anti-socialist institutions, but not necessarily Christian values.

Even left-wing socialists like Rosa Luxemburg and Anton Pannekoek did not stir up anti-religious sentiments in the party. Rosa Luxemburg wrote that it was Social Democracy's explicit aim to defend freedom of conscience and freedom of belief and she insisted on the convergence of the teachings of Christ with the demands of Social Democracy.[172] Pannekoek believed that Christianity would finally be overcome by socialism, but he stressed that this would not be due to any enmity towards religion on the side of the German labour movement.[173] What is more, the movement of free thinkers was never able to make an impact on Social Democracy either. Although free thinkers stressed their commitment to socialism, the SPD did not integrate their basic demands.[174] For the party, free thinking remained one amongst a variety of possible personal orientations. Another personal orientation was Christianity.

The post-1918 era certainly saw an easing of tensions between Social

---

[170] W. v. Schnehen, 'Jesus und der Sozialismus', *NZ* 24 (1905–6), 108–16. Also E. S. [Edmund Scheuer?], 'Sozialismus und Christentum', *NZ* 24 (1905–6), 369–71.

[171] Adolf Levenstein (ed.), *Proletariers Jugendjahre* (Berlin, 1909), 62. For Kleinspehn see Walter, Dürr, and Schmidtke, *Die SPD in Sachsen und Thüringen*, 244.

[172] Rosa Luxemburg, 'Die Kirche und der Sozialismus', in IGA/ZPA, papers of Rosa Luxemburg, NL 2/6, 90–137.

[173] Anton Pannekoek, *Religion und Sozialismus* (Bremen, 1906).

[174] Jochen-Christoph Kaiser, *Arbeiterbewegung und organisierte Religionskritik: Proletarische Freidenkerverbände in Kaiserrich und Weimarer Republik* (Stuttgart, 1981), 35–7, 86–9, 115–18, 338–40.

Democrats and Christians. After the First World War it was no longer seen as improper for an SPD leader to belong to a Christian church.[175] In 1919 an election leaflet of the party expressed clearly: 'We want everyone to be able to keep his belief and his religious convictions and to practice them freely.'[176] Konrad Haenisch, after 1918 minister of culture of Prussia (jointly with Adolph Hoffmann, who tried to prohibit religious instruction in state schools and had to resign over the issue[177]), stressed the need for religious tolerance by the SPD and avoided any confrontation with the churches. Religious ethics, he claimed, could fit into socialist ethics easily, as both beliefs had much in common.[178] There were even efforts from within the SPD to overcome the old enmity between socialists and Catholics, for example Wilhelm Sollmann's article of 1927:

Catholics and socialists for a generation lay in the trenches. At least amongst the workers in both armies the heads go up slowly over the walls and wire entanglements, they lower their weapons and search for the look of the brothers. It dawned on the most fervent believers in socialism and the most fervent believers in Catholicism . . . that they have a great deal in common . . .[179]

Georg Beyer in 1929 also sensed 'a convergence of socialism and Catholicism and a deeper understanding of socialism amongst Catholics.'[180] It clearly emerged in the Weimar Republic that few Social Democrats had radically broken with religion.[181]

Uniting secularists and 'religious' socialists in both countries was the belief that socialism constituted a new religion. Bebel himself has been characterized as a preacher whose socialism has major parallels to early Christian teachings, namely to strive for equality, universal brotherhood, and mutual charity.[182] Christian values and norms were propagated by party literature.[183] It was the party philosopher Joseph Dietzgen who popularized the idea of Social Democracy as a new religion: 'The

---

[175] J. Siemann, 'Die sozialdemokratischen Arbeiterführer in der Zeit der Weimarer Republik' (University of Göttingen Ph.D. 1955), 50 f.

[176] IGA/ZPA, Handbill Collection DF/VI/34, 1.

[177] Winkler, *Von der Revolution*, 92 f.

[178] Konrad Haenisch, *Neue Bahnen der Kulturpolitik*, 166–82.

[179] Wilhelm Sollmann, 'Katholizismus und Sozialismus: Ein Versuch zur Klärung', *Vorwärts* (28 Dec. 1927).

[180] Georg Beyer, 'Die Probleme zwischen Katholizismus und Sozialismus', *SM* 35 (1929), 289 f.

[181] Winkler, *Der Schein der Normalität*, 158.

[182] Vernon Lidtke, 'Bebel, Social Democracy and the Churches', *Journal of the History of Ideas*, 27 (1966) 262 and 264.

[183] See, for example, Edmund Scheuer, *Die Religion und der Sozialismus* (Berlin, 1921), 5 f.

tendencies within Social Democracy comprise the material for a new religion . . . the belief of the proletariat begins to become religious, it grips the believers with their whole heart, their whole soul and their whole nature.'[184] Party journals and papers echoed this idea: 'For the worker the party means something different than for the bourgeois. For the worker the party is more. His belief in mankind, his religion he gives to the party.'[185] For the rank and file this religious identification with the party was important, as it gave them hope and orientation.[186]

For Britain Stephen Yeo has argued convincingly that socialism in the 1880s and 1890s was surrounded by the 'language and style of religiosity'.[187] In the Bermondsey ILP: 'The whole membership entered on their task as a great crusade, visualising it as a work of social salvation. To Alfred Salter and his friends socialism was a religion.'[188] The ILP in Leicester called their recruitment campaigns 'mission drives' before 1914[189] and R. J. Campbell wrote of the Labour Party in 1907: 'In the primitive sense of the word, the Labour Party is itself a Church, because it is bent upon the realization of a moral ideal and had become the instrument of the cosmic purpose towards this end.'[190] Robert Blatchford justified his attacks on established religion with the argument that he was not out to make religion obsolete, but that he wanted to build up a better religion than Christianity.[191] Bruce Glasier wrote: 'Political Socialism in our own day inevitably assumes a religious complexion in the minds of its more earnest advocates.'[192] and H. G. Wells completely agreed: 'to me it [socialism] is a religion, in the sense, that it gives a work to do that is not self-seeking, . . . that it supplies that imperative craving of so many human souls, a devotion.'[193] Keir Hardie, anticipating Bebel's words in 1912, argued in 1907: 'There is in the Socialist movement more of that asceticism, that simplicity of life and love of the natural, which characterised the early Christian movement than there is in the churches.'[194]

Probably the most interesting phenomenon in the history of the

---

[184] *Die Religion der Sozialdemokratie: Kanzelreden von Joseph Dietzgen* (Berlin, 1903), 3.

[185] *Die Genossin*, 1/5 (1 Nov. 1924), 135.

[186] Klaus Saul, Jens Flemming, Dirk Stegmann, P. C. Witt (eds.), *Arbeiterfamilien im Kaiserreich: Materialien zur Sozialgeschichte in Deutschland, 1871–1914* (Königstein im Taunus, 1982), 256 and 268.

[187] Yeo, 'A New Life', 17–19.   [188] Brockway, *Bermondsey Story*, 33.

[189] Cox, 'The Labour Party in Leicester', 203–5.

[190] R. J. Campbell, 'The Labour Movement and Religion', *Labour Leader* (25 Jan. 1907).

[191] Fincher, 'The Clarion Movement', 289.

[192] Glasier, *The Meaning of Socialism*, 149.   [193] Wells, *New Worlds for Old*, 138.

[194] Keir Hardie, 'Socialism and the Churches', *Labour Leader* (18 Jan. 1907).

'religion of socialism' were the Labour Churches. It was largely a pre-1914 phenomenon of the industrial north of Britain. Between 1891 and 1914 at least 121 Labour Churches were founded, but in 1914 only thirteen survived and by the 1930s only the Stockport and Hyde branches were left. At the peak of the movement it had hardly more than 2,000 full members (yet attendance was by no means confined to members).[195] One of the longest-surviving Labour Churches, in Stockport, was founded in 1904 out of

the feeling that the labour movement was something more, something deeper than mere politics . . . [the Labour Church should] devote itself to the development of the idea that the Labour movement was, in the truest sense, a religious movement. [Its members looked forward to] the time when all our children will be inspired by the wonderful vision of a New World whose foundation shall be love. [For them] Socialism is the future hope of England and . . . of the whole world. Co-operation in all means to life, and a world-wide brotherhood, are our ultimate aims.[196]

Most Labour Churches set up Socialist Sunday Schools, in which the children were taught the 'Socialist Ten Commandments', which reflected the yearning for the society to come. This religion of socialism in Britain—as in Germany—was not necessarily Christian: 'That the religion of the Labour Movement is not necessarily theological, but respects each individual's personal convictions upon this question.'[197]

There is no simple conclusion to the ambiguous relationship between churches and working-class parties in Britain and Germany. It has been argued that the churches in Germany were more united against the working-class party than the churches in Britain, even if the latter could be fervently anti-socialist at certain places in certain times. Equally, German Social Democracy, which saw itself as the inheritor of the liberals' secularism, was more irreligious than the British Labour Party, some of whose members remained influenced by religious thought, even if it was more of an ethical-utopian than of a theological nature. On the other hand there remained a strong tradition of outspoken secularism in the British labour movement, whereas the SPD was reluctant to campaign heavily on anti-religious issues, realizing the importance of winning over those parts of the working class who were still actively religious. Even where SPD

---

[195] McLeod, *Religion and the Working Class*, 48 f.
[196] C. Glithero, 'The Stockport Labour Church', in *Official Handbook*, ed. by the Stockport Labour Church (Stockport, 1907), 15, 19, and 21.
[197] *Official Handbook*, 77.

activists denounced organized religion, their attitude towards the values of Christianity might have been more positive. What is more, many comrades in both parties believed in socialism as a 'new religion' that would be able rationally to command the devotion of its disciples. As has been seen, religious imagery and symbolism crept into the language of Labour in Britain and Germany and blended with its inherent utopianism into a firm, if vague system of belief for the rank and file. In the centre of such imagery stood the 'new society'—sometimes referred to as the 'new Jerusalem' in Britain—which was synonymous for a perfect socialist world. As Edwin Muir remembered about his socialist conversion:

> my conversion to socialism . . . was not . . . the result of an intellectual process, but rather a sort of emotional transmutation. . . . I read books on socialism, because they delighted me and were an escape from the world I had known with such painful precision. Having discovered a future in which everything, including myself, was transfigured, I flung myself into it, lived in it, though every day I still worked in the office of the beer bottling factory . . .[198]

The difference between the two working-class parties in their attitudes towards religion was thus rather one of degree than of substance. It was, then, not only in terms of organization and structure that the working-class parties in Britain and Germany were more similar than hitherto observed, the same can be said for both parties' ideology: the 'Marxist' SPD and the 'Labourist' Labour Party were more alike than the labels would suggest.

[198] Muir, *An Autobiography*, 113.

6
Relations between the Working-Class Parties in Britain and Germany from about 1890 to 1933

T H E prevalent view in the historiography of European Labour is that the British Labour Party was parochial, that it had few contacts with international socialists from other countries, and that it was not particularly interested in European socialism. Douglas J. Newton has portrayed British trade unions as outrightly hostile to the International, and the Labour Party as struggling to come to terms with continental socialism without much success and enduring love: 'the British Labour Party bosses failed to establish close and friendly relations with the German socialists. This persistence of cool relations arose principally from the great ideological distance which separated the two parties . . .'.[1] This chapter will show that such a view is misplaced. In previous chapters it has been argued that the concentration on the differences between the Labour Party and the SPD have so far blocked the view of an underlying consensus and a similarity of outlook. If that was the case then it would be surprising had there not been closer contacts between the two parties.

6.1. Personal relations

Karl Marx and Friedrich Engels both lived and worked in Britain for most of their lives. Ernest Belfort Bax was a close friend of Engels in the British labour movement.[2] Kausky later wrote of Bax's relationship with Engels that 'they constantly sat together in London'.[3] In 1925 Bax wrote

---

[1] Douglas J. Newton, *British Labour, European Socialism and the Struggle for Peace, 1889–1914* (Oxford, 1985), 228 f.

[2] Eduard Bernstein, *My Years of Exile: Reminiscences of a Socialist* (London, 1921), 200. Bax himself gave a description of his friendships with Engels, Bebel, Motteler, Liebknecht, Singer, and Kautsky—almost the complete leadership cadre of the SPD before 1905—in his autobiography. See Ernest Belfort Bax, *Reminiscences and Reflections of a Mid and Late Victorian* (London, 1918), 139–43.

[3] IGA/ZPA, SPD, PV, II, 145/49, no. 58: letter from Kautsky to Gustav Mayer, 19 Sept. 1925.

to Gustav Mayer: 'At the time I knew Engels, he was far removed from ... the English labour movement, although he superficially knew some of its personalities.'[4] Those he knew included John Burns, Tom Mann, Keir Hardie, Maltman Barry, H. H. Champion, Margaret Harkness, Edward Aveling, and Eleanor Marx. Engels's own letters to other social-ists in Germany and France do not support Bax's view; on the contrary, they demonstrate Engels's interest in the British labour movement. In 1889 he actively, but unsuccessfully, tried to win over English socialists for the Marxist foundation conference of the Second International. In 1890, in a letter to Laura Lafargue, he stressed the importance of wooing the English trade unions, despite their shaky socialist convictions. Cor-rectly, he saw that the trade unions represented the strongest potential for the development of any socialist organization in Britain.[5] Regularly and enthusiastically Engels reported strikes and May Day demonstrations in Britain. By 1895 he was convinced: 'Here a socialist feeling develops within the masses . . .'.[6] In the 1920s a veteran of the Battersea branch of the SDF remembered Engels as a person who was constantly engaged in drawing British socialists into the orbit of the International.[7] Engels had some part in the foundation of the Socialist League through his contacts with William Morris,[8] and it was certainly due to Engels's efforts that Bebel's *Frau* was translated into English in 1885.[9] To speak of Engels as totally removed from British socialism, as Bax did, therefore seems unsustainable.

One of Marx's daughters was another link between the British and the German movements. She worked in a secretarial capacity and as a trans-lator of the Miners' International and for the Second International. For the preparation of the London conference of the Second International in 1896 Eleanor Marx and her lover Edward Aveling formed the personal link between the committee and the continental Socialists. In 1892 she successfully mediated in a conflict between German and Scottish miners in the Ayrshire mines in Cumnock, where the Germans were

[4] IGA/ZPA, SPD, PV, II, 145/49, no. 1: letter from Bax to Gustav Mayer, 11 Nov. 1925.

[5] Waltraud Opitz and Uwe de la Motte (eds.), *Friedrich Engels: Die Zweite Internationale und der 1. Mai* (Berlin, 1989), 157–61.

[6] Ibid. 193.

[7] 'Ushering in the Dawn. Stray Reminiscences of a Propagandist', *Labour Magazine*, 4 (1925–6), 163–5.

[8] A. L. Morton and G. Tate, *The British Labour Movement* (London, 1956), 176 f.

[9] Hölscher, *Weltgericht*, 318. For Engels's and Marx's contacts in Britain see also Rose-mary Ashton, *Little Germany: Exile and Asylum in Victorian England* (Oxford, 1986), 56–71 and 97–138.

undercutting wages. She had very good contacts with Wilhelm Liebknecht, whom she persuaded in 1896 to come to Britain in order to give a series of lectures. Together with Edward Aveling they toured the country and spoke in Glasgow, Edinburgh, Bradford, Manchester, Liverpool, and in the East End of London. Eleanor Marx spent much of her life campaigning to introduce what she saw as the achievements of the German socialists to British trade unionists and socialists. She wrote regularly about the German movement in her 'International Notes', published in *Justice* every week, and she gave numerous speeches on the topic.[10] After the antisocialist law was lifted in 1890, she apparently helped to raise money for the SPD in Britain, so that the German party could more effectively contest the election of 1893.[11]

A meeting-place of British and German socialists in London was the Communistische Arbeiterbildungsverein (Communist Workers' Educational Association) in Fitzroy Square to which few historians have made any reference so far.[12] In an article written after the 1889 conference of the International, Bernstein mentioned the Association as a prime example of the international spirit prevailing amongst the British and German socialists in London.[13] The activities of the association included the publication of a German weekly (from 1909 to 1914) as well as active participation in the London May Day demonstrations.[14] Julius Motteler, the long-time secretary of the club, was several times selected as one of the London May Day speakers and his office naturally brought him into contact with British socialists. He knew Herbert Burrows, Harry Quelch, Theodore Rothstein, and J. B. Askew well. When the club celebrated sixty years of its existence a delegation of the SDF spoke of the admiration British socialists felt for their German comrades. Bernstein in return recalled the efforts of the club to help a British socialist movement into existence.

Most of those British socialists who knew the SPD came to admire the party's organization. Keir Hardie, for example, found in the German

---

[10] Chushichi Tsuzuki, *The Life of Eleanor Marx, 1855–1898: A Socialist Tragedy* (Oxford, 1967), 192, 219–21, 236, 282 f.

[11] Letter of Eleanor Marx concerning the German election appeal to international socialism, see: Labour Party Archive, PIC/1.

[12] Some information can be found in Henry Collins and Chimen Abramsky, *Karl Marx and the British Labour Movement* (London, 1965), and in Max Nettlau, 'Londoner deutsche kommunistische Diskussionen 1845. Nach dem Protokollbuch des CABV', *Archiv für die Geschichte des Sozialismus und der Arbeiterbewegung*, 10 (1922), 362–91.

[13] For the article, see Opitz and de la Motte, *Friedrich Engels*, 54–67.

[14] For a 1899 London May Day pamphlet in German see IGA/ZPA, Handbill Collections, V DF/III/61, no. 9.

SPD a model to follow for the Labour Party. Before 1914 he, like many other socialists all over Europe, put his hope for peace on the *entente* between British and German socialists.[15] He met Engels in 1887 and was a close friend of August Bebel, although his own writings tended rather to support Bernstein and the revisionists. In a letter to the German socialist Lilly Braun[16] he declared his lack of understanding of the SPD's doctrinal battles. His way of arguing the case for socialism was different, but this did not prevent him from forging close links with a movement whose ultimate aims and motivations, he rightly assumed, were very similar to those of his own party.

Bertrand Russell discussed German Social Democracy extensively in six lectures he delivered at the LSE in February and March 1896 which were subsequently published as a book. Like Hardie, he was especially delighted with the party's organization: 'The new organization was a masterpiece of ingenuity and efficiency.'[17] In his diary of a winter spent in Berlin (he stayed from 5 November to 21 December 1895), Russell noted all the meetings he had with major and minor officials of the party and the trade unions. He called on Liebknecht, Bebel, and Legien, as well as on several men of trust of the party, and also on simple party members and workmen. His first and foremost contacts were the Social Democrats Lily and Heinrich Braun in Berlin. Russell was especially impressed with the cultural standards of the simple workmen organized in the SPD. On 15 November he noted:

Called on Frl. Ottilie Baaden, a seamstress. We found her having tea with her old father and two little nephews in a small stuffy room with two beds and a sewing machine. Everything was very clean and there were books and papers about . . . Frl. B. told us that she had a little leisure that afternoon because she had not been able to get any sewing to do, and she was reading *Vorwärts* and *Breslauer Protokoll* while her father read *Die Neue Zeit* and the children worked at their lessons. We talked about Liebknecht's trial . . .[18]

Fred Jowett, the Labour MP for Bradford for sixteen years and one of the founding fathers of the Bradford ILP, not only admired the SPD's organization, he also believed in a special relationship between the British and the German socialists. 'He gained an impression, which lived with him during the long series of international conferences which followed,

[15] Morgan, *Keir Hardie*, 181 f.

[16] Printed in *Frankfurther Volksstimme*; see Robert Michels, 'Die deutsche Sozialdemokratie im internationalen Verbande', *AfSWP* 25 (1907), 312.

[17] Bertrand Russell, *German Social Democracy: Six Lectures* (London, 1896), 116.

[18] B. Russell, 'Diary of a Winter spent in Berlin', in LSE, Coll. Misc. 296, 15 Nov. 1895.

that "for self-possession, patience and tenacity of purpose, the British and German delegations were most alike".[19] His sympathies for the German socialists were reinforced by his friendship with the German socialist Robert Pohl. Pohl was a teacher at Bradford Technical College, a fervent believer in international brotherhood and working-class solidarity. Interned in the war, he was deported to Germany afterwards. There he established a War Resister's League in imitation of the NCF which he had come to admire in Bradford.[20]

Herbert Morrison's reorganization of the London Labour Party after 1918 was almost certainly influenced by Morrison's 1910 visit to Hamburg, Berlin, Leipzig, Frankfurt, and Cologne. He came back full of admiration for the German Socialists' organizational talents and proved himself their equal after 1918.[21] In 1931, John Paton, 'possibly the ablest organizer in the ILP',[22] was equally struck by the impression of efficiency that the SPD's organization made on him. 'The long desire to see something of the organization of the German party'[23] led him to spend a six-week vacation in Germany just before the start of the Vienna congress of the Labour and Socialist International (LSI). He visited the SPD strongholds of Berlin, Dresden, and Hamburg where the width and breadth of party organizations made a lasting impression upon him. Such expression of admiration, combined with the actual contacts that British socialists had with their German comrades, do not support the view that there was estrangement and alienation between a British and a continental type of socialism. What is more, such admiration helps to explain some of the changes introduced within the Labour Party after 1918 (e.g. machine-building; community-oriented party).

Yet not everybody within the British labour movement admired the SPD. H. M. Hyndman, who had met many Social Democrats before the First World War through his work in the International Socialist Bureau (ISB), regarded German socialists as despots and nationalists. He attacked them in conservative papers like the *Morning Post* and *The Times*. J. B. Askew, an SDF member, wrote to Kautsky in 1902: 'Hyndman was very cross with the German party—you are entirely bad and also wholly

---

[19] Fenner Brockway, *Socialism over Sixty Years: The Life of Jowett of Bradford* (London, 1946), 63. Bradford had been a centre for German-Jewish immigration in the nineteenth century. Amongst the immigrants there were several German socialists.

[20] Ibid. 136.

[21] Donoughue and Jones, *Herbert Morrison*, 32–4. For the influence of the SPD organization on Morrison see also above, pp. 96–7.

[22] Robert Dowse, *Left in the Centre*, 84.

[23] Paton, *Left Turn*, 342–8.

insignificant and ignorant people who live with the same illusions as William II.'[24] This appears the more surprising, as the SDF, which Hyndman led, was an orthodox Marxist party in Britain. Hyndman's hostility is to be explained not in ideological but in personal terms. Marx and Engels both disliked him, because Marx thought that Hyndman had plagiarized *Capital*.[25] Even after Engels's death, there was no real understanding between Hyndman and the leaders of the SPD. Speaking the language of Marxism, Hyndman was to remain antipathetic to the German SPD.

Robert Blatchford wrote a series of anti-German articles in the *Daily Mail* before the war and reserved a whole chapter of his autobiography for German-bashing.[26] Unlike Hyndman he originally did not dislike the German SPD, but he—quite prophetically—did not believe in the power of the SPD to stop an aggressive German military machine: 'the Socialist theory of joint action by the British and German socialists for the prevention of war . . . is one of those harmless games with which some Labour statesmen amuse themselves on dull days.'[27] Blatchford had few international contacts and he remained too much of a 'little Englander' to worry about that.[28] On the whole Hyndman's and Blatchford's views were minority ones in the British labour movement.[29] In fact, Hyndman, after deviating too far from the sanctioned Labour Party course, was not re-elected to the ISB by an ILP-dominated delegation in 1910 where he found himself totally isolated.[30] Viewed in this light it is apparent that Newton has put too much stress on Hyndman's 'German Menace' campaign to demonstrate the difficult relationship between British and German socialists. He exaggerates the importance of Hyndman and other anti-SPD forces for the Labour Party at large.[31]

[24] IISG, Kautsky papers, letter Askew to Kautsky, 15 Jan. 1902.

[25] Chushichi Tsuzuki, *H. M. Hyndman and British Socialism* (London, 1961), 32–66.

[26] Robert Blatchford, *My Eighty Years* (London, 1931), 223 and the chapter 'Who caused the war?', esp. p. 248.

[27] Robert Blatchford, *Germany and England: Articles reprinted from the Daily Mail* (London, 1909), 15.

[28] For his obsession with England's dependency on 'foreigners' and his programme of creating an England based on economic autarky see Robert Blatchford, *Merrie England* (London, 1895), 34.

[29] Kenneth E. Miller, *Socialism and Foreign Policy: Theory and Practice in Britain to 1931* (The Hague, 1967), 42–5.

[30] Glasier 'declared that the re-election of Hyndman after his Jingo utterances would be an outrage upon International Socialist sentiment. Anderson and Hardie both spoke strongly on the same side. Quelch, Irving and others defended Hyndman while not approving his views.' See Liverpool University Library, Glasier papers 1910/32, letter Glasier to his wife, 30 Aug. 1910.

[31] Newton, *British Labour*, 139–78 and 212–27.

The 'official' view was better reflected by leaders like Ramsay MacDonald, whose intellectual indebtedness to Eduard Bernstein is beyond doubt. 'Tight and long bonds of friendship'[32] connected them. Bernstein was not only a frequent visitor at 3, Lincoln's Inn Fields, where MacDonald settled after marriage,[33] but the two also worked actively for peace and a better understanding between their two people before the First World War. Bernstein translated an article by MacDonald on *England and Germany* which appeared in the *Sozialistische Monatshefte* in 1908. Here MacDonald distanced himself from 'a small group of English socialists . . . for instance Hyndman who never had abandoned their anti-German chauvinism'[34] and he called on the British and German labour movements to set an example to their people and abandon the mutual mistrust prevalent among the two people.[35] In 1911 Bernstein in return wrote a little booklet entitled *Die englische Gefahr und das deutsche Volk*, in which he looked at the Anglo-German rivalry from a historical per-spective condemning the 'most shortsighted and most foolish policy which makes the great English nation our enemy'.[36] Many of Bernstein's regular contributions to the left-liberal weekly *The Nation* before 1914 aimed at improving Anglo-German relations.[37] They maintained contact with one another even in the difficult circumstances of war. In September 1917 Bernstein wrote to MacDonald from Denmark, raising the faint possibil-ity of negotiating for peace and rebuilding the International.[38]

Apart from Bernstein's contact with MacDonald, he knew virtually all the prominent Fabians and was especially friendly with Sidney and Beatrice Webb, Hubert Bland, E. R. Pease, and G. B. Shaw, who took first place among British socialists in Bernstein's memoirs. He further met Hyndman, William Morris, John Burns, and Will Thorne. He described Beatrice and Sidney Webb as 'people whose chief delight is research work' and

---

[32] Helmut Hirsch, *Der Fabier Eduard Bernstein* (Bonn, 1977), 81. Also David Marquand, *Ramsay MacDonald*, 56 f., 164.

[33] In his memoirs Bernstein recalled the ' "at home" days' of the MacDonalds, when they would be entertaining their friends. When Bernstein left Britain in 1901, they organized a farewell party for him at their home. See Bernstein, *My Years of Exile*, 246 f.

[34] Ramsay MacDonald, 'England und Deutschland', *SM* 17 (1908), 1033.

[35] Ibid. 1035.

[36] Eduard Bernstein, *Die englische Gefahr und das deutsche Volk* (Berlin, 1911), 47 f.

[37] F. L. Carsten, *Eduard Bernstein 1850–1932: Eine politische Biographie* (Munich, 1993), 109.

[38] Marquand, *Ramsay MacDonald*, 260. In 1916 Bernstein also published the last letter he had received from Keir Hardie, 17 May 1914 in which he had expressed hope in the international strength of socialism. See E. Bernstein, 'Ein Brief Keir Hardies: Zum Gedächtnistage seines Todes', *Vorwärts* (26 Sept. 1916).

about Sidney Webb he wrote: 'He is absolutely a walking encyclopedia, a fact which is particularly to be remarked when he has to answer questions or is heckled in debate . . . He is manifestly the most powerful brain to be found among the Fabians, and today he gives the full impression of being the man of learning that he is.'[39] The warm relationship he manifestly enjoyed with the Webbs was kept-up all through his life. After the war Sidney Webb invited him to a Fabian summer school, and in a personal letter accompanying the formal invitation he remarked:

How many times in the last six calamitous years have we not spoken about you in this house, and wished that we could have the opportunity of talking this over with you? . . . I need hardly say what pleasure it would give to your English friends if you could accept this invitation . . .[40]

In a further letter which he wrote on 5 April 1930 Sidney Webb informed Bernstein that

we have finally quit our home at 41 Grosvenor Road, Westminster, where we have lived since 1893, and where we have had the pleasure of receiving you, and so many other German friends and comrades . . . [and he ended his letter:] . . . With kindest regards and best wishes from us both, I am, to you as to other friends, still yours sincerely Sidney Webb (though officially Lord Passfield).[41]

Beatrice and Sidney Webb took a great interest in the development of the German labour movement. In an introduction to a book about the German trade unions written by W. S. Sanders, Sidney Webb stated that the German unions could be a model for the British in many ways:

The German workmen learnt their Trade Unionism from this country, but in many points they have known how to improve on their instructors. . . . There are many lessons in this book for British Trade Unions. The wonderful development of the central Trade Union offices, with their expert staff; the skill and wisdom with which they obtain and utilize their own statistical information; their really remarkable efforts for the education of their members; their training schools for Trade Union officials—all this is in striking contrast with the haphazard methods of British wage-earning Democracy.[42]

Bernstein was certainly the most prominent German socialist to stay for any length of time in Britain. The *Encyclopedia Britannica* asked him

---

[39] Bernstein, *My Years of Exile*, 242.
[40] IISG, Bernstein papers D 816: letter S. Webb to E. Bernstein, 19 Apr. 1920.
[41] Ibid.: letter S. Webb to E. Bernstein, 5 Apr. 1930.
[42] W. S. Sanders, *Trade Unionism in Germany* (Westminster, 1916), 3 f.

to write an article about Karl Marx for them[43] and the German foreign office wanted to use his British contacts.[44] Before and after the war British organizations asked him to speak at their meetings, e.g. the Cobden Club in 1913 and the League of Nations Union in 1923.[45] When Bernstein was finally able to return to Germany from his British exile in 1901, several letters from British Labour organizations congratulated him, e.g. there is a message of the ILP Edinburgh branch signed by John Davidson, its secretary, from 23 January 1901: 'We rejoice that your sphere of useful-ness should have been so extended and trust you may be long spared to work on behalf of our common cause.'[46] Even after his return to Germany he loved to come back to Britain. In 1909, for example, he engaged in a lecture tour to Edinburgh, Glasgow, and Manchester.[47] The wish to forge close links with British socialism was not restricted to Bernstein only. Lothar Erdmann, editor of the theoretical ADGB journal *Die Arbeit* from 1923 to 1933, chose to live in Britain before the First World War (around 1910), where he joined the Fabian Society and became a disciple of George Bernard Shaw.[48] Johann Sassenbach, secretary and later general secretary of the IFTU in Amsterdam from 1922 to 1930, first came into contact with Ramsay MacDonald and other Labour Party leaders in June 1909, when a Labour Party commission travelled to Cologne and other German cities. In the spring of 1914 Sassenbach was invited to spend two months at Ruskin College, Oxford, where he made many contacts in Labour circles and became particularly friendly with W. A. Appleton, general secretary of the General Federation of Trade Unions. On the invitation of Sassenbach, Appleton and Ben Tillett visited the free trade union congress in Munich in June 1914. Before the congress, Appleton and Sassenbach spent a week's holiday together in the Bavarian Alps.[49] In the inter-war period prominent Social Democrats continued to live and work in Britain. Amongst them were the party journalists Egon Wertheimer and Viktor Schiff, who had a distinguished career with the *Daily Herald*, Julius Braunthal, the historian of the International, Hermann Badt, a

---

[43] IISG, Bernstein papers, D 148.

[44] Ibid. D 24.

[45] Ibid. D 396 and D 660.

[46] Ibid. D 127: letter Davidson to Bernstein, 23 Jan. 1901.

[47] *Labour Leader* (26 Mar. 1909), 201.

[48] Gerhard Beier, *Schulter an Schulter. Schritt für Schritt: Lebensläufe deutscher Gewerkschafter* (Cologne, 1983), 42.

[49] Otto Scheugenpflug, *Johann Sassenbach: ein Beitrag zur Geschichte der deutschen und internationalen Arbeiterbewegung nach Aufzeichnungen Sassenbachs* (Hanover, 1959), 44 f., 54–6 and 118 f.

one-time aide to Albert Grzesinski in the Prussian Ministry of the Interior and many others.[50]

If we now return to MacDonald we see that after the war he kept up his contacts with German socialists. On his eightieth birthday in 1930 Bernstein wrote to MacDonald: 'The feeling that only possesses me is thankfulness, undescribable thankfulness to the party where I have got so much happiness, and to the comrades who have presented me with so many proofs of benevolent amity. This feeling you have, dear friend, to a high degree contributed to create in me.'[51] MacDonald also corresponded with Eugen Diederichs who published his book *Socialism and Government* in German, with Joseph Bloch, in whose *Sozialistische Monatshefte* MacDonald wrote, and with Südekum whom he probably met on the event of Südekum's 1906–8 lecture tours through England.[52] Before the First World War he travelled to Germany several times to study the German labour movement and social conditions there. He knew most of the SPD leaders well. When Ebert died in 1925, MacDonald sent a letter of condolence to his wife: 'Grieved beyond words at death of my old friend . . . Not only Germany but Europe has lost a wise and patient servant.'[53]

After a visit in July 1920[54] MacDonald went to Berlin again in 1928 to meet the Social Democratic chancellor Hermann Müller and other Social Democrats.[55] On the event of MacDonald's election victory in 1929 and his taking office, Müller congratulated him on a 'glorious victory . . . I know that we are in perfect harmony, that all must be done, to save the peace of Europe, which guarantees the welfare of all nations.'[56] And MacDonald replied: 'As you know, one of my greatest desires is to help to have peace behind me as the contribution which this generation makes to civilization. . . . I too rejoice that at this moment we should both hold the positions we do.'[57] The bonds of personal contact seemed to have been strongest amongst German revisionists and British socialists. Georges

---

[50] See the list in Anthony Glees, *Exile Politics during the Second World War: The German Social Democrats in Britain* (Oxford, 1982), 29. Glees' book is the most extensive history of the party relations between Labour Party and SPD for the period 1933–45.

[51] PRO, MacDonald papers, 30/69, 752/12–13.

[52] BA, Südekum papers, NL 91.

[53] PRO, MacDonald papers, 30/69, 1170/1/394. For correspondence with Südekum, Bloch and Diederichs see ibid. 992/7, 1150/15, 988/6–10, and 992/49.

[54] Marquand, *Ramsay MacDonald*, 260.

[55] FES, Müller papers, Box 1, 56, letter MacDonald to Müller, 9 July 1928 Box 4, 284, letter Müller to MacDonald, 26 Sept. 1928.

[56] Ibid., Box 4, 285, letter Müller to MacDonald, 8 June 1929.

[57] Ibid., Box 1, 59, letter MacDonald to Müller, 13 June 1929.

Haupt has written about South Eastern European socialists being more interested in German marxists, like Kautsky and Luxemburg.[58] In that respect Labour Party–SPD relations were based on that 'other' tradition within the SPD: the reformist tradition.

Apart from personal contacts, international summer schools were held frequently by the Fabian Society, the ILP, the SPD, the trade unions, and international labour organizations. Because of a lack of archival material, one can only get glimpses of the schools' organization and atmosphere. So, for instance, Beatrice Webb recorded how at the Fabian summer school of September 1920 at Priorsfield, Godalming, Adolf Braun 'in an address of one and a half hours . . . achieved his purpose of harrowing the feelings and rousing the sympathies of the audience by a vivid account of the desperate material and moral condition of the German people'.[59] Maria Hodann, who fled Nazi Germany in 1933 and became a British citizen under the name of Mary Saran, wrote of the International Trade Union Summer School at Ruskin College in Oxford and her stay with a family at Kentish Town in London: 'I could not have had a better introduction to the London of the Cockneys, their humour and warm hospitality.'[60] IFTU summer schools were held in Berlin (1930), Oxford (1924, 1926, 1931), and various other places in Europe after 1918. Normally there were a series of lectures on international trade unionism and the school would finish after a fortnight, sometimes even after a week. Many German unions remained sceptical about the practical value of summer schools in comparison to their relatively high costs. Language problems were especially hard to overcome.[61] Yet the executive of the ADGB stressed the usefulness of summer schools in terms of a stronger internationalism of the labour movements of the world. For the participants they were an opportunity to look beyond their rather narrow national, sometimes local or regional horizon and to get to know labour movements of other countries.[62]

Summer schools were also held by the International People's College in Denmark. A Danish foundation with strong links to the Danish labour movement, it found support particularly amongst British and German

[58] Georges Haupt, *Aspects of International Socialism 1871–1914* (Cambridge, 1986), 63.
[59] *The Diaries of Beatrice Webb 1912–1924*, ed. Margaret Cole (London, 1952), 189.
[60] Mary Saran, *Never Give up* (London, 1976), 30.
[61] See the sceptical response of many German unions to the call of the ADGB to send representatives to international summer schools in the 1920s in Historische Kommission, NB 78, 29–48.
[62] Historische Kommission, NB 78, no. 36: letter from the ADGB executive to the textile union, 22 Nov. 1924.

socialists whose delegations were regularly the largest ones in Helsingfør. Eduard Bernstein and George Lansbury headed committees in Germany and Britain whose task it was to further the interests of the College.[63] The British and German socialist travel organizations also worked together in the 1920s to ensure 'that the participants of study and holiday trips should get in close touch with the workers beyond the national boundaries, so that the idea of international solidarity would be transformed into reality'.[64] Fifty years after Harry Grey had visited Germany with the No More War Movement, he was still impressed with the methodical ways the German socialists had. Out of a two-week stay with a German socialist family, contacts developed which lasted until after the Second World War.[65] Similar rank-and-file contacts were organized via the Socialist Youth International. In 1923, for example, fifteen German and Austrian youths went to Britain for two weeks. They toured the country, giving performances of socialist songs and German folk dances.[66] Such an exchange of youth groups was paralleled by the organization of correspondence with penfriends through the Bureau of the Youth International. Many German requests asked for pen-friends in Britain and there seemed to have been a considerable number of contacts between individual young socialists. In a report to the Bureau one of the participants of the international exchange of letters recalled his positive experiences:

Besides the more general exchange of ideas about the labour and youth movement, feelings of friendship and comradeship developed through the exchange of letters. If mutual visits did not come about this summer, it was mainly because of the economic situation. Through mutual help it should be possible to overcome these difficulties next year.[67]

It is impossible today to quantify the significance of such rank-and-file contacts, but they seemed to have brought life into the abstract statements of British and German socialist leaders about international solidarity and

---

[63] W. H. Marwick, 'The International People's College in Denmark', *Labour Magazine*, 3 (1924–5), 300 f.

[64] Pamphlet of the Reichsausschuß für sozialistische Bildungsarbeit in IGA/ZPA, SPD, PV, II, 145/27, no. 4. See ibid. for a conference of the International on organized workers' holidays and the correspondence between Reichsausschuß and WTA on the occasion of a visit of German socialists to Britain in 1929. Woolwich docks and factory works in Birmingham were amongst the sights as well as the Houses of Parliament and the Tower of London.

[65] Interview with Harry and Kitty Grey, 30 Apr. 1990.

[66] IISG, files on the Socialist Youth International, no. 37a: letter from Ollenhauer to Pendry, 19 Apr. 1923.

[67] Ibid., no. 357/5, letter from Felix Kyora to the Bureau of the Socialist Youth International, 22 Aug. 1931.

brotherhood. They multiplied and mirrored the friendships and contacts of socialist leaders of Britain and Germany. If, as has been argued, both the leaders of British and German working-class parties and their rank and file enjoyed good personal contacts, it seems difficult to uphold Newton's proposition that British socialists were isolated, different from and alien to 'continental' socialism.

6.2. Institutionalized relations

Personal friendships and contacts were one side of the relations between the British Labour Party and the German SPD. As has been seen in the last section, numerous personal contacts can be found. Often such contacts led to more official visits and delegations that involved the two party organizations, whilst the socialist press in both countries decisively formed the mutual perceptions of the organized working class in Britain and Germany.

Party journalism

Robert Dell, who joined the Fabian Society in 1889, became foreign correspondent for the *Manchester Guardian* and other papers, among them the *New Statesman*, in Geneva (1920–1), Berlin (1922–4), Paris (1925–32), and again Geneva (1932–9). In his letters back home to his daughter Sylvia and in his articles about Germany, Labour's positive and generous view of Germany is reflected.[68] Here we touch upon an important potential for British–German socialist contacts: the socialist press. As the *New Statesman* had its journalists in Germany, so some of the German Labour papers and journals had their journalists in Britain. They made various contacts with representatives of the labour movement within the foreign country and often enough acted as bridge-builders between the two movements. Two such bridge-builders were Max Beer and William John.

After moving to London in 1895, Beer worked as the London correspondent of *Vorwärts* from the middle of 1901 to the beginning of 1911. Before the First World War, he wrote in his autobiography: 'all my journalistic work for *Vorwärts* and *Neue Zeit*, so far as it dealt with foreign affairs, was mainly guided by the desire to apprise my readers . . . of the growing antagonism between Britain and Germany and the possibility of a European war.'[69] However, he also got heavily involved in British

---

[68] LSE, Dell Papers, 1/9 and 5/11.
[69] Max Beer, *Fifty Years of International Socialism* (London, 1935), 121.

Labour Politics, helping to defend the ILP against attacks from the Marxist SDP, reassuring Glasier: 'you will always find me on your side. I am determined to contribute my share in this fight.'[70] As one of the first students at the LSE before the war, he befriended some of the leading Fabians. Graham Wallas, Sidney Webb, and R. H. Tawney all helped Beer at the outbreak of the First World War, when Beer found himself stranded in London.[71] In the war Beer moved back to Berlin and worked as a translator for the committee in charge of international trade union work. After the war he remained in touch with British socialists. In his papers there are letters from G. D. H. Cole, Harold J. Laski, Arthur J. Penty, Marion Philipps, R. H. Tawney, S. Webb, and H. G. Wells.[72] His relations with Laski and Tawney were especially cordial. The former wrote to him on the occasion of Beer's flight from National Socialism to Britain on 14 July 1933: 'It was good to know . . . that you escaped from that cursed tyranny. . . . we shall want you to come to dinner and have a long talk . . . Please assume that I belong unchangeably to those (not a few) who hold you in warm esteem and regard.'[73] And Tawney wrote on 14 September 1941: 'Your friendship has meant a great deal for me—more than I can express. I feel the deepest gratitude to you for it. I will not say more'.[74] It was also Tawney, together with Page-Arnot, who made sure that Beer's book on the early British labour movement could be published in Britain after the First World War.[75]

On the British side one example of a journalist who became an important figure in Anglo-German working-class party relations was William John. John was an ILP member who lived in Hamburg from 1904 to 1918. He became the official representative of the British Labour press in Germany and wrote for the *Labour Leader*[76] and the *Daily Citizen*. During the war he was interned in Germany. After his release he suffered from ill-health and returned home. He never resumed his contacts with German socialists afterwards, due to his disappointment about many of

[70] Liverpool University Library, Glasier Papers, 1909/6 and 1909/24, letters Beer to Glasier, 31 Mar. and 19 Apr. 1909.

[71] LSE, Wallas Papers, corresp., 1/48. And LSE, Tawney Papers, no. 26/2: letter Beer to Tawney, 3 Sept. 1919.

[72] IISG, Beer papers, Dr van der Leeuw was preparing an inventory at the IISG in Amsterdam for Beer's papers in 1988.

[73] Ibid., letter Laski to Beer, 14 July 1933.

[74] Ibid., letter Tawney to Beer, 14 Sept. 1941.

[75] LSE, Tawney Papers, no. 26/2: letter Beer to Tawney, 3 Sept. 1919. Max Beer, *History of British Socialism*, 2 vols. (London, 1921; repr. 1953) remains an extremely detailed, readable, and scholarly work on the early British labour movement.

[76] LSE, Miscellaneous Collections, Coll. Misc. 686: letter Glasier to John, 20 June 1908.

his German socialist friends, who easily swapped sides from internationalism to jingoism in 1914.[77]

When he first went over to Germany, he carried a letter of introduction from Keir Hardie to Bernstein, who put him in touch with Oskar Peterssen, one of the SPD officials in Hamburg. Before the war, John was enthusiastically engaged in the efforts of British Labour to better Anglo-German relations. His idea of organizing a visit of a Labour deputation to Hamburg was eagerly taken up by Bruce Glasier, the editor of the *Labour Leader*, who wrote to him on 20 November 1909: 'The idea which you mention of having a deputation of the Labour Party to Hamburg is excellent, and I hope it will be realised. There ought to be a constant exchange of speakers from different countries.'[78] John provided MacDonald with information published in Germany about the British labour movement,[79] and he served as link between the British and the German labour movements to other Labour figures. For instance he proposed to Keir Hardie that he accept German money in order to set up a Labour daily in Britain. Hardie declined, out of 'pride', as he wrote to John on 5 November 1910: 'Thanks for your suggestion re finance. I do not, however, propose to approach the German party except as a very last resort.'[80] Harry Elvin, the General Secretary of the National Union of Clerks, wrote to John on 3 June 1910 of his plans to visit Germany in the hope that John could somehow arrange a meeting with representatives of the German Clerk's Association.[81]

It is hardly an exaggeration to say that journalists like Dell, John, and Beer did much to bring the British and German labour movements closer together. The socialist press in Britain and Germany—especially its representatives in foreign countries—were important in shaping the perceptions of the two parties in regard to the other. The socialist press in Germany regularly reported on the movement in Britain, the party, and trade union conferences, and it followed the major debates within the British socialist organizations with interest.[82] Reports about anti-socialist

---

[77] LSE, letter from Petersson to John, 1919 (without precise date).
[78] Ibid., letter Glasier to John, 20 Nov. 1909. In fact Glasier had already suggested 'a frequent exchange of leading Socialist speakers among the different countries' at a Bureau meeting of the Second International in 1908. See Liverpool University Library, Glasier papers, 1909/85 letter Glasier to Johnson, 27 Feb. 1909.
[79] Ibid., letter MacDonald to John, 18 Jan. 1911.
[80] Ibid., letter Hardie to John, 5 Nov. 1910.
[81] Ibid., letter Elvin to John, 3 June 1910.
[82] ZStA Merseburg, CBS no. 140, and 307/11, and 86/11-V, where social democratic press cuttings about the Labour Party are collected.

organizations and tendencies in Britain[83] can be found as well as reports about the International's efforts to unite the various socialist parties in Britain,[84] obituaries of British socialists like Harry Quelch,[85] and reports of jubilees of Labour organizations.[86]

Orthodox German Marxists tended to see the Labour Party as a socialist party in its infancy. In 1886 Kautsky wrote to Bernstein: 'Socialism [in Britain] should first of all create a viable literature then one can start taking it seriously. Now it is only sentimental philanthropy, nothing else.'[87] Commenting on the lack of electoral success of the Labour Party in 1910 *Vorwärts* wrote: 'England today demonstrates how important a strict programme and strict guide-lines are for a political party. Only a specifically socialist programme can give the Labour Party any right of existence today.'[88] If the Labour Party was a child, it was constantly growing up. Victor Grayson's victory in Colne Valley in 1907 was seen as a decisive step in the direction of socialism, as far as *Vorwärts* was concerned.[89] For Clara Zetkin both the International conference of 1896 in London and the miners' strike in 1912 were clear indications that the British labour movement was joining its continental socialist brothers.[90] The Labour Party's reorganization after 1918 was equally seen as a move towards more centralization and towards a more homogeneous party organization and greeted as a further step towards a socialist party in Britain.[91]

Contrary to the Marxist view of British Labour, the reformists within the SPD often admired the Labour Party as a model of tolerance and pragmatic policy-making, free from the sectarian dogmatism of their own party. Already by 1900 Karl Kautsky was pointing out that German revisionism was following an 'English model'.[92] Egon Wertheimer, in the inter-war period, found it 'characteristic of this British Socialist movement that . . . there were . . . individuals, all with their own particular

---

[83] *Vorwärts*, 244 (18 Oct. 1907), and *LVZ* 255 (2 Nov. 1907).

[84] *Vorwärts*, 214 (20 Aug. 1913).

[53] *Vorwärts*, 245 (20 Sept. 1913).

[86] *Vorwärts*, 138 (23 May 1914) for a report about the jubilee of the Fabian Society.

[87] IGA/ZPA, Bernstein papers, NL 23/8, no. 104: letter from Kautsky to Bernstein, 18 Jan. 1886.

[88] *Vorwärts*, 30 (5 Feb. 1910).

[89] *Vorwärts*, 170 (24 July 1907).

[90] Clara Zetkin, 'Der internationale sozialistische Arbeiter- und Gewerkschaftskongreß in London', *Die Gleichheit* (5 Aug. 1896), 121; Clara Zetkin about the 1912 miners' strike in *Die Gleichheit* (1 Apr. 1912), 209 f.

[91] Max Beer, 'Der 21. Parteitag der britischen Arbeiter', *NZ* (1920–1), 368–71.

[92] Karl Kautsky, 'Akademiker und Proletarier', *NZ* 19 (1900–1), 89–91.

style, not, as with us, one traditional party style, which the officials of the
party, under penalty of the loss of their authority, dare not depart from.
Here, even within the domain of a workers' party, . . . was Liberty Hall.'[93]
Wertheimer wanted the SPD to adopt much of what he saw as undogmatic, pluralistic socialism which would incorporate the middle classes of
society.[94]

British socialists frequently contributed articles about the British
labour movement to the German party press. MacDonald, Snowden,
Glasier, Shaw, Hardie, and Barnes all contributed to the *Sozialistische
Monatshefte*, Rothstein, Askew, and Brockle wrote for the *Neue Zeit* before
the war, and Delisle Burns for *Die Gesellschaft* thereafter. The revisionist
Sozialistische Monatshefte and its editor J. Bloch were keen on British
socialism because they saw it as a possible counterweight to Marxism
within their own party. In Kautsky's *Neue Zeit* only British Marxists
wrote about Britain. The split that went right through the SPD before
1914 also determined the attitude towards the British Labour Party.
Revisionists tended to be enthusiastic about its achievements, Marxists
were critical of its shortcomings and looked forward to its transformation
into a really socialist party. Newton's argument, however, that little was
known about the Labour Party in German socialist circles[95] seems unreal-
istic when seen against the evidence from SPD journals.

If we now consider the British labour movement's perception of their
German comrades, it becomes equally clear that the notion of the insularity of British Labour has been exaggerated.[96] The foreign news coverage
of the official Labour daily before the war, the *Daily Citizen*, was neither
extensive nor detailed, the main reason for this being its poverty. Nevertheless the paper had a daily column, 'Labour Abroad', until January
1913.[97] Henry Pelling has already pointed to the fact that much of the
British interest in Socialism in the 1880s sprang from the success of
the German SPD.[98] And H. N. Brailsford recalled his feelings towards
the SPD: 'I shared the respect which all who knew them felt for the

[93] Wertheimer, *Portrait of the Labour Party*, p. xi.

[94] Egon Wertheimer, 'Sozialismus für unsere Generation', *Die Gesellschaft*, 3 (1926),
444–57.

[95] Newton, *British Labour*, 250.

[96] See, for example, Stephen Yeo, 'Socialism, the State and some Oppositional Englishness', in R. Colls and P. Dodd (eds.), *Englishness: Politics and Culture, 1880–1920* (London,
1986), 312: 'there was a lot of . . . "Englishness" about in labour and socialist circles during
the late nineteenth and early twentieth centuries.'

[97] Ichikawa, 'The Daily Citizen', 63–6.

[98] Henry Pelling, *The Origins of the Labour Party, 1880–1900* (London, 1954), 13–22 and
219.

organizing talent and the disciplined steadiness of the Germans.'[99] Indeed, British socialists followed the development of the German party rather closely before and after the First World War. When the *Umsturzvorlage* was discussed in the Reichstag in 1895, *Vorwärts* published letters of solidarity from all over the world, amongst them several from English and Scottish Labour organizations.[100] When the Social Democrats did well in the 1898 elections almost all socialist parties in Britain and even some individual branches sent letters of congratulation to Berlin.[101] After 1918 not only Lenin expected the socialist transformation to begin in Germany. British socialists, like Beatrice Webb, looked with great expectations to Germany. She noted in her diary on 24 June 1919 (on the event of the scuttling of the German fleet at Scapa Flow): 'The Germans will sink other things besides their fleet before the Allies repent this use of victory: the capitalist system for instance. The Germans have a great game to play with Western civilization if they choose to play it, if they have the originality and the collective determination to carry it through . . .'[102]

It is by no means difficult to find references to the SPD in the British Labour Press. Again, the prime object of admiration was the organizational skill of the Germans: 'Our German comrades are perfect demons of organization.'[103] In 1909 W. John published a series of favourable articles about the German SPD in the *Labour Leader* and regular exchanges of peace greetings between the two parties were also published in the press.[104] Time and again local Labour Parties and socialist organizations had SPD visitors.[105] As British socialists wrote for the SPD press, German socialists wrote for the Labour Party press. Bernstein published articles in nearly every socialist journal; the official *Labour Magazine* in the 1920s had contributions from Viktor Schiff, Max Beer, Rudolf Breitscheid, Friedrich Stampfer, Karl Kautsky, Max Westphal, Theodor Cassau, Richard Seidel, Siegfried Aufhäuser, Hermann Schlimme, Paul Hertz, Max Fechner, and Fritz Naphtali. The *Labour Organizer* drew attention to the good electoral

---

[99] H. N. Brailsford in his introduction to Julius Braunthal, *In Search of the Millennium*, 8

[100] *Vorwärts*, 217 (17 Aug. 1895).

[101] ZStA Merseburg, CBS, Rep. 77, no. 466, vol. i, nos, 31, 33, 35–7.

[102] *The Diaries of Beatrice Webb, 1905–1924*, ed. by Jeanne and Norman MacKenzie (London, 1984), iii. 345.

[103] *Labour Leader* (11 Jan. 1907), 534.

[104] For example: *Labour Leader* (2 Apr. 1909), 217; *Vorwärts*, 107 (4 May 1913).

[105] *Labour Leader* (2 and 9 Mar. 1906), 586 and 601; Kenneth Richardson, *20th Century Coventry* (London, 1972), 190; E. and R. Frow, *To Make that Future—Now!*, 37 f.

organization of the SPD in 1922.[106] The *Socialist Review* carried a number of articles about Germany after 1918, all favourable to the country and its agonies; Karl Kautsky as well as Eduard Bernstein contributed to the *Socialist Review*.

Party delegations

Apart from journalistic links, socialists in Britain and Germany kept in contact through mutual delegations to their respective yearly conferences. Newton has stressed that the Labour Party never sponsored a fraternal delegate to any of the SPD's annual congresses up to 1914.[107] However, even if there were no official fraternal delegates, individual British socialists visited the German party conferences. Keir Hardie, for example, visited both the 1910 and 1913 SPD party conferences.[108] Bruce Glasier was also present at Jena in 1913 recalling a long meeting with 'my good friend Eduard Bernstein, Dr Frank and Dr Südekum.[109] Newton also fails to report about German socialists attending British conferences. Hardie wrote twenty-one years after Bernstein had attended the foundation conference of the ILP in Bradford on 13–14 January 1893: 'You do not quite visualize the worth of your presence at our conference (in 1893), I believe. It was some sort of perfecting of it and it gave to it a legitimation which contributed considerably to our success.'[110] It was not the last time that he attended ILP conferences. In 1909 Bernstein, for example, was enthusiastically received by the Edinburgh conference of the ILP. Hermann Molkenbuhr visited the twelfth party conference of the Labour Party in 1912 and Hermann Müller attended the ILP conference in 1913. Fritz Heine observed the 1929 general elections in Britain on behalf of the SPD executive committee.

After the war there were British delegates to the SPD conferences of 1922 and 1924. At the unity conference of MSPD and USPD on 24 September 1922 in Nurenberg, Ammon and Davies were welcomed by Wels as 'representatives of the English working class which to an ever

[106] 'Der Tag', in *Labour Organizer* (Nov. 1922), 3.

[107] Newton, *British Labour*, 250.

[108] For the 1910 congress see Liverpool University Library, Glasier papers, 1910/35, letter Glasier to his wife, 7 Sept. 1910. For the 1912 congress see John Eichmanis, 'The British Labour Movement and the Second International, 1889–1914' (University of London M.Phil. 1982), 323.

[109] Liverpool University Library, Glasier papers 1913/12, letters Glasier to his wife, 15 Sept. 1913.

[110] Letter from Keir Hardie to Bernstein, 17 May 1914, repr. in translation in *Vorwärts* (26 Sept. 1916).

increasing degree had put itself alongside the German working class',[111] thereby emphasizing the special role of the British labour movement for the German one after the First World War. In their report back to the Labour Party conference in 1923 both men stated: 'it is obvious that the German working classes are expecting release from their intolerable economic conditions through the help of the British Labour Party . . .'.[112] In 1924 Mrs Bell from the Labour Party attended the SPD annual congress in Berlin. She heard Crispien thank the British Labour Party for its support in the Ruhr struggle: 'we can note with satisfaction that Comrade MacDonald has been one of the most eager colleagues on our international conferences, that he tried again and again to mobilize weapons against the policy of Poincaré.'[113]

Apart from fraternal delegations at conferences there had been special delegations to Germany. In 1908 George Barnes, J. R. Clynes, and Arthur Henderson went to Düsseldorf, Cologne, Berlin, Frankfurt, and Strasburg to study the industrial conditions in the country. Amongst the German socialists they met were Eduard Bernstein and J. Sassenbach, who was later to become secretary of the IFTU.[114] In May 1910 another Labour Party delegation including George Barnes, G. H. Roberts, G. Wardle, A. Henderson, and J. Parker visited the SPD to look into the effects of tariffs on the living standards of German workers. In their concluding report they stressed that 'The great economic boom in Germany resulted from the German talent of organization [*sic*] and not from tariffs . . .'.[115] In 1908 and 1912 there were peace delegations of British socialists to the SPD, and in 1908 Kautsky and Ledebour paid a return visit to Britain on the invitation of the ILP. Albert Südekum also went on a lecturing tour of Britain addressing large meetings in all major British towns.[116] In 1909 another Labour Party delegation caused embarrassment amongst international socialists. The delegation which included prominent Labour Party members, like MacDonald, Barnes, Henderson, Crooks, Jowett, Clynes, Middleton, and Appleton met Bethmann-Hollweg and other political

---

[111] *Protokoll des SPD Einheitsparteitags 1922* (Berlin, 1922), 193.

[112] *Report of the Annual Conference of the Labour Party 1923* (London, 1923), 28.

[113] *Protokoll des SPD Parteitags 1924* (Berlin, 1924), 47 f.

[114] G. N. Barnes and A. Henderson, *Unemployment in Germany* (Westminster, 1908). For Clynes's separate visit see J. R. Clynes, *Memoirs, 1869–1924*, i (London, 1937), 156.

[115] ZStA Potsdam, Reichsarbeitsministerium, 39.01, no. 10/6560, vol. ii, fo. 3, no. 80 and no. 88

[116] *Vorwärts*, 179 (2 Aug. 1908), and IGA/ZPA, SPD, PV, II, 145/3, nos. 1–2 for the 1912 delegation. For the 1908 visit of SPD representatives to Britain see Liverpool University Library, Glasier papers, 1909/85: letter Glasier to Johnson, 27 Feb. 1909. For Südekum's visit also: BA Roblenz, Papers of Albert Südekum, NL 190, 91/41.

opponents of the SPD. Because of such contacts with the 'class-enemy', the SPD and the ADGB officially refused to meet the delegation. How had such an apparent gaffe become possible?

Apparently British socialists were keen to go to Berlin and meet German socialists in a common gesture for peace and goodwill. It was Bebel who told them not to come. In a letter to Molkenbuhr from 20 August 1908 he noted: 'I have told the English in the most energetic way not to honour us with delegations. The whole affair is ridiculous. If a war is impossible at any moment, it is now . . .'.[117] MacDonald on the other hand was not amused by Bebel's snub to the Labour Party's desire to send a delegation to Germany. He wrote to John:

They [the SPD] were asked last September, if they would arrange for a visit from us. The letter making the request was written to Bebel, couched in terms which makes it simply dishonest for him or anybody else to say he did not understand it was an official communication . . . The question therefore came up: Were we to be kept out of Germany simply because the Executive of the German Social Democratic Party thought we ought to remain away?[118]

In the end the SPD decided to invite the British section of the International to send a peace delegation to Germany, but the Labour Party regarded this as unacceptable, as it would have involved the SDF. Consequently the Labour Party decided not to wait for a proper invitation from the SPD, but to follow an invitation of the German-English Conciliation Committee, in which German Liberals were prominent.[119]

The Labour Party delegation finally met SPD officials 'in a private and most friendly conference'[120] and Bruce Glasier called on the SPD as a one-man delegation at about the same time, in order to soothe the storm that had arisen. In Berlin he met Südekum, Sassenbach, Bernstein, Legien, Molkenbuhr, Hermann Müller, and Friedrich Ebert, who showed him the town, the parliament, and the party premises.[121] Nevertheless the whole affair left a bitter after-taste amongst socialists of both countries. Theodore Rothstein, in the 1910 *Socialist Annual*, probably expressed the feelings of many German Social Democrats when he wrote: 'The Labour

[117] IGA/ZPA, Bebel papers, NL 22/132, no. 23.

[118] LSE, Miscellaneous Collections, Coll. Misc. 686: letter MacDonald to John, 17 June 1909.

[119] For the events surrounding the 1909 delegation see also Eichmanis, 'The British Labour Movement', 294–7.

[120] Margaret MacDonald, 'The Labour MPs' visit to Germany', *Labour Leader* (11 June 1909), 374.

[121] Bruce Glasier, 'Peace Pilgrimage to Berlin' and 'With the Socialists in Berlin', *Labour Leader* (4 June 1909 and 11 June 1909), 358 and 369.

Party distinguished itself in a somewhat foolish fashion by its visit to Germany, where it ignored the Social Democrats and hob-nobbed with their enemies . . .'.[122] And *Vorwärts* seemed to be only too keen to point out that the German government denied MacDonald the right to speak at an SPD assembly only weeks after he had stood on the same platform with Bethmann-Hollweg: 'Probably the English comrades . . . will now understand German Social Democracy's apprehension concerning any official contact with ministers. And now they can also evaluate the friendliness that the German government bestowed onto them at a time when it suited the government.'[123]

Yet, this incident showed not so much the difficult relationship between British and German working-class parties,[124] but, rather, threw a dubious light on Bebel, whose brisk rejection of the Labour Party's wish to come to Germany seemed to have set off the whole affair. It seems to underline Peter Nettl's view of Bebel as an example for a German jingo socialist à la Hyndman.[125] Certainly Bebel was convinced that the first place amongst the socialist parties of the world belonged to the German SPD. As he wrote in *Die Frau*:

In the enormous struggle of the future, German socialists have taken the lead. Germany . . . is predestined for such leadership. It is not by chance that it was Germans who discovered the laws of modern society . . . It is not by chance that the German socialist movement is the most important of the world . . . It is furthermore not by chance that Germans are the pioneers who bring the socialist idea to the workers of the various people of the world.[126]

Such views certainly made for authoritarianism in Bebel's attitude to foreign working-class parties. That this was not necessarily anti-English has been shown by R. J. Crampton, who has pointed out that Bebel conveyed often secret and confidential information to the British Foreign Office. He even offered to Grey to include anything in his speeches which Grey might think beneficial to better relations between the two countries.[127]

After 1918 there were three main issues on which the Labour Party sent delegations to Germany: the situation directly after the war and the

---

[122] Theodore Rothstein (ed.), *The Socialist Annual 1910* (London, 1910), 46.

[123] *Vorwärts*, 192 (19 Aug. 1909).

[124] As argued by Newton, *British Labour*, 229–32.

[125] Nettl, 'The German Social Democratic Party', 81.

[126] Bebel, *Die Frau und der Sozialismus*, 379.

[127] R. J. Crampton, 'August Bebel and the British Foreign Office', *History*, 58 (1973), 218–32.

effects of the Versailles treaty, the Ruhr occupation, and finally the rise of Nazism in Germany. From January to July 1919 the ILP's *Labour Leader* carried special articles about 'The Situation in Germany' nearly every week—largely about the struggle of the Social Democrats for a peaceful transition to democracy. It was from its Wilsonian standpoint that the Labour Party was outraged at the treatment of Germany in Versailles. There was a Labour Party manifesto against the peace terms of the *entente* which was promptly translated and published by the Social Democrats' *Buchhandlung Vorwärts* in 1921 under the title *Die englischen Arbeiter gegen die Ententeforderungen: Ein Manifest der Labour Party über Arbeitslosigkeit, Frieden und Entschädigungsfrage.*

In the same year Ben Riley and Emanuel Shinwell of the ILP went to Munich to address a meeting of the USPD and declared their party's opposition to the Versailles treaty.[128] In 1922, Tom Shaw, the secretary of the International Federation of Textile Workers from 1911 to 1929 and the secretary of the Labour and Socialist International from 1923 to 1925, granted an interview to *Vorwärts* in which he stressed the support of the Labour Party for the German demand of a revision of the Versailles treaty.[129] The SPD in the 1920s readily admitted the important role of the British labour movement in bringing about a more conciliatory attitude of the Allies concerning reparations. At the SPD conference in 1929 Crispien said: 'That this [a change to the better concerning the reparations question] has been possible, we owe to the existence of the English Labour government . . .'.[130]

Many pro-Germans, like E. N. Bennett, Dorothy F. and Charles Roden Buxton, Prof. R. Beazley, G. Young, and E. D. Morel sat on the Advisory Council for International Questions of the Labour Party (ACIQ) and tried to do their best to arouse interest in the German situation after 1918, even if this meant driving a wedge between the British and their world war ally, France. In the British labour movement there was much suspicion of French political objectives and sympathy for Germany that amounted almost to Francophobia.[131] Charles Roden Buxton's views can be seen as exemplary. Anglo-German relations were 'the major concern of

---

[128] Francis L. Carsten, *Britain and the Weimar Republic* (London, 1984), 66.
[129] 'Die Stimmung in England: Unterredung mit dem Genossen Tom Shaw', *Vorwärts*, (28 Aug. 1922).
[130] *Protokoll des SPD Parteitags 1929* (Berlin, 1929), 218.
[131] Robert E. Dowse, 'The ILP and Foreign Politics, 1918–1923', *IRSH* 7 (1962), 33–46. For pro-German attitudes in the Labour Party after 1918 see also Wolfgang Krieger, *Labour Party und Weimarer Republik, ein Beitrag zur Außenpolitik der britischen Arbeiterbewegung zwischen Programmatik und Parteitaktik, 1918–1924* (Bonn, 1978).

his political life',[132] and in 1921 he went to Essen, living with a German miner's family for a week and writing the ILP pamphlet *In a German Miner's Home* afterwards. His major aim was to demonstrate the economic effects of Versailles on the German worker and to create a sense of solidarity between the British and the German workers:

By the end of our stay we had come to be very familiar with one another. Heinz became more talkative, and behind his rather stiff exterior, his warm, human feelings came to sight. It became more difficult to remember that we belonged to two different nations. There seemed to be no particular reason, why we should.[133]

Ernest Bevin was another example of an influential Labour leader extremely interested in international socialism after 1918. An influential member in the Joint International Committee of Labour Party and TUC, whose task it was to reorganize the Second International after 1918, he paid his first visit to Central Europe in 1922 and 'he was highly interested by what he observed of the leaders of European socialism'.[134] MacDonald was one of the chief proponents of the theory of the two Germanies. He denied any sole war guilt of Germany, maintained that Germany had changed, and that the new Germany could not be made responsible for the faults of the old Germany. The Weimar Republic embodied the 'better Germany'.[135] George Young, a member of the ACIQ, made the same point in his account of the German revolution, written after he had returned from Germany in 1919.[136]

During the Ruhr conflict there were at least three British Labour delegations to the Ruhr. In February 1923 J. Wheatley, J. Maxton, D. Kirkwood, and C. Stephen, all four leading figures in the ILP, went to the Ruhr. In a leaflet published after their visit they pleaded that Labour should stand by France, as the German capitalist class, who did not want to pay reparations, was behind the whole conflict.[137] This remained the

---

[132] Victoria de Bunsen, *Charles Roden Buxton: A Memoir* (London, 1948), 151.

[133] Dorothy F. and Charles Roden Buxton, *In a German Miner's Home* (London, 1921), 14.

[134] Alan Bullock, *Ernest Bevin*, i. 232. For a second visit to the SPD in 1929 see ibid. 509.

[135] D. Aigner, *Das Ringen um England: Das deutsch-britische Verhältnis. Die öffentliche Meinung, 1933–1939. Tragödie zweier Völker* (Munich, 1969), 27.

[136] George Young, *The New Germany* (London, 1920), 4.

[137] *Why Labour should stand by France*, ed. by the ILP (London, 1923). Much research concerning the Ruhr occupation would support such a view. See J. Bariéty, *Les Rélations franco-allemandes après la première guerre mondiale* (Paris, 1977), and J. Jacobson, 'Strategies of French Foreign Policy after World War I', *Journal of Modern History*, 55 (1983), 78–95.

minority view within the Labour Party. Ben Tillett, A. Creech-Jones, and Samuel Warren, who went to the Ruhr as a delegation of the Transport and General Workers' Union, brought back different findings. The consequences of French aggression were described as impoverishment, inflation, rising costs of living, and falling consumption of foodstuffs.[138] Tom Shaw, secretary of the Labour and Socialist International until 1925, went to Germany with a delegation of the PLP in August 1923 and reported back to the TUC General Council much in the same way.[139] At a meeting of the Joint International Department in December 1923, he ended his description of the effects of inflation on the German socialist party and trade unions: 'I therefore earnestly appeal to you to do what you can to help the two central organizations (the SPD and the ADGB) in this period of exceptional, even fantastic difficulty.'[140] Shaw had been in contact with Wels and the PV before his trip, which was organized by the SPD.[141] The PV urged Shaw to inform the British government about the real situation in Germany, so that he then could put pressure on the governments in Paris and Brussels.[142] In the following months the Labour Party campaigned consistently against the French occupation. The Joint International Department of TUC and Labour Party issued a resolution called 'The International Situation', in which it urged the British government to put more pressure on France, as France's aim was to become the new hegemonial power on the continent.[143] Even more strongly worded but of the same content was a resolution of the ACIQ.[144] In the *New Leader* Brailsford and Angell demanded an anti-French alliance between Britain, Germany, and the Soviet Union. Morel's Fancophobia found an outlet in a series of articles in *Foreign Affairs*.[145]

It was particularly in times of crisis that the SPD could call upon the Labour Party for support: in 1918, 1923, and again in 1932. When Friedrich Voigt of the SPD learned from Ellen Wilkinson that she might spend a fortnight's holiday in Germany, he wrote a seven-page letter to her, describing the desperate situation of the SPD, asking:

---

[138] Ben Tillett, A. Creech-Jones, and Samuel Warren, *The Ruhr: The Report of a Deputation of the TGWU* (London, 1923), 18.

[139] TUC Library, Files on Germany.

[140] Labour Party Archive, LSI file 14/15/1.

[141] IISG, LSI files, no. 1408: letter from a representative of Shaw to Braun, 26 June 1923.

[142] Ibid., no. 1408/3: letter from the Parteivorstand to Shaw, 8 June 1923, 2–3.

[143] Ibid., no. 1408, 'The International Situation', issued by the Joint International Department of TUC and Labour Party.

[144] Ibid.

[145] Krieger, *Labour Party und Weimarer Republik*, 264 ff.

I wonder if you could give part of it [her holiday] to the German elections . . . Some recognition, some sign of solidarity coming from the British labour movement would have the most heartening effect here. It would reach the remotest industrial villages, and would do something to relieve the isolation so great that I can hardly understand how they [his German comrades] endure it.[146]

Wilkinson agreed to come and telegrams from Germany expressed much delight.[147] The Labour Party, following Voigt's proposal, sent a message of solidarity, fraternal greetings, and good wishes signed by Citrine on behalf of the General Council of the TUC, by George Latham on behalf of the NEC of the Labour Party, and by George Lansbury on behalf of the PLP. It was published in all major and minor SPD and trade union newspapers, mostly on the front page. Wilkinson on her tour handed over a flag of solidarity to the Social Democrats and delivered several speeches in several German towns.[148]

Looking at these three examples it might be said that the British labour movement was genuinely concerned for their German comrades. Yet, apart from a genuine idealistic socialist internationalism the Labour Party's position was also much effected by economic self-interest. Its leaders realized that the fall of the mark would badly damage the British export economy. Part of the Labour Party's interest in Germany was grounded in the fear of rising unemployment at home and pressure from British employers to lower wages, given the low wages and high international competitiveness of the German economy.[149] Many Labour leaders were also seriously worried about the danger of another war and saw French policy towards Germany as the major threat to the stabilization of peace in Europe. Their attitudes were due to a principled foreign policy approach, as embodied in MacDonald's 'New Diplomacy'.[150]

Mutual financial help

Relief actions for foreign labour movements in times of distress were a common feature of the international labour movement ever since the First International had been founded. British socialists supported the German party financially during the period of the Anti-Socialist

---

[146] Labour Party Archive, International Department Files, ID/GER/7, letter Voigt to Wilkinson from 1932 (no precise date given).

[147] Ibid., telegrams from Hilferding/Breitscheid to Wilkinson, 27–8 June 1932.

[148] Modern Records Centre, Coventry, MSS 209: Press cutting of Ellen Wilkinson.

[149] Krieger, *Labour Party und Weimarer Republik*, 196 ff.

[150] See Elaine Windrich, *British Labour's Foreign Policy* (London, 1952), 31–47, ch. 5: 'The New Diplomacy'.

Law.[151] The German movement helped the ASE during the lock-out of 1897 when money was urgently needed to uphold the union's capacity to pay benefits to its members.[152] The SPD and the socialist trade unions in Germany collected 120,000 marks (approximately £300,000 in 1991) for their colleagues in the ASE.[153] Barnes wrote on the 15 November 1897: 'It is more important than ever that we have the hearty support of our fellow workers. I am glad to say that the stream of support increases in volume, especially from Germany.'[154]

In 1910 the conference of the Second International heavily criticized inadequate financial solidarity on the part of the British labour movement towards its Swedish comrades who had been fighting a general strike. A resolution of the SPD accused the British movement of neglecting its commitment to give financial support to members of the International in need.[155] In an article in the *Volkswacht* Carl Severing summed up the feelings of the German delegates in Copenhagen: 'The attitude of the English is even less understandable, if one thinks of the great strike of the English engineers, in which the whole of Europe made sacrifices to help them. The English have to fulfil the duty of international solidarity towards other nations to the same degree.'[156]

The British labour movement did exactly this in helping its German comrades substantially after the First World War. Directly after the war there had been relief efforts, and British Labour again sent £23,047 (approximately £700,000 in 1991) during the great inflation in 1923.[157] The ILP ran a parallel campaign of collecting money for the striking workers of the Ruhr. From February to October 1923 Margaret M. Green forwarded £310 (approximately £10,000 in 1991) to Hermann Kube of the ADGB.[158] In addition, socialist groups all over Britain sent letters of support to the striking Ruhr workers.[159] The German unions, in

---

[151] Jutta Seidel, 'Internationale Solidaritätsaktionen für den Kampf der deutschen Arbeiterpartei während des Sozialistengesetzes', *Jahrbuch für Geschichte*, 22 (Berlin, 1981), 143.

[152] Hugh A. Clegg, A. Fox, and A. F. Thompson, *A History of British Trade Unionism since 1889*, i: *1889–1910* (Oxford, 1964), 161–6.

[153] *Protokoll der 10. Sitzung des Gewerkschaftsausschusses der Gewerkschaften Deutschlands*, 7 July 1898.

[154] IISG, Kleine Korrespondenz der SPD, letters from Barnes to Karpeles.

[155] *Vorwärts*, 204 (1 Sept. 1910) and 205 (2 Sept. 1910).

[156] *Volkswacht* (6 Sept. 1910).

[157] TUC Library, 'Report of the Meeting of the International Committee of the TUC', 10 Dec. 1923; *Report of the Annual Conference of the TUC 1924* (Hull, 1924), 261.

[158] Historische Kommission, ADGB papers, NB 163, nos. 43 ff.

[159] Ibid., NB 168, no. 68 and NB 169, no. 13.

turn, supported the British unions financially in the General Strike of 1926. The ADGB decided to collect money and prefinance the payment to the British unions through loans. All in all 900,000 marks (approximately £1.3 million in 1991) was collected and sent to Britain.[160] There were well over a hundred demonstrations of solidarity with the British miners in nearly every large town in Germany and everywhere money, clothes, and food were collected for the strikers in Britain.[161] Yet the General Strike was regarded as a mistake by both the SPD and the ADGB. When Crispien gave an overview of the international socialist movement at the 1929 SPD conference, he described the event as an example of short-sighted Bolshevist radicalism.[162] Within the *Ausschuß* of the ADGB at its meeting on 7 May 1926 there was harsh criticism of the British movement. Tarnow criticized the new British trade union leadership for its lack of discipline and Müntner hoped that the strike would soon be called off.[163]

So far it has been demonstrated that individual friendships between socialists in Britain and Germany were not the sum total of contacts between the two working-class parties. They found additional expression in financial help during strikes or political suppression, in fraternal conference delegations as well as in special delegations, and were reflected by frequent reports about the British movement in the German socialist press and vice versa, as well as in the bridge-building function of socialist journalists living abroad. The relations between the Labour Party and the SPD were further enhanced by the hostility of the Labour Party to the post-war settlement in Europe, as reflected in the Versailles treaty. In times of special hardship for the SPD, as in the Ruhr occupation of 1923 as well as the rise of National Socialism, the Labour Party actively tried to help its German comrades, partly out of internationalist and humanitarian sentiment, partly from economic domestic reasons. Yet it was not only in bilateral contacts that the strong bonds which connected the British and the German working-class parties became visible. Another

---

[160] *Protokoll der Sitzung des Gewerkschaftsausschusses* (11 Nov. 1926), 779.

[161] B. M. Zabarko, 'Die internationale Solidarität mit dem Bergarbeiterstreik in Großbritannien', *BZG* 28 (1986), 630–4. For a report about a protest rally held in Solingen on 18 Sept. 1926 in which a seventeen-man strong British miners' choir participated see IGA/ZPA, St. 12/103, no. 209 f.

[162] *Protokoll des SPD Parteitags 1929* (Berlin, 1929), 214–15. Also Max Schippel, 'Die Tragödie des englischen Generalstreiks', *SM* 32 (1926), 368–72.

[163] *Die Gewerkschaften von der Stabilisierung bis zur Weltwirtschaftskrise, 1924–1930*, rev. Horst A. Kuckuck and Dieter Schiffmann (Cologne, 1986), 666–72.

forum for their co-operation, which will be examined in the next section, was the International, both before and after 1918.

6.3. Relations within the International

In the period from 1889 to 1933 the British and the German parties were vital for the existence of the Socialist International and they often dominated its conferences and actions. The SPD reached its zenith of international influence before 1914 whereas the Labour Party's influence became most important after the First World War.[164] Contrary to Newton's efforts to portray the Labour Party and the SPD as worlds apart, German socialists were keen on British participation before 1914. Engels's efforts to win British socialists for the foundation conference of the Second International have already been mentioned. At the 1896 London conference of the International Bebel called on the British trade unionists and socialists to organize into a great party of Labour: 'Lead your brothers on the continent and the flag of socialism will fly.'[165] This not only indicated that Bebel was well aware of ILP efforts to win the trade unions to the idea of an independent socialist party, it also showed the importance that Bebel attached to such a party in Britain. Yet Newton is right that the 1896 conference marked the withdrawal of British trade unionism from the International and up to 1918 the TUC showed no further interest in its proceedings.[166] German socialists' hopes for stronger participation by the British trade unions in the International were not fulfilled.

This should not, however, be taken to imply that the British labour movement withdrew completely from the international scene. The British labour movement was far from marginal to the Second International well before 1914.[167] Whilst the SPD always found it difficult to recruit enough delegates for the international conferences, at the 1904 Amsterdam

---

[164] See generally for the pre- and inter-war periods James Joll, *The Second International, 1889–1914* (2nd edn., London, 1974); Robert Sigel, *Die Geschichte der Zweiten Internationale, 1918–1923* (Frankfurt am Main, 1986); Werner Kowalski, *Geschichte der Sozialistischen Arbeiter-Internationale (1923–1940)* (Berlin, 1985).

[165] *Vorwärts*, 178 (1 Aug. 1896).

[166] Newton, *British Labour*, 35–9.

[167] Eichmanis, 'The British Labour Movement', esp. ch. 11.2: 'The Role of Engels and Continental Developments', ch. IV.1: 'Internationalism and British Socialists', ch. V.2: 'Wilhelm Liebknecht in Britain', ch. VIII.4: 'Status of the Labour Party within the International'. Also Chris Wrigley, 'Widening Horizons? British Labour and the Second International 1893–1905', *Labour History Review*, 58 (1993), 8–13.

conference of the International, the British delegation was the largest. Three years later, at the 1907 Stuttgart conference 130 British delegates—including prominent trade unionists, Fabians, and ILPers as well as the leaders of the SDF—formed the second-biggest delegation after that of the hosts. Long before 1914 the leaders of British socialism, including not only Hyndman and Quelch but also Keir Hardie and Glasier, enthusiastically took part in the regular meetings of the ISB, where they worked together with Auer, Singer, Bebel, Kautsky, Molkenbuhr, and other German socialists. Douglas Newton's judgment that 'the struggle for full recognition of the ILP and the Labour Party [in the International] was to be long and difficult'[168] exaggerates the isolation of mainstream British socialism from their continental comrades. A clear indication that the SPD would go a long way to integrate the mainstream of British Labour into the International, was Kautsky's 1908 formula for the inclusion of the Labour Party into the International. According to the rules of the International any party which wanted to affiliate had to stand on the basis of the class struggle. Precisely because of the Labour Party's refusal to accept the theory of the class struggle the SDF objected to the Labour Party's affiliation. Yet Kautsky pressed for a compromise solution: 'The British Labour Party is admitted to International Socialist Congresses, because, while not expressly accepting the proletarian class struggle, in practice the Labour Party conducts this struggle, and adopts its standpoint, inasmuch as the party is organized independently of the bourgeois parties.'[169]

One example of how the Second International was able to establish good relations between the British and German socialists, just by providing a forum for discussion, is the case of W. S. Sanders, a member of the SDF, a Fabian, and an NEC member of the Labour Party 1913–15. At the 1891 Brussels congress of the International he came into direct contact with the leaders of the German movement:

At Brussels I had the privilege of being one of a little company who, with Liebknecht, Bebel, and Singer, met every evening after the Congress at the café *Les Trois Suisses*, to discuss, over a glass of lager or a cup of coffee, the situation of the Socialist movement and general political and social matters. I thus came in direct contact with the German Socialist movement through its chief men, and this created an interest for me which has never lapsed.[170]

---

[168] Newton, *British Labour*, 43.

[169] *Vorwärts*, 194 (21 Aug. 1908). Also in Labour Party Archive, NEC minutes, 15 Dec. 1908.

[170] W. S. Sanders, *Early Socialist Days* (London, 1927), 92.

The impression these talks made on him were so influential that he finally decided to go to Germany, in order to study its labour movement. In his publications in Britain, which sought to bring the German movement closer to the consciousness of British Labour, he was full of praise for its strong socialist class-consciousness on the one hand and for its organizational skills on the other. Yet for Sanders and for many of those who came to admire the German socialist movement before 1914, the war was a source of bitter disappointment. In a pamphlet, published in 1918 he denounced the SPD's efforts

to harmonize the aims of Pan-Germanism and socialism. . . . The party which formerly prided itself upon its intense international spirit is now equally proud of its intense national spirit. . . . By giving wholehearted support to the war-policy of the government, and making peace without terms with the Kaiser, the great majority of the German Social-Democrats voluntarily joined forces with those who, they had declared, were not only the enemies of the German working-class, but a menace to the whole world. . . . The great movement built up by August Bebel and Wilhelm Liebknecht . . . has become the willing captive of the power that it set out to conquer . . . the revolutionaries have been revolutionised into apostles of the gospel of Junkerdom.[171]

Such statements foreshadowed how difficult it would be for German Social Democracy to regain some of its pre-war recognition in the International after 1918.

When the war came, nationalism proved to be a stronger force than socialist internationalism in every European socialist party except the Russian and Italian. Yet a minority everywhere tried to keep alive the pre-war ideas of international solidarity and brotherhood. The anti-war factions of both working-class parties tried to get in contact with one another, realizing and appreciating the existence of like-minded people and organizations in the other country. Fenner Brockway, the chairman of the No Conscription Fellowship (NCF) and co-founder of the War Resisters' International who knew most German socialists from several pre-and post-war visits to the country, stood at the forefront of British anti-war efforts, together with Clifford Allen. He received letters from Liebknecht, Luxemburg, and Zetkin, all expressing their determination to keep up the spirit of socialist internationalism. Their letters, together with another one by Franz Mehring, were all published in December 1914 in the *Labour Leader*.[172]

---

[171] W. S. Sanders, *Pan-German Socialism* (London, 1918), 3, 22, 24.
[172] Brockway, *Inside the Left*, 50 ff. and 134.

Vorwärts in 1915 reported favourably about the anti-war stand of MacDonald and Keir Hardie.[173] The 1916 ILP conference declared its 'sympathetic attitude . . . towards bona fide peace sentiment in the German socialist movement . . . the ILP has signified its warm appreciation of the courageous stand for peace and international principles taken up by our comrades Clara Zetkin, Liebknecht, Haase, Ledebour, Bernstein and other members of the party.'[174] When news of Ludwig Frank's death reached Glasier he wrote in his diary: 'A great loss this. He was a splendid fellow and fully in sympathy with our Labour Party.'[175] Glasier tried in vain to convince Huysmans in the war that a meeting of the ISB should be convened and the German socialists invited.[176] In 1916 Glasier wrote a pamphlet entitled 'German Socialists and the War: A Record and a Contract'. His major aim was to 'help greatly to modify the feeling against the German socialists'.[177] When Glasier, together with Francis Johnson and Fred Jowett, wanted to travel to the Zimmerwald conference in 1915 to meet fellow German socialists, they were not allowed to leave the country. Yet a peace manifesto was smuggled out and it was read at the conference.[178] British socialists were also not allowed out for the second meeting of the Zimmerwald socialists, but this time they were represented by an English socialist, living in Switzerland, who had received instructions from the ILP.[179] In 1915 Clara Zetkin organized an International Socialist Women's Conference in Berne. British socialists living abroad attended, but two representatives from the ILP did not receive passports. Marion Philipps and Clara Zetkin corresponded via the Dutch socialist Helen Ankersmit during the war and Zetkin published the messages received from Philipps in her paper *Gleichheit*, before the party took it away from her.[180] Zetkin, as secretary of the Socialist Women's

[173] *Vorwärts*, 49 (18 Feb. 1915).

[174] *Report of the Annual Conference of the ILP in 1916*, 12.

[175] Quoted from Thompson, *The Enthusiasts*, 208.

[176] Thompson, *The Enthusiasts*, 212 f.

[177] Liverpool University Library, Glasier papers 1916/61, letter Glasier to Johnson, 15 Sept. 1916.

[178] IGA/ZPA, St. 10, 229, no. 12: report to the Ministry of the Interior about the Zimmerwald conference.

[179] Ibid., nos. 63–5. For the ILP's support of Zimmerwald see also *Vorwärts*, 280 (10 Oct. 1915).

[180] IGA/ZPA, Zetkin papers, NL5/107, nos. 10–14; NL5/85, nos. 4–10; NL5/69, nos. 7, 19, 23–7, 48, 54. Also *Die Gleichheit*, 10 (5 Feb. 1915). From 1907 *Gleichheit* had been the international journal of the Socialist Women's International. The latter was founded at the 1907 conference of the International under the spiritual guidance of Clara Zetkin. Zetkin joined the communists after the First World War, but the Women's International was finally rebuilt in 1927 through the initiative of Marion Philipps, Toni Sender, and Gertrud Hanna. See Marion Philipps, 'Socialist Women Meet in Switzerland', in *Labour Magazine*, 8 (1929–30), 54 f.

International from 1907 to 1917, also enjoyed a close friendship with Dora Montefiore of the British SDF. She visited Britain in 1909, where she came into contact with many British socialists.[181]

One of the few socialists in either country who supported the war effort, but was also interested in maintaining contacts with 'enemy' socialists, was Arthur Henderson, who even served in the war cabinet. In 1915 Haase was reported to have contacts with Henderson and in a social democratic assembly in Berlin he spoke of his hope for a meeting with Henderson in the near future.[182] The social democratic press bureau reacted positively to Henderson's efforts in 1918 to bring about peace through negotiations.[183] Henderson's international commitment became even stronger after the war, when he became chairman of the International. Resigning from this post in 1929 he stressed his continued commitment to socialist internationalism.[184] Henderson published two pamphlets on foreign policy in 1922 and 1933, in which he stressed heavily the importance of international action for world peace.[185] If Kautsky was trying to mediate before the war between the ideologies, Henderson had to mediate after the war between the nationalities. At the first international conference at Berne in February 1919, there were heated debates over the question of the behaviour of the German Majority Socialists during the War. Time and again, at Berne and elsewhere, Henderson intervened to prevent a breakup of the International.[186] His mediation efforts, in particular between the French and the German socialists, were of crucial importance in guaranteeing the success of the conference and, ultimately, the success of rebuilding the International after 1918.[187]

The British delegation to Berne, which had given the impulse to the

---

[181] Kaven Hunt, 'British Women and the Second International', *Labour History Review*, 58 (1993), 25–29.

[182] ZStA Potsdam, Heine papers, 90 He 1, no. 6, nos. 80 f.: letter Heine to Scheidemann, 7 July 1915.

[183] IGA/ZPA, SPD, PV, II/145/13: note of social democratic press bureau to all editor's offices, 13 Sept. 1918.

[184] IGA/ZPA, SAI papers, I, 6/2/31, no. 19: letter Henderson to Adler, 1929.

[185] Arthur Henderson, *Labour and Foreign Affairs* (London, 1922), and id., *Labour's Foreign Policy* (London, 1933). The role of Henderson in laying out a foreign policy concept of the Labour Party after 1918 has been especially stressed by Henry R. Winkler, 'The Emergence of a Labour Foreign Policy in Great Britain, 1918–1929', *Journal of Modern History*, 28 (1956), 255.

[186] *Report of the Conference of the International Permanent Commission at Luzerne, 2–9 August 1919*, reprinted in *Die Zweite Internationale, 1918–1919*, ed. G. A. Ritter (Berlin, 1980), 645.

[187] Mary Agnes Hamilton, *Arthur Henderson: A Biography* (London, 1938), 194 f. Also Konrad von Zwehl, 'Zur Zerspaltenheit der Internationalen Arbeiterbewegung (ca. 1917–1921)', in *Internationale Tagung der Historiker der Arbeiterbewegung. 15. Linzer Konferenz 1979* (Vienna, 1981), 172.

conference, organized it and influenced its agenda as well as its results, put itself side by side with the German delegation in demanding an end to the discussions about war guilt: 'We are of the opinion that this question of responsibilities will have to be discussed at some time, but we are also of the opinion that this is not the time. . . . We are here to carry out the mandate of Labour and Socialism all over the world and we shall not be carrying out that if we waste time in useless and mischievous discussions.'[188] A remarkable consensus between British and German socialists over nearly all issues characterized the proceedings of the conference. As in Berne, the British and the German delegation were especially close to each other at the Geneva conference of the LSI in August 1920. As Beatrice Webb recalled in her diary: 'There was, in fact more comradeship between the Germans and the British than between any other nationalities.'[189] In the debate about Central Europe MacDonald's speech left 'an especially deep impression' on the German delegates. He demanded British help for Germany and argued the case for a policy of economic help in order to make the peace more secure.[190] Time and again the British delegates acted at various international conferences as mediators, assuring that the German Social Democrats could join the International without too much obloquy.

Not surprisingly, Otto Wels had good relations with the British socialists in the International, especially with MacDonald, who replaced Shaw as secretary of the LSI in 1925, and with whom Wels sat on the International's executive.[191] They worked together over the question of reuniting the International[192] and over the issue of Upper Silesia.[193] When it became known to Wels that MacDonald wanted to resign from the LSI executive, he wrote:

I am really alarmed at the news that you want to give up your work for the International. That would be the severest blow that we could receive. Your moral authority through your attitude during the war is such a strong factor in favour of our contact with the Vienna Union, that we must keep you in the Second International under any circumstances . . . You have purified the air and prepared the ground; and only those who think it is possible to reap before the seed is sown and the harvest time has come can misjudge the real effects of your labours. . . . I

---

[188] *Report of the Berne Conference in 1919*, reprinted in: *Die Zweite Internationale*, ed. Ritter, 264.

[189] *The Diaries of Beatrice Webb, 1912–1924*, ed. Cole, 186.

[190] A. Braun, *Der Internationale Kongreß zu Genf 1920* (Berlin, 1920), 30 f.

[191] H. J. Adolph, *Otto Wels und die Politik der deutschen Sozialdemokratie, 1894–1934* (Berlin, 1971), 195.

[192] IISG, LSI Files, no. 88/35, no. 88/50, and no. 86/8.

[193] Ibid., no. 85/11: letter from Wels to MacDonald, 20 Oct. 1921.

beg you earnestly, if my advice carries any weight with you, do not leave us in the lurch, but help us cover the next few years . . .[194]

That the SPD was indebted to the Labour Party for the latter's efforts in reintroducing German socialists into the community of the International after 1918 as quickly as possible was realized by leading Social Democrats.[195] MacDonald himself recalled the thankfulness of the SPD to the Labour Party: '[they] cordially paid tribute in many a conversation and interview to the help rendered to them by us . . .'.[196]

At the conferences of the MSPD and the USPD in 1919, as well as at the Labour Party Conference, the results of the Berne Conference and the role of the Labour Party were widely discussed. Eduard Bernstein reported to the MSPD stressing the comradely spirit of the Berne conference.[197] In the debate it became clear that two factions existed within the party, one which put its hopes on a close alliance with Britain and one which looked more favourably to continental countries, notably France. Bernstein spoke sharply against those 'activists in the SPD who demand a continental policy against the Anglo-Saxon world'.[198] The debate was taken up again at the party conference of 1920,[199] yet the position of *Kontinentalpolitik* never seemed to have much impact on the party policy. At the USPD conference in 1919 Kautsky also stressed the importance of the British Labour Party for the German SPD: 'English socialism is going to achieve more, it will become attractive for the whole world. That is only going to be of advantage for us.'[200]

Nearly all the important internationalists of German Social Democracy belonged to the side which favoured close ties with Britain—Breitscheid, H. Müller, Löbe, Carl Severing. Especially for Breitscheid, who became the leading foreign policy expert of the SPD in the 1920s, good relations

[194] IISG, LSI Files, no. 102/16, letter Wels to MacDonald, 28 June 1922.
[195] See for example letter from Adolf Braun to Paul Löbe, 29 July 1922, in IGA/ZPA, Löbe papers, NL 110/97, no. 25.
[196] Ramsay MacDonald, 'Outlook', *SR* 16 (1919), 114.
[197] *Protokoll des SPD Parteitags 1919*, 240–9.
[198] *Protokoll des SPD Parteitags 1919*, 248. The supporters of *Kontinentalpolitik*, grouped around the *SM*, looked for a 'coalition of the continental European states who should form a stabilizing power factor in world politics that would be directed against Britain'. See R. Klinkhammer, 'Die Außenpolitik der SPD in der Zeit der Weimarer Republik' (University of Freiburg im Breisgau Ph.D. 1955), 51. As J. F. P. Wrynn, *The Socialist International and the Politics of European Reconstruction, 1919–1930* (Amsterdam, 1976), 170, pointed out they 'had long favoured a Pan-European federation based on a Paris–Berlin axis and excluding the whole of *Angelsachsentum*.'
[199] *Protokoll des SPD Parteitags 1920*, 56 and 81.
[200] *USPD Protokoll der Verhandlungen des außerordentlichen Parteitages vom 2.–6. März 1919 in Berlin* (Berlin, 1919), 127.

with the British Labour Party were most important. In August 1924 he went as observer to the London conference, where the Dawes plan was accepted and the end of the French occupation of the Ruhr was agreed. Together with MacDonald, he contributed considerably to the success of the conference.[201] In the late 1920s he became more and more involved with the LSI. William Gillies, the International Secretary of the Labour Party, unsuccessfully tried to bring Breitscheid to England in 1933. There were efforts to collect money for him, in order to allow him to live in London, and the Labour Party also offered Breitscheid the opportunity of editing a German exile paper in London which was to be financed by the Labour Party.[202]

The Labour Party's conferences of 1918 and 1919 reflected its efforts to reconstitute the LSI. At Southport in 1919 there were extensive reports on the international conferences at Berne and Amsterdam and it was frequently stressed in the discussions that there should be no punishment for the German workers. The right to self-determination for all peoples was stressed with a view towards rejecting any dismemberment of Germany.[203] At the ILP conference in 1919 Margaret Bondfield moved a resolution which welcomed the Berne conference and called for the reconstruction of the International. Wallhead reminded the audience of Liebknecht's and Bebel's stand against the annexation of Alsace-Lorraine in 1871: 'The mantle of Liebknecht and Bebel had fallen upon the socialists of 1919.'[204]

Otto Wels, Ramsay MacDonald, and Tom Shaw were probably most important in uniting the LSI and the Vienna Union in 1923. On 9 July 1922 the IFTU invited the executives of both Internationals to a meeting where joint measures to support the German workers against political reaction were to be discussed. Wels immediately saw the great potential of such a meeting. He wrote to MacDonald to make sure there would be British representatives: 'I beg you urgently that you, Tom Shaw and Henderson come to Amsterdam on the 20th of this month: it could after

---

[201] Kenneth E. Miller, *Socialism and Foreign Policy* (The Hague, 1967), 118–19. For Breitscheid as an Anglophile and for his foreign policy activities see Peter Pistorius, *Rudolf Breitscheid, 1874–1944: Ein biographischer Beitrag zur deutschen Parteiengeschichte* (Cologne, 1970), esp. 22, 94 f., 211–29.

[202] Labour Party Archive, Breitscheid file. As international secretary, Gillies was certainly the wrong choice. His obstinacy and lack of expertise in international affairs is most fully investigated by Christine Collette, 'British Labour Attitudes to Europe, 1918–1939, with Special Reference to the Role of the Labour Party International Secretary (University of Oxford M. Litt., 1992). Also Anthony Glees, *Exile Politics*, 121 and 125 ff.

[203] *Report of the Annual Conference of the Labour Party in 1919*, esp. 196–204.

[204] *Report of the Annual Conference of the ILP in 1919*, 66–8.

all mean that the whole work which London has so far invested, finds its culmination.'[205] At the conference itself both Shaw and Wels made barely hidden approaches in direction of the Vienna Union. Shaw stated: 'The Majority Socialists and the Independent socialists in Germany have been brought together under the stress of circumstances. The same should be possible in regard to the international movement. Our guiding thought should be the unity of all workers' organizations.' Their efforts succeeded and at a joint meeting of the executives of the two Internationals in Prague on 12–13 August 1923 the decision was taken to hold a joint conference.[206] The reunification congress was held in Hamburg from the 21 to 25 May 1923. In his closing speech Wels referred most warmly to Arthur Henderson, who had fallen ill: 'Henderson belongs to those comrades, who directly after the war have brought together the International again in Berne and who have been busy ever since to erect the work that we here in Hamburg have brought to a certain end.'[207]

In the second part of the 1920s several commissions of the LSI or joint commissions of the LSI and the IFTU were set up on which British and German socialists served together. In April 1926 a disarmament commission was appointed by the LSI to undertake a thorough study of the problem of disarmament, on which Cramp and Müller worked together. Later they were replaced by Gillies and Wels (who was replaced by Breitscheid after 1928). The commission drafted a disarmament resolution which was accepted by the 1928 conference of the LSI and presented to the disarmament conference in Geneva. In February 1927 a commission of enquiry into the conditions of political prisoners was appointed. Its most important task was to agitate for the abolition of the death penalty. Crispien, Wels, Cramp, Gillies, and Brockway were representatives of their respective labour movements. Collaboration with the IFTU[208] found expression in several joint commissions regarding disarmament and world economic problems, in which Breitscheid, Leipart, Gillies, and Citrine served. From 1928 there was also a commission for the democratization of the League of Nations, in which Breitscheid and Gillies found themselves working together once again.

[205] IISG, LSI files: letter from Wels to MacDonald, 13 July 1922.
[206] For Shaw's statement at the Berlin conference and all events connected with it otherwise see Sigel, *Die Geschichte der Zweiten Internationale, 1918–1923*, 79–85.
[207] *Protokoll des Ersten Internationalen Sozialistischen Arbeiterkongresses in Hamburg, 21. bis 25. Mai 1923* (Berlin, 1923), 88.
[208] The LSI had strong links with the IFTU. At the end of the 1920s and even more so at the beginning of the 1930s mutual conferences and meetings of leading figures of both Internationals took place. See Kowalski, *Geschichte der SAI (1923–1940)*, 54.

The USPD, and later on the left wing of the SPD which was to break away from the party in 1931 to form the Sozialistische Arbeiterpartei (SAP), and the ILP certainly had contacts with one another in the 1920s and 1930s. Yet it is difficult to trace them as no USPD archive remains.[209] In 1925 at the Marseilles congress, Brockway and Jowett of the ILP took up informal contacts with SPD dissenters like Max Seydewitz, Kurt Rosenfeld, and Paul Levi.[210] From that time on the ILP wanted to organize a distinct left-wing group within the International. At the end of the 1920s the relations between the Labour Party and the ILP and between the SPD and its left wing had already soured. The Labour Party and the SPD were uniting in the International to fight a left-wing challenge from within their own parties. When, for example, the ILP attacked the SPD over the latter's policy of tolerating Brüning, the Labour Party speaker George Latham declared his party's support for the SPD:

> Their [the ILP's] attempt to lecture and instruct the great German Socialist movement is regarded by us as an impertinence. The British Labour Party has confidence in the German Socialists. We extend to them all the sympathy and confidence which they need. We declare our solidarity with them at the moment when they are endeavouring to protect European democracy.[211]

In May 1930 the first international meeting of left socialists took place in the Netherlands, organized by the ILP, and this led to the formation of an association of left-wing groups within the International itself. The first time that German socialists came into contact with this group was in August 1930 when representatives of the German 'class-war group' (*Klassenkampfgruppe*) visited the ILP summer school in Letchworth. Dora Fabian and Kurt Rosenfeld were present at the meeting there, which decided to form a closer association. John Paton of the ILP became permanent secretary, responsible for keeping the members in touch. The ILP sent sixteen delegates to Vienna in order to get into contact with as many European comrades as possible. Among the German left Max Seydewitz, Ernst Eckstein, Karl Böchel, and Toni Sender were represented

---

[209] Robert F. Wheeler, *USPD und Internationale: Sozialistischer Internationalismus in der Zeit der Revolution*, (Frankfurt am Main, 1975), 130 visited over eighty archives in eight countries to find out about the international contacts between the ILP, the BSP, and the USPD—without any success. All he could establish was that contacts had been made in the early 1920s.

[210] Willy Buschak, *Das Londoner Büro: Europäische Linkssozialisten in der Zwischenkriegszeit* (Amsterdam, 1985), 9. See generally 30–65.

[211] LSI. *Fourth Congress of the LSI at Vienna, 25 July to 1 August 1931* (London, 1931), 130 f.

in Vienna. All in all, the organizational links had been formed in the 1920s which later led to the formation of the Socialist Bureau in London.[212]

6.4. Conclusion

Despite a historiographical tradition to the contrary, there existed many contacts and relations between the two biggest and most important European labour movements of the twentieth century. Often, these relations were dependent on the initiative of individuals (Roden Buxton), or due to exile (Bernstein), or they were the results of party/trade union delegations or enquiry committees (Ruhr delegations). Sometimes personal friendships could lead to official missions, like Wilkinson's trip to Germany in 1932. Of course the various Internationals were important meeting-places. Here views could be exchanged, actions could be planned and connections could be made. Some of the contacts between high ranking officials of the Labour Party and the SPD seemed to have resulted from LSI conferences, e.g. the contact between Gillies and Breitscheid. It should also not be forgotten that the contacts were made on the highest level as well as on the level of the rank and file. Working-class party leaders like Otto Wels, Hermann Müller, Ramsay MacDonald, Arthur Henderson, and Sidney Webb have been mentioned as well as ordinary rank-and-file activists like Harry Grey and Mary Saran. In many ways British socialists, like Herbert Morrison and Keir Hardie, were influenced by what they saw as the superior organization of the SPD. As has been demonstrated in chapters 2 and 3 they tried to implement much of the SPD 'model' organization in Britain. On the other hand German socialists, especially reformists like Bernstein and Wertheimer were influenced by what they perceived as a constructive, tolerant, and undogmatic British socialism.

If the relations between British and German socialist in the first three decades of this century are compared with the relations between British and German liberals or conservatives, the impression of tight bonds between socialists of both countries is further confirmed. As there is no book about liberal or conservative Anglo-German relations at that time, it is difficult to say anything definite, but contacts seemed to have been rare. Anglophile German liberals like Brentano, Weber, and Barth almost certainly were the exception. Brentano undertook a study tour to Britain

---

[212] For Willy Brandt's contacts with Brockway and Maxton in the 1930s over the Socialist Bureau and Brandt's 1936 visit to an ILP summer school see Brandt, *Links und Frei*, 164 f.

from 1868 to 1869 and he found the economic freedom and the parliamentary system especially attractive.[213] Amongst his many British correspondents were Applegarth, the Buxtons, John Burns, John Malcolm Ludlow, Sir Alfred Mond, E. D. Morel, Lord Parmoor, Lord Ponsonby, Sidney and Beatrice Webb, and G. B. Shaw.[214] In a letter to Brentano's family after the latters' death, Sidney Webb emphasized his 'gratitude and admiration' for Brentano,[215] who had suggested the Webbs for an honourary doctorate awarded to them by Munich University in 1926.[216] Yet Brentano was not necessarily representative of German liberals. Werner Sombart, for example, was rather an Anglophobe, therein joining most German conservatives who shared Hegel's well-known distaste for Britain. That the forces of extreme nationalism found it difficult to look beyond their borders for contacts and friendship is underlined by a statement of the British ASU: 'the difficulties in the way of an international Anti-Socialist movement are considerable . . . Anti-Socialists, as we are proud to acknowledge, are intensely patriotic, and to look outside their country for sympathy and help would be more or less distasteful to most of them . . .'.[217] All in all, it would be extremely helpful to research further into German liberal and conservative relations to Britain, but from the limited information available at present, it can be said that such contacts were rare and due to individual Anglophilia.

The socialists in both countries, on the contrary, made internationalism a creed, and even if a majority of socialists failed in crucial situations, like the First World War, to live up to their ideals, there were plenty of examples of international solidarity and friendship on all levels of the two movements. If French and Austrian socialists had more contacts with the German SPD in the 1870s and 1880s, the relationship with British socialists became increasingly important from the 1890s onwards. From 1890 to 1900 the *Neue Zeit* published 363 reports about foreign labour movements (in twenty-seven countries). More reports were published about

---

[213] Sheehan, *The Career of Lujo Brentano*, 22–5. Also E. P. Hennock, 'Lessons from England: Lujo Brentano on British Trade Unionism', *German History*, 11 (1993), 141–60. The differences between the social liberalism in Britain and Germany are stressed by Karl Rohe, 'Sozialer Liberalismus in Großbritannien in Komparativer Perspektive', in Karl Holl, Günter Trautmann, Hans Vorländer (eds.), *Sozialer Liberalismus* (Göttingen, 1986), 110–25.

[214] The complete correspondence of Brentano can be found in the BA Koblenz. In his autobiography Brentano himself stressed his many friendships with British radicals: Lujo Brentano, *Mein Leben im Kampf um die soziale Entwicklung Deutschlands* (Jena, 1931), 45.

[215] BA Koblenz, Brentano papers, letters, 14 July 1929 and 4 Nov. 1931.

[216] BA Koblenz, Brentano papers, letter from Sidney Webb to Brentano, 27 Nov. 1926.

[217] 'Should Anti-Socialists be International?', *Anti-Socialist*, 6 (July 1909), 66.

the British labour movement (66) than about any other.[218] Furthermore, Jürgen Rojahn has recently stressed that the contacts between the SPD and other continental socialist parties should not be overemphasized. Contrary to an established opinion in comparative Labour historiography, he has found little evidence that the SPD served as a model for socialist parties in other continental countries.[219] That is not to say that the SPD's relations with the socialist parties in Austria and Scandinavia were not stronger than those with the Labour Party, yet, if such a long chapter about the relations between the British and the German socialists can be written, it further supports the thesis that the gulf between the two movements was not as big as is often assumed in the literature.

[218] On the importance of British–German socialist links in comparison with other socialist parties see also Jutta Seidel, *Internationale Stellung und internationale Beziehungen der deutschen Sozialdemokratie, 1871–1895/96* (Berlin, 1982), 46–54, 229–232, 245.

[219] Jürgen Rojahn, 'War die deutsche Sozialdemokratie ein Modell für die Parteien der Zweiten Internationale?', *IWK* 27 (1991), 291–302. For the older view see Geary, *European Labour Politics*, 2.

7
Conclusion

In the three decades from 1900 to 1930 the Labour Party and the SPD were working-class parties which looked similar in more ways than one. The hypothesis that organizational and ideological differences made the Labour Party an altogether different type of working-class party from the one to which the SPD belonged cannot easily be sustained. This hypothesis and its variants were all set within the historiographical context of *Sonderweg* theories. The point of departure for many comparative studies about European labour movements has been the dictum that either the German or the British labour movement had its peculiar, more or less unique features when compared with other European labour movements, as Germany or Britain, respectively, had taken a different political, economic, and social development, i.e. a *Sonderweg*, from other European nation states.[1]

Apart from the various *Sonderweg* theories, to the importance of which we will have to return, the only other influential theoretical framework for the study of political parties has been Robert Michels's theory of the 'iron law of oligarchy'. Michels largely ignored the contexts of nation-states and their development, arguing that certain developments were inherent in party structures as such, notwithstanding the society in which the party developed. With the growing organization of parties, the power of the leadership increased and intra-party democracy vanished; any control over the leadership by the rank and file became illusory. According to Michels, tendencies of party bureaucratization and centralization were accelerated and a party hierarchy emerged which implemented a strong party discipline. The party leadership ossified and became increasingly independent of the rank and file.[2]

Michels's findings resemble some of the findings of this thesis remarkably

---

[1] For the notion of a German *Sonderweg* see Tenfelde, 'Geschichte der deutschen Arbeiter und Arbeiterbewegung', 469–83. For the notion of a British *Sonderweg* see Geary, 'Introduction', in id., *Labour and Socialist Movements*, 4, Breuilly, *Labour and Liberalism*, esp. chs. 4, 6 and 7; Bernd Weisbrod, 'Der englische "Sonderweg" in der neueren Geschichte', *GG* 16 (1990), 243 f.

[2] Michels, *Zur Soziologie*, esp. 33–53.

closely. Chapter 3, for example, has demonstrated that both working-class parties tried hard to centralize and bureaucratize their organizational structures. The strong opposition of the Labour Party to any devolution of power to the regions, and the growing number of full-time, fully-paid organizers in both parties only underlined these tendencies. Real power became more and more concentrated in the leadership which remained virtually unchanged, often for decades, and which became ever more autonomous. Party conferences found it increasingly difficult to control the leaders. The willingness of the rank and file in both parties to follow their much admired leaders was far stronger than their willingness to criticize them. Finally, the trade union leadership markedly influenced party decisions in both the Labour Party and the SPD.

If the Labour Party could not centralize and bureaucratize its party structure to the same degree as the SPD, and if party discipline in the parliamentary party of the SPD was stronger than in the PLP, this was not so much due to the conscious rejection of bureaucratization, centralization, and hierarchization by the Labour Party, as to lack of opportunities to implement such measures. It lacked such opportunities, because it remained distrustful of the regions and because it continued to be financially dependent on trade union funds. Whereas the SPD centralized and bureaucratized its structure most effectively at the regional level, the Labour Party tried to centralize its organization at the national level. This made an efficient control of and constant contact with the constituencies hardly possible, and led to the relative independence of local organizations from head office in London. Head office also never had the financial means to divert resources to those areas which needed most development. The failure to centralize funds at the national party level meant that local organizations remained dependent on strong financial backing in the localities. They had this backing only where either trade unionism or political radicalism was strong. Although Labour Party leaders intended to make the organization stronger, and looked especially to the German SPD for a model, they failed to do so, largely because of the failure to regionalize the party and to centralize funding. Because of the more effective bureaucratization and centralization of the SPD at regional level, Michels's theory is indeed far more applicable to the SPD than it is to the Labour Party whose centralization at national level paradoxically led to greater autonomy at local level.

If Michels's arguments are attractive, it is because of his own experience and rich knowledge of the workings of the SPD and other European working-class parties. Much of his most fascinating material is based on empirical evidence and his own acute awareness of organizational trends within many European working-class parties. His authoritarian conclusions—owing much to the élite theories of Mosca and Pareto—make his book unattractive and help to explain his later fascination with Mussolini and Italian fascism. He has argued, for example, that there is no alternative to the authoritarian, oligarchic structure of an all-powerful party bureaucracy; first, because of the necessity for organization, and secondly, because of a 'natural longing' of the masses to be led. Instead it could equally be stressed that better organization meant higher efficiency.[3] Already Eduard Bernstein vigorously opposed Michels' criticism of the oligarchic tendencies of the SPD bureaucracy, stressing instead the functional usefulness of bureaucracies.[4] Paul Kampffmeyer emphasized the sacrifices of social democratic leaders for the movement and the sheer necessity of a professional and strong leadership confronting the increasingly complex economic, political, and social questions of the times.[5] Furthermore, the degree of isolation of the leaders from the rank and file should not be overestimated: many rank and file supported their leaders because the latter had established themselves in positions of authority which remained throughout democratically accountable. In the last resort Michels's iron law of oligarchy' should be seen as the deeply pessimistic flight into mass psychology of a one-time syndicalist who had believed in the revolutionary instincts of the working class.

While some of the evidence presented in this book confirms at least part of Michels's argument, the explanatory value of his argument is limited precisely because it largely ignores the social contexts in which European Labour developed. Instead, it resorts to psychology and ultimately unprovable theories about the nature of man. Therefore it is to the efforts of historians to connect the nature of European working-class parties with the nature of the various European nation states that we have to return.

Dick Geary has tried to formulate four general principles to describe the relationship between national society and labour movement: (1) the more liberally a state reacts towards emerging working-class organizations, the more moderate and integrated the working-class party will be; (2) the

---

[3] Nolan, *Social Democracy and Society*, 118 has emphasized that a centralized and bureaucratized party structure was essential for the organizational success of the SPD in Düsseldorf. Furthermore bureaucratization and centralization did not lead to political conservatism. Düsseldorf remained a stronghold of the intra-party left.

[4] Eduard Bernstein, 'Die Demokratie in der Sozialdemokratie', *SM* 12/3 (1908), 1106–14; id., 'Zur Reorganisation der Partei', *SM* 16/2 (1912), 910–14.

[5] Paul Kampffmeyer, 'Masse und Führer—Historisches zu einem aktuellen Problem', *SM* 38 (1932), 3–9.

more affluent a nation-state and the more willing to secure a decent standard of living for the working class, the more politically moderate its labour movement; (3) the more employers' organizations accept working-class organizations and are willing to deal with them, for example to agree to wage agreements by collective bargaining, the more integrated the working class becomes and the less attracted it is to a radical political organization; (4) the stronger confessional allegiances are in a nation-state the more difficult it is for a non-religious working-class party to mobilize the working class.[6] Generally the findings of this thesis do not contradict the correctness of these tentative generalizations. Where comparative historians like Geary, Mommsen, and Mitchell[7] have been too forthright is in the specific distinction between Britain and Germany in the light of such general statements.

In terms of economic development both nation-states were rather similar, if compared with other European states, and the situation of the working class in both countries compared favourably with that of most other European nations.[8] Yet Geary and others have rightly stressed the importance of other than economic factors for the development of labour movements, namely the importance of the state. A strong, often illiberal, German state, which takes over areas of the economy and substitutes market regulation with planning, has been juxtaposed to a weak and liberal British state which did not intervene in the economy.[9] Of course, there can be little doubt that powerful bureaucracies had a long tradition in Germany at a time when the expansion of bureaucratic apparatuses in Britain had only just started. The state was more of a factor in its own right in Germany than in Britain, and Peter Lösche has rightly pointed to the fact that the bureaucratic, hierarchic structure of the SPD owed much to the model of the German state.[10] Yet, as has been argued, the

[6] Geary, 'Introduction', in id., *Labour and Socialist Movements*, 4. For a more detailed and complex model which enlists many more variables which determine the character of working-class parties see Seymour Martin Lipset, 'Radicalism or Reformism: The Source of Working-Class Politics', *APSR* 77 (1983), 1–18.

[7] See above, pp. 13–6.

[8] Wladimir Woytinsky, 'Industrielle Entwicklung Großbritanniens und Deutschlands', *Die Gesellschaft*, 5 (1928), 509–32. The well-established Gerschenkronian argument about the relative backwardness of the German economy and its implications for labour movement history have been criticized by P. K. O'Brien, 'Do We Have a Typology for the Study of European Industrialization in the Nineteenth Century?', *Journal of European Economic History*, 15 (1986), 291–333.

[9] For such arguments see Heinrich August Winkler (ed.), *Organisierter Kapitalismus: Voraussetzungen und Anfänge* (Göttingen, 1974).

[10] Peter Lösche, 'Arbeiterbewegung und Wilhelminismus: Sozialdemokratie zwischen Anpassung und Spaltung', *GWU* 20 (1969), 519–33.

rise of the Labour Party marked the decline of the 'British' tradition of abstaining from any form of state intervention in the economy. Partly drawing upon British thinkers who had demanded stronger state intervention, like Ruskin, partly drawing upon the model of Germany, Labour was preoccupied with the building up of a strong state machinery for the provision of better living standards. The Labour Party's bureaucratic inclinations have been traced via its ideology (Chapter 5) as well as via its leaders' notions of party organization (Chapter 3).

The argument that the labour movement in Britain had to suffer less repression than its German counterpart, and that socialists therefore did not form any culturally, socially, and ideologically sectarian ghettos within their society, seems also to be based on rather shaky grounds. As has been argued in Chapter 2, the British labour movement had to face severe persecution at times, which did not help it to integrate into the British state more positively than the SPD was integrated into the German. Not only did the early labour movement suffer from massive state persecution, but the development of the Labour Party was accompanied by explicitly anti-socialist organizations, by paternalistic employers, by the difficulty of attracting middle-class support, and by the outright enmity of the British judiciary. Following Blackbourn and Eley, it has been argued that the economic, social, cultural, and political developments of Britain and Germany were not as different as has often been maintained in the past by *Sonderweg* historians. It has been demonstrated in Chapters 3–5 that the working class parties of both countries were also much closer than so far assumed. Arguments about the different character of British and German Labour which largely rest on *Sonderweg* notions have to be re-evaluated. The Labour Party has been described by many historians as a model of political and ideological moderation and as a political party in the narrowest sense, i.e. as an electoral machine without much of a surrounding subculture. The SPD, exactly to the contrary, has often been seen as a model of ideological and organizational sectarianism, enmeshed in a subculture that cared for its members 'from the cradle to the grave'. Within that subculture debates about Marxist theory and its revolutionary consequences barred the party from a pragmatic and power-oriented policy approach that was in turn regarded as being characteristic for the Labour Party. This view of an almost opposite development of the British and German working-class parties has come under attack in the preceding pages.

If a lack of positive integration means a concentration on an existing subculture, it is not surprising that much information on a labour movement culture could be presented in Chapter 4. Far from being a kind of trade union appendix without a life of its own, the Labour Party in many localities strove to be that 'community of solidarity' with which the SPD is widely associated. Both parties put heavy emphasis on education and saw a strong working-class press as the best means of educating the unconverted. Drama, music, and sports' societies blossomed within the working-class party milieu in both Britain and Germany. Women's and youth organizations came to play an important role in local parties in both countries and club life as well as the festival culture within both parties looked rather alike. In quantity the Labour Party could not compete with the SPD and here indeed the SPD's ancillary organizations often seemed to be in a different class, but the whole mental world of the working-class parties in Britain and Germany nevertheless closely resembled each other. Here, as on almost all levels of party organization (Chapter 3), the Labour Party strove to copy that wider SPD culture and structure.

Comparative historians have not only neglected the subcultural aspects of the British Labour Party, they have also exaggerated the idea that the Labour Party was little more than a trade union interest group in parliament. This seemed another basic difference from the continental labour movement, and especially the German one, where the party seemed less trade unionized. In Chapter 3, it has been argued that such a distinction between a trade union party in Britain and an independent socialist party in Germany cannot be sustained. Whereas the trade union movement in Germany increasingly influenced the SPD in the direction of reformism and pragmatic policy-making, the trade union leaders in Britain seldom intervened with the policies of the Labour Party leaders, although the affiliated unions, which in more than one way *were* the Labour Party, wielded substantial formal powers within the NEC and the structure of the Labour Party generally. Whereas trade union leaders often sat in parliament for the SPD, a high trade union office was regarded by many British union leaders as incompatible with a seat in parliament. Yet ultimately the fall of the Müller and the MacDonald governments in 1930 and 1931 respectively over a trade union veto on cuts in unemployment benefit showed the potential power of the trade unions in both parties. In this area, therefore, the differences between the Labour Party and the SPD were also much less clear cut than hitherto assumed.

As the British Labour Party was less well integrated into its native society and the German SPD better integrated into its respective society than many *Sonderweg* historians have so far argued, it can hardly be surprising that the findings in Chapter 5 not only showed organizational similarities, but also ideological ones. Ideologically, the Marxism of the

SPD and its consequences have been overemphasized by historians. As both parties originated as protest movements against a society which was understood to be unjust and immoral, they were both reluctant to work within that system. The majority within both parties finally overcame these doubts, although substantial minorities clung to the older transformatory aims of both parties and seceded in 1917/1920 (foundation of USPD/KPD and the CPGB) and at the beginning of the 1930s (disaffiliation of the ILP, foundation of SAP). On the level of ideology from below, represented by party literature and party propaganda, it has been argued, that in both parties similar keywords can be found. Amongst others, a belief in the historical inevitability of the victory of the working-class party, an obsession with the scientific nature of socialism and the belief in socialism as a 'new religion' have been identified as central themes in the literature and rhetoric of both the Labour Party and the SPD.

That the British and the German working-class parties were not divided by organizational and ideological differences was underlined by Chapter 6, in which the often close relationships between representatives of the two parties have been examined. Where the Labour Party often admired the SPD's organization (and rejected its dogmatism), the reformist wing of the SPD admired the Labour Party's pragmatic policy approach. Personal friendships, as well as party delegations and bilateral contacts over such questions as the maintenance of peace before the war and the revision of Versailles thereafter led to a close understanding between the two parties. In comparison with the SPD's relations with other parties of the International, and despite a historiographical tradition to the contrary—arguments about weak contacts between Labour Party and SPD cannot be sustained.

The similarities that have been discovered in the organization and ideology of Labour Party and SPD make it difficult to sustain the existing typology of labour movements which differentiates between a syndicalist continental, a Marxist, German-dominated continental, and an Anglo-Saxon type. This thesis can only provide a negative check on such a typology, yet it might suggest that in the future it will be more appropriate to speak of a European labour movement including both the Labour Party and the SPD and altogether different non-European labour movements, like the American labour movement.[11] Such a typology would

---

[11] The differences between working-class organizations in Britain and the USA have been stressed by Ira Katznelson, 'Working-Class Formation and the State: Nineteenth Century England in American Perspective', in Peter B. Evans, Dietrich Rueschemeyer, and Theda Skocpol (eds.), *Bringing the State back in* (Cambridge, Mass., 1985), 257–84.

coincide with efforts to emphasize the similarities between the social experiences of Western European nations, including Britain, in the twentieth century.[12] Furthermore it would support the argument of those historians, like David Blackbourn and Geoff Eley, who have suggested that one cannot speak of a German *Sonderweg* in history. Certainly, specific characteristics remain, like the early and high degree of bureaucratization in Germany and—connected with that—the stronger tradition of state intervention. Yet, the same problems and questions had to be solved in the industrialized European nations and the answers to those problems resembled each other to the same degree that the questions resembled each other. Therefore the questions that historians will have to ask in the future are not primarily those which deal with the specific histories of nation states in Europe (although these will remain important), but those which deal with their common history.

---

[12] Hartmut Kaelble, *A Social History of Western Europe 1880–1980* (London, 1990).

Select Bibliography

BIBLIOGRAPHICAL NOTE

The bibliography includes only the most important titles that have been found useful in the formation of the book's argument. Articles in edited volumes are not mentioned separately, unless there is only one particular article of interest in any one given volume. Otherwise, only the edited volume will be listed.

A good review of the more recent research on the social history of the German labour movement can be found in Richard J. Evans, 'The Sociological Interpretation of German Labour History', in Richard J. Evans, *Rethinking German History: Nineteenth-Century and the Origins of the Third Reich* (London, 1987), 191–220. The *IWK* regularly publishes a report on all current research that is undertaken on Labour history in German and abroad (as far as it is made known to the journal). Further useful bibliographies for the German labour movement in the period under discussion here include Hans-Ulrich Wehler, *Bibliographie zur neueren deutschen Sozialgeschichte* (Munich, 1993), esp. 370–84, G. A. Ritter and Klaus Tenfelde, *Bibliographie zur Geschichte der deutschen Arbeiterschaft und Arbeiterbewegung, 1863–1914: Berichtszeitraum 1945–1975* (Bonn, 1981) and Kurt Klotzbach, *Bibliographie zur Geschichte der deutschen Arbeiterbewegung, 1914–1945: Sozialdemokratie. Freie Gewerkschaften. Christlich-soziale Bewegungen. Kommunistische und linke Splittergruppen* (Bonn, 1974). For a most useful comparative review of international Labour research see also Klaus Tenfelde (ed.), *Arbeiter und Arbeiterbewegung im Vergleich: Berichte zur internationalen historischen Forschung* (Munich, 1986). For British Labour history the *SSLH/Labour History Review* regularly publishes a list of recently completed theses. A useful bibliography is provided by Harold Smith, *The British Labour Movement to 1970: A Bibliography* (London, 1981). See also F. L. M. Thompson (ed.), *Cambridge Social History of Britain 1750–1950*, 3 vols. (Cambridge, 1990).

MANUSCRIPT SOURCES

Amsterdam: International Institute of Social History
    Files of the Socialist Youth International,
    Kleine Korrespondenz der SPD,
    LSI Files,
    Papers of Max Beer,
      Eduard Bernstein,
      Rudolf Breitscheid,

G. D. H. Cole,
Wolfgang Heine,
Karl Kautsky,
James S. Middleton,
Wilhelm Sollmann.

Berlin: Geheimes Staatsarchiv
Reichs- und Staatsministerium des Inneren: Überwachung der SPD.

Berlin: Historische Kommission
ADGB Restakten.

Berlin [O]: Institut für die Geschichte der Arbeiterbewegung, (formerly: Institut für Marxismus-Leninismus)
Handbill collections,
Papers of August Bebel,
Eduard Bernstein,
Karl Liebknecht,
Paul Löbe,
Rosa Luxembourg,
Clara Zetkin,
Reichsministerien Papers:
St. 10/228,
St. 10/229,
St. 12/101,
St. 12/103,
St. 22/6,
St. 22/16,
St. 22/28,
St. 22/37,
St. 22/38,
St. 22/75,
SAI Papers,
SPD Parteivorstand Papers:
PV II 145.

Bonn: Friedrich-Ebert Stiftung, Archiv für soziale Demokratie
Emigration Archive of the SPD
Papers of August Bebel,
Wilhelm Dittmann,
Wolfgang Heine,
Hermann Molkenbuhr,
Julius Motteler,
Hermann Müller,

Carl Severing,
Otto Wels,
SAJ Archive.

Cambridge: Churchill College
Bevin Papers,
Noel-Baker Papers.

Koblenz: Bundesarchiv
Papers of Lujo Brentano,
Wolfgang Heine,
Albert Südekum,
Zeitgeschichtliche Sammlung 1 and 2.

Liverpool: University Library
Papers of John Bruce Glasier

London: Labour Party Archive
Advisory Council of International Questions, Minutes,
Breitscheid File,
Darlington Labour Party, Minutes, 1926–32,
General Correspondence,
Gillies, W., Correspondence,
International Department Files,
International Sub-Committee, Minutes and Documents,
Local Labour Party Files,
LSI Files,
Middleton Papers,
National Joint Council of Labour, Minutes,
NEC Minutes,
Organization Subcommittee, Minutes 1932–3,
PIC/1: letter Eleanor Marx re German elections.

London: London School of Economics, British Library of Political and Economic
Science
Coll. Misc. 296: Bertrand Russell, 'Diary of a Winter Spent in Berlin',
Coll. Misc. 686: Papers of W. John,
Papers of Robert Dell,
George Lansbury,
R. H. Tawney,
Graham Wallas.

London: Public Record Office
MacDonald Papers.

London: Trades Union Congress Library, Transport House
Files on Germany 1927–39,
Meetings of the International Committee of the TUC
General Council, Minutes 1923–33.

Merseburg: Zentrales Staatsarchiv
  Papers from:
    CBS, Rep. 77: newspaper cuttings re labour movement,
    CBP, Rep. 77: newspaper cuttings re socialists
  Papers of politicians:
    no. 28: August Bebel,
    no. 108: Eduard Bernstein,
    no. 291: Philipp Scheidemann.

Oxford: Nuffield College Library
  Fabian Papers
  Papers of G. D. H. Cole,
    Stafford Cripps,
    Herbert Morrison.

Potsdam: Zentrales Staatsarchiv
  Papers of Theodor Barth,
    Konrad Haenisch,
    Wolfgang Heine,
    Carl Legien,
    Heinrich Müller.
  Papers from:
    01.01.: Reichstag,
    07.01.: Reichskanzlei,
    09.01.: Auswärtiges Amt,
    15.01.: Reichsministerium des Inneren,
    15.07.: Reichskommissar für die Überwachung der öffentlichen Ordnung,
    39.01.: Reichsarbeitsministerium.

Warwick, University of: Modern Records Centre
  Newspaper Cuttings Ellen Wilkinson.

Interviews:
Harry and Kitty Grey, Labour Party activists in the 1920s and 1930s from Nuneaton; on 30 April 1990.
Herbert Rogers, Labour Party agent for the Bristol East Constituency in the 1920s and 1930s.; on 30 March 1990.

PRIMARY SOURCES

Journals and Newspapers

Anti-Socialist, 1909–10.
Die Arbeit, 1924–33.
Daily Herald, 1912–33 (selected issues).
Dresdner Volkszeitung, 1908–12, 1919–23.
Elberfelder Freie Presse, 1925–8.

Die Genossin: Informationsblätter der weiblichen Funktionäre der SPD, July 1924–Mar. 1932.

Die Gesellschaft, 1924–32.

Die Gleichheit, 1896 and 1912 and 1915.

Hamburger Echo, 1914–19.

Labour Leader, 1905–10.

Labour Magazine, 1918–33.

Labour Organizer: The Official Journal of the National Association of Labour Registration and Election Agents, ed. Herbert Drinkwater 1920–33.

Labour Party Bulletin, 1920 and 1925–33.

Labour Prophet, 1892.

League of Youth Bulletins, 1930–2

Leipziger Volkszeitung, 1900–32 (selected issues).

Liberty, 1910–12.

London Labour Chronicle, Sept. 1918–Oct. 1924.

London News, Nov. 1924–Dec. 1932.

Mitteilungen des Vereins Arbeiterpresse, 1900–33.

Mitteilungsblatt der VSPD, 1924–8.

Die Neue Zeit, 1887–1923.

Socialist Review, 1917–24.

Sozialistische Lebensgestaltung, 1921–3.

Sozialistische Monatshefte, 1897–1933.

SPD Nachrichten für die Funktionäre, 1921–2.

Vorwärts, 1891–1933 (selected issues).

Der Weg, 1927–33.

Other Publications

ALLEN, CLIFFORD, Is Germany Right and Britain Wrong? (London, 1914).

ALTENBERGER, ERICH (ed.), *Arbeiters Weihnachten: Ein Haus- und Handbuch für freie Menschen* (Waldenburg im Schlern, 1927).

——(ed.), *Herbst- und Jahreswende* (Waldenburg im Schlern, 1929).

——(ed.), *Revolution und Nie Wieder Krieg* (Waldenburg im Schlern, 1929).

Annual Report Presented by the GMC to the Individual Members of the Westminster Labour Party 1925 (Westminster, 1925).

Annual Report of the Sheerness Trades Council and Labour Party, 1926 (Sheerness, 1926).

Annual Reports of the EC of the LLP (1924/5–1932/3).

Annual Reports of the London Labour Party (1918–33).

Arbeiterführer für Leipzig und Umgebung: Nachschlagewerk, xi, ed. Richard Lipinski (Leipzig, 1909).

Außerordentlicher Internationaler Sozialistenkongreß zu Basel am 24. und 25. November 1912 (Berlin, 1912).

BAILEY, W. MILNE (ed.), *Trade Union Documents* (London, 1929).

——*Trade Unions and the State* (London, 1934).

BALLOD, KARL, *Der Zukunftsstaat: Produktion und Konsumtion im Sozialstaat* (2nd edn., Stuttgart, 1919).

BARNES, G. N., and HENDERSON, ARTHUR, *Unemployment in Germany* (Westminster, 1908).

BEBEL, AUGUST, *Die Frau und der Sozialismus* (10th edn., Stuttgart, 1891).

——*Gewerkschaftsbewegung und politische Parteien* (Stuttgart, 1900).

BEER, MAX, *History of British Socialism*, 2 vols. (London, 1921; repr. 1953).

BELLAMY, EDWARD, *Ein Rückblick aus dem Jahr 2000 auf das Jahr 1887*, ed. and trans. Klara Zetkin (Stuttgart, 1914).

Bericht über die Tätigkeit des Bezirksvorstands der sozialdemokratischen Partei Leipzigs, 1911/12 (Leipzig, 1912).

Bericht über die Tätigkeit des Bezirksvorstands der sozialdemokratischen Partei Leipzigs, 1913/14 (Leipzig, 1914).

BERNSTEIN, EDUARD, *Parlamentarismus und Sozialdemokratie* (Berlin, 1906).

——*Evolutionary Socialism: A Criticism and Affirmation* (London, 1909).

——*Die englische Gefahr und das deutsche Volk* (Berlin, 1911).

——*Die Internationale der Arbeiterklasse und der europäische Krieg* (Tübingen, 1915).

——*Die Voraussetzungen des Sozialismus und die Aufgaben der Sozialdemokratie* (repr. of the 1921 edn., Bonn, 1977).

——*Das Görlitzer Programm der Sozialdemokratischen Partei Deutschlands, eingeleitet und allgemein verständlich erläutert* (Berlin, 1922).

BEVIN, ERNEST, *The Britain I Want to See* (London, n.d.).

BIELIGK, FRANZ (ed.), *Die Organisation im Klassenkampf: Die Probleme der politischen Organisation der Arbeiterklasse* (Berlin, 1931).

BLANK, R., 'Die soziale Zusammensetzung der sozialdemokratischen Wählerschaft Deutschlands', *AfSWP* 20 (1905), 513–24.

BLATCHFORD, ROBERT, *Merrie England* (8th edn., London, 1895).

——*Britain for the British* (London, 1902).

——*God and my Neighbour* (London, 1903).

——*Not Guilty: A Defence of the Bottom Dog* (London, 1906).

——*Germany and England: Articles Reprinted from the Daily Mail* (London, 1909).

BRAUN, ADOLF, *Gewerkschaften und Sozialdemokratie* (Berlin, 1914).

——*Gewerkschaftliche Betrachtungen und Überlegungen während des Weltkrieges* (Leipzig, 1915).

——*Der internationale Kongreß zu Genf, 1920* (Berlin, 1920).

——(ed.), *Das Programm der Sozialdemokratie: Vorschläge für seine Erneuerung* (Berlin, 1920).

——(ed.), *Programmentwurf der Sozialdemokratischen Partei: Ein Kommentar* (Berlin, 1921).

BUDDEBERG, THEODOR, 'Das soziologische Problem der Sozialdemokratie', *AfSWP* 49 (1922), 108–32.

The Burston School Strike, ed. by the ILP (London, 1915).

BUXTON, CHARLES R., and BUXTON, DOROTHY F., *In a German Miner's Home* (London, 1921).

CANT, KATHERINE, *Die Bergarbeiterfrauen Englands im Kampf*, ed. Klara Zetkin (Hamburg, 1927).

CARPENTER, EDWARD (ed.), *Forecasts of the Coming Century* (London, 1897).

Christentum und Sozialismus: Eine religiöse Polemik zwischen Herrn Kaplan Hohoff in Hüsse und dem Verfasser der Schrift 'Die parlamentarische Tätigkeit des deutschen Reichstages' (Leipzig, 1874).

Christentum, Zentrum und Sozialdemokratie (n.p., n.d.).

CITRINE, WALTER, *The Labour Chairman and Speaker's Companion* (London, 1921).

CRIPPS, STAFFORD, *Can Socialism Come by Constitutional Methods* (London, 1932).

Darf ein Katholik Sozialdemokrat sein? (Breslau, n.d.).

DELL, ROBERT, *Socialism and Personal Liberty* (London, 1921).

The Diaries of Beatrice Webb, 1912–1924, ed. Margaret Cole (London, 1952).

The Diaries of Beatrice Webb, 1924–1932, ed. Margaret Cole (London, 1956).

The Diaries of Beatrice Webb, 1905–1924, ed. Jeanne and Norman MacKenzie, vols. i–iii (London, 1984).

The Diary of Fred Knee, ed. David Englander, SSLH Bulletin Supplement 3 (Warwick, 1977).

Dokumente aus geheimen Archiven: Übersichten der Berliner politischen Polizei über die allgemeine Lage der sozialdemokratischen und anarchistischen Bewegung, i: *1878–1889*, ed. Dieter Fricke and R. Knaack (Cologne, 1982), ii: *1890–1906*, ed. F. Beck (Weimar, 1989), iv: *1914–1918* (Weimar, 1987).

DÜCKERSHOFF, ERNST, *How the English Workman Lives* (London, 1899).

DUTT, RAJANI PALME, *The Labour International Handbook* (London, 1921).

Engels, Friedrich: Die zweite Internationale und der 1. Mai, ed. Waltraud Opitz and Uwe de la Motte (Berlin, 1989).

Die englischen Arbeiter gegen die Ententeforderungen: Ein Manifest der Labour Party über Arbeitslosigkeit, Frieden und Entschädigungsfrage (Berlin, 1921).

Exposure of the Socialist Conspiracy: The Socialist Secret Plan of Campaign, ed. by the Anti-Socialist Union (London, 1911).

The Failures of Socialism, ed. by the ASU (London, 1909).

Fifty Years History of the Woolwich Labour Party (Woolwich, 1953).

FRICKE, FRITZ, *Zehn Jahre gewerkschaftlicher Bildungsarbeit in Berlin: Die Berliner Gewerkschaftsschule* (Berlin, 1932).

GAMMAGE, ROBERT, *Reminiscences of a Chartist*, ed. W. H. Maehl, SSLH Bulletin Supplement 4 (Warwick, 1983).

GEIGER, THEODOR, *Die soziale Schichtung des deutschen Volkes: Soziographischer Versuch auf statistischer Grundlage* (Stuttgart, 1932).

——'Die Mittelschichten und die Sozialdemokratie', *DA* 13 (1931), 619–35.

Die Gewerkschaften von der Stabilisierung bis zur Weltwirtschaftskrise, 1924–1930, rev. Horst A. Kuckuck and Dieter Schiffmann (Cologne, 1986).

Die Gewerkschaften in der Endphase der Republik, 1930–1933, rev. Peter Jahr unter Mitarbeit von Detlev Brunner (Cologne, 1988).

GLASIER, J. BRUCE, *The Meaning of Socialism* (Manchester, 1919).

GÖHRE, PAUL, *Drei Monate Fabrikarbeiter und Handwerksbursche* (Leipzig, 1891).
——*Wie ein Pfarrer Sozialdemokrat wurde* (Berlin, 1909).
GRIFFITHS, DAN, *The Real Enemy and Other Socialist Essays*, with a foreword by Ramsay MacDonald (London, 1923).
——(ed.), *What is Socialism? A Symposium* (London, 1924).
HAENISCH, KONRAD, *Neue Bahnen der Kulturpolitik: Aus der Regierungspraxis der deutschen Republik* (Berlin, 1921).
Handbuch für die Ortsvereine: Eine Anweisung für die Erledigung der Aufgaben der Ortsvereine (Berlin, 1930).
HANSOME, MARIUS, *World Workers' Educational Movement* (New York, 1931).
HARDIE, KEIR, *From Serfdom to Socialism* (London, 1907).
HEILMANN, ERNST, *Geschichte der Arbeiterbewegung in Chemnitz und dem Erzgebirge* (Chemnitz, 1912).
HENDERSON, ARTHUR, *Prussian Militarism* (London, 1917).
——*The Aims of Labour* (London, 1918).
——'The Outlook for Labour', *Contemporary Review*, 113 (Feb. 1918), 121–30.
——*Labour and Foreign Affairs* (London, 1922).
——*Labour in Action* (London, 1932).
——*Labour's Foreign Policy* (London, 1933).
——and MACDONALD, JAMES RAMSAY, *Notes on Organization and the Law of Registration and Elections* (London, n.d.).
HERTZKA, THEODOR, *Freiland: Ein soziales Zukunftsbild* (10th edn., Dresden, 1896).
HILFERDING, RUDOLF, *Für die soziale Republik* (Berlin, 1924).
——*Die Aufgaben der Sozialdemokratie in der Republik* (Berlin, 1927).
History of the Colne Valley Labour Party, 1891–1941: Jubilee Souvenir (Colne Valley, 1941).
Internationale Arbeitsgemeinschaft sozialistischer Parteien (ed.), *Beschlüsse der internationalen sozialistischen Konferenz* (Vienna, 1921).
Internationale Arbeitsgemeinschaft sozialistischer Parteien, Neunerkomitee (ed.), *Protokoll der Konferenz der drei internationalen Exekutivkomitees vom 2.4.–5.4. 1922 in Berlin* (Berlin, 1922).
Jahrbuch der SPD (1927–33).
Jahresbericht des Bezirksverbands der SPD Berlin (1925–31).
Ein katholischer Pfarrer als Sozialdemokrat, ed. *Vorwärts* (Berlin, 1906).
KAUTSKY, KARL, *Patriotismus und Sozialdemokratie* (Leipzig, 1907).
——*Der Weg zur Macht: Politische Betrachtungen über das Hineinwachsen in die Revolution* (Berlin, 1909).
Kongreßprotokolle der Zweiten Internationale, repr. J. Dietz Verlag, Bonn 1977 ff.: Amsterdam, 1904; Stuttgart, 1907; Copenhagen, 1910; Basle, 1912;
Kongreßprotokolle des ADGB, (1918–31).
Labour and the Nation (London, 1928).
Labour and the New Social Order: A Report on Reconstruction (London, 1918).

Labour and the Peace Treaty (London, 1919).

Labour and the Ruhr: Report of the British Labour Party Delegation Appointed by the Parliamentary Labour Party to Visit the Ruhr District to Investigate Conditions There under French Military Occupation (London, 1923).

Labour and Socialist International: Second Congress of the Labour and Socialist International at Marseilles, 22–27 August 1925 (London, 1925).

Labour and Socialist International: Third Congress of the Labour and Socialist International at Brussel, 5–11 August 1928 (London, 1928).

Labour and Socialist International: Fourth Congress of the Labour and Socialist International at Vienna, 25 July to 1 August 1931 (London, 1931).

Labour and Socialist International: Fifth Congress of the Labour and Socialist International at Paris, 21–25 August 1933 (London, 1933).

The Labour Party Constitution (London, 1918).

Labour Party Propaganda and Education in London: A Memorandum for the Consideration of Local Labour Parties (London, 1932).

LANSBURY, GEORGE, *Miracle of Fleet Street* (London, 1925).

LASKI, HAROLD, *The Crisis and the Constitution: 1931 and After* (London, 1932).

LEGIEN, CARL, *Die Organisationsfrage* (Hamburg, 1891).

——and THIMME, FRIEDRICH (eds.), *Die Arbeiterschaft im neuen Deutschland* (Leipzig, 1915).

LEIPART, THEODOR, *Die kulturelle und volkswirtschaftliche Bedeutung der Gewerkschaften* (Berlin, 1926).

——*Auf dem Weg zur Wirtschaftsdemokratie* (Berlin, 1928).

LEVENSTEIN, ADOLF (ed.), *Proletariers Jugendjahre* (Berlin, 1909).

——*Die Arbeiterfrage: Mit besonderer Berücksichtigung der sozialpsychologischen Seite des modernen Großbetriebes und der psycho-physischen Auswirckungen auf die Arbeiter* (Munich, 1912).

LIEBKNECHT, KARL, *Rechtsstaat und Klassenjustiz: Vortrag, gehalten zu Stuttgart am 23. August 1907* (Stuttgart, 1907).

LIEBKNECHT, WILHELM, *Kein Kompromiß, kein Wahlbündnis* (Berlin, 1899).

LIPINSKI, RICHARD, *Bericht des Bezirksvorstandes der sozialdemokratischen Partei Leipzigs im Jahr 1913/14* (Leipzig, 1914).

MACDONALD, JAMES RAMSAY, *Labour and Empire* (London, 1907).

——*Socialism and Government* (London, 1909).

——*The Socialist Movement* (London, 1911).

——*Socialism: Critical and Constructive* (London, 1921).

——*The Foreign Policy of the Labour Party* (London, 1923).

——*Die auswärtige Politik der englischen Arbeiterpartei*, ed. and trans. Egon Wertheimer (Hamburg, 1924).

——*Why Socialism must Come* (London, 1924).

MAN, HENDRIK DE, *Die Intellektuellen und der Sozialismus* (Jena, 1926).

—— *Der Sozialismus als Kulturbewegung* (Berlin, 1929).

——*Die sozialistische Idee* (Jena, 1933).

MAURENBRECHER, MAX, *Die Gebildeten und die Sozialdemokratie* (Leipzig, 1904).

MAXTON, JAMES, and COOK, A. J. , *Our Case for a Socialist Revival* (London, 1928).

The Meaning of May Day, ed. by the Labour Research Department, Labour White Papers 42 (London, 1929).

MICHELS, ROBERT, 'Die deutsche Sozialdemokratie: I. Parteimitgliedschaft und soziale Zusammensetzung', *AfSWP* 23, NS 5 (1906), 471–556.

——'Die deutsche Sozialdemokratie: II. Die deutsche Sozialdemokratie im internationalen Verband', *AfSWP* 25, NS 7 (1907), 148–231.

——*Zur Soziologie des Parteiwesens in der modernen Demokratie: Untersuchungen über die oligarchischen Tendenzen des Gruppenlebens* (1st pub. 1911, repr. of the 2nd edn., Stuttgart, 1957).

MORRIS, WILLIAM, *News from Nowhere and Selected Writings and Designs* (Harmondsworth, 1962).

MORRISON, HERBERT, *Organization Points* (London, 1918 ff.).

——*London Labour Party, Organization in London* (London, 1921).

——*Labour Party Organization in London* (London, 1930).

MÜLLER, HERMANN, *Geschichte der Arbeiterbewegung in Sachsen-Altenburg* (Jena, 1923).

——*Sozialdemokratie und Staat* (Berlin, n.d.).

——*Der Werdegang des sozialdemokratischen Programms* (Berlin, n.d.).

Der nationalliberale Parteitag und die Sozialdemokratie: Rede des Reichstagsabgeordneten August Bebel in der Volksversammlung vom 16. Oktober 1907 in 'Kellers Festsälen' in Berlin (Berlin, 1907).

NETTLAU, MAX, 'Londoner deutsche Communistische Diskussionen 1895, Nach dem Protokollbuch des CABV', in *Archiv für die Geschichte des Sozialismus und der Arbeiterbewegung*, 10 (1922), 362–91.

Official Handbook, ed. by the Stockport Labour Church (Stockport, 1907).

Official Report of the Conference between the Executives held at Berlin, 2 April 1922 and Following Days (London, 1922).

Origins and Developments of the Labour Party, ed. by D. G. Clark (EP, Microfilm, Wakefield, 1980).

Our Struggle for Socialism in Barrow: Fifty Years Anniversary, ed. by the Barrow Labour Party (Barrow, 1950).

PANNEKOEK, ANTON, *Religion und Sozialismus* (Bremen, 1906).

Programmatische Dokumente der deutschen Sozialdemokratie, ed. Dieter Dowe and Kurt Klotzbach (Berlin, 1973).

Programme of the Great Victory Demonstration to Celebrate Labour's Municipal Election and By-Election Victories (London, 1934).

Protokoll des Ersten Internationalen Sozialistischen Arbeiterkongresses in Hamburg vom 21.–25. Mai 1923 (Berlin, 1923).

Protokoll der Internationalen Sozialistischen Konferenz in Wien vom 22.–27. Februar 1921 (repr. 2nd edn., Bonn, 1978).

Protokolle der Sitzungen des Gewerkschaftsausschusses der Gewerkschaften Deutschlands (1896–1932).

Protokolle der SPD Parteitage (1891–1931).

Protokolle der USPD Parteitage (1918–22).

Quellen zur Geschichte der deutschen Gewerkschaftsbewegung im 20. Jahrhundert, founded by Erich Mathias, ed. Hermann Weber, Klaus Schönhoven, and Klaus Tenfelde, 6 vols. (Cologne, 1985–8).

RADBRUCH, GUSTAV, *Kulturlehre des Sozialismus* (Berlin, 1922).

RADLOF, LUDWIG, *Vaterland und Sozialdemokratie* (Munich, 1915).

Report and Balance Sheet of Barrow-in-Furness LRC, 1905–06 (Barrow-in-Furness, 1906).

Report on Membership Organization, ed. by the Southampton Labour Party (Southampton, 1936).

Reports of the Annual Conferences of the ILP (1893–1933).

Reports of the Annual Conferences of the LRC (1900–5).

Reports of the Annual Conferences of the Labour Party (1906–33).

Reports of the Annual Conferences of the TUC (1890–1933).

REXHÄUSER, LUDWIG, *Gewerkschaftliche Neutralität* (Leipzig, 1908).

REYNOLDS, STEPHEN, WOOLLEY, BOB, and WOOLLEY, TOM, *Seems So! A Working-Class View of Politics* (London, 1913).

ROTHSTEIN, THEODORE (ed.), *The Socialist Annual 1910* (London, 1910).

RUSKIN, JOHN, *Unto this Last: Four Essays on the First Principles of Political Economy* (7th edn., London, 1890).

RUSSELL, BERTRAND, *German Social Democracy: Six Lectures* (London, 1896).

SANDERS, W. S., *Trade Unionism in Germany* (London, 1916).

——*Pan-German Socialism* (London, 1918).

SASSENBACH, JOHANN, *25 Years of International Trade Unionism* (Amsterdam, 1926).

SCHEUER, EDMUND, *Die Religion und der Sozialismus* (Berlin, 1921).

Das Schuldkonto der deutschen Sozialreform, pamphlet no. 1 of the Reichsverband, pub. 5 Jan. 1906.

SCHWARZ, SALOMON, *Handbuch der deutschen Gewerkschaftskongresse* (Berlin, 1928).

SHAW, G. B. (ed.), *Fabian Essays in Socialism* (London, 1889, and 3rd edn., London, 1920).

——'Die englischen Fabier und die deutsche Sozialdemokratie', *Deutsche Worte*, 24 (1904), 367–78.

——*Socialism and the Labour Party: A Lecture Delivered on January 29th 1920* (London, 1920).

——*Socialism: Principles and Outlook and Fabianism* (London, 1930).

Socialism and Religion, ed. S. D. Headlam, P. Dearmer, J. Clifford, and J. Woolman (London, 1908).

Socialism Exposed, ed. by the ASU (London, 1914).

Socialism in Our Time (London, 1926).

Socialist Educational International, 1922–1939 (n.p., 1939).

Socialist Youth International: Objects, Structure and Activity (Berlin, n.d.).

SOMBART, WERNER, *Der proletarische Sozialismus* (Jena, 1924).

Die Sozialdemokratie im Urteile ihrer Gegner (Berlin, 1911).

Sozialdemokratische Antworten auf Flugblätter des Reichsverbandes gegen die Sozialdemokratie, ed. by the Party Executive (n.p., n.d.).

Sozialdemokratische Parteikorrespondenz, 1923–1928: Ergänzungsband (Berlin, 1928).

Der sozialdemokratische Zukunftsstaat: Verhandlungen des deutschen Reichstags am 31. Januar, 3., 4., 6., und 7. Februar 1893 (Berlin, 1893).

Sozialistische Kulturarbeit: Bericht über das Jahr 1928, ed. by the Reichsausschuß für sozialistische Bildungsarbeit (n.p., n.d.).

SPENGLER OSWALD, *Preußentum und Sozialismus* (Munich, 1922).

TAWNEY, R. H., 'The Choice before the Labour Party', *Political Quarterly*, 3 (July–Sept. 1932), 323–45.

TEISTLER, HERMANN, *Der Parlamentarismus und die Arbeiterklasse* (Berlin, 1892).

TILLETT, BEN, *Trades Unionism and Socialism* (London, 1897).

——*Is the Parliamentary Labour Party a Failure?* (London, 1908).

——CREECH-JONES, A., and WARREN, SAMUEL, *The Ruhr: The Report of a Deputation from the Transport and General Workers Union* (London, 1923).

Trade Unionists and Politics, Fabian Tract 65 (London, 1895).

TRESSELL, ROBERT, *The Ragged Trousered Philanthropists* (1st pub. 1914, repr. London, 1965).

TROELTSCH, WALTER, and HIRSCHFELD, P., *Die deutschen sozialdemokratischen Gewerkschaften: Untersuchungen und Materialien über ihre geographische Verbreitung* (Berlin, 1905).

Twenty-Five Years History of the Woolwich Labour Party, 1903–1928 (Woolwich, 1928).

UMBREIT, PAUL, *Die Bedeutung und Aufgaben der Gewerkschaftskartelle* (Berlin, 1903).

Vierteljahrhundertfeier der internationalen Gewerkschaftsbewegung, ed. by the IFTU (Berlin, 1926).

War Resistance: A Practical Policy: An Account of the Movement which Extends into Fifty-Six Countries and Has Organized Sections in Twenty-Four (New York, 1931).

Was ist, was will der Sozialismus?, ed. by the Party Executive of the SPD (Berlin, 1919).

WEBB, SIDNEY, *The new Constitution of the Labour Party: A Party of Handworkers and Brainworkers: The Labour Programme and Prospects* (London, 1918).

——and WEBB, BEATRICE, *The Principles of the Labour Party* (London, 1919).

————*A Constitution for the Socialist Commonwealth of Great Britain* (repr. of the 1920 edn., Cambridge, 1975).

Der Weg des Sozialismus: Quellen und Dokumente vom Erfurter Programm 1891 bis zur Erklärung von Havanna 1962, ed. Konrad Farmer and Theodor Pinkus (Reinbek, 1964).

WELLS, H. G., *New Worlds for Old* (London, 1908).

——*The Outline of History* (rev. edn., London, 1923).

——*The Discovery of the Future* (rev. edn., London, 1924).

WENDEL, HERMANN, *Sozialdemokratie und anti-kirchliche Propaganda* (Leipzig, 1907).

WERTHEIMER, EGON, *Portrait of the Labour Party* (2nd edn., London, 1930).

Why Labour Should Stand by France, ed. by the ILP (London, 1923).

WILKINSON, ELLEN, *Clash* (London, 1929, repr. 1989).

WOLTMANN, LUDWIG, *Die Stellung der Sozialdemokratie zur Religion* (Leipzig, 1901).

Yearbook of the International Federation of Trade Unions (London 1922, 1923/4, 1925, 1926, 1927, and 1930).

YOUNG, GEORGE, *The New Germany* (London, 1920).

Zehn Jahre Reichsverband: Festgabe der Hauptstelle des Reichsverbandes gegen die Sozialdemokratie in Berlin zum 9. Mai 1914 (Berlin, 1914).

Die Zweite Internationale 1918–1919, ed. G. A. Ritter (Berlin, 1980).

SECONDARY SOURCES

ABELSHAUSER, WERNER, 'Lebensstandard im Industrialisierungsprozeß: Britische Debatte und deutsche Verhältnisse', *Scripta Mercaturae*, 16 (1982), 71–92.

ABENDROTH, WOLFGANG, *Sozialgeschichte der europäischen Arbeiterbewegung* (8th edn., Frankfurt am Main, 1972).

ABRAMS, LYNN, *Workers' Culture in Imperial Germany: Leisure and Recreation in the Rhineland and Westphalia* (London, 1992).

ABRAMSKY, CHIMEN, and COLLINS, HENRY, *Karl Marx and the British Labour Movement* (London, 1965).

ACHTEN, UDO, *Illustrierte Geschichte des Ersten Mai* (Oberhausen, 1979).

——*Mein Vaterland ist international: Internationale Geschichte des Ersten Mai* (Oberhausen, 1986).

ADAMS, A. J., 'Working-Class Organization, Industrial Relations and the Labour Unrest, 1914–1921' (University of Leicester Ph.D. 1988).

ADOLPH, H. J., *Otto Wels und die Politik der deutschen Sozialdemokratie, 1894–1939* (Berlin, 1971).

ANDERSON, PERRY, 'The Figures of Descent', *NLR* 161 (1987), 20–77.

ASHPLANT, T. G., 'The Working Mens' Club and Institute Union and the ILP: Working Class Organization, Politics and Culture, 1880–1914' (University of Sussex Ph.D. 1983).

ASHTON, ROSEMARY, *Little Germany: Exile and Asylum in Victorian England* (Oxford, 1986).

BAIN, G. S., and PRICE, ROBERT, *Profiles of Union Growth: A Comparative Statistical Portrait of Eight Countries* (Oxford, 1980).

BAJOHR, STEFAN, *Vom bitteren Los der kleinen Leute: Protokolle über den Alltag Braunschweiger Arbeiterinnen und Arbeiter 1900–1933* (Cologne, 1984).

BARKER, BERNARD, 'The Anatomy of Reformism: The Social and Political Ideas of the Labour Leadership in Yorkshire', *IRSH* 18 (1973), 1–27.

BARNES, G. N., *From Workshop to War Cabinet* (London, 1924).

BAUMANN, ZYGMUNT, *Between Class and Elite: The Evolution of the British Labour Movement. A Sociological Study* (Manchester, 1972).

——*Socialism: The Active Utopia* (London, 1976).

BAX, ERNEST BELFORT, *Reminiscences and Reflections of a Mid and Late Victorian* (London, 1918).

BAXTER, R., 'The Liverpool Labour Party, 1918–1963' (University of Oxford D.Phil. 1969).

BEALEY, FRANK, *The Social and Political Thought of the Labour Party* (London, 1970).

——and PELLING, HENRY, *Labour and Politics, 1900–1906: A History of the LRC* (London, 1958).

BEER, MAX, *Fifty Years of International Socialism* (London, 1935).

BEIER, GERHARD, *Geschichte und Gewerkschaft: Politisch-historische Beiträge zur Geschichte sozialer Bewegungen* (Cologne, 1981).

BELCHEM, JOHN, *Industrialization and the Working Class* (London, 1990).

BENDIX, REINHARD, *Nation-Building and Citizenship: Studies of Our Changing Social Order* (Berkeley, Calif., 1964).

BENSON, JOHN, *The Working Class in Britain, 1850–1939* (London, 1989).

BERADT, CHARLOTTE, *Paul Levi: Ein demokratischer Sozialist in der Weimarer Republik* (Frankfurt, 1969).

BERG, WERNER, *Wirtschaft und Gesellschaft in Deutschland und Großbritannien im Übergang zum 'Organisierten Kapitalismus'. Unternehmer, Angestellte, Arbeiter und Staat im Steinkohlebergbau des Ruhrgebietes und von Süd-Wales, 1850–1914* (Bielefeld, 1980).

BERLANSTEIN, GEORGE L., 'Liberalism and the Progressive Alliance in the Constituencies, 1900–1914: Three Case Studies', *Historical Journal*, 26 (1983), 617–40.

BERNSTEIN, EDUARD, *My Years of Exile: Reminiscences of a Socialist* (London, 1921).

BERRIDGE, V. S., 'Popular Journalism and Working Class Attitudes 1859–1886: A Study of Reynolds' Newspaper, Lloyd's Weekly Newspaper, and the Weekly Times' (University of London Ph.D. 1976).

BIAGINI, E. F., and REID, ALASTAIR (eds.), *Currents of Radicalism: Popular Radicalism, Organized Labour and Party Politics in Britain 1850–1914* (Cambridge, 1991).

BIRD, STEPHEN, 'History of the BWSA', *SSLH* 50 (1985), 7–9.

BIRKE, ADOLF M., and KETTENACKER, LOTHAR (eds.), *Wettlauf in die Moderne: England und Deutschland seit der Industriellen Revolution* (Munich, 1988).

——and KLUXEN, KURT (eds.), *Viktorianisches England in deutscher Perspektive* (Munich, 1983).

BLACKBOURN, DAVID, and ELEY, GEOFF, *The Peculiarities of German History: Bourgeois Society and Politics in Nineteenth-Century Germany* (Oxford, 1984).

BLATCHFORD, ROBERT, *My Eighty Years* (London, 1931).

BLAXLAND, GREGORY, *J. H. Thomas: A Life for Unity* (London, 1964).

BLEWETT, NEIL, *The Peers and the People: The General Election of 1910* (London, 1972).

BLOCH, MARC, 'Toward a Comparative History of European Societies' (trans.

Jelle C. Riemersma), in Jelle C. Riemersma and Frederic C. Lane (eds.), *Enterprise and Secular Change: Readings in Economic History* (London, 1953), 494–521 (first pub. 1928 in *Revue de Synthèse Historique*, 46: 15–50).

BOLL, FRIEDHELM, *Massenbewegungen in Niedersachsen, 1906–1920: Eine sozialgeschichtliche Untersuchung zu den unterschiedlichen Entwicklungstypen Braunschweig und Hannover* (Bonn, 1981).

——(ed.), *Arbeiterkulturen zwischen Alltag und Politik: Beiträge zum europäischen Vergleich in der Zwischenkriegszeit* (Vienna, 1986).

BONDFIELD, MARGARET, *A Life's Work* (London, 1950).

BORSDORF, ULRICH, 'Deutsche Gewerkschaftsführer: biographische Muster', in Ulrich Borsdorf, O. Hemmer, Gerhard Leminsky, and Heinz Markmann (eds.), *Gewerkschaftliche Politik: Reform aus Solidarität. Zum 60. Geburtstag von Heinz Oskar Vetter* (Cologne, 1977), 11–41.

——*Hans Böckler: Arbeit und Leben eines Gewerkschaftlers von 1875–1945* (Cologne, 1982).

BOUGHTON, J., 'Working-Class Politics in Birmingham and Sheffield, 1918–1931' (University of Warwick Ph.D. 1985).

BRANDT, PETER, and RÜRUP, REINHARD, *Volksbewegung und demokratische Neuordnung in Baden 1918/19: Zur Vorgeschichte und Geschichte der Revolution* (Sigmaringen, 1991).

BRANDT, WILLY, *Links und Frei: Mein Weg, 1930–1950* (Hamburg, 1982).

BRAUNTHAL, GERALD, *Socialist Labor and Politics in Weimar Germany: The General Federation of German Trade Unions* (Hamden, Conn., 1978).

BRAUNTHAL, JULIUS, *In Search of the Millenium*, introd. H. N. Brailsford (London, 1945).

——*Geschichte der Internationale*, ii: *1914–1943* (Hanover 1963).

BREITMAN, RICHARD, *German Socialism and Weimar Democracy* (Chapel Hill, NC, 1981).

BRENTANO, LUJO, *Mein Leben im Kampf um die soziale Entwicklung Deutschlands* (Jena, 1931).

BREUILLY, JOHN, *Labour and Liberalism in Nineteenth Century Europe: Essays in Comparative History* (Manchester, 1992).

BRIGGS, ASA, and SAVILLE, JOHN (eds.), *Essays in Labour History* (London, 1960).

BROCKWAY, FENNER, *Inside the Left* (London, 1942).

——*Socialism over Sixty Years: The Life of Jowett of Bradford* (London, 1946).

——*Bermondsey Story* (London, 1949).

BROMME, MORITZ, *Lebensgeschichte eines modernen Fabrikarbeiters* (Jena, 1905).

BRONDER, D., 'Organisation und Führung der sozialdemokratischen Arbeiterbewegung im Deutschen Reich, 1890–1914 (University of Göttingen Ph.D. 1952).

BROWN, K. D. (ed.), *Essays in Anti-Labour History* (London, 1974).

——(ed.), *The First Labour Party* (London, 1985).

BRÜGGEMEIER, F. J., *Leben vor Ort: Ruhrbergleute und Ruhrbergbau, 1889–1919* (Munich, 1983).

BUCHWITZ, OTTO, *50 Jahre Funktionär der deutschen Arbeiterbewegung* (Düsseldorf, 1949).

BULLOCK, ALAN, *The Life and Times of Ernest Bevin*, i: *Trade Union Leader, 1881–1940* (London, 1960).

BULLOCK, IAN, 'Socialists and Democratic Form in Britain, 1880–1914' (University of Sussex Ph.D. 1981).

BUNSEN, VICTORIA DE, *Charles Roden Buxton: A Memoir* (London, 1948).

BURGESS, KEITH, *The Challenge of Labour, Shaping British Society, 1850–1930* (London, 1980).

BURKE, CATHERINE, 'Working Class Politics in Sheffield, 1900–1920: A Regional Study in the Origins and Early Growth of the Labour Party' (Sheffield City Polytechnic Ph.D. 1983).

BURNS, ROB, and WILL, WILFRIED VAN DER, *Arbeiterkulturbewegung in der Weimarer Republik* (Frankfurt am Main, 1982).

BUSCHAK, WILLY, *Das Londoner Büro: Europäische Linkssozialisten in der Zwischenkriegszeit* (Amsterdam, 1985).

BUSE, D. K. (ed.), *Parteiagitation und Wahlkreisvertretung: Eine Dokumentation über Friedrich Ebert und seinen Reichstagswahlkreis Elberfeld/Barmen, 1910–1918* (Bonn, 1975).

——'Party Leadership and the Mechanisms of Unity: The Crisis of German Social Democracy Reconsidered, 1910–1914', *Journal of Modern History*, 62 (1990), 477–502.

CALKINS, K. R., 'The Uses of Utopianism: The Millenarian Dream in Central European Social Democracy Before 1914', *Central European History*, 15 (1982), 124–48.

CALLCOTT, M., and CHALLINOR, R. (eds.), *Working-Class Politics in North-East England* (Newcastle upon Tyne, 1983).

CARPENTER, L. P., *G.D.H. Cole: An Intellectual Biography* (Cambridge, 1973).

CARSTEN, FRANCIS L., *War against War: British and German Radical Movements in the First World War* (London, 1982).

——*Eduard Bernstein 1850–1932: Eine politische Biographie* (Munich, 1993).

CHAPPIUS, CHARLES W., 'Anglo-German Relations, 1929–1933: A Study of the Role of Great Britain in the Achieving of the Aims of German Foreign Policy' (University of Notre Dame Ph.D. 1966).

CITRINE, WALTER, *Men at Work: An Autobiography* (London, 1964).

CLARK, DAVID, *Colne Valley: Radicalism to Socialism, 1890–1910* (London, 1981).

——*Labour's Lost Leader: Victor Grayson* (London, 1985).

CLARKE, P. F., *Lancashire and the New Liberalism* (Cambridge, 1971).

——'Liberals, Labour and the Franchise', *EHR* 92 (1977), 582–90.

——*Liberals and Social Democrats* (Cambridge, 1978).

CLEGG, H. A., *A History of British Trade Unionism Since 1911*, vol. ii (Oxford, 1985).

——FOX, A. and THOMPSON, A. F., *A History of British Trade Unionism since 1889*, vol. i (Oxford, 1964).

CLINTON, ALAN, *The Trade Union Rank and File: Trades Councils in Britain, 1900–1940* (Manchester, 1977).

CLYNES, J. R., *Memoirs, 1869–1924*, 2 vols. (London, 1937).

COLE, G. D. H., *A History of the Labour Party from 1914* (London, 1948).

COLE, G. D. H., *A History of Social Thought, 1789–1939*, 5 vols. (2nd edn., London 1967–9).

COLE, MARGARET, *Growing up into Revolution* (London, 1949).

COLLETTE, CHRISTINE, *For Labour and for Women: The Women's Labour League, 1906–1918* (Manchester, 1989).

—— 'British Labour Attitudes to Europe, 1918–1939, with Special Reference to the Role of the Labour Party International Secretary' (University of Oxford M.Litt. 1992).

COLLISON, W., *The Apostle of Free Labour* (London, 1913).

COX, DAVID, 'The Labour Party in Leicester', *IRSH* 6 (1961), 197–211.

CREW, D. F., *Town in the Ruhr: A Social History of Bochum, 1860–1914* (New York, 1979).

CRONIN, JAMES, *Labour and Society in Britain, 1918–1979* (London, 1984).

—— 'Neither Exceptional nor Peculiar: Towards the Comparative Study of Labour in Advanced Society', *IRSH* 38 (1993), 59–74.

CROSSICK, GEOFF, and HAUPT, GEORGES (eds.), *Shopkeepers and Master Artisans in Nineteenth Century Europe* (London, 1986).

CUNNINGHAM, HUGH, *Leisure in the Industrial Revolution, c.1780–1880* (London, 1980).

DAHRENDORF, RALF, *Gesellschaft und Demokratie in Deutschland* (Munich, 1965).

DALTON, HUGH, *Call Back Yesterday, Memoirs 1887–1931* (London, 1953).

DENNIS, N., HENRIQUES, F., SLAUGHTER, C., *Coal is Our Life* (London, 1969).

DITT, KARL, *Industrialisierung, Arbeiterschaft und Arbeiterbewegung in Bielefeld, 1850–1914* (Dortmund, 1982).

DONOUGHUE, B., and JONES, G. W., *Herbert Morrison* (London, 1973).

DOWSE, R. E., *Left in the Centre: The Independent Labour Party, 1893–1940* (London, 1966).

DRUCKER, H. M., *Doctrine and Ethos in the Labour Party* (London, 1979).

DRUMMOND, D. K., 'Crewe: Society and Culture of a Railway Town, 1842–1914' (University of London Ph.D. 1986).

DURBIN, ELIZABETH, *New Jerusalems: The Labour Party and the Economics of Democratic Socialism* (London, 1985).

DUVERGER, MAURICE, *Political Parties: Their Organization and Activity in the Modern State* (2nd edn., London, 1959).

EBERLEIN, ALFRED (ed.), *Die Presse der Arbeiterklasse und der sozialen Bewegungen* (Frankfurt, 1968).

EICHMANIS, JOHN, 'The British Labour Movement and the Second International, 1889–1914' (University of London M.Phil. 1982).

EISENBERG, CHRISTIANE, *Deutsche und englische Gewerkschaften: Entstehung und Entwicklung bis 1878 im Vergleich* (Göttingen, 1986).

——'The Comparative View in Labour History. Old and New Interpretations of the English and German Labour Movements Before 1914', *IRSH* 34 (1989), 403–32.

EKSTEINS, MODRIS, 'The German Democratic Press and the Collapse of Weimar Democracy' (University of Oxford D.Phil. 1970).

EMIG, BRIGITTE, *Die Veredelung des Arbeiters: Sozialdemokratie als Kulturbewegung* (Frankfurt am Main, 1980).

ENGELHARDT, ULRICH, *'Nur vereinigt sind wir stark': die Anfänge der deutschen Gewerkschaftsbewegung 1862/63–1869/70* (Stuttgart, 1977).

ENGELSBERGER, R. M., 'Gewerkschaften—gestern und heute. Entwicklung und Gegenüberstellung der Erfolge in England, Deutschland und Österreich' (University of Graz Ph.D. 1958).

EPPE, HEINRICH, and UELLENBERG VAN DAWEN, WOLFGANG, *Kleine Chronik der deutschen und internationalen sozialistischen Kinder- und Jugendorganisationen, 1900–1940* (Bonn, 1982).

EUCHNER, WALTER, 'Sozialdemokratie und Demokratie: zum Demokratieverständnis der SPD in der Weimarer Republik', *AfS* 26 (1986), 125–78.

EVANS, RICHARD J. (ed.), *The German Working Class, 1888–1933: The Politics of Everyday Life* (London, 1982).

——*Comrades and Sisters: Feminism, Socialism and Pacifism in Europe, 1870–1945* (New York, 1987).

——*Proletarians and Politics: Socialism, Protest and the Working Class in Germany before the First World War* (New York, 1990).

FARRAR, E., 'The British Labour Party and International Organisation: A Study of the Party's Policy towards the League of Nations, the United Nations and Western Union' (University of London Ph.D. 1952).

FAULENBACH, BERND, and HÖGL, GÜNTHER (eds.), *Eine Partei in ihrer Region: Zur Geschichte der SPD im westlichen Westfalen* (Essen, 1988).

FINCHER, J. A., 'The Clarion Movement: A Study of a Socialist Attempt to Implement the Co-operative Commonwealth' (University of Manchester MA 1971).

FISCHER, BENNO, *Theoriediskussionen der SPD in der Weimarer Republik* (Frankfurt am Main, 1987).

FISCHER, CONAN, *The German Communists and the Rise of Nazism* (London, 1991).

FLETCHER, ROGER, *Revisionism and Empire: Socialist Imperialism in Germany, 1897–1914* (London, 1984).

——(ed.), *Bernstein to Brandt: A Short History of German Social Democracy* (London, 1987).

FLÜGEL, SIEGFRIED, 'Die Entwicklung des Arbeitergesangs im Raum Halle, Weißenfels und Zeitz zwischen 1890 und 1933' (University of Halle Ph.D. 1965).

FOOTE, GEOFFREY, *The Labour Party's Political Thought: A History* (2nd edn., Beckenham, 1986).

FOWKES, BEN, *Communism in Germany under the Weimar Republic* (London, 1984).

Fox, K. O., 'The Emergence of the Political Labour Movement in the Eastern Section of the South Wales Coalfield, 1894–1910' (University of Wales MA 1965).

Francis, Hywel, and Smith, David, *The Fed: A History of the South Wales Miners in the Twentieth Century* (London, 1980).

Francis, Pat, 'The Labour Publishing Company, 1920–1929', *HWJ* 18 (1984), 115–29.

Franzen, Hans Joachim, *Auf der Suche nach politischen Handlungsspielräumen: die Diskussion um die Strategie der Partei in den regionalen und lokalen Organisationen der badischen Sozialdemokratie zwischen 1890–1914*, 2 vols. (Frankfurt am Main, 1983).

Freeden, Michael, *The New Liberalism, 1880–1914* (Oxford, 1978).

——*Liberalism Divided: A Study in British Political Thought, 1914–1939* (Oxford, 1986).

Fricke, Dieter, 'Der Reichsverband gegen die Sozialdemokratie von seiner Gründung bis zu den Reichstagswahlen von 1907', *ZfG* 7 (1959), 237–80.

——*Bismarcks Prätorianer: Die Berliner politische Polizei im Kampf gegen die deutsche Arbeiterbewegung (1871–1898)* (Berlin, 1962).

——*Die deutsche Arbeiterbewegung, 1869–1914: ein Handbuch über ihre Organisation und Tätigkeit im Klassenkampf* (Berlin, 1976).

——*Kleine Geschichte des Ersten Mai: die Maifeier in der deutschen und in der internationalen Arbeiterbewegung* (Frankfurt am Main, 1980).

——*Handbuch zur Geschichte der deutschen Arbeiterbewegung, 1869–1917*, 2 vols. (Berlin, 1987).

Frow, Edmund, and Frow, Ruth, *'To Make that Future Now': A History of the Manchester and Salford Trades Council* (Manchester, 1976).

Fyfe, Hamilton, *Sixty Years of Fleet Street* (London, 1949).

Gay, Peter, *The Dilemma of Democratic Socialism* (New York, 1952).

Geary, Dick, *Labour Protest in Europe, 1848–1939* (London, 1981).

——*Karl Kautsky* (Manchester, 1987).

——(ed.), *Labour and Socialist Movements in Europe before 1914* (Oxford, 1989).

——'Employers, Workers and the Collapse of the Weimar Republic', Ian Kershaw (ed.), *Weimar: Why did German Democracy Fail?* (London, 1990), 92–120.

——*European Labour Politics from 1900 to the Depression* (London, 1991).

Gerschenkron, Alexander, *Economic Backwardness in Historical Perspective* (Cambridge, Mass., 1966).

Gewerkschaftsbewegung im 20. Jahrhundert im Vergleich: Forschungskolloquium Wintersemester 1984/1985, ed. the Institut zur Geschichte der Arbeiterbewegung an der Ruhr-Universität Bochum (Bochum, 1985).

Gillespie, J. A., 'Economic and Political Change in the East End of London during the 1920s' (University of Cambridge Ph.D. 1984).

Glees, Anthony, 'The SPD, the Labour Party and the Foreign Office' (University of Oxford D.Phil. 1979).

—— *Exile Politics during the Second World War: The German Social Democrats in Britain* (Oxford, 1982).

GOLDSTEIN, R. J., *Political Repression in Nineteenth Century Europe* (London, 1983).

GORMAN, JOHN, *Images of Labour: Selected Memorabilia from the National Museum of Labour History* (London, 1985).

GOSPEL, H. F., 'Employers' Organizations: Their Growth and Function in the British System of Industrial Relations in the Period 1918–1939' (University of London Ph.D. 1974).

GOSS, SUE, *Local Labour and Local Government, Southark 1919–1982* (London, 1988).

GREBING, HELGA, *Der 'deutsche Sonderweg' in Europa, 1806–1945: Eine Kritik* (Stuttgart, 1986).

GREW, RAYMOND, 'The Case for Comparing Histories', *AHR* 85 (1980), 763–78.

GROH, DIETER, *Negative Integration und Revolutionärer Attentismus: Die deutsche Sozialdemokratie am Vorabend des 1. Weltkrieges* (Frankfurt am Main, 1973).

—— and BRANDT, PETER, *'Vaterlandslose Gesellen': Sozialdemokratie und Nation 1860–1990* (Munich, 1992).

GROSCHOPP, HORST, *Zwischen Bierabend und Bildungsverein: Zur Kulturarbeit in der deutschen Arbeiterbewegung vor 1914* (2nd edn., Berlin, 1987).

GUTTSMAN, W. L., *The German Social Democratic Party, 1875–1933: From Ghetto to Government* (London, 1981).

—— *Workers' Culture in Weimar Germany: Between Tradition and Commitment* (New York, 1990).

HAGEMANN, KAREN, *Frauenalltag und Männerpolitik: Alltagsleben und gesellschaftliches Handeln von Arbeiterfrauen in der Weimarer Republik* (Bonn, 1990).

HAIMSON, LEOPOLD, and TILLY, CHARLES (ed.), *Strikes, Wars, and Revolutions in an International Perspective: Strike Waves in the Late Nineteenth and Early Twentieth Centuries* (Cambridge, 1989).

HALL, ALEX, 'By Other Means: The Legal Struggle against the SPD in Wilhelmine Germany, 1890–1900', *Historical Journal*, 17 (1974), 365–86.

—— *Scandal, Sensation and Social Democracy: The SPD Press and Wilhelmine Germany, 1890–1914* (Cambridge, 1977).

HAMILTON, M. A., *Arthur Henderson* (London, 1938).

HANSON, A. H., 'The Labour Party and the House of Commons Reform', *Parliamentary Affairs*, 10 (1956–7), 454–68 and 11 (1957–8), 39–56.

HAUPT, GEORGES, *Aspects of International Socialism, 1871–1914* (Cambridge, 1986).

HAUPT, H.-G., 'Zur gesellschaftlichen Bedeutung des Kleinbürgertums in westeuropäischen Gesellschaften des 19. Jahrhunderts', *GG* 16 (1990), 296 317.

HECKART, BEVERLY, *From Bassermann to Bebel: The Grand Bloc's Quest for Reform in the Kaiserreich, 1900–1914* (New Haven, Conn. 1974).

Herkunft und Mandat: Beiträge zur Führungsproblematik in der Arbeiterbewegung (Frankfurt am Main, 1976).

HERZIG, ARNO, and TRAUTMANN, GÜNTER (eds.), *'Der kühnen Bahn nur folgen wir . . .': Ursprünge, Erfolge und Grenzen der Arbeiterbewegung in Deutschland*, 2 vols. (Hamburg, 1989).

HINTON, JAMES, *Labour and Socialism: A History of the British Labour Movement 1867–1974* (Brighton, 1983).

HIRSCHFELDER, HEINRICH, *Die bayrische Sozialdemokratie, 1864–1914*, 2 vols. (Erlangen, 1979).

HÖBER, JOHANNNES, 'Die Nachkriegsentwicklung der englischen Arbeiterbewegung' (University of Heidelberg Ph.D. 1930).

HOBSBAWM, ERIC J., *Labouring Men* (London, 1964).

——*Worlds of Labour: Further Studies in the History of Labour* (London, 1984).

——'Labour in the Great City', *NLR* 166 (Nov.–Dec. 1987).

HODGE, CARL CAVANAGH, 'The Trammels of Tradition: Social Democratic Parties in Britain, France and Germany 1863–1937 (University of London Ph.D. 1987).

HODGES, FRANK, *My Adventures as a Labour Leader* (London, 1925).

HODGKINSON, GEORGE, *Sent to Coventry* (London, 1970).

HOGGART, RICHARD, *The Uses of Literacy* (London, 1957).

HOLFORD, JOHN, *Reshaping Labour: Organization, Work and Politics: Edinburgh in the Great War and After* (London, 1988).

HÖLSCHER, LUCIAN, *Weltgericht oder Revolution: Protestantische und sozialistische Zukunftsvorstellungen im deutschen Kaiserreich* (Stuttgart, 1989).

HOMBACH, BODO, and NIETHAMMER, LUTZ (eds.), *'Die Menschen machen ihre Geschichte nicht aus freien Stücken, aber sie machen sie selbst.' Einladung zu einer Geschichte des Volkes in Nordrhein Westfalen* (Berlin, 1984).

HOWARD, CHRISTOPHER, 'Expectations Born to Death: Local Labour Party Expansion in the 1920s', J. Winter (ed.), *The Working Class in Modern British History* (Cambridge, 1983), 65–81.

HOWELL, DAVID, *British Workers and the ILP, 1888–1906* (Manchester, 1983).

——*A Lost Left: Three Studies in Socialism and Nationalism* (Manchester, 1986).

HOWKINS, ALUN, 'Edwardian Liberalism and Industrial Unrest: A Class View of the Decline of Liberalism', *HWJ* 4 (1977), 143–61.

HÜLLBÜSCH, URSULA, 'Gewerkschaften und Staat: Ein Beitrag zur Geschichte der Gewerkschaften zu Anfang und zu Ende der Weimarer Republik' (University of Bonn Ph.D. 1958).

HUNT, RICHARD N., *German Social Democracy, 1919–1933* (New Haven, Conn., 1964).

ICHIKAWA, T., 'The Daily Citizen, 1912–1915: A Study of the First Labour Daily Newspaper in Britain' (University of Wales, Aberystwyth, MA 1985).

JEMNITZ, JANOS, 'A Comparative Historical Sketch of the Early European May 1 Celebrations', in Andrea Panaccione (ed.), *May Day Celebration* (Venice, 1988), 191–206.

JOHN, MICHAEL, 'The Peculiarities of the German State: Bourgeois Law and Society in the Imperial Era', *PP* 119 (1988), 105–31.

——*Politics and the Law in Late 19th Century Germany: The Origins of the Civil Code* (Oxford, 1989).

JOLL, JAMES, *The Second International, 1889–1914* (2nd edn., London, 1974).

JONES, BARRY, and KEATING, MICHAEL, *Labour and the British State* (Oxford, 1985).

JONES, GARETH STEDMAN, *Languages of Class: Studies in English Working-Class History, 1832–1982* (Cambridge, 1983).

JONES, G. W., *Borough Politics: A Study of the Wolverhampton Town Council, 1888–1964* (London, 1969).

JONES, S. G., 'The British Labour Movement and Working Class Leisure, 1918–1939' (University of Manchester Ph.D. 1983).

——*Workers at Play: A Social and Economic History of Leisure, 1918–1939* (London, 1986).

——*The British Labour Movement and Film* (London, 1987).

——'The Survival of Industrial Paternalism in the Cotton Districts: A View from the 1920s', *Journal of Regional and Local Studies*, 7 (1987), 1–13.

——'The European Workers' Sport Movement and Organized Labour in Britain Between the Wars', *EHQ* 18 (1988), 3–32.

——*Sport, Politics and the Working Class: Organized Labour and Sport in Interwar Britain* (Manchester, 1988).

KAELBLE, HARTMUT, 'Der Mythos von der rapiden Industrialisierung in Deutschland', *GG* 9 (1983), 106–18.

——'Wie feudal waren die deutschen Unternehmer im Kaiserreich? Ein Zwischenbericht', in R. H. Tilly (ed.), *Beiträge zur quantitativen vergleichenden Unternehmensgeschichte* (Stuttgart, 1985), 148–74.

——*A Social History of Western Europe 1880–1980* (London, 1990).

KAMINSKY, THOMAS, 'Grundzüge der internationalen Beziehungen der deutschen Sozialdemokratie in der Zeit nach dem Stuttgarter bis zum Kopenhagener Kongress der II. Internationale (1907–1910)' (University of Leipzig Ph.D. 1987).

KANDLER, ROBERT, 'The Effects of Economic and Social Conditions on the Development of the Free Trade Unions in Upper Franconia, 1890–1914' (University of Oxford D.Phil. 1986).

KATZNELSON, IRA, 'Working Class Formation and the State: 19th Century England in American Perspective', in Peter B. Evans, Dietrich Rueschemeyer, and Theda Skocpol (eds.), *Bringing the State back in* (Cambridge, Mass., 1985), 257–84.

——and ZOLBERG, A. R. (eds.), *Working Class Formation: Nineteenth-Century Patterns in Europe and the U.S.* (Princeton, NJ, 1986).

KEIL, WILHELM, *Erlebnisse eines Sozialdemokraten*, 2 vols. (Stuttgart, 1947–8).

KENDALL, WALTER, *The Labour Movement in Europe* (London, 1975).

——*The Revolutionary Movement in Britain, 1900–1921* (London, 1969).

KENNEDY, P. M., 'Idealists and Realists: British Views of Germany, 1864–1939', *Transactions of the Royal Historical Society*, 5th ser., 25 (1975), 137–56.

KIRBY, DAVID, *War, Peace and Revolution* (Aldershot, 1986).

KIRK, NEVILLE, ' "Traditional" Working-Class Culture and "the Rise of Labour":

Some Preliminary Questions and Observations', *Social History*, 16 (1991), 203–16.

KLARMAN, MICHAEL J., 'The Osborne Judgement: A Legal/Historical Analysis' (University of Oxford D.Phil. 1987).

KLAUS, G. H. (ed.), *The Rise of Socialist Fiction, 1880–1914* (New York, 1987).

KLENKE, DIETMAR, LILJE, PETER, and WALTER, FRANZ, *Arbeitersänger und Volksbühnen in der Weimarer Republik* (Bonn, 1992).

KLINKHAMMER, REIMUND, 'Die Außenpolitik der SPD in der Zeit der Weimarer Republik' (University of Freiburg im Breisgau Ph.D. 1955).

KOCKA, JÜRGEN (ed.), *Europäische Arbeiterbewegungen im 19. Jahrhundert: Deutschland, Österreich, England und Frankreich im Vergleich* (Göttingen, 1983).

——*Klassengesellschaft im Krieg: Deutsche Gesellschaftsgeschichte, 1914–1918* (Göttingen, 1983).

——*Lohnarbeit und Klassenbildung: Arbeiter und Arbeiterbewegung in Deutschland, 1800–1875* (Berlin, 1983).

——(ed.), *Arbeiter und Bürger im 19. Jahrhundert: Varianten ihres Verhältnisses im europäischen Vergleich* (Munich, 1986).

——(ed.), *Bürgertum im 19. Jahrhundert: Deutschland im europäischen Vergleich*, 3 vols. (Munich, 1988).

——*Geschichte und Aufklärung* (Göttingen, 1989).

——*Weder Stand noch Klasse: Unterschichten um 1800—Arbeiterverhältnisse und Arbeiterexistenzen: Grundlagen der Klassenbildung im 19. Jahrhundert*, 2 vols. (Bonn, 1990).

Konflikt und Kooperation: Strategien europäischer Gewerkschaften im 20. Jahrhundert, ed. by the Institut zur Erforschung der europäischen Arbeiterbewegung (Essen, 1988).

KÖNKE, GÜNTHER, *Organisierter Kapitalismus, Sozialdemokratie und Staat: Eine Studie zur Ideologie der sozialdemokratischen Arbeiterbewegung in der Weimarer Republik, 1924–1932* (Stuttgart, 1987).

KOSZYK, KURT, *Die Presse der deutschen Sozialdemokratie: Eine Bibliographie* (Hanover, 1966).

KOTOWSKI, GEORG, *Friedrich Ebert: Eine politische Biographie* (Wiesbaden, 1963).

KOWALSKI, WERNER, *Geschichte der SAI (1923–1940)* (Berlin, 1985).

KRIEGER, WOLFGANG, *Labour Party und Weimarer Republik, ein Beitrag zur Außenpolitik der britischen Arbeiterbewegung zwischen Programmatik und Parteitaktik, 1918–1924* (Bonn, 1978).

KUCZYNSKI, JÜRGEN, *Studien zur Geschichte des deutschen Imperialismus*, ii: *Propagandaorganisationen des Monopolkapitals* (Berlin, 1950).

LANCASTER, BILL, *Radicalism, Co-operation and Socialism: Leicester Working Class Politics, 1860–1906* (Leicester, 1987).

LANGEWIESCHE, DIETER, 'Arbeiterbildung in Deutschland und Österreich: Konzeption, Praxis und Funktionen', in Werner Conze and Ulrich Engelhardt (eds.), *Arbeiter im Industrialisierungsprozeß: Herkunft, Lage und Verhalten* (Stuttgart, 1979), 439–64.

——'Freizeit und Massenbildung: Zur Ideologie und Praxis der Volksbildung in der Weimarer Republik', in Gerhard Huck (ed.), *Sozialgeschichte der Freizeit* (Wuppertal, 1980), 223–48.

——and SCHÖNHOVEN, KLAUS, 'Arbeiterbibliotheken und Arbeiterlektüre im Wilhelminischen Deutschland', *AfS* 16 (1976), 135–204.

——(eds.), *Arbeiter in Deutschland: Studien zur Lebensweise der Arbeiterschaft im Zeitalter der Industrialisierung* (Paderborn, 1981).

LANSBURY, GEORGE, *My Life* (London, 1928).

LAYBOURN, K. and REYNOLDS, J., *Liberalism and the Rise of Labour* (London, 1984).

LEHNERT, DETLEF, *Reform und Revolution in den Strategiediskussionen der klassischen Sozialdemokratie* (Bonn, 1977).

——*Sozialdemokratie und Novemberrevolution: Die Neuordnungsdebatte 1918/1919 in der politischen Publizistik von SPD und USPD* (Frankfurt am Main, 1983).

LEPSIUS, RAINER, 'Parteiensystem und Sozialstruktur: Zum Problem der Demokratisierung der deutschen Gesellschaft', in *Wirtschaft, Geschichte und Wirtschaftsgeschichte*, ed. by Wilhelm Abel, Knut Borchardt, Hermann Kellenbenz, and Wolfgang Zorn (Stuttgart, 1966), 371–93.

LIDTKE, VERNON, *The Outlawed Party* (Princeton, NJ, 1966).

——*The Alternative Culture: Socialist Labor in Imperial Germany* (New York, 1985).

LINDEMANN, ALBERT S., *A History of European Socialism* (New Haven, Conn., 1983).

LINDEN, MARCEL VAN DER, 'The National Integration of European Working Classes (1871–1914)', *IRSH* 33 (1988), 285–311.

——and ROJAHN, JÜRGEN (eds.), *The Formation of Labour Movements 1870–1914: An International Perspective*, 2 vols. (Leiden, 1990).

LINDER, MARC, *European Labor Aristocracies: Trade Unionism, the Hierarchy of Skill and the Stratification of the Manual Working Class Before the First World War* (Frankfurt am Main, 1985).

LIPSET, S. M., 'Radicalism or Reformism: The Source of Working-Class Politics', *APSR* 77 (1983), 1–18.

LORECK, JOCHEN, *Wie man früher Sozialdemokrat wurde: Das Kommunikationsverhalten und die Konzeption der sozialistischen Parteipublizistik durch August Bebel* (Bonn, 1977).

LÖSCHE, PETER, 'Arbeiterbewegung und Wilhelminismus: Sozialdemokratie zwischen Anpassung und Spaltung', *GWU* 20 (1969), 519–33.

——and WALTER, FRANZ, 'Zur Organisationskultur der sozialdemokratischen Arbeiterbewegung in der Weimarer Republik: Niedergang der Klassenkultur oder solidargemeinschaftlicher Höhepunkt?', *GG* 15 (1989), 511–36.

——'Auf dem Weg zur Volkspartei? Die Weimarer Sozialdemokratie', *AfS* 29 (1989), 75–136.

——*Die SPD: Klassenpartei—Volkspartei—Quotenpartei* (Darmstadt, 1992).

LUCAS, ERHARD, *Zwei Formen von Radikalismus in der deutschen Arbeiterbewegung* (Frankfurt am Main, 1976).

LUEBBERT, G. M., *Liberalism, Fascism or Social Democracy: Social Classes and the Political Origins of Regimes in Interwar Europe* (New York, 1991).

LUTHARDT, WOLFGANG (ed.), *Sozialdemokratische Arbeiterbewegung und Weimarer Republik: Materialien zur gesellschaftlichen Entwicklung, 1927–1933*, 2 vols. (Frankfurt am Main, 1978).

——*Sozialdemokratische Verfassungstheorie in der Weimarer Republik* (Opladen, 1986).

McCARRAN, MARGARET, 'Fabianism in the Political Life of Britain, 1919–1931' (Catholic University of America, Washington, Ph.D. 1952).

McKENZIE, R. T., *British Political Parties: The Distribution of Power within the Conservative and the Labour Party* (2nd edn., London, 1963).

McKIBBIN, ROSS, 'James Ramsay MacDonald and the Problem of the Independence of the Labour Party, 1910–1914', *Journal of Modern History*, 42 (1970), 216–35.

——*The Evolution of the Labour Party, 1910–1924* (Oxford, 1974).

——'The Economic Policy of the Second Labour Government, 1929–1931', *PP* 68 (1975), 95–123.

——'Arthur Henderson as a Labour Leader', *IRSH* 23 (1978), 79–101.

——'Why was there no Marxism in Great Britain?', *EHR* 99 (1984), 297–331.

——*The Ideologies of Class: Social Relations in Britain 1880–1950* (Oxford, 1990).

——KAY, J. A., and MATTHEW, H. C. G., 'The Franchise Factor in the Rise of the Labour Party', *EHR* 91 (1976), 723–52.

MACINTYRE, STUART, *A Proletarian Science: Marxism in Britain, 1917–1933* (Cambridge, 1980).

McLEAN, IAIN, *The Legend of Red Clydeside* (New York, 1983).

McLEOD, HUGH, *Religion and the Working Class in 19th Century Britain* (London, 1984).

——'Religion in the British and German Labour Movements, c.1890–1914: A Comparison', *SSLH* 55 (1986), 25–35.

MACNAIR, JOHN, *James Maxton: The Beloved Rebel* (London, 1955).

MAEHL, W. H., *August Bebel: Shadow Emperor of the German Workers* (Lawrence, Kan., 1980).

——*The German Socialist Party: Champion of the First Republic, 1918–1933* (Philadelphia, 1986).

MARKS, G. W., 'Trade Unions in Politics: Trade Union Political Activity and its Development in Britain, Germany and the United States in the 19th and early 20th Centuries' (University of Stanford Ph.D. 1982).

MARQUAND, DAVID, *Ramsay MacDonald* (London, 1977).

MARTIN, D. E., and RUBINSTEIN, DAVID (eds.), *Ideology and the Labour Movement: Essays Presented to John Saville* (London, 1979).

MARTIN, KINGSLEY, *Harold Laski: A Biographical Memoir* (London, 1953).

MARTIN, R. M., *TUC: The Growth of a Pressure Group, 1868–1976* (Oxford, 1980).

MARTINY, MARTIN, *Integration oder Konfrontation? Studien zur Geschichte der sozialdemokratischen Rechts- und Verfassungspolitik* (Bonn, 1976).

MARWICK, ARTHUR, *Clifford Allen, the Open Conspirator* (London, 1962).

MATHIAS, ERICH, and PIKART, EBERHARDT, *Die Reichstagsfraktion der deutschen Sozialdemokratie, 1898 bis 1918* (Düsseldorf, 1966).

——and SCHÖNHOVEN, KLAUS (eds.), *Solidarität und Menschenwürde: Etappen der deutschen Gewerkschaftsgeschichte von den Anfängen bis zur Gegenwart* (Bonn, 1984).

MAYER, GUSTAV, *Erinnerungen: Vom Journalisten zum Historiker der deutschen Arbeiterbewegung* (Munich, 1949).

MEACHAM, STANDISH, *A Life Apart: The English Working Class, 1890–1914* (Cambridge, Mass., 1977).

MEYER, THOMAS and HEIMANN, HORST (eds.), *Reformsozialismus und Sozialdemokratie: Zur Theoriediskussion des Demokratischen Sozialismus in der Weimarer Republik* (Berlin, 1982).

MEYNELL, HILDAMARIE, 'The Second International, 1914–1923' (University of Oxford B.Litt. 1956).

MILIBAND, RALPH, *Parliamentary Socialism* (London, 1961).

MILLAR, J. P. M., *The Labour College Movement* (London, 1979).

MILLER, SUSANNE, *Das Problem der Freiheit im Sozialismus: Freiheit, Staat und Revolution in der Programmatik der Sozialdemokratie von Lasalle bis zum Revisionismusstreit* (Frankfurt am Main, 1964).

——*Burgfrieden und Klassenkampf* (Düsseldorf, 1974).

——'Grundwerte in der Geschichte der deutschen Sozialdemokratie', *aus politik und zeitgeschichte*, 11 (1976), 16–31.

——*Die Bürde der Macht: Die deutsche Sozialdemokratie, 1918–1920* (Düsseldorf, 1978).

——and POTTHOFF, HEINRICH, *A History of German Social Democracy: From 1848 to the Present* (Leamington Spa, 1986).

MINKIN, LEWIS, *The Labour Party Conference: A Study in the Politics of Intra-Party Democracy* (London, 1978).

——*The Contentious Alliance: Trade Unions and the Labour Party* (Edinburgh, 1991).

MITCHELL, H. and STEARNS, P., *Workers and Protests: The European Labor Movement, the Working Classes and the Origins of Social Democracy, 1890–1914* (Ithaca, NY, 1971).

MOMMSEN, HANS, 'Arbeiterbewegung', in C. D. KERNIG (ed.), *Sowjetsystem und demokratische Gesellschaft: Eine vergleichende Enzyklopädie*, vol. i (Freiburg, 1966), 274–311.

——(ed.), *Industrielles System und politische Entwicklung in der Weimarer Republik* (Düsseldorf, 1974).

——(ed.), *Sozialdemokratie zwischen Klassenbewegung und Volkspartei* (Frankfurt, 1974).

——'Zum Problem der vergleichenden Behandlung nationaler Arbeiterbewegungen am Beispiel Ost- und Südostmitteleuropas', *IWK* 15 (1979), 31–4.

——(ed.), *Arbeiterbewegung und industrieller Wandel: Studien zu gewerkschaftlichen Organisationsproblemen im Reich und an der Ruhr* (Wuppertal, 1980).

MOMMSEN, HANS, and BORSDORF, ULRICH (eds.), *Glück Auf, Kameraden* (Cologne, 1976).

MOMMSEN, WOLFGANG J., *Britain and Germany, 1800–1914: Two Developmental Paths towards Industrial Society* (London, 1986).

——and HUSUNG, HANS GERHARDT (eds.), *Auf dem Wege zur Massengewerkschaft: Die Entwicklung der Gewerkschaften in Deutschland und Großbritannien, 1880–1914* (Stuttgart, 1984).

——and MOCK, WOLFGANG (ed.), *The Emergence of the Welfare State in Britain and Germany, 1850–1950* (London, 1981).

MORGAN, JANE, *Conflict and Order: The Police and Labour Disputes in England and Wales, 1900–1939* (Oxford, 1987).

MORGAN, KENNETH O., *Keir Hardie* (London, 1975).

——*Labour People: Leaders and Lieutenants Hardie to Kinnock* (Oxford, 1987).

MORRISON, HERBERT, *An Autobiography* (London, 1960).

MOSES, JOHN A., *Trade Unionism in Germany from Bismarck to Hitler*, 2 vols. (London, 1982).

MÜLLER, ANDREAS, 'Die groß-hannoversche Sozialdemokratie vom Vorabend des 1. Weltkrieges bis zur Novemberrevolution', *Hannoversche Geschichtsblätter*, NS 33 (1979), 143–86.

MUIR, EDWIN, *An Autobiography* (London, 1964).

NA'AMAN, SHLOMO, *Die Konstituierung der deutschen Arbeiterbewegung 1862/1863: Darstellung und Dokumentation* (Assen, 1975).

NAIRN, TOM, 'The Nature of the Labour Party', *New Left Review* (Sept.–Oct. 1964), 38–65 and (Nov.–Dec. 1964), 33–62.

NAßMACHER, K. H. (ed.), *Kommunalpolitik und Sozialdemokratie: Der Beitrag des Demokratischen Sozialismus zur kommunalen Selbstverwaltung* (Bonn, 1977).

NETTL, PETER, 'The German Social Democratic Party, 1890–1914 as a Political Model', *PP* 30 (1965), 65–95.

——*Rosa Luxemburg* (abridged edn., Oxford, 1969).

NEUMANN, SIEGMUND, *Die Parteien der Weimarer Republik* (Stuttgart, 1965).

NEWTON, DOUGLAS J., *British Labour, European Socialism and the Struggle for Peace, 1889–1914* (Oxford, 1985).

NIPPERDEY, THOMAS, *Die Organisation der deutschen Parteien vor 1918* (Düsseldorf, 1961).

——'Sozialdemokratie und Geschichte', in H. Horn, A. Schwan, and T. Weingartner (eds.), *Sozialismus in Theorie und Praxis: Festschrift für Richard Löwenthal* (Berlin, 1978), 493–517.

NOLAN, MARY, *Social Democracy and Society: Working Class Radicalism in Düsseldorf, 1890–1920* (Cambridge, 1981).

O'BRIEN, P. K., 'Do we Have a Typology for the Study of European Industrialization in the 19th Century?', *Journal of European Economic History*, 15 (1986), 291–333.

OPITZ, WALTRAUD, and DE LA MOTTE, UWE (eds.), *Friedrich Engels: Die Zweite Internationale und der 1. Mai* (Berlin, 1989).

PATON, JOHN, *Left Turn* (London, 1936).

PELLING, HENRY, *The Origins of the Labour Party, 1880–1900* (London, 1954).

——*Popular Politics and Society in Late Victorian Britain* (London, 1968).

——*A Short History of the Labour Party* (8th edn., London, 1986).

PETERS, J. N., 'Anti-Socialism in British Politics, c.1900–1923: The Emergence of a Counter-Ideology' (University of Oxford D.Phil. 1992).

PETZINA, DIETMAR (ed.), *Fahnen, Fäuste, Körper: Symbolik und Kultur der Arbeiterbewegung* (Essen, 1986).

PEUKERT, D. J., 'Zur Regionalgeschichtsschreibung der Arbeiterbewegung', in *Das Argument*, 110 (1978), 546–60.

PHILIPPS, GORDON, *The Rise of the Labour Party 1893–1931* (London, 1992).

PIERSON, STANLEY, *Marxism and the Origins of British Socialism: The Struggle for a New Consciousness* (New York, 1973).

——*British Socialists: The Journey from Fantasy to Politics* (Cambridge, Mass., 1979).

——*Marxist Intellectuals and the Working-Class Mentality in Germany 1887–1912* (Cambridge, Mass., 1993).

PISTORIUS, PETER, *Rudolf Breitscheid, 1874–1944: Ein biographischer Beitrag zur deutschen Parteiengeschichte* (Cologne, 1970).

PORE, R. E., 'The German Social Democratic Women's Movement, 1919–1933' (University of Morgantown Ph.D. 1977).

POSTGATE, R. W., *The Life of George Lansbury* (London, 1951).

POTTHOFF, HEINRICH, 'Freie Gewerkschaften und sozialistische Parteien in Deutschland', *AfS*, 26 (1986), 49–85.

——*Freie Gewerkschaften, 1918–1933: Der ADGB in der Weimarer Republik* (Düsseldorf, 1987).

PRACHT, ELFI, *Parlamentarismus und deutsche Sozialdemokratie, 1867–1914* (Pfaffenweiler, 1990).

PRICE, RICHARD, 'Labour, State and Society in Britain Before 1914', paper given at the International Colloquium, Graz, 5–9 June 1989.

PRINZ, MICHAEL, 'Wandel durch Beharrung: Sozialdemokratie und "neue Mittelschichten" in historischer Perspektive', *AfS* 29 (1989), 35–73.

PRYNN, D. L., 'The Socialist Sunday Schools, the Woodcraft Folk and Allied Movements' (University of Sheffield MA 1972).

PRZEWORSKI, ADAM, *Capitalism and Social Democracy* (Cambridge, 1985).

PUGH, MARTIN, *The Tories and the People, 1880–1935* (Oxford, 1985).

QUATAERT, J. H., 'The German Socialist Women's Movement, 1890–1918: Issues, Internal Conflicts and the Main Personages' (University of Los Angeles Ph.D. 1974).

RABE, BERND, *Der sozialdemokratische Charakter: Drei Generationen aktiver Parteimitglieder in einem Arbeiterviertel* (Frankfurt am Main, 1978).

RABENSCHLAG-KRÄUßLICH, JUTTA, *Parität statt Klassenkampf? Zur Organisation des Arbeitsmarktes und Domestizierung des Arbeitskampfes in Deutschland und England, 1900–1918* (Frankfurt am Main, 1983).

RADICE, L., *Beatrice and Sidney Webb* (London, 1984).

RAUH, MANFRED, *Föderalismus und Parlamentarismus im Wilhelminischen Reich* (Düsseldorf, 1973).

——*Die Parlamentarisierung des Deutschen Reiches* (Düsseldorf, 1977).

REID, ALASTAIR, 'Class and Organization', *HJ* 30 (1987), 225–38.

——*Social Classes and Social Relations in Britain, 1850–1914* (London, 1992).

REID, J. H. STEWARD, *The Origins of the British Labour Party* (Minneapolis, 1955).

REMME, IRMGARD, 'Die internationalen Beziehungen der deutschen Frauenbewegung vom Ausgang des 19. Jahrhunderts bis 1933' (University of Berlin Ph.D. 1955).

RENSHAW, PATRICK, 'Anti-Labour Politics in Britain, 1918–1927', *Journal of Contemporary History*, 12 (1977), 693–705.

REULECKE, JÜRGEN (ed.), *Arbeiterbewegung an Rhein und Ruhr* (Wuppertal, 1974).

RIECHERS, CHRISTIAN, *Antonio Gramsci: Marxismus in Italien* (Frankfurt am Main, 1970).

RIMLINGER, G. V., *Welfare Policy and Industrialization in Europe, America and Russia* (New York, 1971).

RITTER, FRANZ, *Theorie und Praxis des Demokratischen Sozialismus in der Weimarer Republik* (Frankfurt am Main, 1981).

RITTER, G. A., 'The British Labour Movement and its Policy Towards Russia from the First Russian Revolution Until the Treaty of Locarno' (University of Oxford B.Litt. 1958).

——'Zur Geschichte der britischen Labour Party, 1900–1918: Die Umbildung einer parlamentarischen Pressure Group in eine politische Partei', in *id.*, *Parlament und Demokratie in Großbritannien: Studien zur Entwicklung und Struktur des politischen Systems* (Göttingen, 1972), 125–81.

——*Arbeiterbewegung, Parteien und Parlamentarismus: Aufsätze zur deutschen Sozial- und Verfassungsgeschichte des 19. und 20. Jahrhunderts* (Göttingen, 1976).

——(ed.), *Arbeiterkultur* (Königstein im Taunus, 1979).

——(ed.), *Die Zweite Internationale, 1918–1919* (Berlin, 1980).

——*Sozialversicherung in Deutschland und England: Entstehung und Grundzüge im Vergleich* (Munich, 1983).

——'Die Sozialdemokratie im deutschen Kaiserreich in sozialgeschichtlicher Perspektive', *HZ* 249 (1989), 259–362.

——(ed.), *Der Aufstieg der deutschen Arbeiterbewegung: Sozialdemokratie und freie Gewerkschaften im Parteiensystem und Sozialmilieu des Kaiserreichs* (Munich, 1990).

——*Der Sozialstaat im internationalen Vergleich* (2nd edn., Munich 1991).

——and TENFELDE, KLAUS, *Arbeiter im deutschen Kaiserreich 1871–1914* (Bonn, 1992).

ROBERTS, ROBERT, *The Classic Slum: Salford Life in the First Quarter of the Century* (Manchester, 1971).

ROJAHN, JÜRGEN, 'War die deutsche Sozialdemokratie ein Modell für die Parteien der Zweiten Internationale?', *IWK* 27 (1991), 291–302.

ROSE, G. C., 'Locality, Politics and Culture: Poplar in the 1920s' (University of London Ph.D. 1989).

ROTH, GÜNTHER, *The Social Democrats in Imperial Germany: A Study in Working-Class Isolation and National Integration* (Totowa, NJ, 1963).

ROWETT, J. S., 'The Labour Party and Local Government: Theory and Practice in the Inter-War Years' (University of Oxford D.Phil. 1979).

ROWLINSON, M. C., 'Cadbury's New Factory System, 1879–1919' (University of Aston Ph.D. 1987).

RUPPERT, WOLFGANG (ed.), *Die Arbeiter: Lebensformen, Alltag und Kultur von der Frühindustrialisierung bis zum Wirtschaftswunder* (Munich, 1986).

SAAGE, RICHARD (ed.), *Solidargemeinschaft und Klassenkampf: Politische Konzeptionen der Sozialdemokratie zwischen den Weltkriegen* (Frankfurt am Main, 1986).

SALDERN, ADELHEID VON, *Vom Einwohner zum Bürger: Zur Emanzipation der städtischen Unterschicht Göttingens, 1890–1920: Eine sozial- und kommunalhistorische Untersuchung* (Berlin, 1973).

——'Wilhelminische Gesellschaft und Arbeiterklasse: Emanzipations- und Integrationsprozesse im kulturellen und sozialen Bereich', *IWK* 13 (1977), 469–505.

——*Auf dem Wege zum Arbeiter-Reformismus: Parteialltag in sozialdemokratischer Provinz, Göttingen 1870–1920* (Frankfurt am Main, 1984).

——'Arbeiterradikalismus—Arbeiterreformismus: Zum politischen Profil der sozialdemokratischen Parteibasis im Deutschen Kaiserreich. Methodischinhaltliche Bemerkungen zu Vergleichsstudien', *IWK* 20 (1984), 483–97.

SALVADORI, MASSIMO, *Karl Kautsky and the Socialist Revolution, 1880–1938* (London, 1979).

SANDERS, W. S., *Early Socialist Days* (London, 1927).

SARAN, MARY, *Never Give Up* (London, 1976).

SAUL, KLAUS, *Staat, Industrie und Arbeiterbewegung im Kaiserreich: Zur Innen- und Sozialpolitik des Wilhelminischen Deutschland, 1903–1914* (Düsseldorf, 1974).

——FLEMMING, JENS, STEGMANN, DIRK and WITT, P.-C. (eds.), *Arbeiterfamilien im Kaiserreich: Materialien zur Sozialgeschichte in Deutschland, 1871–1914* (Königstein im Taunus, 1982).

SAVAGE, M. A., 'The Social Bases of Working-Class Politics: the Labour Movement in Preston, 1890–1940' (University of Lancaster Ph.D. 1984).

SAVAGE, MICHAEL, *The Dynamics of Working-Class Politics: The Labour Movement in Preston, 1880–1940* (Cambridge, 1987).

SAVILLE, JOHN, *1848: The British State and the Chartist Movement* (Cambridge, 1987).

SCHADT, JÖRG, and SCHMIERER, WOLFGANG (eds.), *Die SPD in Baden-Württemberg und ihre Geschichte: Von den Anfängen der Arbeiterbewegung bis heute* (Stuttgart, 1979).

SCHEIDEMANN, PHILIPP, *Memoirs of a Social Democrat*, 2 vols. (London, 1929).

SCHNEER, JONATHAN, *George Lansbury* (Manchester, 1990).

SCHÖNHOVEN, KLAUS, *Expansion und Konzentration: Studien zur Entwicklung der Freien Gewerkschaften im Wilhelminischen Deutschland, 1890 bis 1914* (Stuttgart, 1980).

—— 'Selbsthilfe als Form von Solidarität: Das gewerkschaftliche Unterstützungswesen im Deutschen Kaiserreich bis 1914', *AfS* 20 (1980), 147–93.

—— *Reformismus und Radikalismus: Gespaltene Arbeiterbewegung im Weimarer Sozialstaat* (Munich, 1989).

SCHORSKE, CARL E., *German Social Democracy, 1905–1917: The Development of the Great Schism* (Cambridge, Mass., 1955).

SCHRÖDER, W. H., *Arbeitergeschichte und Arbeiterbewegung: Industriearbeit und Organisationsverhalten im 19. und frühen 20. Jahrhundert* (Frankfurt am Main, 1978).

—— *Sozialdemokratische Reichstagsabgeordnete und Reichstagskandidaten, 1898–1918: Biographisch-statistisches Handbuch* (Düsseldorf, 1986).

SCHULT, JOHANNES, *Geschichte der Hamburger Arbeiter, 1890–1918* (Hamburg, 1967).

SCHULZE, HAGEN, *Otto Braun oder Preußens demokratische Sendung: Eine Biographie* (Frankfurt am Main, 1977).

SCHUSTEREIT, H., *Linksliberalismus und Sozialdemokratie in der Weimarer Republik* (Düsseldorf, 1975).

SCHWARZ, MAX, *MdR: Biographisches Handbuch der Reichstage* (Hanover, 1965).

SCHWARZMANTEL, JOHN, *Socialism and the Idea of the Nation* (London, 1991).

SEABROOK, JEREMY, *What Went Wrong? Working People and the Ideals of the Labour Movement* (London, 1978).

SEEBACHER-BRANDT, BRIGITTE, *Erich Ollenhauer: Biedermann und Patriot* (Berlin, 1984).

—— *Bebel: Künder und Kärrner im Kaiserreich* (Berlin, 1988).

SEIDEL, JUTTA, *Internationale Stellung und internationale Beziehungen der deutschen Sozialdemokratie, 1871–1895/96* (Berlin, 1982).

SEVERING, CARL, *Mein Lebensweg*, 2 vols. (Cologne, 1950).

SHEEHAN, JAMES J., *The Career of Lujo Brentano: A Study of Liberalism and Social Reform in Imperial Germany* (Chicago, 1966).

SHEPHERD, G. W., 'The Theory and Practice of Internationalism in the British Labour Party, with Special Reference to the Inter-War Period' (University of London Ph.D. 1952).

SIEMANN, JOACHIM, 'Die sozialdemokratischen Arbeiterführer in der Zeit der Weimarer Republik' (University of Göttingen Ph.D. 1955).

SIGEL, ROBERT, *Die Geschichte der II. Internationale, 1918–1923* (Frankfurt, 1986).

SILKIN, JOHN, *Changing Battlefields: The Challenge to the Labour Party, 1923–1987* (London, 1987).

SMITH, JOAN, 'Labour Tradition in Glasgow and Liverpool', *HWJ* 17 (1984).

SNOWDEN, PHILIPP, *An Autobiography*, 2 vols. (London, 1934).

SPOONER, R. T., 'The Evolution of the Official Programme of the Labour Party, 1918–1939' (University of Birmingham MA 1949).

SPRINGHALL, JOHN, *Youth, Empire and Society* (London, 1977).

STAMPFER, FRIEDRICH, *Erfahrungen und Erkenntnisse: Aufzeichnungen aus meinem Leben* (Cologne, 1957).

STEARNS, PETER, 'Adaptation to Industrialization: German Workers as a Test Case', *Central European History*, 3 (1970), 303–31.

STEENSON, GARY P., *Karl Kautsky, 1854–1938: Marxism in the Classical Years* (Pittsburgh, 1978).

—— *'Not one Man—Not one Penny': German Social Democracy, 1863–1914* (Pittsburgh, 1981).

STEINBACH, PETER, *Sozialdemokratie und Verfassungsverständnis: Zur Ausbildung einer liberal-demokratischen Verfassungskonzeption in der Sozialdemokratie seit der Mitte des 19. Jahrhunderts* (Opladen, 1983).

STEINBERG, H. J., 'Worker's Libraries in Germany Before 1914', *HWJ* 1 (1976), 166–80.

—— *Sozialismus und deutsche Sozialdemokratie: Zur Ideologie der Partei vor dem 1. Weltkrieg* (5th edn., Berlin, 1979).

STÜBLING, RAINER, *Kultur und Massen: Das Kulturkartell der modernen Arbeiterbewegung in Frankfurt am Main, 1925–1933* (Offenbach, 1983).

TANNER, DUNCAN, *Political Change and the Labour Party, 1900–1918* (Cambridge, 1990).

TAYLOR, R. K. S., and JOWITT, J. A. (eds.), *Bradford 1890–1914: The Cradle of the ILP* (Bradford, 1980).

TEANBY, K., '"Not Equal to the Demand": Major Concerns of the Doncaster Divisional Labour Party, 1918–1939' (University of Sheffield M.Phil. 1985).

TENFELDE, KLAUS, 'Geschichte der deutschen Arbeiter und Arbeiterbewegung: Ein Sonderweg', in *Der Aquädukt 1763–1988. Ein Almanach aus dem Verlag C. H. Beck im 225. Jahr seines Bestehens* (Munich, 1988), 469–83.

—— 'Großstadt und Industrieregion: Die Ausbreitung der deutschen Arbeiterbewegung in Grundzügen', in Sabine Weiss (ed.), *Historische Blickpunkte: Festschrift für Johann Rainer* (Innsbruck, 1988), 687–700.

THANE, PAT, *The Foundation of the Welfare State* (London, 1982).

THIERINGER, ROLF, 'Das Verhältnis der Gewerkschaften zu Staat und Parteien in der Weimarer Republik: Die ideologischen Verschiedenheiten und taktischen Gemeinsamkeiten der Richtungsgewerkschaften. Der Weg zur Einheitsgewerkschaft' (University of Tübingen Ph.D. 1954).

THOMAS, J. H., *My Story* (London, 1937).

THOMAS, TOM, 'The WTM: Memoirs and Documents', introd. Raphael Samuel, *HWJ* 4 (1977), 102–42.

THOMPSON, C. P., 'The Remscheid Workers' Movement from 1914 to 1945' (University of Warwick Ph.D. 1983).

THOMPSON, E. P., 'The Peculiarities of the English', *Socialist Register* (1965), 311–62.

THOMPSON, L. V., *Robert Blatchford: Portrait of an Englishman* (London, 1951).

—— *The Enthusiasts: A Biography of J. and K. B. Glasier* (London, 1971).

THOMPSON, PAUL, 'London Working-Class Politics and the Formation of the London Labour Party, 1885–1914' (University of Oxford D.Phil. 1963).

——*Socialists, Liberals and Labour: The Struggle for London, 1885–1914* (London, 1967).

THORNE, WILL, *My Life's Battles* (London, 1926).

TILLY, CHARLES, *Big Structures, Large Processes, Huge Comparisons* (New York, 1985).

TSUZUKI, CHUSHICHI, *H. M. Hyndman and British Socialism* (London, 1961).

——*The Life of Eleanor Marx 1855–1898: A Socialist Tragedy* (Oxford, 1967).

TURNER, JOHN (ed.), *Businessmen and Politics: Studies of Business Activity in British Politics 1900–1945* (London, 1984).

TURNER, MICHAEL, *A History of the Workers' Educational Association: Western District, 1911–1986* (Bristol, 1986).

ÜBERHORST, HORST, *Frisch, Frei, Stark und Treu: Die Arbeitersportbewegung in Deutschland, 1893–1933* (Düsseldorf, 1973).

ULAM, A. B., *Philosophical Foundations of English Socialism* (Cambridge, Mass., 1951).

UNGER, DAVID, 'The Roots of Red Clydeside: Economic and Social Relations and Working-Class Politics in the West of Scotland, 1900–1919' (University of Texas, Austin Ph.D. 1979).

VERNON, B. D., *Ellen Wilkinson* (London, 1982).

VERNON, RAYMOND, *Big Business and the State: Changing Relations in Western Europe* (London, 1974).

WACHENHEIM, HEDWIG, *Vom Großbürgertum zur Sozialdemokratie: Memoiren einer Reformistin* (Berlin, 1973).

WAITES, BERNARD, *A Class Society at War: England 1914–1918* (Leamington Spa, 1987).

WALKER, H. J., 'The Outdoor Movement in England and Wales, 1900–1939' (University of Sussex Ph.D. 1987).

WALLER, ROBERT J., *The Dukeries Transformed: The Social and Political Development of a Twentieth Century Coalfield* (Oxford, 1983).

WALTER, FRANZ, *Sozialistische Akademiker- und Intellektuellenorganisationen in der Weimarer Republik* (Bonn, 1990).

——DENECKE, VIOLA, and REGIN, CORNELIA, *Sozialistische Gesundheits- und Lebensreformverbände* (Bonn, 1991).

——DURR, TOBIAS, and SCHMIDTKE, KLAUS, *Die SPD in Sachsen und Thüringen zwischen Hochburg und Diaspora: Untersuchungen auf lokaler Ebene vom Kaiserreich bis zur Gegenwart* (Bonn, 1993).

WARDE, ALAN, 'Conditions of Dependence: Working Class Quiescence in Lancaster in the 20th Century', *IRSH* 35 (1990), 71–105.

WATERS, CHRIS, *British Socialists and the Politics of Popular Culture, 1884–1914* (Manchester, 1990).

WEARMOUTH, R. F., *The Social and Political Influence of Methodism in the 20th Century* (London, 1957).

WEDGWOOD, JOSIAH, *Memoirs of a Fighting Life* (London, 1940).

WEHLER, H.-U., *Sozialdemokratie und Nationalstaat: Die deutsche Sozialdemokratie und die Nationalitätenfragen in Deutschland von Karl Marx bis zum Ausbruch des ersten Weltkrieges* (Würzburg, 1962).

——*Das deutsche Kaiserreich 1871–1918* (Göttingen, 1973).

——(ed.), *Klassen in der europäischen Sozialgeschichte* (Göttingen, 1979).

WEISBROD, BERND, *Schwerindustrie in der Weimarer Republik: Interessenpolitik zwischen Stabilisierung und Krise* (Wuppertal, 1978).

WEITZ, E. D., 'Conflict in the Ruhr: Workers and Socialist Politics in Essen, 1910–1925' (University of Boston Ph.D. 1983).

WELLS, H. G., *Experiment in Autobiography*, 2 vols. (Cape, 1969).

WENDT, BERNDT-JÜRGEN, '"Deutsche Revolution—Labour Unrest": Systembedingungen der Streikbewegungen in Deutschland und England, 1918–1921', *AfS* 20 (1980), 1–55.

WHITE, D. S., 'Reconsidering European Socialism in the 1920s', *Journal of Contemporary History*, 16 (1981), 251–272.

WICKHAM, JAMES, 'The Working-Class Movement in Frankfurt a.M. During the Weimar Republic' (University of Sussex Ph.D. 1979).

——'Working-Class Movement and Working-Class Life', *Social History*, 8 (1983), 315–43.

WILLIAMS, C. M., 'Democratic Rhondda: Politics and Society, 1885–1951' (University of Wales Ph.D. 1991).

WILLIS, KIRK, 'The Introduction and Critical Reception of Marxist Thought in Britain 1850–1900', *Historical Journal*, 20 (1977), 417–59.

WINKLER, H. A., 'Klassenbewegung oder Volkspartei? Zur Programmdiskussion in der Weimarer Sozialdemokratie, 1920–1925', *GG* 8 (1982), 9–54.

——*Von der Revolution zur Stabilisierung: Arbeiter und Arbeiterbewegung in der Weimarer Republik, 1918–1924* (Berlin, 1984).

——*Der Schein der Normalität: Arbeiter und Arbeiterbewegung in der Weimarer Republik, 1924–1930* (Berlin, 1985).

——*Der Weg in die Katastrophe: Arbeiter und Arbeiterbewegung in der Weimarer Republik, 1930–1933* (Berlin, 1987).

WINKLER, JÜRGEN, 'Die soziale Basis der sozialistischen Parteien in Deutschland 1912–1924', *AfS* 29 (1989), 137–71.

WINTER, J. M., *Socialism and the Challenge of War: Ideas and Politics in Britain, 1912–1918* (London, 1974).

WRIGLEY, C. (ed.), *A History of British Industrial Relations* (Brighton, 1982).

WRYNN, J. F. P., *The Socialist International and the Politics of European Reconstruction, 1919–1930* (Amsterdam, 1976).

WUNDERER, HARTMUT, *Arbeitervereine und Arbeiterparteien: Kultur- und Massenorganisationen in der Arbeiterbewegung, 1890–1933* (Frankfurt am Main, 1987).

YEO, EILEEN, and YEO, STEPHEN (eds.), *Popular Culture and Class Conflict, 1590–1914* (Brighton, 1981).

YEO, STEPHEN, 'A New Life: The Religion of Socialism in Britain, 1883–1896', *HWJ* 4 (1977), 5–56.

——'Socialism, the State and some Oppositional Englishness', in Robert Colls and Philip Dodd (eds.), *Englishness: Politics and Culture, 1880–1920* (London, 1986), 308–69.

YOUNG, J. D., 'Elitism, Authoritarianism and Western Socialism', *SSLH* 25 (1972), 68–71.

——*Socialism and the English Working Class: A History of English Labour, 1883–1939* (Hemel Hempstead, 1989).

YOUNG, NIGEL, 'Prometheans or Troglodytes? The English Working Class and the Dialectics of Incorporation', *Berkeley Journal of Sociology*, 12 (1967), 1–43.

ZEITZ, ALFRED, *Zur Geschichte der Arbeiterbewegung der Stadt Brandenburg vor dem 1. Weltkrieg* (Potsdam, 1965).

ZWAHR, HARTMUT, *Die Konstituierung des Proletariats als Klasse* (Berlin, 1978).

——'Die deutsche Arbeiterbewegung im Länder- und Territorialvergleich 1875', *GG* 13 (1987), 448–507.

Index